Improving Student Thinking
A Comprehensive Approach

Barry K. Beyer
George Mason University

ALLYN AND BACON

Boston   London   Toronto   Sydney   Tokyo   Singapore

Related Titles of Interest

Teaching Thinking Skills: A Handbook for Elementary School Teachers
Barry K. Beyer
ISBN 0–205–12796–7

Teaching Thinking Skills: A Handbook for Secondary School Teachers
Barry K. Beyer
ISBN 0–205–12797–5

Interdisciplinary High School Teaching: Strategies for Integrated Learning
John H. Clarke and Russell M. Agne
ISBN 0–205–15710–6

The Thinking Classroom: Learning and Teaching in a Culture of Thinking
Shari Tishman, David N. Perkins, and Eileen Jay
ISBN 0–205–16508–7

For more information or to purchase a book, please call 1–800–278–3525.

Allyn & Bacon
A Viacom Company
Needham Heights, MA 02194

Internet: www.abacon.com
America Online: keyword: College Online

Library of Congress Cataloging-in-Publication Data
Beyer, Barry K.
    Improving student thinking : a comprehensive approach / Barry K.
Beyer.
        p.   cm.
    Includes bibliographical references and index.
    ISBN 0–205–15062–4
    1. Thought and thinking—Study and teaching—United States.
    2. Interdisciplinary approach in education—United States.
    I. Title.
LB1590.3.B486   1997   96–39375
                                               CIP

Printed in the United States of America
10 9 8 7 6 5 4 3 2 1   01

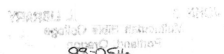

For

WILLY
Kurt and Becky
Stacey, Jimmy, and Greg
with love

Contents

Foreword

What makes humans uniquely human is their insatiable quest for meaning. Humans have a passion for problem finding, cooperating together to create new solutions and communicating their results. Innate within every human being is the drive for greater efficacy, flexibility, consciousness, craftsmanship, interdependence, and spirituality.

Although every individual human being comes equipped with these capacities, if left to their own devices, these capacities may not develop to their fullest potential due to environmental conditions or physiological constraints. These capacities must be continually mediated, encouraged, modeled, and enhanced.

An analogy might serve to illustrate. Most all human beings move. Some of us move with precision, style, and grace; others of us are awkward, clumsy, or ungainly. It takes years of practice, concentration, and coaching to become a powerful gymnast, a lively ice-skater, or a graceful ballerina. Improvement is demonstrated by the increasing mastery of complex and intricate maneuvers performed repeatedly on command with sustained and seemingly effortless alacrity. The distinction between awkwardness and agility is readily apparent to even the most undisciplined observer.

Like agile, graceful movement, good thinking is hard work. And like the development of agility of movement, refinement of thinking requires practice, concentration, and coaching. Unlike athletics, however, thinking is most often individual and covert, and therefore assessment is more elusive than in the direct observation of performance as in athletics or dance. To the trained observer, however, distinctions between awkward and polished thinking are readily apparent. Awkward thinkers tend to be gullible and impulsive, they distort ideas, delete information, and overgeneralize. They fail to think about their own thinking, are reluctant to take risks, and are dependent on others for solutions. They are unable to generate new ideas, are egocentric in their outlooks, and resist changing their minds even with the addition of compelling information. Improving and refining thinking seek to overcome these cognitive weaknesses.

Besides the development of those human potentials to which each child is entitled, society is increasingly demanding trained and agile thinkers. As we enter a world in which knowledge doubles in less than five years (the projection is that by the year 2020, it will double every 73 days), it is no longer feasible to anticipate our future information requirements. This trend requires a movement away from an exclusively content-driven curriculum to one that also provides individuals with the skills necessary to engage in life-long learning.

Students entering the workplace of the future must come fully equipped with the skills that enable them to be systems thinkers and continuous learners. They must bring into the workplace their abilities to think for themselves, to be self-initiating, self-modifying, and self-directing thinkers. Organizations will only survive in the future if they adopt a new way of managing that is based on a capacity to learn and change consciously, continuously, and quickly. They will need to go beyond just fixing problems to anticipating what might happen. Their workers must possess a wide variety of cognitive skills, including the disposition of searching continuously for more creative solutions.

Educators today realize that new goals for the next century are becoming increasingly apparent as survival skills for our children's future, for the continuity of our democratic institutions, and even for our planetary existence. Content can no longer be the sole result of schooling but rather a tool by which people learn to make meaning for themselves and to solve problems for which they do not have answers. These twenty-first-century goals include the following:

- The capacity for continued learning
- Knowing how to behave when answers to problems are not immediately apparent
- Cooperativeness and team building
- Precise communication in a variety of modes
- An appreciation for disparate value systems
- Problem solving that requires creativity and ingenuity
- Enjoyment of resolving ambiguous, discrepant, and paradoxical situations
- The generation and organization of an overabundance of technologically produced information
- Pride and craftsmanship of product

- High self-esteem
- Personal commitment to larger organizational and global values

These new goals need to drive the instructional, curriculum, and assessment practices in our schools of the future. The delivery system—curriculum materials, instructional strategies, and the school organization—need to embody these goals. Furthermore, these goals are valid not only for students but for all of the school's inhabitants, as well. Achieving these goals requires changes in our educational procedures, outcomes, standards, and policies.

Barry Beyer decries the unschooled mind. He is one of those who strongly believe that every human being has the right to have his or her intellectual capacities developed to the fullest and asserts that schools have the responsibility to enhance these cognitive skills, operations, and dispositions. He has confidence that, with proper instruction, effective human thought processes can become more broadly applied, more spontaneously generated, more precisely focused, more intricately complex, more metaphorically abstract, and more insightfully divergent.

The question that Beyer addresses in this book is: What constitutes proper instruction?

Children come to school fully equipped with an insatiable drive to explore and experiment, yet our educational institutions are currently oriented predominantly toward controlling rather than learning and toward rewarding individuals for performing for others rather than cultivating their natural curiosity and impulse to learn. Teachers are often more highly influenced by the values of the school culture, the influence of other teachers, the contents of the testing program, and the chapters of textbooks than from what they know about human development, learning, and enhancing inquiry or even the structure and modes of inquiry of the disciplines themselves. Unfortunately, school environments, culture, and traditions send mixed signals to teachers, support staff, parents, students, and the community, which, in turn, causes confusion in practice—for example:

- We want students to think, but some communities and parents demand improvement of scores on low-level cognitive standardized tests.
- We value creativity and risk taking, but students are administered, evaluated, and rewarded for high scores on multiple-choice tests.
- We want students to learn to work cooperatively with one another, but when they are tested, they must work individually, quietly, and not look at each other's papers.
- We want students to take the time to explore issues in depth, consider consequences, and identify assumptions, but school curricula must be

covered rapidly in preparation for graduation, a test, college entrance exams, or passing to the next grade level.
- We value student thinking, but school rewards are given for athletics, attendance, high grades, and citizenship.
- Teachers are admonished to teach for thinking, but they are evaluated on their performance of a limited range of instructional behaviors that have been correlated mainly with high test scores.

Thus, teachers' values often seem to be more influenced by the cues from their environment and school culture as to what is important to teach and assess. Traditionally structured schools, classrooms, testing procedures, and curricula send confusing and complicating signals to the staff, students, and community about what is truly valued and rewarded in school.

Since the origins of the "thinking skills" renaissance in the early 1980s, a plethora of approaches, programs, points of view, and platforms have been produced professing how best to teach for, assess, and organize a curriculum intended to develop students' intellectual prowess. Unfortunately, there is no common core of concepts, agreed-upon structure, or set of strategies for teachers and other curriculum workers for achieving this goal. Over 30 different published curricula intended to teach critical thinking, problem solving, decision making, learning to learn, metacognition, remedial thinking, and creative thinking compete. Each claims profound results.

How such programs are best taught is elusive. Out of this disparateness, many conflicting points of view have been championed by numerous outspoken and influential leaders in the field: Reuven Feuerstein, Edward deBono, Richard Paul, Jack Lochhead, David Perkins, Fred Newmann, Lauren Resnick, Beau Fly Jones, Jay McTighe, Art Whimbey, and Barry Beyer, himself, to mention a few.

Some of their agonizing but friendly debates have raised many thoughtful inquiries for further research, experimentation, and development: Should thinking be integrated with subject matter or taught as a separate subject? How should it be assessed? Should it be tested, performed, observed, exhibited, or inferred? Should thinking skills be taught directly or infused in the curriculum? What are the roles of dispositions and habits of mind of the effective thinker and how should they be taught and assessed? How should effective thinking processes be defined, categorized, and sequenced? What is the relationship between the content of the disciplines and modes of thinking? How should effective thinking practices be manifested throughout a learning environment? What is the role of the teacher in modeling, teaching, and reinforcing effective thinking? How should the curriculum be adapted so as to be developmentally appropriate for students' emergent thinking capacities? What is the influence of the home environment in shaping student thinking skills, habits, and dispositions?

In this book, Barry Beyer provides us with a new coherence that touches on many of these questions. What is unique about this book is that it synthesizes many of the existing divergent and sometimes apparently antithetical points of view regarding the ways and means of teaching our youth to become more effective thinkers. Beyer has compiled a vast, comprehensive, but very user-friendly vision of how to teach for, of, and about these new outcomes. He has transcended the many "schools of thought" to present a fresh and coherent, comprehensive, and integrated approach to improving not only student thinking abilities but also those of adults who have responsibility to influence them.

In the decades ahead, schools as well as universities will change more and more drastically than they have in the past 300 years. These changes are being brought about because of new technology, because of the demands of a knowledge-based society in which organized learning has become a lifelong process, and because of new theories and understandings about how human beings learn. Beyer's contribution here will prove invaluable to teachers, staff developers, administrators, teacher educators, program specialists, and curriculum workers in their inquiry into and quest for restructuring curriculum, instruction, and learning for the next millennium.

Arthur L. Costa, Ed.D.
Professor Emeritus
California State University, Sacramento
and Codirector
Institute for Intelligent Behavior, Berkeley, California

Preface

The most important goal of schooling is to learn. And learning, as numerous educators have repeatedly pointed out, is a consequence of thinking.[1] Our students' success in school is thus heavily dependent on their inclinations as well as their abilities to think skillfully. This also holds true for success in the workplace and in most areas of civic and social life. One way to ensure that students learn more and better than they do now, and to help ensure their success in out-of-school life as well, is to help them improve the quality of their thinking. This book explains what we, as educators, can do to accomplish this goal.

My purpose here is twofold: to explain four approaches we can—and should—employ in our teaching to improve the quality of our students' thinking and to demonstrate how these can be combined into a comprehensive instructional program to achieve this end. These approaches consist of:

1. Providing thoughtful classroom learning environments
2. Making visible and explicit the invisible substance of thinking
3. Supporting and guiding student practice of thinking
4. Integrating these approaches with each other and with continuing instruction in subject matter

Improving the quality of student thinking in our schools requires doing *all* the above, for these approaches to improving thinking are not mutually exclusive. In fact, no single one of these approaches by itself provides all the conditions and instructive supports essential for improving student thinking. Raising the quality of student thinking involves making sustained, deliberate, systematic schoolwide classroom efforts to combine all of these four approaches into a comprehensive instructional effort directed at all students. *Only by integrating these four approaches into classroom and curricular practices can we create and provide the meaningful opportunities, insights, support, guidance, and instruction required by students to improve the quality of their thinking.*

The pages that follow describe and explain each of the preceding four instructional approaches and provide specific, practical suggestions for how to carry them out. Part I provides some snapshots of thoughtful classrooms, identifies some essential features of these learning environments, and explains what can be done to establish and maintain such classrooms. Part II provides examples of four powerful techniques for making thinking visible and explicit. Ways to use selected techniques and materials for scaffolding, cueing, and otherwise guiding and supporting student thinking are explained and exemplified in Part III. Part IV explains various approaches to integrating the use of these methods of instruction in thinking with each other and with instruction in any subject matter at any grade level. Taken together, these four approaches constitute a comprehensive approach to improving the quality of student thinking.

Undoubtedly, incorporating these approaches into regular classroom teaching requires some effort and a high degree of commitment, as well as perhaps experimentation and training. However, when all have been effectively implemented, integrated, and institutionalized into an instructional program, any teacher or school can be sure that it has in place a program that will provide the essential elements for making a positive and significant difference in the quality of their students' thinking, learning, success in the workplace, and civic competence. Bringing about this improvement begins with a systematic effort to understand and employ the teaching techniques described here.

ACKNOWLEDGMENTS

Completion of this book would not have been possible without the generous assistance, advice, and support of a number of individuals as well as the graduate faculty of George Mason University.

I am, first and foremost, especially indebted to my wife Judy for her continuing assistance in producing the various drafts that preceded this volume. Given the fact that my idea of hi-tech is a number-2 pencil with a soft rubber eraser, it was her word-processing skills that got the manuscript drafts and revisions into our computer, which then eventually coughed up the final version that follows. She also read, reread, and critiqued with a kind but sharp eye what I wrote and rewrote. I could not have produced this without her unflagging keyboard skills, constructive criticism, patience, and encouragement, for all of which I will be forever grateful.

I am also indebted to colleagues who so kindly gave their time and expertise to review the various drafts of this manuscript. Barbara Presseisen, formerly of Research for Better Schools and now Vice President of Education at Nobel Education Dynamics, Inc. in Media, Pennsylvania, provided an amazingly detailed, incisive, and constructive review of the initial manuscript. Her suggestions proved invaluable in many ways. Loretta Hannum of the Williamsburg–James City County, Virginia, Public Schools; Ann Hutchinson of the Middlesex County Board of Education, Ontario, Canada; and Jay McTighe, Director of the Maryland Assessment Consortium, also provided candid and insightful critiques, suggestions, and encouragement. Their comments and recommendations contributed much to shaping the contents of the pages that follow.

To my colleague and friend, Art Costa, goes my special and profound appreciation for so willingly providing the Foreword to this book—a statement that sets this topic in the broader context of today's drive for educational improvement. Art, indeed, is one of the most outstanding, stimulating, enthusiastic, and active shakers and movers in education today. His contributions to improving the quality our children's learning, particularly in the area of thinking, are matched by few. It is a privilege to have his views lead off these pages.

I also deeply appreciate the assistance of a number of fellow educators in locating or providing materials for use here. Fred Newmann, of the University of Wisconsin–Madison, alerted me to the case studies that appear in the overview to Part I. Educators Art Whimbey and Jack Lochhead allowed me to reprint a significant excerpt from their classic *Problem Solving and Comprehension.* Frank Lyman, Coordinator of the University of Maryland/Howard County Professional Development School Center, graciously gave permission to include his Think Trix. Shelby Walker, librarian in the Randolph Henry High School in Charlotte County, Virginia, helped me track down the original of the poem that concludes this book. Educational consultant Bena Kallick kindly allowed me to reprint the student statement that appears in the closing pages here. I am very thankful for the assistance provided by each and all. I also thank the graduate faculty and administration of George Mason University and its Graduate School of Education for providing me with a faculty study leave to conduct much of the research on which this book is based.

Finally, I wish to acknowledge the encouragement given this effort by Allyn and Bacon's Mylan Jaixen and Nancy Forsyth. My thanks, too, go especially to Lynda Griffiths for her careful, and caring, editing of this manuscript.

To all these individuals, my most sincere thanks for all their encouragement, patience, support, and assistance.

Barry K. Beyer
Professor Emeritus
Graduate School of Education
George Mason University
Fairfax, Virginia

ENDNOTE

1. John Dewey, *How We Think* (Boston: D. C. Heath, 1910); John R. Hayes, *Cognitive Psychology: Thinking and Creating* (Homewood, IL: Dorsey Press, 1978); David Perkins, *Smart Schools* (New York: The Free Press, 1992), pp. 34 ff; Lauren Resnick, *Education and Learning to Think* (Washington, DC: National Academy Press, 1987); Lauren Resnick, "Learning in School and Out," *Educational Researcher* (December 1987): 3–20.

Introduction: Improving Student Thinking

That the quality of student thinking needs improving is rarely disputed. Our students simply do not think as well as they could or should.[1] Addressing this situation in a positive, purposeful fashion is one of the major challenges facing society today. The current attention to setting and raising standards for school achievement, as well as rapidly increasing, easy access to, and use of massive electronic databases gives increased urgency to efforts to meet this challenge.

Interestingly, improving the quality of student thinking is one of those "good news/bad news" situations. The good news is that the need to improve student thinking does not arise because youngsters cannot or do not think. All of them can think. And they do. Even the youngest preschoolers engage in what is for them sophisticated intellectual activity.[2] Indeed, Piaget notwithstanding, research indicates that even very young children can and do engage in serious reasoning and problem solving.[3] All human beings are able to, and on occasion do, engage or attempt to engage in even the most complex thinking, starting at a very young age.

The bad news is that, unfortunately, most school-age youngsters (and, indeed, many adults) do not think as well as they are capable of thinking, especially where complex thinking tasks are involved.[4] Too many jump to conclusions instead of suspending judgment. Too many consider only one or two rather than all relevant alternatives in making important decisions.

Too many view a problematic situation from one point of view only (usu-ally theirs) rather than looking at it from a variety of viewpoints. Too many accept uncritically their own hasty conclusions as well as those of other people.[5]

Furthermore, most school-aged youngsters are not strategic in their thinking. They do not plan what they are going to do mentally to carry out a thinking task before launching into it. They do not clarify a problem they wish to resolve or clarify a goal they wish to achieve before setting out to resolve it. They do not consciously attend to, evaluate, and alter a mental process they are using to execute a thinking task as they engage in it. They often just are not aware of what they are doing mentally. This means that they are unable to spot errors in their thinking in time to remedy them or improve what they are doing so they can do it more efficiently.[6]

Yet, in a way, this situation has a "good news" side, too. These flaws in the way students think do not occur because of inherent mental deficiencies. Rather, they occur because it seems to be human nature to behave in these ways. Poor thinking seems to be quite natural. As cognitive specialist David Perkins, educator Art Costa, and others point out, it is good thinking that is rather unnatural—that goes against many of the natural inclinations of human beings.[7] Happily, though, good thinking—skillful thinking—*can* be made more a part of one's natural behavior. In fact, human thinking can be dramatically improved in quality and can be made a part of one's normal behavior with a little serious attention and effort.[8] As teachers, we *can* help youngsters think better than they are apt to if left to their own natural de-vices and inclinations. We *can improve* the *quality* of student thinking.

QUALITY THINKING

What do we mean by the *quality* of thinking? Quality, in the sense used here, means the degree to which the characteristics of thinking considered essen-tial to its smooth and effective functioning are present in any act of think-ing. In thinking of high quality these characteristics are obviously and con-sistently present. In low- or poor-quality thinking, they are absent, incomplete, or otherwise flawed.

A number of researchers and specialists have attempted to define high-quality thinking. Researcher Raymond Nickerson, for instance, asserts that high-quality thinking is intentional, efficiently carried out, consistent, deep, and productive.[9] Psychologist Arthur Whimbey and educator Jack Loch-head claim that high-quality thinking is distinguished by the following:[10]

- A concern for accuracy and understanding of the facts and relation-ships of a problem

- A systematic, step-by-step procedure by which a thinking task is carried out, including breaking the thinking task into smaller parts and starting at a point at which one can make sense of it
- Careful attention to directions, data, and procedure, with continuous assessment of what is being done, used, and produced
- An active effort that includes using a variety of props (such as diagrams, models, mental images, self-questioning) to carry out one's thinking
- Confidence in one's ability to carry out a thinking task successfully

Educators Benjamin Bloom and Lois Broder, Arthur Costa, Reuven Feuerstein, Matthew Lipman, and David Perkins, among others, assert that, furthermore, high-quality thinking is characterized by these attributes:[11]

Intentionality

Persistence

Deliberateness rather than impulsiveness

Precision

Deliberate consideration from a variety of points of view

A desire to be well informed

Seeking and giving reasons and evidence

Open-mindedness, suspending judgment

Objectivity

Willingness to change a position when evidence and reason warrant doing so

Judging in terms of situations, issues, purposes, and consequences rather than in terms of dogma, self-interest, or wishful thinking

Clearly, all of these attributes mark high-quality, skillful thinking. But there are other qualities, as well. For instance, consider the following:

The speed at which one thinks

The elegance or economy of procedure and effort utilized

The degree of automaticity

The practice of engaging simultaneously in metacognitive as well as cognitive operations

Troubleshooting successfully when one's thinking breaks down

Persistent application of a wide range of alternative procedures when temporarily stymied

Continuing self-criticism

Skilled use of a large repertoire of cognitive procedures

The inclination as well as ability to think metacognitively about one's own thinking

The knowledge, inclination, willingness, and ability to execute cognitive operations appropriate to the task at hand

High-quality thinking is distinguished by all of these characteristics. Thinking of high quality, in short, is the inclination and ability to carry out a wide range of cognitive (thinking) operations—including especially complex, higher-order operations—in a rapid, accurate, expert, self-critical, and self-correcting manner; in a wide variety of contexts, including unfamiliar ones; and in a comfortable and confident manner to produce sound, accurate thinking products. Thinking that exhibits the characteristics described here is in considerable demand today, as a learning skill, as a survival skill, and as a skill for bettering oneself and the world.

IMPROVING THE QUALITY OF STUDENT THINKING

To improve the quality of student thinking means to raise it to a level of performance in academic contexts as well as civic and personal life that consistently exhibits the characteristics of high-quality thinking as defined above. Fortunately, doing this does not mean teaching thinking from scratch, for, as noted earlier, all our students *can* and *do* think. What it does mean is helping them become more skilled in carrying out their thinking, helping them exhibit more regularly the characteristics of good thinking, and helping them become better able and willing to engage in complex thinking on their own initiative when and where it is appropriate to do so. Yes, this is a tall order, but not nearly as impossible or as difficult as it might at first appear!

Happily, there are plenty of things we can do to improve the quality of student thinking. Unfortunately, making youngsters think or making them "think deeper" or "think harder" is not among them. But the approaches to improving thinking described in these pages are. This book seeks to make readily accessible some practical information and materials that can be used to implement these approaches.

Research and exemplary practice suggest that in improving significantly the quality of their thinking, learners of any age benefit markedly from four things: a *thoughtful learning environment; seeing or hearing what is actually done to execute cognitive operations they are trying to improve; guidance and support of their initial efforts to carry out these operations until they can carry them out on their own initiative and in a self-directed way; and something worth thinking about.*[12] These constitute the essential elements of any effort to improve student thinking that is most likely to produce positive results.

A thoughtful learning environment is one that provides frequent, repeated occasions for engaging in the kinds of thinking students need to improve. Because thinking is hard work and often requires considerable sustained effort, this environment also provides stimulation and encouragement to take advantage of these occasions. And, since thinking—especially complex, higher-order thinking—is often risky, a thoughtful classroom environment minimizes the risks and frustrations inherent in early efforts to engage in it. Such a classroom is not only *thinking centered* but it is *thinker friendly*, as well.[13]

Seeing or hearing how thinking works means making thinking explicit and visible. Doing this enables students to become more aware of how they think, which, in turn, helps them to realize what they are doing does or does not work well, and what, if anything, needs fixing. Seeing and hearing what others do to carry out the same cognitive tasks in which they are engaged makes students aware of how to correct flaws in their own thinking processes or how to execute these processes with greater expertise and less mental effort. Such awareness serves as the essential foundation of any effort to improve the quality of anyone's thinking.[14]

Moreover, students engaged any kind of thinking new to or difficult for them rarely can do it, even to their own satisfaction, without some *guidance* and *support* by others more knowledgeable or expert in how to do it than they.[15] They benefit immensely from being directly or indirectly walked through the process of actually doing it as they engage in this thinking. They benefit equally from other kinds of structured support, scaffolding, or cueing as they refine their performances through continued practice and reflection and become more autonomous in their thinking.

Finally, students care most about thinking when they engage in thinking about subjects or issues they consider to be *worthwhile*, meaningful, or useful. Furthermore, thinking is informed by the content of what is being thought about and by the context in which it is carried out. Meaningless thinking drill and practice is no substitute for thinking about something students find interesting, meaningful, and of value. Thus, providing students with topics or content that they perceive to be of value to them sharply enhances their efforts to think better as well as their motivation to do so. Efforts to improve student thinking pay off best when they are tied to the study of subjects and issues students care about and realize they need to understand or master.[16]

Therefore, we can best improve the quality of student thinking by ensuring that these four elements are built into the curricula and instruction provided to all students in all schools at all levels. Any or all of these can be incorporated into existing classroom instruction and curricula in any grade, in any subject, for virtually any students. No special, separate courses or programs need to be created to do this. Student thinking can be improved simply by making these conditions an integral part of already existing subjects and classes.

In order to do this in any class or subject or grade level, we can:

1. Establish and maintain a thoughtful classroom—one that nourishes thinking as well as minimizes the risks inherent in efforts to engage in and to improve one's thinking.
2. Make visible and explicit the thinking of our students and of others already skilled in doing it.
3. Guide and support student efforts at thinking by various techniques that serve to provide continuing scaffolding and cues for that thinking.
4. Integrate the practice and use of and instruction in thinking with meaningful instruction in major subjects across the curriculum.

None of these approaches is new. All have been recommended by a number of respected educators for at least the past decade or so.[17] Indeed, some of us and even some of our school systems have already attempted to implement one or more of these approaches. For a variety of reasons, however, many efforts at improving student thinking have often been directed at implementing only *one* or, at best, two of these approaches. Many of us have generally viewed or treated these approaches as "either-or" options, competitive with or substitutes for each other and thus mutually exclusive. Consequently, we have sought—or continue to seek—to identify and select one, single approach that appears to be "best" for our students.[18] As a result, our efforts have generally not accomplished their intended goals as well as they might. Improving the quality of student thinking requires more of us than simply selecting "one of the above!" It requires, at the very least, incorporating all four of these approaches throughout our classrooms and curricula.

ENDNOTES

1. Barry K. Beyer, *Developing a Thinking Skills Program* (Boston: Allyn and Bacon, 1988); Barry K. Beyer, *Practical Strategies for the Teaching of Thinking* (Boston: Allyn and Bacon, 1987); Arthur L. Costa, *The School as a Home for the Mind* (Palatine, IL: Skylight Publishing, 1991).

2. Barbara Means, Carol Chelemer, and Michael S. Knapp (Eds.), *Teaching Advanced Skills to At-Risk Students: Views from Research and Practice* (San Francisco: Jossey-Bass, 1991), p. 9; Penelope Peterson, Elizabeth Fennema, and Thomas Carpenter, "Using Children's Mathematical Knowledge" in Means, Chelemer, and Knapp, p. 74; Robert S. Siegler, *Children's Thinking* (Englewood Cliffs, NJ: Prentice-Hall, 1986).

3. Robbie Case, *The Mind's Staircase* (Hillsdale, NJ: Lawrence Erlbaum, 1992); Robbie Case, *Intellectual Development* (Orlando: Academic Press, 1985); Matthew Lipman, *Thinking in Education* (New York: Cambridge University Press, 1991); David Perkins, *Smart Schools* (New York: The Free Press, 1992), p. 62; Siegler, *Children's Thinking,* pp. 1–95.

4. Raymond Nickerson, "On Improving Thinking through Instruction," *Review of Research in Education,* Vol. 15 (Washington, DC: American Educational Research Association, 1988–89), pp. 4–5; Perkins, *Smart Schools,* pp. 28–29.

5. Benjamin Bloom and Lois Broder, *Problem-Solving Processes of College Students* (Chicago: University of Chicago Press, 1950); Lipman, *Thinking in Education,* pp. 9–18; David Perkins, "Foreword," in Beyer, *Practical Strategies,* pp. xii–xiii.

6. Beau Fly Jones, Annemarie Sullivan Palinscar, Donna Sederburg Ogle, and Eileen Glynn Carr, (Eds.), *Strategic Teaching and Learning* (Alexandria, VA: Association for Supervision and Curriculum Development, 1987); Means, Chelemer, and Knapp, *Teaching Advanced Skills,* pp. 9–11; Michael Pressley and Karen R. Harris, "What We Really Know about Strategy Instruction," *Educational Leadership 48* 1 (September 1990): 31–34.

7. Perkins, in Beyer, *Practical Strategies,* pp. xi–xiii; Grant Wiggins, "Creating a Thought-Provoking Curriculum," *American Educator 11* 4 (Winter 1987): 11, 16.

8. Walter Doyle, "Academic Work," *Review of Educational Research 53* 2 (Summer 1983): 159–199; Nickerson, "On Improving Thinking," pp. 3–57; Gaea Leinhardt, "What Research on Learning Tells Us about Teaching," *Educational Leadership 49* 7 (April 1992): pp. 20–25; David Perkins, "Mindware: The New Science of Learnable Intelligence," Paper presented at the Fourth Annual International Conference on Thinking, San Juan, Puerto Rico, August, 1989; Robert J. Sternberg, "How Can We Teach Intelligence?" *Educational Leadership 42* 1 (September 1984): 38–48; Arthur Whimbey with Linda Shaw Whimbey, *Intelligence Can Be Taught* (New York: Basic Books, 1975).

9. Nickerson, "On Improving Thinking," p. 4.

10. Arthur Whimbey and Jack Lockhead, *Problem Solving and Comprehension* (3rd ed.) (Philadelphia: The Franklin Institute Press, 1982), pp. 18–19, 28–29; see also Whimbey and Whimbey, *Intelligence Can Be Taught.*

11. Bloom and Broder, *Problem-Solving Processes, passim*; Costa, *The School as a Home, passim*; Reuven Feuerstein, *Instrumental Enrichment* (Baltimore: University Park Press, 1980); Lipman, *Thinking in Education, passim.*; Perkins, "Mindware."

12. Barry K. Beyer, "Common Sense about Teaching Thinking Skills," *Educational Leadership 41* 3 (November 1983): 44–49; Barry K. Beyer, "Improving Thinking Skills: Defining the Problem," *Phi Delta Kappan 65* 7 (March 1984): 486–490; Doyle, "Academic Work," pp. 159–199; Nickerson, "On Improving Thinking," pp. 3–57.

13. Wiggins, "Creating a Thought-Provoking Curriculum," pp. 11–16; Nickerson, "On Improving Thinking," p. 39.

14. Arthur L. Costa, "Mediating the Metacognitive," *Educational Leadership 42* 3 (November 1984): 57–62.

15. Beau Fly Jones, Minda Rae Amiran, and Michael Katims, "Teaching Cognitive Strategies and Text Structures within Language Arts Programs," in Judith W. Segal, Susan F. Chipman, and Robert Glaser (Eds.), *Thinking and Learning Skills: Relating Instruction to Research* (Hillsdale, NJ: Lawrence Erlbaum, 1985), pp. 259–295; Pressley and Harris, "What We Really Know," pp. 31–34.

16. Robert Glaser, "Education and Thinking: The Role of Knowledge," *American Psychologist* 29 2 (February 1984): 93–104; Leinhart, "What Research on Learning Tells Us," pp. 20–25; Perkins, *Smart Schools*; Lauren Resnick, "Literacy in School and Out," *Daedalus* 119 2: 169–185.

17. John Barell, *Teaching for Thoughtfulness* (New York: Longman, 1991); Arthur Costa, *The School as a Home*; Jay McTighe and Frank T. Lyman, Jr., "The Promise of Theory Embedded Tools," *Educational Leadership* 45 7 (April 1988): 18–24; Perkins, *Smart Schools*; Robert J. Swartz and D. N. Perkins, *Teaching Thinking: Issues and Approaches* (Pacific Grove, CA: Critical Thinking Press, 1989).

18. Larry Cuban, "Policy and Research Dilemmas in the Teaching of Reasoning: Unplanned Designs," *Review of Educational Research* 54 4 (Winter 1984): 655–681.

PART I

PROVIDING A THOUGHTFUL CLASSROOM

Good thinking does not develop overnight, nor does it develop in hostile settings. Just as crops require adequate soil, minerals, sunshine, water, and other nutrients as well as cultivation and protection to grow and develop, so, too, does the skillful, effective execution of thinking—especially of complex, higher-order thinking—require stimulation, support, and protection of a hospitable, friendly setting. Specialists refer to such settings as *thoughtful classrooms*. Establishing and maintaining classrooms as thoughtful classrooms—whatever the grade level, subject, or type of students we teach—is absolutely essential to improving the quality of thinking and thus the academic achievement of the students in our schools today.

What is a thoughtful classroom? And why is it so essential to improving student thinking?

A thoughtful classroom is a classroom that engages students continuously in purposeful thinking in the pursuit of meaningful learning. Simultaneously, it provides the encouragement, support, and other nutrients—the "rich surround" as cognitive specialist David Perkins has described them[1]

—needed to "grow" or develop that thinking. In these classrooms, the primary focus is on turning information into knowledge. The principal activity is thinking, of all kinds, including higher-order thinking. What do such classrooms look like? Here's one example—a fifth-grade thoughtful classroom in action:

> Students estimated, without paper and pencil, products of numbers such as 56 × 37, 83 × 52, and 505 × 1,495. The teacher supplied no strategies, procedures, or answers. Students worked alone or in groups. The teacher asked the students to explain their reasoning and their strategies. She often helped students to articulate their reasoning by asking, "Is that reasonable?" This encouraged students to interpret and analyze the relative magnitudes of their factors and answers.
>
> The teacher encouraged students to be aware of multiple solutions. In one problem, when students used two different solution methods, she accepted both methods and pushed the students to explain why each method had worked. For another problem, students offered three substantially different solutions—250,000, 750,000, and 1,500. Each group had to explain how they got their answers and why theirs was the preferable answer.[2]

Here's another example of a thoughtful classroom—an eighth-grade social studies class considering the impact on a community of workers being laid off from work:[3]

> After helping the students define certain terms related to the issue—such as "lay-off," "unemployment compensation" and so on—the teacher briefly presented information about the economies of their community and of two other communities of similar size but with different types of businesses and employment.
>
> Students then worked in small groups to answer this question: "What generalizations can you state about each local economy?" After studying the given data and discussing their findings, students reported, explained and defended their generalizations. They noted, for example, that the communities differed in that one was a two industry city while another was a one industry city, based largely on the military. In speculating about cutbacks in federal military spending, the students agreed, generally, that a community was better off if it was not too dependent on any one business or type of employment.
>
> In the course of the discussion, students noted the potential impacts on other local businesses—such as car dealerships—and on peoples' health by the loss of salaries and fringe benefits, such as health care. In concluding their lesson, the students generalized about the impact of the loss of jobs on local economies and people, especially in communities based on single types of business or industry.

Classrooms like these are, indeed, thought-*full!* In such classrooms, active engagement in thinking is essential for achieving class learning goals and is thus a major, continuing learning activity. Virtually all that goes on is intended to contribute to the advancement of thinking and the knowledge it produces. Students do not recite previously read or given information. Rather, they *use* that information to produce new insights or to construct new understandings. Students freely manipulate ideas about the information they consider by hypothesizing, evaluating, making relationships, analyzing, and generalizing, among other things. They engage continuously in these kinds of thinking as a natural, normal, integral part of everyday learning. The teacher focuses especially on facilitating, stimulating, and encouraging such thinking. These classrooms are, indeed, thinking-friendly places.

Thoughtful classrooms are also thinker-friendly. In these classrooms, both teacher and students encourage and support each other in their efforts to engage in the often difficult and demanding thinking required. They willingly engage in thinking, feel free to do so, and feel safe in doing so. Moreover, they willingly scrutinize their own thinking as well as submit it to the critical scrutiny of their peers. Students also feel comfortable in sharing their thinking with others to carry their learning forward. These are difficult and sometimes risky undertakings. They require not only effort but initiative and, often, courage. In thoughtful classrooms teachers and students provide an atmosphere conducive to students engaging in thinking; they also provide whatever kinds of encouragement will make such engagement more efficient and productive. Such classrooms are as thinker-friendly or supportive of those who *do* the thinking as they are supportive of the thinking itself.

Thoughtful—thinking-friendly and thinker-friendly—classrooms are essential to improving thinking for two major reasons. First, such classrooms provide students with repeated, continuous, opportunities to apply and practice the kinds of higher-order thinking which most of them need to improve. Second, by providing these opportunities, thoughtful classrooms provide us, as teachers, with repeated authentic opportunities to intervene in the process. We intervene by providing students with support that encourages them to invest in the effort required to engage in such thinking as well as providing instructional assistance that can improve their abilities to carry out these operations. Without a thoughtful classroom, efforts to improve the quality of student thinking would not have the fertile ground needed to accomplish this goal.

Of course, not all classrooms in our schools are thoughtful. Indeed, a great many, unfortunately, are not. But any classroom—at any grade level in any subject for students of any ability—can become a thoughtful classroom. By incorporating into our classrooms the features that distinguish thoughtful from more conventional, traditional, recitation classrooms, we can establish and maintain the kind of thinking and thinker friendly learning settings so essential for improving student thinking and, for that matter, student learning as well.

So, what exactly makes a thoughtful classroom thoughtful? And what is it that we can do to establish and maintain thoughtful classrooms of our own? The chapters that follow here in Part I address these questions. Chapter 1 identifies the behaviors and conditions that typify thoughtful classrooms and identifies three essential features of these classrooms. Chapters 2 and 3 then present what we can do to incorporate these features into our classrooms and to ensure that our own classrooms remain as thoughtful as possible. Accomplishing these goals is crucial to any serious and sustained effort to improve the quality of thinking of our students as well as their learning.

ENDNOTES

1. David Perkins, "Mindware: The New Science of Learnable Intelligence," paper presented at the Fourth International Conference on Thinking, San Juan, Puerto Rico, August 1989; D. N. Perkins, "Foreword," in Barry K. Beyer, *Practical Strategies for the Teaching of Thinking* (Boston: Allyn and Bacon, 1987), pp. xi–xiii.

2. From Fred M. Newmann, Walter G. Secada, and Gary G. Wehlage, *A Guide to Authentic Instruction and Assessment: Visions, Standards and Scoring* (Madison, WI: Wisconsin Center for Education Research, 1995), pp. 29–30.

3. Abridged from Newmann, Secada, and Wehlage, *A Guide to Authentic Instruction and Assessment*, pp. 30–31.

1

The Essential Features of a Thoughtful Classroom

The elements of a thoughtful classroom that make such a setting especially conducive to student thinking and to efforts to improve the quality of that thinking are closely intertwined with what goes on in such a classroom. Identifying the activities that typify these thoughtful classrooms and the conditions that make these activities possible enables us to identify those features that are essential to the continued existence of such classrooms. This chapter seeks to accomplish this goal. Replicating the resulting image can then serve as an inspiration as well as a target for any effort to establish and maintain thoughtful classrooms of our own.

THE NATURE OF THOUGHTFUL CLASSROOMS

A number of specialists have devoted considerable attention to identifying exactly what distinguishes thoughtful classrooms from other kinds of classrooms. Some of their analyses are based on firsthand observation of students and teachers in actual classroom settings that claim to demand, provoke, stimulate, and engage students in increasingly complex thinking. Other analyses present features inferred by specialists from what *they believe* is involved as students carry out critical thinking, problem solving, decisionmaking, and similar kinds of higher-order cognitive operations employed in learning. Generally, all these analyses present thoughtful classrooms in terms of two major elements: (1) the behaviors of students and teachers and (2) the nature of what is being studied. A careful examination of these analyses, each presented from a different point of view, can help clarify exactly what makes a thoughtful classroom thoughtful.

Thoughtful Student and Teacher Behaviors

Five different studies and reports provide rather clearly focused "snapshots" of student and/or teacher behaviors that are asserted to typify a thoughtful classroom. Fred Newmann and his colleagues at the University of Wisconsin–Madison National Center for Effective Secondary Schools observed a number of classrooms in recent years to find out what goes on in thoughtful classrooms.[1] In such classrooms, these observers noted the following:

The Students:

- Offer "explanations and reasons for their conclusions."
- Generate "original and unconventional ideas, explanations, hypotheses and solutions."
- Assume the roles of questioners and critics.
- Contribute in relevant, articulate ways that are related to the discussion at hand.
- Are involved in considerable numbers in the on-going discussion.
- Spend considerable time in discussion with each other, testing and refining ideas.
- Demonstrate genuine involvement (are attentive, interrupt to raise substantive questions or issues, make extended comments) in the substance of the lesson.

The Teachers:

- Allow an "appropriate amount of time" for students to think.
- Provide "challenging questions" and challenging, structured tasks.
- Press students to "justify and clarify their assertions."
- "Carefully consider" student-offered "explanations and reasons for their conclusions."
- Encourage "students to generate original and unconventional ideas, explanations [and] solutions."
- Acknowledge that not all assertions made by authoritative sources are absolutely accurate or certain.
- Integrate relevant student experiences into lessons.
- Model thoughtfulness.

Rexford G. Brown, a senior policy analyst for the Education Commission of the States, has presented another analysis of a thoughtful classroom.

During the late 1980s, he and his colleagues interviewed experts, analyzed research, and conducted school visits throughout the United States and Canada to identify policies and programs they believed were conducive to thoughtfulness.[2] His "snapshot" of a thoughtful classroom depicts the following:

- Considerable student talk, especially student-to-student discussion and debate of ideas, takes place.
- Teacher and student questioning includes numerous open, hypothetical questions.
- Teacher facilitation and probing encourages students to clarify and expand ideas and to build bridges between knowledge and the students themselves as knowledge seekers.
- Sustained discussion includes teacher and students giving reasons and evidence to support comments and opinions, self-critiques of discussions and syntheses, and summaries of points made.
- Courtesy and sensitivity are evidenced by active listening, polite interactions, and the acceptance and acknowledgment of conflicting viewpoints.
- Students are actively engaged in the learning at hand, as opposed to sleeping or fidgeting, daydreaming, passing notes, and other forms of nonengagement.
- There is self-regulation or reflection about what is happening, what is being learned, and how or how well the class is moving toward its learning goals.
- Risk taking encourages and supports creative problem solving, brainstorming, and the use of mistakes to generate more learning.

Cognitive researcher David Perkins has also contributed to efforts to describe thoughtful classrooms. In his book *Smart Schools*[3] he presented a snapshot of classrooms that exhibit complex thinking, or, as he called it, thinking for understanding. In this kind of classroom, the following can be seen:

The Students:

- Have a choice in what to study and how to learn.
- Interact with each other in ways that distribute cognition among many learners.
- Engage in the active use of knowledge.
- Demonstrate understanding by explaining, analyzing, and generalizing about topics studied in depth.

The Teachers:

- Teach for understanding of the significant rather than for retention of the trivial.
- Model the dispositions of good thinking.
- Provide students with clear information, thoughtful practice, informative feedback, and support.
- Teach for transfer.

Researcher Jere Brophy's analysis of thoughtful classrooms is more general than the preceding snapshots. Deriving his analysis primarily from theory and research, Brophy has described a thoughtful classroom as one in which the following take place:[4]

The Students:

- Develop expertise in an application context.
- Construct meaning.
- Develop higher-order thinking by engaging in authentic (real world) tasks that call for the application of knowledge through problem solving, decision making, and/or critical thinking.

The Teachers:

- "Scaffold and respond" to student ideas as well as contribute their own ideas.
- Join with students to create a genuine learning community.

A fifth snapshot of a thoughtful classroom is presented by philosopher Matthew Lipman, developer and author of a popular critical thinking program, Philosophy for Children. Lipman's snapshot describes student behaviors that typify a thoughtful classroom primarily in terms of the behaviors associated with critical thinking. In such classrooms, which he calls communities of inquiry, students do the following:

- Question one another
- Request of each other reasons for beliefs [or claims]
- Build on one another's ideas
- Deliberate among themselves
- Offer counter-examples to the hypotheses of others
- Point out possible consequences of one another's ideas
- Cooperate in the development [and use] of rational problem-solving techniques[5]

Given these snapshots, what kinds of student and teacher behaviors typify a thoughtful classroom? Close examination and comparison of these features reveal that students and teachers in thoughtful classrooms are actively—even aggressively—engaged in the collection, analysis, evaluation, and synthesis of information. Students ask as well as answer questions, pose as well as test hypotheses, and search for, produce, and evaluate information, knowledge claims, and arguments. They are reflective rather than impulsive, and they exhibit curiosity and a desire to explore rather than being content simply to accept and absorb. Students also demonstrate a persistent desire for statements to be supported by plausible reasoning and evidence.[6]

In a thoughtful classroom, almost all students are deeply involved in sustained dialogue and debate about issues of substance and methodology as they seek to go beyond the given information and knowledge claims to produce new knowledge. They venture, carefully consider, and evaluate ideas and explanations and critically examine them in terms of evidence, reasoning, assumptions, and implications. And they use the contributions of all class members to advance toward achieving shared learning goals. A spirit of interdependence permeates the classroom, as contributions from all are expected, actively sought, carefully scrutinized, and attentively considered. This is evidenced as students and teacher construct complex, meaningful solutions, decisions, concepts, understandings, or other kinds of knowledge. Even responses or claims that turn out to be inadequate, inaccurate, or otherwise flawed serve to move the class onward toward accomplishing its learning goals.[7]

Thoughtful Curricula

According to some observers,[8] a thoughtful classroom consists of more than the behavior of teachers and students. Some observers claim that *what* students study—the curricula—as well as the kinds of learning tasks in which they engage also contribute significantly to the degree of thoughtfulness exhibited by any classroom.

Newmann's[9] snapshot of a thoughtful curriculum, for example, asserts that such a curriculum meets the following criteria:

- It provides "sustained examination of a few topics rather than superficial coverage of many" different topics.
- It consists of lessons that display "substantive coherence and continuity."
- It integrates relevant student experiences into lessons.

Virtually all experts agree with Newmann's assertions that a thoughtful curriculum provides in-depth study of a limited number of topics rather than broad, general coverage of many.[10] In addition, Brophy has asserted that (1) a thoughtful curriculum also seeks to develop knowledge, skills,

and attitudes useful outside of as well as inside school; (2) content is organized around a limited number of powerful ideas; and (3) learning tasks are
built around the application of conceptual understanding and the use of
self-regulated skills.[11] Furthermore, Brown has claimed that providing students with firsthand experiences also constitutes an important element of a
thoughtful curriculum.[12] To these features, educator Arthur Costa has
added that in a thoughtful curriculum, content is selected because of its contribution to the process of thinking and that such a curriculum is "aligned,
coordinated and developmentally appropriate."[13]

Unlike these analyses, those of David Perkins and Grant Wiggins have
described a thoughtful curriculum in terms of what it is *not*. Their snapshot
"negatives" identify curricular and instructional features that inhibit thinking and understanding. In Perkins's judgment, these thought*less* learning
environments are characterized by a short answer/right-wrong syndrome
he calls the "trivial pursuit approach" to learning.[14] In his view,[15] thought-
less curricula or instruction are revealed by the following:

- Missing, inert, trivial, naive, and routinized knowledge
- Overemphasis on fact-learning and memorization
- Knowledge telling rather than knowledge using
- Poor or low-level thinking
- Failure to use the language of thinking
- Superficial coverage (breadth over depth)
- Ability-centered rather than effort-centered teaching and learning
- Testing for fact retention rather than understanding performances
- "Entity" (one item of unrelated information at a time), rather than in-
  cremental, teaching and learning

Researcher Grant Wiggins has claimed that thought*less* curricula consider "facts as the remedy of ignorance and accurate recall as the only sign
of knowledge."[16] In studying such curricula, students have no control over
what they learn or how they learn, according to Wiggins. Information and
skills are drilled and tested, and only rarely applied.[17]

Curricula distinguished by features cited by Perkins and Wiggins obviously limit or prevent student thinking and active construction of knowledge. Such curricula certainly offer little, if any, opportunity for students to
engage in thinking much above the level of simple recall. Nor do these types
of curricula offer the kinds of stimulation, encouragement, and support
needed to sustain even that kind of thinking. A curriculum characterized by
the features noted by Perkins and Wiggins is the antithesis of the kind of
curriculum that could accurately be characterized as thought*ful*.

However, by identifying the opposite of the curriculum features noted
by Perkins and Wiggins, we can identify the elements of a thoughtful cur-

riculum, at least as they see it. Based on the views held by Perkins and Wiggins of a "thought*less*" curriculum, a thought*ful* curriculum is one that meets the following criteria:

- It stresses the development of conceptual knowledge and understanding.
- It engages students in information (fact) *using* rather than fact gathering.
- It emphasizes student generation or construction of knowledge by applying complex thinking.
- It seeks to develop meaningful understanding rather than routine memorization.
- It requires student effort—with adequate time, support, and instruction—to meet high expectations.
- It stresses substantive coherence and incremental knowledge building.

These, as well as other attributes inferred from the Perkins and Wiggins analyses, can be added to the features of a thoughtful curriculum identified by Newmann, Brophy, Brown, and Costa. The resulting composite is a curriculum in which students seek to construct their own understanding and meaning from purposeful "thinking through what they are learning about"[18] as they actively apply complex thinking, conceptual knowledge, and the critical spirit in a quest for what appears to be reasonably true or most accurate. A thoughtful curriculum demands the *use* of thinking as well as the *use* of information and the knowledge claims of others. It is one in which learning is incremental rather than fragmentary, as students and teacher explore a few selected topics in depth rather than superficially cover a large number of topics. Such a curriculum seeks to develop relationships and connections, to build rather than simply to remember, and to produce something new rather than regurgitate something already given.

Thoughtful Classrooms as Thinking Places

Thoughtful classrooms, of course, exhibit many of the characteristics of any conventional classroom and they engage students and teachers in many of the same behaviors and activities, as well. As in most all classrooms, attendance is taken, teachers give directions, tests are administered, and grades are assigned. Yet, thoughtful classrooms do differ considerably from more traditional, less thoughtful, recitation-oriented classrooms. Figure 1.1 summarizes the most significant of these differences. They are not inconsequential. Thoughtful classrooms differ from traditional classrooms by the

Figure 1.1 Major Features of Thoughtful and Traditional Classrooms

Typical Behaviors or Conditions	Thoughtful Classrooms	Traditional Classrooms
Students	Ask and answer questions	Answer questions
	Remember and report information	Remember, repeat, and report information
	Collect, analyze, evaluate, and synthesize information and ideas	Collect and arrange information
	Produce and construct knowledge	Reproduce information
	Accept and take thinking risks	Avoid thinking risks
	Work in groups and individually	Work individually
	Engage in sustained discussion, deliberation, and inquiry	Engage in recitation and drill
	Interact with each other and the teacher	Respond to the teacher
Teachers	Guide student use of information	Provide information to be learned
	Seek clarification, elaboration, evaluation, and justification	Seek correct answers
	Stimulate, encourage, facilitate, and support learning	Direct and referee learning
	Model complex thinking	Model reporting, recording, and remembering
	Join with students in learning	Stand above students
Curriculum	In-depth study of limited number of topics	Superficial coverage of many topics
	Incremental, conceptual, integrated learning	Fragmentary, episodic, entity learning
	Integrates learning with student experience	Information learning as an end in itself
	Utilizes multiple sources of information	Utilizes single source of information

Figure 1.1 *Continued*

Typical Behaviors or Conditions	Thoughtful Classrooms	Traditional Classrooms
Class	Considerable student talk	Considerable teacher talk
	Considerable student-to-student interaction	Limited or no student-to-student interaction
	Builds knowledge as a group as well as individually	Accumulate information individually
	Requires considerable mental inquiry and effort	Requires limited mental inquiry and effort

kinds of learning and curricula they feature and the extent to which students engage in purposeful, higher-order thinking to learn.

As noted in Figure 1.1, thoughtful classrooms center on thinking. These classrooms honor both curiosity and skepticism. There is a general disposition for claims to be supported by reasons and evidence, and a reflective deliberate consideration of information, claims, and ideas. Thoughtful classrooms are also characterized by flexibility—a willingness to entertain alternatives and options regardless of how far fetched they may initially appear, as well as a willingness to alter positions when evidence and reason warrant. Another feature of thoughtful classrooms is that they are interactive. Students engage with information, each other, and the teacher to produce insights, understandings, and other forms of knowledge. The knowledge developed is socially constructed, as all members of the class contribute to its development. The thinking that produces this knowledge is distributed through the entire class. Each individual is both teacher and student, in that each individual gives and receives assistance in learning.[19] Thoughtful classrooms, in sum, are classrooms in which students and teacher actively think to learn.

ESSENTIAL FEATURES OF THOUGHTFUL CLASSROOMS

Of all the features that distinguish thoughtful from traditional classrooms, three in particular stand out as essential to the existence and operation of these classrooms:

- The production of knowledge through continuous application of higher-order thinking

- Active, continuous, intellectual engagement of students and teacher with information and with each other
- A commitment to and an emphasis on truth and proof as standards of knowledge production and learning

In fact, these three features encapsulate all the behaviors, activities, and conditions that make a thoughtful classroom thoughtful.

Knowledge Production

In a thoughtful classroom, the majority of time and effort is devoted to student production of knowledge new to them rather than to the *re*production of knowledge or information they previously have been given. In these classrooms, information is not treated as an end in itself or as something simply to be stored for recall or reproduction later.[20] Instead, information and the knowledge claims of others—whether presented by or secured from textbooks, reference materials, lectures, films, videos, electronic databases, teachers, or peers—are *used* by students and teacher to *construct meanings and understandings* that were not initially explicit or apparent to them.

This means that students and teacher reorganize, restructure, or transform existing information and what others claim to be knowledge into new explanations, concepts, hypotheses, conclusions, understandings, and generalizations. They use the ideas they are developing, as well as their own knowledge and prior experience, to reflect on and manipulate this information to generate, elaborate, test, evaluate, and revise their emerging ideas and understandings into new forms of knowledge.[21]

For example, instead of simply memorizing what a teacher or text asserts are the causes of the American Revolution, students analyze sources from the revolutionary period (such as the Declaration of Independence, diaries, newspaper accounts, letters, and treatises). Students then infer or identify probable causes and test their inferences against additional primary and secondary sources, such as period histories by Jared Sparks and Henry Bancroft, accounts by actual participants in the events of the period, and recent secondary historical studies and interpretations.

Engaging in learning activities like these involves more than simply trying to memorize what someone or some text presents or remember what was presented or asserted yesterday and last week. Producing knowledge requires sustained application of and engagement in *higher-order thinking*—application, analysis, synthesis, and evaluation—as well as in lower-order thinking such as recall and translation.[22] In thoughtful classrooms, students apply thinking skills, concepts, principles, and theories to make sense out of information. They take information apart and analyze it to identify its parts, relationships, patterns, and organizing principles. Students then synthesize (or formulate or create) hypotheses, conclusions, predictions, generalizations, concepts, theories, paragraphs, poems, paintings, plays, and musical compositions. They evaluate the quality of the materials they use and the products they generate by judging the accuracy of information, the validity of hypotheses, the credibility of sources, the strength of arguments, the beauty of paintings, the quality of written works, and so on. The use of higher-order thinking is central to producing meaning, understanding, and other forms of knowledge.

Interestingly, applying higher-order thinking to processing prior knowledge, given information, and experience into new forms enables students not only to produce new understandings but also to remember the information used to generate these new insights. Higher-order thinking also helps students make sense of unfamiliar information encountered later.[23] According to Perkins, these actions evidence deep understanding of a topic, subject, or idea.[24] Thoughtful classrooms are *not* settings where lessons are heard or information is simply committed to memory. They are settings where knowledge, meaning, and understanding are constructed.

Active, Sustained, Intellectual Engagement

Knowledge and understanding are constructed or produced by *active* intellectual and verbal engagement with information, subject matter, and other individuals, and sometimes by experiential engagement, as well. In a thoughtful classroom, students and teacher engage in intentional, effortful, generative, and reflective manipulation and analysis of information to produce the kinds of understandings and new knowledge they seek to develop.

For example, rather than simply reading descriptions of how people's actions affect the environment, students identify the ways people interact with the environment (such as having fireplace fires; disposing of trash in landfills; using insecticides or fertilizers on lawns, fields, or gardens; altering the landscape; and so on) and then identify and trace by observation, measurement, and experiments the results of such actions. The conclusions drawn from such firsthand investigation result from *doing* something *to* and *with* data or information beyond simply reading it or committing it to memory.

Constructing or producing new knowledge requires, at the very least, active mental effort, sustained processing of information, intellectual initiative, persistence, and reflection.[25] It also requires sustained student-to-student and student-to-teacher-to-student deliberation. Students analyze given information, extend and elaborate on it, evaluate it critically, and move it around to identify patterns, relationships, and connections within the information. They also relate it to other information of which they are aware and to their own personal experiences in and outside of school.[26] In doing this, students (1) ask questions of the information and of each other; (2) seek, generate, analyze, and evaluate answers, claims, definitions, explanations, and hypotheses and the reasoning, evidence, assumptions, and viewpoints on which they are based; and (3) apply or process in many different ways what they find out. Students engage in subject matter individually and with each other, sometimes seeking individual learning goals and other times cooperating with classmates in efforts to achieve common learning goals or to share special insights and discoveries. A thoughtful classroom is distinguished by continuous student engagement and interaction with information as well as with each other. It is not a place for spectators!

Commitment to and Emphasis on Truth and Proof

There is more to a thoughtful classroom than simply constructing knowledge that is new or unique to students. Although diversity, alternatives, and uniqueness are valued—indeed, encouraged—not just anything goes. In a thoughtful classroom, student inquiry and deliberation are conducted according to the highest standards of truthfulness, accuracy, proof, and soundness. Information and knowledge claims of whatever origin are treated with caution as well as with open minds.

In thoughtful classrooms, most learning is not a search for answers someone has already determined are "right." Rather it is a search for defensible, well-reasoned claims built on relevant, accurate, and sufficient evidence. The validity of an assertion or claim is not determined by the title or position of the individual making the assertion, nor is it determined by the enthusiasm, vigor, or loudness with which the assertion is made, nor by the degree of power one may hold over others. The validity of an assertion is determined by the quality of the reasoning and evidence upon which it is grounded.

For example, rather than accepting or rejecting a claim such as "Artificial light is not as good as natural sunlight for growing vegetables," teacher and students push for clarification, evidence, assumptions, and reasoning related to the claim and may even conduct experiments to test its validity. In using a newspaper account of a political speech, students evaluate it for accuracy by comparing it to other accounts of the same speech, to a copy of the speech, and to a recording of the speech. They also analyze the account and its author's credentials for evidence of partisanship or other forms of misrepresentation or error.

In a thoughtful classroom, students and teacher critically analyze and evaluate the inferences, hypotheses, conclusions, concepts, and generalizations they and others construct as well as the information they use for this purpose.[27] They evaluate knowledge claims, information, and sources for accuracy, credibility, bias, stereotyping, and unstated assumptions. Because arguments are only as strong as their supporting reasoning and evidence, they, too, are evaluated for the soundness of their reasoning, as well as for the accuracy, sufficiency, and relevance of the evidence backing them up. In addition, students reflect on and analyze the methods by which they and their peers have collected and processed this information as well as the sources from which it was taken.

In carrying out these crucial thinking operations, students, *on their own initiative*, give and seek reasons and evidence in support of their claims and those of others. They clearly state the criteria they are using to make judgments and they use criteria accepted by experts as well as class-generated criteria. To ensure that they use and develop the most accurate and plausible understandings possible, students subject their own thinking and the products of their thinking to the same kinds of standards and evaluations that they apply to others. This is done always with the intent to use the most accurate, truthful, and thorough information accessible to them in constructing what they are learning.[28]

These three features—the production of knowledge through higher-order thinking, active intellectual engagement, and a commitment to truth and proof—sum up the essence of a thoughtful classroom. By building a classroom around these features, we can establish and maintain precisely the kind of thoughtful learning environment so essential for the exercise—and potential improvement—of student thinking. If we can accomplish this, we will automatically incorporate all the other features of a thoughtful classroom into our classrooms as well.

Most, if not all, of the features that distinguish thoughtful classrooms from conventional recitation classrooms are embedded in or presupposed by the three core features of a thoughtful classroom just described. Students cannot, for example, construct or produce knowledge without studying topics in depth. Nor can they construct knowledge without intellectual inquiry, discussion, and deliberation. Nor can they study a topic in depth without using multiple sources of information. Nor can they demonstrate a commitment to truth and proof without asking questions, seeking clarification, and justification, or making reasoned judgments. Knowledge-producing classrooms that involve active intellectual engagement and a commitment to truth and proof also exhibit the other features of thoughtfulness identified here.

THOUGHTFUL CLASSROOMS: A SUMMARY

Thoughtful classrooms nourish thinking by making it possible as well as necessary. They support student efforts at thinking by making classrooms personally safe and natural to engage in. As a result, in thoughtful classrooms, student thinking is a normal, expected, and nonthreatening learning activity; it is also the major learning activity. By being so thinking-friendly and thinker-friendly, thoughtful classrooms provide need, opportunity, and stimulus to think. These conditions are absolutely essential to the sustained student engagement in thinking so necessary to improving their skill in executing it.

We can establish and maintain thoughtful classrooms like those described in this chapter by concentrating primarily on two things. First, we can create and provide continuing and enticing opportunities for students to engage in the kinds of thinking at which they need to improve. Second, we can provide the encouragement—in the broadest sense of the term—that will best enable students to take advantage of these opportunities to think and to improve their skills of how to do so. The next two chapters describe and explain techniques for providing such opportunities and encouragement for thinking.

ENDNOTES

1. Fred M. Newmann, "Higher Order Thinking in Teaching Social Studies: A Rationale for the Assessment of Classroom Thoughtfulness," *Journal of Curriculum Studies 22* 1 (January-February 1990): 41–56.

2. Rexford G. Brown, *Schools of Thought* (San Francisco: Jossey Bass, 1991), especially pp. xiv–xv; see also Rexford G. Brown, "Cultivating a Literacy of Thoughtfulness," *Thinking: The Journal of Philosophy for Children 9* 4, pp. 5–12.

3. David Perkins, *Smart Schools* (New York: The Free Press, 1992).

4. Jere Brophy, "Probing the Subtleties of Subject-Matter Teaching," *Educational Leadership 49* 7 (April 1992): 4–8.

5. Matthew Lipman, *Thinking in Education* (Cambridge: Cambridge University Press, 1991), p. 52.

6. Fred M. Newmann, "Higher Order Thinking in the School Curriculum," *National Association of Secondary School Principals' Bulletin 72* 508 (May 1988): 58–64.

7. Newmann, "Higher Order Thinking in Teaching Social Studies"; Brown, "Cultivating a Literacy of Thoughtfulness," *passim*; Lipman, *Thinking in Education*, p. 52.

8. Brophy, "Probing the Subtleties," p. 6; Arthur L. Costa, *The School As a Home for the Mind* (Palatine, IL: Skylight, 1991), pp. 7–10; Newmann, "Higher Order Thinking in Teaching Social Studies," pp. 52–56; Perkins, *Smart Schools*, pp. 165–166; Grant Wiggins, "Creating a Thought-Provoking Curriculum," *American Educator 11* 4 (Winter 1987): 10–17.

9. Newmann, "Higher Order Thinking in Teaching Social Studies," pp. 50–52.

10. Mary Bryson and Marlene Scardamalia, "Teaching Writing to Students at Risk for Academic Failure," in Barbara Means, Carol Chelemer, and Michael S. Knapp (Eds.), *Teaching Advanced Skills to at-Risk Students* (San Francisco: Jossey-Bass, 1991), pp. 141–163; Brophy, "Probing the Subtleties," p. 6; Brown, *Schools of Thought*, *passim*; Frank N. Dempster, "Exposing Our Students to Less Should Help Them

Learn More," *Phi Delta Kappan 74* 5 (February 1993): 433–437; Perkins, *Smart Schools, passim*; Richard S. Prawat, "The Value of Ideas: The Immersion Approach to the Development of Thinking," *Educational Researcher 70* 2 (August–September 1993): 5–16; Grant Wiggins, "The Futility of Trying to Teach Everything of Importance," *Educational Leadership 47* 3 (November 1989): 44–59.

11. Brophy, "Probing the Subtleties," p. 6.

12. Brown, "Cultivating a Literacy of Thoughtfulness," p. 6.

13. Costa, *The School As a Home*, pp. 7, 10.

14. Perkins, *Smart Schools*, pp. 31–34, 41.

15. *Ibid.*, pp. 21–41.

16. Wiggins, "The Futility," p. 48.

17. Wiggins, "Creating a Thought-Provoking Curriculum," *passim*.

18. Perkins, *Smart Schools*, p. 7.

19. Bryson and Scardamalia, "Teaching Writing," pp. 141–163; Newmann, "Higher Order Thinking in the School Curriculum," pp. 58–64; Lipman, *Thinking in Education*, p. 52.

20. Ronald Brandt, "On Teaching for Understanding: A Conversation with Howard Gardner," *Educational Leadership 50* 7 (April 1993): 4–7.

21. Richard S. Prawat, "The Value of Ideas: The Immersion Approach to the Development of Thinking," *Educational Leadership 70* 2 (August–September 1993): 10.

22. Benjamin Bloom, Max D. Engelhart, Edward J. Furst, Walker H. Hill, and David R. Krathwohl, *Taxonomy of Educational Objectives—Handbook 1: Cognitive Domain* (New York: David McKay, 1956).

23. Robert Marzano, "Fostering Thinking across the Curriculum through Knowledge Restructuring," *Journal of Reading 34* 7 (April 1991): 518–525; Fred M. Newmann, "Can Depth Replace Coverage in the High School Curriuclum?" *Phi Delta Kappan 70* 5 (January 1988): 396; Hilda Taba, "Learning by Discovery," *Elementary School Journal 63* 6 (March 1963): 311, 313.

24. Perkins, *Smart Schools, passim.*

25. Brophy, "Probing the Subtleties," pp. 4–8; Brown, "Cultivating a Literacy of Thoughtfulness," p. 6; John Dewey, *Experience and Education* (New York: Macmillan, 1963, 1971); Marzano, "Fostering Thinking," pp. 518–525; Perkins, *Smart Schools*, p. 45.

26. Brophy, "Probing the Subtleties," p. 5; Taba, "Learning by Discovery," p. 309.

27. Brown, "Cultivating a Literacy of Thoughtfulness," p. 6; Lipman, *Thinking in Education, passim.*

28. Barry K. Beyer, *Critical Thinking—What Is It?* (Bloomington: Phi Delta Kappa Educational Foundation, 1995); Robert Ennis, "A Logical Basis for Measuring Critical Thinking Skills," *Educational Leadership 43* 2 (October 1985): 44–48; Lipman, *Thinking in Education, passim*; Richard Paul, *Critical Thinking* (Rohnert Park, CA: Center for Critical Thinking and Moral Critique, 1990).

2

Providing Opportunities for Student Thinking

A thoughtful classroom could not exist without plenty of opportunities for students to engage in higher-order thinking. Without such opportunities, students would not be able to practice the kinds of thinking that are most in need of improvement. Moreover, without frequent opportunities to engage in such thinking, any serious effort to improve the quality of that thinking would be virtually impossible. Thus, ensuring that a classroom offers numerous and repeated opportunities to engage in higher-order thinking is essential to the development of student thinking.[1] This chapter describes and explains what can be done to build these thinking opportunities into any classroom teaching and learning.

TURNING OCCASIONS TO THINK INTO OPPORTUNITIES FOR THINKING

Most classrooms, including traditional recitation classrooms, present occasions for students to think. However, these occasions are usually sporadic, are often unrelated to the subject-matter learning that is supposed to be going on, and rarely involve higher-order thinking. A thoughtful classroom, on the other hand, not only provides numerous occasions for students to engage in different kinds of higher-order thinking but it also provides repeated occasions to engage in whatever kind of thinking the students need to improve. This enables students to build on successive applications of that particular kind of thinking so that they can improve their proficiency in carrying it out. In addition, these thinking occasions are a natural, authentic part of the substantive learning that is going on, thus motivating students to want to improve their abilities to execute it. Most significantly, in a thoughtful classroom these occasions for thinking are encountered as *opportunities* to be taken advantage of.

In a thoughtful classroom, thinking occasions are not "time to think" add-ons. Rather, they are occasions that *demand* thinking, as Vygotsky has noted, by making it necessary for students to engage in such thinking in order to succeed or move on.[2] These occasions *stimulate* student engagement in thinking by providing interesting and meaningful things to think about. In fact, these occasions actually *provoke* thinking, by triggering it and calling it into play.[3] By inviting thinking, these occasions become engaging *opportunities* for students to think—and for teachers to help students improve their abilities to do so.

Ensuring that such thinking opportunities exist in any classroom is as much a planning or design task as it is an instructional one. As teachers, we can create and provide these opportunities by focusing especially on two major aspects of teaching: the learning tasks or activities in which our students engage and the subjects or topics about which they seek to learn.

Attention to learning tasks or activities is essential because unless these tasks consist of natural and necessary occasions for engaging in the kind of thinking to be improved, students are not likely to invest the kind of effort in thinking that is required to improve it. Likewise, we as teachers are not likely to be able to provide the kinds of meaningful instruction and coaching that will help students make such improvement. Attention to the subjects of study in any classroom is essential because unless these subjects provoke, stimulate, and engage student interest, students are not likely to invest the effort or time required to carry out rather complex thinking or to produce the degree of understanding to which a thoughtful classroom aspires.[4] We can attend to both of these aspects of teaching by the ways we frame or structure student learning.

To provide compelling opportunities for higher-order thinking in our classrooms, we can do the following:

- Frame learning with thoughtful questions.
- Provoke puzzlement or dissonance.
- Engage students in knowledge-producing activities.
- Structure learning around knowledge-producing strategies.

Any or all of these techniques can provide opportunities to engage students in higher-order thinking to construct new and meaningful learning. Each stimulates student engagement in a particular way, but some sustain engagement longer than others. When several of these are combined, however, they reinforce each other and are more likely to compel students to take advantage of and sustain engagement in the thinking opportunities that arise in the course of their study and learning. All of these techniques can be employed, in different combinations with each other, to promote both thinking and learning. Explanations of what can be done specifically to apply these techniques in any classroom follow.

FRAME LEARNING WITH THOUGHTFUL QUESTIONS

Productive, higher-order student thinking can be initiated and structured in a number of ways. One way is by questions, but not just any kind of question will do for this purpose. For example, the question, When did Columbus discover America? differs considerably from the question, Who discovered Columbus? Both questions trigger thinking, but the former usually triggers recall and generally produces a quick and brief response. The latter triggers puzzlement as well as recall, and then hypothesizing and hypothesis testing interspersed by new, student-asked questions. It is this latter type of question that proves so useful in launching and stimulating increasingly complex student thinking. Teaching specialists refer to such questions as *thoughtful questions*.

Thoughtful questions may be employed in a variety of ways to create opportunities for sustained higher-order thinking and the thoughtful learning that results. Because these questions imply or embody additional subordinate questions that must be asked and answered in order to generate appropriate responses, thoughtful questions can structure, or organize, as well as initiate and stimulate thinking. Thoughtful questions may thus be used to frame entire curricula or major units of study within a curriculum or course. This may be done by building and sequencing learning activities or tasks around the subordinate questions that the major thoughtful question implies or generates. Thoughtful questions may also be used just as effectively to initiate and organize daily lessons, projects, or short units of several days' duration. Because thoughtful questions are so useful, designing and selecting them becomes an important aspect of any effort to create a thoughtful classroom.

The Nature of Thoughtful Questions

A thoughtful question is a question that stimulates or encourages student thinking beyond the level of recall or translation. It requires students to go mentally where they have not been before, to use information they may not have yet encountered, or to restructure information with which they are already familiar in order to produce something they did not know when that question was raised. Thoughtful questions make students think deeply and keep on thinking!

To develop a sense of what a thoughtful question is, consider the questions in Figure 2.1. Which question—number 1 or number 2—is more thoughtful, according to the preceding description of a thoughtful question? Clearly, question 2 requires more thinking to answer than does question 1. More importantly, the kind of thinking required to respond to question 2 is qualitatively different from the kind of thinking required to answer question 1. To develop an acceptable response to question 1 most likely requires recall. To develop an acceptable answer to question 2 requires, at the very least, making and testing hypotheses, analyzing information, evaluating data, and producing a sound argument—all types of higher-order thinking.

Now, which question—3 or 4—is more thoughtful? Why? Which question—5 or 6—is more thoughtful? Why? To what degree are the remaining questions thoughtful? Beyond the fact that they appear tougher to answer

Figure 2.1 Thoughtful and Thoughtless Questions

1. In what year did Christopher Columbus first sail to the New World?

2. If Christopher Columbus was so important, why aren't North and South America called North and South Columbia?

3. What are three democratic features of the United States today?

4. Is the United States more or less democratic today than it was at Independence?

5. What were three causes of the Civil War?

6. To what extent was the Civil War a "just" war?

7. How do outsiders—in any group or country—get to be insiders?

8. What and who make "great books" great? How? Why?

9. What if gravity were a horizontal rather than vertical force?

10. Who determines what is "just"? How? By what right?

Sources: Fred M. Newmann, "Higher Order Thinking in Teaching Social Studies," *Journal of Curriculum Studies* 22 1 (January–February 1990): 41–56; Herb Rosenfeld, "Commentary," in Barbara Means, Carol Chelemer, and Michael S. Knapp (Eds.), *Teaching Advanced Skills to At-Risk Students* (San Francisco: Jossey-Bass, 1991), pp. 246, 252; Rebecca Simmons, "The Horse Before the Cart? Assessing for Understanding," *Educational Leadership* 51 5 (February 1994): 22; Grant Wiggins, "Creating a Thought-Provoking Curriculum," *American Educator* 11 4 (Winter 1987): 12–13.

and more complicated, what specifically makes a thoughtful question thoughtful?

A thoughtful question is clearly *not* a question that can be answered simply by recall or with a single word or phrase. Nor is it a question to which most people in the room already know the preferred or "right" answer. Rather, a thoughtful question is one that stimulates students to think further and deeper than recall; it generates a variety of views and opinions; and it fosters discussion and exchange of information and views. Answering a thoughtful question necessitates finding and reorganizing information and data as well as evaluating the data and the questions derived from or based on them.

Educator Grant Wiggins claims that thoughtful questions are questions that do these things and more. He asserts that the most thoughtful question is one that meets the following criteria:[5]

- Deals with the most controversial and important topics or issues of a discipline or subject
- Has no obvious, single, prescribed correct answer
- Requires analysis, evaluation, and/or synthesis, as well as other types of complex thinking
- Allows personalized responses because there is no one correct way to go about developing an adequate response
- Requires the production or construction of new knowledge—knowledge presumably unknown by the students prior to receiving the question
- Advances students toward a deeper understanding of the subject on which they focus

Thoughtful questions, then, are questions that inspire—or require—complex thinking. These questions provide challenging opportunities for students to engage in a sustained way in a variety of kinds of thinking and especially in higher-order thinking as they seek to answer them. In fact, one of the most important tests of any question that purports to be a thoughtful question is the extent to which it requires use of various kinds of complex thinking such as analysis, evaluation, synthesis, nonroutine problem solving, and so on. Questions that can be answered by recall alone or by reference to readily accessible, authoritative sources—such as, How many homeless were there in America's five largest cities in 1996?—do not meet this test. A question such as, Who is responsible for the homeless in America? does meet the necessary requirements. Productive learning can easily be initiated by engaging students in developing well-supported responses to questions that meet these criteria.

Figure 2.2 lists some questions that experienced educators have proposed as thoughtful questions. Do you agree? To what extent do each of

Figure 2.2 Sample Thoughtful Questions

1. Who owns America?
2. Why was Euclid's set of postulates accepted over competing postulates as the basis for the geometry we study?
3. What era or incident from (given century) show (a people) at their *best* and *worst*? How so?
4. Why was 10 selected as a base for our number system?
5. To what extent would the American men and women who died in (the American Revolution/World War II/the Viet Nam War) think (your/our) generation (is/was) worth the sacrifices they made?
6. Why are some words and objects considered feminine or masculine in many languages?
7. Must everything that goes up come down?
8. What would genuine world peace look like? How would people have to change if they were truly committed to world peace?
9. To what extent was (any turning point or event) progress or a step backward?
10. When did (will) civilization start?

Sources: Martin Krovetz, David Casterson, Charlene McKowne, and Tom Willis, "Beyond Show and Tell," *Educational Leadership 50* 7 (April 1993): 74; Fred M. Newmann, "Higher Order Thinking in Teaching Social Studies," *Journal of Curriculum Studies 22* 1 (January– February 1990): 41–56; Grant Wiggins, "Creating a Thought-Provoking Curriculum," *American Educator 11* 4 (Winter 1987): 13.

these questions meet the criteria of thoughtful questions? For those questions you believe to be less thoughtful, what revisions would you make to them so that they are more thoughtful in terms of the discussed criteria? What additional thoughtful questions do these suggest?

Multidisciplinary Thoughtful Questions

The questions presented as examples of thoughtfulness up this point have all been subject or topic specific. However, some educators have developed or proposed sets of thoughtful questions that may be appropriately used in a variety of subjects to frame study of any number of topics. One such set of all-purpose thoughtful questions is that developed by the faculty of Central Park East Secondary School in New York. These questions can be asked of any text or source, whether academic, journalistic, literary, or student generated:

1. Whose voice am I hearing? From where is this statement or image coming? What's the point of view?
2. What is the evidence? How do we or they know? How credible is the evidence?
3. How do things fit together? What else do I know that fits with this?

4. What if? Could it have been otherwise? Are there alternatives?
5. What difference does it make? Who cares? Why should I care? [6]

Perkins presents these questions as follows:

1. From whose viewpoint are we seeing or reading or hearing? From what angle or perspective?
2. How do we know what we know? What's the evidence, and how reliable is it?
3. How are things, events, or people connected to each other? What is the cause and what the effect? How do they "fit" together?
4. So what? Why does it matter? What does it all mean? Who cares?[7]

Perkins calls thoughtful questions "thought-demanding" questions because they require complex thinking to produce acceptable responses.[8] These questions require students not only to process data to make it meaningful but also (especially in questions 1 and 2 in both sets) to get behind the data and deal with issues of methodology and point of view. Question 3 in both sets probes context, relationships, patterns, and connections. Questions 4 and 5 probe the implications of the data as well as the meaning made from or given to these data.

Another set of all-purpose thoughtful questions focusing even more on what is behind any given data or assertion may also be useful in provoking thinking and developing understanding:

1. What questions did the author(s)/speaker(s) ask in order to end up with (this/these) information or assertions?
2. What did the author(s)/speaker(s) assume to be true that made him/her/them sure of the accuracy of what is presented? Is it?
3. What could or should the author(s)/speaker(s) have asked but didn't? Why should these questions have been asked?
4. If these additional questions had been asked, what answers (would/ might) have been found or produced? Why? How?

These three sets of all-purpose thoughtful questions do not do the same thing. The first two sets essentially probe given points of view, evidence, relationships, and significance or meaning. The third set goes behind and beyond the given assertions to probe alternatives and assumptions and to generate additional knowledge related to the subject from a variety of different points of view. All, however, are *thought demanding* in the best sense of the term. Any of these combinations of questions can engage students in thoughtful analysis and knowledge production in virtually any subject.

Generating Thoughtful Questions

Creating thoughtful questions is not easy, especially for anyone who has not used them much in the past. To help generate such questions, however, we can do at least four things.

Select a Topic.   First, select a topic that is worth thinking about. The topic or subject embedded in a question is as important in engaging and sustaining student thinking as is the way in which the question itself is phrased. Unfortunately, no magic formula exists for identifying such engaging topics. However, experts have identified some features of thought-provoking topics that can serve as guidelines for identification. Perkins and his colleagues[9] for example, have suggested that potentially engaging topics are those that are:

- Accessible to students, in the sense of fitting students' perceived interests, needs, and goals or their conscious concerns, as well as being somewhat familiar to students and appropriate to their abilities, backgrounds, and experience
- Rich enough in detail, depth of detail, implications and interconnections, and relationships to diverse subjects inside and outside of school to allow students to develop "a rich play of varied extrapolation and connection(s)" through sustained dialogue and exchange of well-supported and critically examined competing points of view
- Open to diverse interpretation and methods of inquiry and lead in diverse substantive directions
- Capable of being entered at any of a variety of points

Even after identifying topics that *might* serve as the focal points of thoughtful questions, however, it is necessary to select the exact topic (or limited number of topics) around which to construct these questions. Although this choice may be directed by teacher and/or student preference to some extent, Newmann and several other specialists[10] suggest other criteria that prove useful in this process. According to them, a topic is worth framing as a thoughtful question if it does the following:

- Has "a critical position in a hierarchy of content"—if failure to understand it will put the students "at risk"
- Requires guidance of a teacher to understand, rather than being something that can be readily learned out side of school or by TV or other media
- Is one that teachers are likely to spend lots of time on, instead of rushing through it

- Contributes directly to the development of meaningful and significant key ideas, explanations, principles, concepts, and generalizations
- Can be learned about in the context of realistic problems
- Fits into the overall curriculum and course and will not be undertaken simply as a special opportunity to "be thoughtful"

Using these criteria to select topics for constructing thoughtful questions helps to ensure that the resulting questions will not only deal with topics of interest to the students but will enable them to develop significant and meaningful learning as well.

Begin at the Global Level.   Next, in considering the selected topic, begin at the top or at the global level when developing a subject-matter idea, or at the major thinking operation level when generating a cognitive task.[11] Global subject-matter questions focus on the big picture. They deal with broad rather than narrow ideas, with ill-defined rather than precisely delineated topics. Consequently, to answer such questions requires students to pose and then answer numerous subordinate questions as they seek to define and probe the initial question in all its implications. By inventing and working through these derivative questions, students generate their own focus, steer what they are learning about their own way, and develop a deep, sophisticated understanding of the topic or topics into which they are inquiring.

   In designing thoughtful learning tasks, we also can start at the global level with questions that require complex skills such as problem solving or evaluation or decision making, rather than questions that require only the application of a single cognitive skill such as classifying, for example. Global cognitive questions require engagement in a host of subordinate cognitive operations without specifying those operations, just as global subject-matter questions require probing into a host of subordinate topics or parts of the main topic. For example, evaluation of anything requires selection and definition of criteria to be used; collection, interpretation, and analysis of relevant data as well as critical assessment of those data; application of concepts and generalizations; and synthesis of well-grounded and sound judgments.

   The question, Was the United States more or less democratic in 1800 than it is today? exemplifies a global, thoughtful question. It is more global, less specific, and less precisely defined than are the questions, What rights are guaranteed in the Bill of Rights? and What rights did Americans have in 1800? Yet, answering the global question also requires generating and answering derivative questions like these. To develop a satisfactory response to a global question requires considerable planning, imagination, research, analysis, evaluation, and a highly divergent, personalized approach. It also involves both creative and critical thinking.

To respond to this particular thoughtful question, students could first define *democracy* as it is defined today and as it was defined in 1800, from the points of view of different ethnic groups, socioeconomic classes, and regions of the country in each period, and in different realms of life. They could then distinguish between democracy in theory and as it was in actual practice for all these groups, regions, and social, economic, and political arenas in each of the two given periods. This involves identifying what are to be accepted as criteria for measuring the extent to which identified democratic features existed, and then uncovering and assessing evidence related to these criteria, finally judging the degree to which and extent that the given features existed. Comparing the results of this inquiry for 1800 and today can lead to the development of a response to the initial question that must then be articulated and buttressed with sound reasoning and appropriate evidence. Preparing responses to this global question and others like it requires considerable time, mental effort, data searching and processing, and reflection. This, of course, produces much more complex thinking than is required to respond to more narrowly focused questions.

Word the Question Provocatively.   Third, thoughtful questions should be worded as provocatively as possible so as to invite student engagement.[12] Questions that present unusual, unanticipated, or unconventional points of view bother people, agitate thinking, spark curiosity, and demand responses. Who discovered Columbus? is a much more provocative question than Who did Columbus discover? It arouses perplexity, curiosity, and interest, and it even invites other questions from students. Instead of asking, What significant contributions has the United States made to the world? consider framing the question to be more provocative, as, for example, this question posed by a prominent, contemporary American author:

> The forces of good generally prevail over the forces of evil. If that's not true, then how the hell did we get to where we are today? The world has never been this good. And we did it. It's largely an American accomplishment.[13]

How thoughtful—and global—and provocative—is this question/statement? Why?

As an alternative to being provocative, a question can be framed so that it stimulates students to examine something from an unusual point of view or at least from one or more points of view other than theirs. Asking students to explain the Civil War from the point of view of, say, a farm boy in Indiana suddenly drafted into the Union army, or a southern plantation owner, or a mother who had lost her only two sons in battle, or a recently freed slave, or another individual affected by this conflict, or from several of these points of view will generate much deeper analysis and comprehension than will the less demanding, perhaps even recitation based, What caused the Civil War?

Engage the Students.   Finally, phrase thoughtful questions so they engage students in thinking about subjects or topics in novel ways. Psychologist Irving Sigel, for example, has asserted that challenging students to think in the "non-present" provokes and develops higher-level thinking.[14] To do this, Sigel recommends that students engage in predicting or planning future conditions or events, reconstructing past events or conditions in new ways, or transcending the present by representing it symbolically. He recommends further that students engage in tasks that require developing alternatives, finding multiple attributes, and establishing temporal and physical connections. Educator Rebecca Simmons believes that thoughtfulness can be furthered by having students reflect about questions before they attempt to answer them or before examining the answers they generated after completing such tasks.[15] Research by Isabel Beck and Margaret McKeown on guiding students to question authors also suggests a set of useful all-purpose questions that may be classified as thoughtful.[16] Such questions may be asked of the contents of textbooks, speeches, or any written product and even of speakers, including other students or teachers themselves.

Figure 2.3 presents a variety of thoughtful question sets that incorporate these suggestions and others. These question sets not only provoke higher-order thinking but they also serve as guideposts by which such thinking is stimulated and sustained.

Generating thoughtful questions need not be solely the teacher's responsibility. Students can invent or help invent such questions, too. Having them respond to questions such as What questions, if answered, would give you a better understanding of this (topic, subject, material)? often produces potentially useful thoughtful questions or ideas that can be converted into such questions.[17] Asking students to complete an "I wonder . . . " sentence before or after some introductory study of any given topic serves the same purpose. Listening to students' questions about subjects being studied and noticing the length of time they spend discussing topics can also identify questions or topics around which thoughtful questions can be constructed. Also, observing things about which students express curiosity or confusion or what they read or discuss when given free time or free-choice assignments can serve this same purpose.

Thoughtful questions, in sum, do more than simply initiate and provide opportunities for higher-order thinking. They also literally beg numerous more specific questions that students must articulate and pursue in order to

Figure 2.3 Selected Multidisciplinary Thoughtful Questions

For Critical Analysis—I

What questions does the information presented here answer?

What questions were not asked? Why not?

What questions do you wish had been asked but were not? Why?

If these questions had been asked, what would have been the answers? How do you know?

For Critical Analysis—II

What questions does this information answer?

How do you know the information is correct, objective, complete?

What other questions could or should have been asked? Why? What answers might you get to these questions?

What kind of person would have asked these questions or come up with these answers? What makes you think so?

How would some other kind of person have answered these? Why?

For Perspective Taking—I

What would have been the opinion a (type of person of the time or place) would most likely have had about this event (or condition)? Why?

What opinion would (another type of person of that same time or place) have most likely had about this event (or condition)? Why?

What can you infer about the major concerns most people of (that time or place) had about this event (or condition)?

For Perspective Taking—II

What are two or three images that come to your mind as you read this selection? What in this reading generated these images?

What would be the response of each of (two or three types of) people (of this time or place) to each of these images? Why?

What images might each of these people have come up with? Why?

For Exploring Alternatives or Options

What options were *not* considered here? Why not?

What might have happened if each option had been chosen?

What would (specific groups involved) have seen as the positives and negatives of each predicted consequence of those options considered? Why? Of those not considered? Why?

continued

Figure 2.3 *Continued*

For Reflecting on Questions

Before: Which questions can be answered definitely?

Which questions might have several answers?

After: Which questions produced the most interesting/useful/relevant responses? Why?

Were some answers better than others? If so, which? Why?

For Helping Students to Represent the Same Thing in Different Ways

What are some alternative ways to do this (actions we could take)?

What are all the different features/properties of this you can see or find?

What connections can you find between this and other things/times (etc.)?

For Thinking in the Nonpresent

In visualizing *X*, what is it you see?

What would be a fun/good story about *X*?

What did you do on your (imaginary) trip to *X*?

For Questioning an Author or Speaker

What does the author/speaker mean by (give a quote)? Why? How can you tell?

What is the author/speaker trying to say? Why? How can you tell?

How does this connect to what the author/speaker wrote or said earlier?

How does what the author/speaker wrote/said differ from what we already know about this? What might account for this difference?

develop the kind of responses required to satisfactorily answer these larger, thought-provoking questions. One way to identify a thoughtful question is to imagine the other, more specific questions that must be asked and answered in order to answer the broader question! Thoughtful questions sustain and direct higher-order thinking, as well as initiate it.

Thoughtful questions provide students with a real need to think, and thus motivate students to attempt to apply—and to improve their skill at executing—cognitive skills needed to carry out the task of responding. Such questions also enable students to use a number of different cognitive operations in combination with each other to accomplish a meaningful task.

And, according to some experts, these questions increase the likelihood that proficiency in more complex thinking and the discrete operations or skills of which it consists will be transferred to an increasingly wider variety of other contexts.[18] Using thoughtful questions to frame and initiate learning can provide an opportunity to start the thinking process and keep it going.

PROVOKE PUZZLEMENT OR DISSONANCE

Although thoughtful learning can be launched by teacher-asked questions or teacher-supplied problems, the most effective learning starts when a student seeks an answer to his or her *own* question, or seeks to resolve a problem of personal concern rather than a question or problem posed by someone else. Such student-asked questions or problems customarily arise out of surprise or perceived discontinuity or dissonance in a situation that a learner cannot accept as presented. It is, as Wiggins asserts, the "jolt of suddenly not understanding what seemed once simple or unproblematic" that leads to deeper thought and understanding.[19] The natural desire for closure, an intolerance for ambiguity, or a desire for things to be or work as one imagines they should drives students to exert effort to eliminate the dissonance or achieve certainty. We can engage students in student-driven, thoughtful classroom learning by putting them into situations in which they are confronted by something that bothers them. Their desire for closure can then lead them to take productive action, such as asking questions to which they will seek answers on their own.[20]

Providing Thought-Provoking "Jolts"

Presenting students with a math problem and three different solutions or solutions worked three different ways invariably leads to a question: Well, which one is right? Presenting a demonstration in which something occurs that is exactly the opposite of what is expected raises an almost spontaneous question: Why did that happen? Providing students with several differing accounts of the same event serves the same purpose in literature or social studies. For instance, by presenting the two paragraphs in Figure 2.4 during a study of the appropriate topic in world history, students can be stimulated to come up with one or more questions of their own to answer.

Confronted with the two accounts given in Figure 2.4, young learners normally are provoked to ask an assortment of questions: So, which one is right? What *really* happened? Which are we supposed to believe? Who wrote these? How can we tell which is true? All these questions can initiate new points of investigation and inspire further thinking. From this point on, students can plan a strategy for answering *their* questions. In the process,

Figure 2.4 Sample Statements for Stimulating Dissonance

Selection A

When chief Mojimba and his people heard that a white man, William Stanley, and his party were coming down the Congo River, they prepared a feast and went to honor him. Dressed in ceremonial garb, they swept along the river in great canoes, amidst the beating of thunderous drums, songs of joy and jubilant dancing. But as they drew near to Stanley's boats, they heard gunshots. Many Africans were shot dead. Mojimba and his people turned and fled back to their village. But the white man's party followed and plundered and burned their village, killing everyone they found.

Selection B

Stanley's expedition was attacked repeatedly by the natives. One time, as his string of canoes reached a wide spot in the Congo, they were attacked by Africans in a flotilla of gigantic canoes which eclipsed in size and number anything they had yet seen. Though outnumbered 10 to 1, Stanley's party drove them off. Then they pursued their attackers to their village, where they carried the fight to the village streets and hunted the inhabitants into the woods.

they will raise more specific, task-defining questions. They will identify the information they need to locate and where they might find it, and decide how best to secure it, how to determine its accuracy, and how to figure out what it means vis-à-vis the given statements.

The element of surprise, for instance, can lead to more thoughtful learning, especially when skillfully guided. The "jolt" that sparks that surprise may be as simple as an unexpected and unusual claim, as in the unveiling of a letter to the editor, such as the following, to launch a celebration of Columbus Day:

> As we celebrate another Columbus Day, we, the original people, will mourn 500 years of oppression. Yes, oppression. We will "celebrate" 500 years of broken treaties, broken promises, massacres, starvation, and enslavement.
>
> Osceola, for one, was captured, under a flag of truce, and jailed at Fort DeSoto, in St. Augustine. This fort, by the way, was built by native American slave labor.
>
> I have been in the very cell in which the great Osceola was kept as a animal in a cage in a zoo.
>
> My own ancestor, Black Hawk, was encaged after his capture, and taken to several mid-Eastern states on exhibition for the white people to gaze upon a red savage.
>
> This is American history. Therefore, we, the original people, will mourn on Columbus Day.
>
> *Signed*

Tampa[21]

The desire to reconcile this claim with the traditionally accepted view of the celebrated "discovery" by Columbus or the desire to determine the validity or accuracy of this claim can spark many a thoughtful learning activity.

A thought-provoking "jolt" may also be provided by a potentially controversial position or statement—one that challenges the point of view commonly accepted by students. How jolting might high school students find this statement by a former president of the American Society of Newspaper Editors?

> If you have information, you print it. If it discloses state secrets, so be it. . . . The newspaper's role in America is to tell the public what's going on. Newspapers aren't supposed to keep secrets; they're supposed to disclose secrets.[22]

To what extent might a statement like this spark or stimulate thoughtful learning? Providing statements such as these often serves the same purpose as asking a thoughtful question. Such statements also have the advantage of stimulating students to pose their own questions—questions to which, because they are *their* questions, students are usually more motivated to respond.

This thought-provoking approach to initiating student learning was widely used in the 1960s in innovative curricula in mathematics, the sciences, English, and social studies—often referred to as the New Social Studies, New Math, New English, and so on. Psychologist Jerome Bruner articulated much of the rationale and cognitive theory behind this approach, called *discovery learning* or *inquiry* by its proponents. Thoughtful classrooms today can easily apply the techniques and theory behind these earlier approaches to stimulate student-initiated questioning and higher-order thinking.[23]

What conditions create the "jolts" that produce dissonance and thus provoke thoughtfulness on the part of most students? Rex Brown identifies the following as especially useful:

Mystery

Uncertainty

Disagreement/contradiction

Ambiguity

Curiosity

Unanswered questions of importance to students[24]

Learning materials, tasks, and situations that incorporate any of these conditions or build on them can initiate and sustain the application of higher-order thinking.

Potential Problems in Provoking Thinking

When creating and planning thought-provoking activities, it is important to remain alert to the pitfalls inherent in using this approach to launching student-directed learning. Three of these pitfalls deserve attention here.

First, all student-generated questions are *not* thoughtful. Many do not require complex analysis or evaluation or synthesis making. Who wrote that? may prompt a search for an author and for information about him or her, but little complex analysis is involved. On the other hand, How could anyone say that? leads to considerably more complex information finding, evaluation, analysis, and hypothesizing or conclusion making. Many student questions tend to be convergent, in search of *the* one correct answer and a simple one at that. We, as teachers, must often guide student questioning into broader, productive thinking areas rather than into narrow, fact-gathering sorties. We can do this by helping students evaluate their questions by using the criteria for thoughtful questions (discussed earlier in this chapter). We then guide them in pursuing those questions and related questions that will get them deepest into the subject and require use of the thinking operations that we believe need to be further developed. Student efforts to answer these questions will provide natural opportunities for our purposeful instructional intervention to improve student execution of these operations.

Second, even though provoked, curious, surprised, puzzled, or otherwise potentially motivated to raise a question for further consideration, many students are reluctant to do so. This is because past experience tells students that when they ask a question, they then have to answer it—and doing that, especially when it requires much mental effort, is not what they prefer to do. Many would much rather be told what the answer is so they can simply recall it for the inevitable test and then forget the whole thing. The reluctance of many students to engage in sustained thinking, at least in academic subjects, sometimes limits frequent use of the most dissonance-producing "jolts."

Third, sometimes puzzling or dissonance-producing activities provoke thoughtful questions but not the kind intended or related to the data already stockpiled for use by the students in pursuing the anticipated thoughtful question. One way to handle such a student-initiated surprise is to engage the students in examining the assumptions underlying their questions. Another is to engage them immediately in planning how to answer the questions raised, including what kind of information they need to find and the locations of the sources of this information. A data-gathering expedition can then be undertaken, interspersed with more thoughtful data analysis, evaluation, interpretation, and further analysis.

Thus, provoking students to articulate their own questions, problems, or issues about which to inquire or about which to construct new insights does not always produce the kind of thoughtful learning opportunity desired or anticipated. Simply presenting students with what we perceive as a potentially puzzling or inherently contradictory question or task (because it worked in last year's class) may be safer and produce the desired results, but it may rob the students of an opportunity to follow a line of inquiry that is especially interesting to them *this* year! We can also combine a provocative "jolt" with a thoughtful follow-up question that makes the answer worth pursuing and thus engages the students in thoughtful learning.

ENGAGE STUDENTS IN KNOWLEDGE-PRODUCING ACTIVITIES

In a thoughtful classroom, learning activities are selected at least as much for their thoughtfulness as for their pedagogical nature. Thoughtful learning activities are those that engage students in producing new (to the students) understandings or other forms of knowledge through the use of various types of thinking with and about information or data. Thoughtful learning activities take students beyond where they were when they started by engaging them in solving new, nonroutine or ill-defined problems; assessing knowledge claims and the methods and data from which they were derived; finding or making relationships or patterns; or doing anything that moves the students beyond their current knowledge or cognitive skill levels.

Transcribing information from an encyclopedia or paraphrasing or summarizing what someone else has asserted is not *pro*ductive because it consists of *re*producing something that already exists. Hypothesizing, concluding, designing experiments, and making critical judgments, however, are *pro*ductive because they result in the construction of knowledge that did not exist prior to engagement in these operations, at least inosfar as the students are aware. Productive thinking activities may be carried out in a variety of ways—as class discussions, through collaborative learning, as part of library research, in the production of term papers, in the form of projects, even with or without textbooks.

Two kinds of knowledge-producing activities are most appropriate for use in a thoughtful classroom. One consists of specific, short-range tasks that involve generating new knowledge, such as hypothesis making and testing or assessing the logic of an argument. The other is a more general, broader activity that incorporates a larger number of cognitive operations and is carried out over a longer period of time in the form of a project. Both types can be stimulating, challenging, and engaging thinking experiences if they are carefully designed and carried out. Both lead to constructing, or producing, new understandings and knowledge. And both provide repeated opportunities for students to engage in a variety of higher-order thinking skills and thus authentic opportunities for us to provide guidance and instruction for improving student execution of these skills.

Short-Term Knowledge-Producing Activities

Figure 2.5 identifies some short-term thoughtful learning tasks that enable students to produce insights and other forms of new knowledge. Most require no more than one or two normal-length class periods to complete;

Figure 2.5 Short-Term Knowledge-Producing Activities

1. Plan and conduct an experiment to test a hypothesis or to discover something.
2. Find accurate, appropriate information about something in a large database.
3. Clarify or define a problem or situation for further study, investigation, or action.
4. Identify the kinds of information needed to substantiate or evaluate a claim or to accomplish another goal.
5. Critique given or found information or assertions to determine their accuracy.
6. Judge the merits of ideas, assumptions, inferences, knowledge claims, and arguments.
7. Develop and support a concept, generalization, explanation, hypothesis, or conclusion.
8. Evaluate the strength—the accuracy and soundness—of arguments.
9. Find patterns or relationships.
10. Determine what *really* happened by analyzing a variety of sources.
11. Analyze a controversial issue to determine the "best" position.
12. Use a specific principle, concept, theory, or generalization to explain a specific event, situation, condition, or process.
13. Articulate and justify or critically evaluate a variety of viewpoints.
14. Construct a workable new procedure or product that solves a problem, meets a significant need, or assists in accomplishing a important goal.
15. Locate and critically evaluate sources of information and the information uncovered.
16. Synthesize information and findings in the form of hypotheses, conclusions, explanations, arguments, concepts, graphic representations, or other forms of knowledge.
17. Plan a strategy for answering a question, resolving a problem, assessing a claim, making a decision, creating a concept or generalization, or developing a well-supported and logically sound position on an issue of importance.
18. Construct a convincing argument in support of a conclusion or claim, plan, or problem solution.

Note: Items 2 and 18 are from Allan Collins, Jan Hawkins, and Sharon M. Carver, "A Cognitive Apprenticeship for Disadvantaged Students," in Barbara Means, Carol Chelemer, and Michael S. Knapp (Eds.), *Teaching Advanced Skills to At-Risk Students* (San Francisco: Jossey-Bass, 1991), pp. 266. 240; item 13 is from Fred M. Newmann, "Can Depth Replace Coverage in the High School Curriculum?" *Phi Delta Kappan 70* 5 (January 1988): 345–348.

some can be completed in less than one. Actual completion time will vary, however, depending on the abilities of the students, the amount of data or cases involved, the number of options considered, and the complexity of the claim or plan developed. Critiquing a single claim, for example, obviously takes less time than critiquing a section of a textbook or a lengthy math proof.

What makes the learning tasks in Figure 2.5 knowledge-producing activities? According to specialists,[25] to be a knowledge-producing activity, a task must:

- Contribute directly to creating new knowledge (something the students did not know or could not do prior to engaging in the activity)
- Require complex, higher-order thinking
- Involve sustained, cognitive effort by the students
- Be open ended and amenable to varied and individualized student approaches, response forms, products, or answers
- Require substantiation of responses, positions, and solutions with evidence and sound reasoning
- Require communicating the results to others

The knowledge-producing activities presented in Figure 2.5 can be developed for use in any subject at almost any grade level. For instance, planning how to determine whether artificial or natural light produces better flowers from seed exemplifies the first kind of knowledge-producing activity in Figure 2.5—planning an experiment. Such an activity is well suited for use in studying science in the elementary grades. Evaluating the accuracy of a statement such as "Living conditions of European settlers in their first five years in any of the original 13 colonies were worse than anything these people experienced in their homelands" exemplifies activity 6 in Figure 2.5 and may be well suited for use in middle school social studies classrooms.

Most of the activities in Figure 2.5 require the application of several related higher-order cognitive operations. For instance, evaluating the strength of an argument (activity 8 in Figure 2.5) consists of judging the accuracy of the information presented and assessing the logic of the argument for consistency, fallacies, and bias. It also involves evaluating the significance and sufficiency of reasons and evidence provided. Yet, all of these operations are essentially types of evaluation—students must apply given or self-invented criteria to judge some quality. Others, such as finding accurate or appropriate information about something in a large database (activity 2 in Figure 2.5) consist essentially of single cognitive tasks. Initial efforts at thoughtful teaching might consist of indepth engagement in only one or two of these as part of a broader study of a subject. However, as students demonstrate an ability to carry out these individual tasks, these tasks can be combined to construct more complete learning tasks, such as producing a meaningful conclusion, understanding, generalization, solution, or other kind of complex knowledge.

One way to accomplish this is to combine the activities in Figure 2.5 into longer, more meaningful knowledge-producing activities. For instance, asking students to *explain* a cause/effect relationship among certain events or conditions would, at the very least, involve them in the following:

- Planning a strategy to complete a task (activity type 1)
- Critiquing given information for accuracy and soundness (activity type 1)
- Finding patterns, relationships, and connections (activity type 6)
- Evaluating assertions against data (activity type 4)
- Judging the merits of ideas (activity type 5)
- Articulating and evaluating competing, relevant viewpoints (activity type 10)
- Constructing an argument in support of a conclusion or claim (activity type 12)

Any thoughtful learning activity, whether one of those listed in Figure 2.5 or one that combines several of these activities, requires intense mental effort and considerable time to complete satisfactorily. Productive learning activities are not single-minded, one-shot, hit-and-run affairs!

Another way to provide for student engagement in productive learning is to involve students in a series of what Perkins calls *understanding performances*. Here, students produce products or demonstrations that call for increasingly deeper understanding of the idea, concept, or generalization or kind of knowledge or skills they are developing. In producing these performances, students engage in a series of thinking tasks that become increasingly more complex and challenging as they get further and further into the subject of their investigation. According to Perkins,[26] understanding performances consist of activities such as the following:

- Explaining or justifying a generalization, concept, or conclusion in one's own words
- Giving and finding examples in contexts not previously encountered
- Making analogies to a novel situation
- Identifying the basic features or principles of something and elaborating them
- Applying a generalization or concept in new contexts to generate further knowledge
- Identifying the relationships of a generalization or concept to other generalizations or concepts and to one's previous knowledge or experience

- Generalizing findings to new examples and contexts
- Representing results in new ways
- Imagining examples, applications, or other incidences of what has been learned

Such demonstrations can be initiated by questions or in the form of directions via worksheets, task cards, or periodic assignments. They may be general or subject specific, and they may be presented all at once or as subtasks of a major task, one subtask at a time.

Long Term Knowledge-Producing Projects

Activities that require students to prepare written or multimedia products or other types of culminating performances can also meet the criteria of thoughtful learning activities. These activities generally take longer than do the short-range activities just described. Activities focused on resolving a meaningful problem or developing a response to a significant question allow students to develop their thinking skills and knowledge.[27] Such longer-range activities provide repeated opportunities to engage in a wide variety of cognitive operations. These are, thus, natural, in-context opportunities for teachers to step in and provide instruction in any new or difficult thinking procedures that are needed to carry out these operations. Denoting these activities as projects underscores their cognitive complexity as well as the time required to carry them out. Organizing topics or units of study as projects provides a realistic, purposeful, *authentic* application context for student thinking.

Essentially, projects are long-term activities that involve the development and presentation of some kind of product, performance, or discourse that demonstrates understanding of a topic, subject, problem, or question. Projects may produce plans, narratives, explanations, arguments, or creative products such as concepts, plays, or solutions to problems of significance. Lilian Katz and Sylvia Chard have distinguished three major types of projects: construction, investigation, and dramatization.[28]

Construction projects consist of the production of models, costumes, pictures, maps, or other student-made products. They involve students in brainstorming and designing these products; planning how and what to do to create them; researching needed information; organizing, monitoring, and carrying out agreed-upon procedures; establishing criteria for and on-going evaluating of the intended product; drafting and revising product prototypes or drafts; and producing the finished product(s). *Investigations*, according to Katz and Chard, consist of defining problems, brainstorming potential solution strategies, and organizing, executing, and evaluating efforts to carry out at least one of these strategies. They often involve creating, conducting, and evaluating the results of library research, surveys and interviews, controlled experiments, explanations, and hypothesis making and testing. *Dramatizations*, which Katz and Chard call *dramatic play*, range from simple reader's theater plays and enacting stories, to role-plays, simulations, and the actual creation, writing, and production of dramatizations. Most of these involve some degree of considerable social interaction, bargaining, resolving disputes, and planning, as well as brainstorming, analyzing, evaluating, and generating syntheses. All of these kinds of projects, in fact, require considerable, sustained thinking of various kinds.

To be useful in any curriculum that seeks to improve student thinking, projects should meet the criteria of knowledge-producing activities (presented earlier). In addition, specialists[29] recommend that projects should:

- Be a long-term effort, requiring extended application of time and effort
- Involve students in making informed choices of what to do, what to use, when to do things, and how to monitor and evaluate what they are doing as they do it
- Incorporate analogical elaborations, problems, or cases in order for students to generalize (transfer) the skills and concepts to a variety of applications
- Incorporate collaborative student planning, execution and evaluation of the procedure(s) used and the product(s) or performances(s) generated
- Include opportunities for periodic reflection on the process as well as on the evolving product
- Share the final product, performance, or demonstration with a specified audience

Many different projects that meet these criteria can be imagined. They may be student or teacher initiated and require only a few hours or several weeks or more, depending on the age and abilities of the students as well as the nature and subject of the project. Figure 2.6 presents examples of such projects.

The kinds of potentially powerful thoughtful projects for use in any grade level or subject by students of any ability are virtually endless. The key to the success of any of these, however, remains the extent to which the projects provide for long-term engagement in complex thinking in a context "likely to be encountered by the youngsters in a real life student or adult life setting or circumstance."[30] Such an activity provides students with opportunities to engage in meaningful learning by applying a variety of higher-order thinking operations. It also provides opportunities for teachers to intervene with direct, instructional assistance in how to carry out those

Figure 2.6 Sample Knowledge-Producing Projects

A Newcomer's Guide

Produce a written and/or multimedia package for orienting newcomers to a school building, community, subject (e.g., American literature, biology, or algebra), the planet Earth, the twenty-first century, a concept (cold or gravity or responsibility), a thing (a book), or any place, time, event, or concept. Interviews, library research, and field studies can be used to locate appropriate information; after it has been evaluated, organized, and pulled together, the results can be produced in the forms of maps, videos, brochures, guide books, photo boards, flowcharts, and similar formats.

"Your are There"

Produce, stage, and enact a TV or radio show or dramatic play on an important event in school, in history, or in an academic subject (e.g., the discovery of some basic scientific principle. Production of this show will involve researching information, conceptualizing and creating a product, writing and staging it, preparing scenery and costumes, and the final performance. In its final form, the show may be videotaped, or presented as a picture book with photographs of the actors, or presented as a live stage show or television performance.

The Great Detective Chase

Assume the role of detective—historian, scientist, literary critic, mathematician—to track down whoever committed a significant historical incident (Who invented democracy?) or the solution to a significant problem (Why do plants need light?) or the author of a particular literary work. The "who" may be a collective, such as a group, nation, or category of people; the "why" may be any phenomena or combination thereof; the time period may be past, present, or future. Teams may start by investigating the scene of the problem or event—perhaps a description of a botched science experiment, an erroneous math proof, several different graphs that claim to represent accurately a given table of data, or conflicting eyewitness accounts of the same event. They brainstorm potential concepts or causes, identify needed evidence, search for it, analyze what is found, and then arrange and present it to a "Grand Jury" (of student peers or parents) using written and multimedia materials.

Design an Exhibit

Design a museum exhibit around a theme studied in a specific course or subject. Select and identify artifacts for display, and justify reasons for not selecting other artifacts. Write captions and explanations for each item to be displayed, and prepare a viewers' guide. The entire display and guide can then be opened to the class in a special preview showing and perhaps even later shared with other classes and/or parents.

continued

Figure 2.6 *Continued*

Let's Go on Tour

Prepare a 15-day, 10-concert (world, North American, or other geographic region) travel itinerary for a favorite musical group. Include a daily travel and major activity schedule, appropriate maps, and information about apparel to be taken, lodging to be used, activities or attractions to visit, "do and don't" information about the areas or cultures to be visited, and an itemized budget (not to exceed a specified amount). A brochure advertising the tour could present the final plan, perhaps to attract potential customers. Setting the tour in a selected historical period can make this project useful in the study of the past, as well.

A Citizenship or Scientist Merit Badge

Create the requirements for a badge for a particular role—such as a responsible citizen of the school or nation, a good thinker, a humanitarian, a scientist, a mathematician, an author, or so on—and the procedures for meeting these requirements. Then prepare samples of the materials required at each stage of the process, including written guides, video demonstrations, flowcharts, how-to-do-it explanations, and models. Another student team can then evaluate a proposed badge by carrying out the requirements as stipulated, and perhaps revising them for later use.

Now's Your Chance

Prepare a written, pictorial, graphic promotional performance program or product that would make people want to solve a specific problem, or live in a particular place, or participate in an important historic event (such as their community 100 years ago, ancient Ghana, a science lab, the senior year of high school, being a Teach America volunteer, etc.). The necessary research, data analysis, evaluation, and synthesis could be presented in a multimedia, written, or performance format, shared with others and recorded for future use.

Note: Design an Exhibit and Let's Go on Tour are adapted from Grant Wiggins, "Creating Tests Worth Taking," *Educational Leadership* 49 8 (May 1992): 26–33.

thinking operations that students are working to improve as they pursue this meaningful learning.

Guidelines for Planning and Conducting Knowledge-Producing Activities

Experts recommend a number of guidelines for planning student-centered, knowledge-producing projects.[31] To ensure success, they suggest the following:

- Initiate the project by engaging students in familiar content and activity in order to show them the legitimacy of their existing knowledge, and to raise this knowledge to a level of consciousness that will make it available as a support for subsequent activities related to completing the overall activity.

- Discuss a variety of different procedures so that students realize that any specific heuristic or process is not the absolute or only way to carry out the activity.
- Have students work jointly in mixed groups, collaborating to achieve a common goal or produce a common product. But allow them also to work individually to complete parts of the overall activity by pursuing their own tasks, devising and executing their own procedures, and then sharing, evaluating, and synthesizing the findings obtained by all members of the group.
- From the beginning, give students examples of work to be done or the products to be produced so they will have a target to shoot at and will understand the criteria that distinguish "in-the-ballpark" products from unacceptable products.
- Ensure that data for student use are real, plentiful, readily available, and in a variety of formats.
- Allow a realistic amount of time for all students to do as thorough a job as possible in completing the project.
- Fit the project into the subject matter or content of the course and the themes or big ideas being developed rather than adding it on.
- Be prepared to provide individual or group instruction, coaching, and other assistance as needed.

Engaging students in knowledge-producing, constructivist activities—whether short or long range—does not mean that we, as teachers, abandon the students. On the contrary, while they work individually or in teams or groups to complete these activities, we can provide assistance, as needed, in terms how to go about finding and thinking about information. We can coach or assist individuals or small groups (or even the entire class) in carrying out their projects, clarifying aspects of the task, helping them connect what they are doing or finding out to what they already know or need to find out, and showing them how to implement cognitive procedures more skillfully. By engaging students in learning activities such as those described here, we can provide continuing, purposeful opportunities for higher-order thinking and for improving this thinking for all students.

STRUCTURE LEARNING AROUND KNOWLEDGE-PRODUCING STRATEGIES

Virtually all worthwhile thinking is strategic. It is done systematically to achieve a specific goal. In a thoughtful classroom, students seek to understand or comprehend something or otherwise produce knowledge that they do not currently possess. Consequently, to improve the quality of student thinking and learning, we can structure learning activities around the major steps of any of the knowledge-producing strategies employed in academic pursuits as well as in civic and everyday life. By doing so, we can engage students in thinking as *integral* parts of purposeful, meaningful, knowledge-producing efforts, and thus avoid fragmenting it into isolated, episodic exercises more typical of skill-drill teaching and learning.

A *strategy* is a plan for achieving a major goal. It is operationalized as a step-by-step procedure, each step of which consists of a routine or set of substeps by which that portion of the overall strategy is or can be carried out. The steps in most procedures are not strictly linear but are, in fact, recursive. However, most people expert in executing these strategies generally move through these procedural steps in a systematic fashion.

Knowledge-producing strategies are cognitive strategies employed to generate or construct knowledge. People utilize such strategies to locate needed information and to validate or authenticate that information to solve problems, to develop conclusions, to generalize, to conceptualize, and so on. Figure 2.7 presents major steps in each of several common knowledge-producing strategies used in and out of school. The procedure listed for each strategy is not the only one by which that strategy can be operationalized, of course. However, these procedures are used by many experts to carry out these particular strategies. As such, they and the subroutines of each major step are worth identifying and sharing with students. This will enable students to use the procedures to help make their thinking and learning more productive.

Each of the strategies presented in Figure 2.7, as well as others like these, can be used to execute a particular kind of knowledge-producing task. To produce a concept of fraction, for instance, students can engage in a lesson or sequence of lessons organized around the strategy of conceptualizing. To judge the quality of a story, they can engage in activities that move them through the strategy of critical evaluation. To determine the relative effects of water, heat, and light on growing plants, they could carry out a series of experiments, each organized along the lines of an experimenting strategy. Learning activities and lessons that are organized by these strategies will provide students with repeated, sustained, and meaningful opportunities to engage in all kinds of useful thinking. Simultaneously, we, as teachers, will be provided with opportunities to help them improve their developing expertise in carrying out this thinking.

Structuring lessons, activities, or units around any knowledge-producing strategy consists of sequencing student learning according to the steps in a procedure for carrying out that strategy. Instead of planning student study in terms of the study activities they will be expected to engage in (e.g., reading a text, listening to a lecture, filling in a worksheet, making a model,

Figure 2.7 Knowledge-Producing Strategies

Problem Solving

1. Identify and clarify a problem.
2. Select or devise a plan (strategy) for resolving the problem.
3. Carry out the plan, monitoring, evaluating, and revising it as necessary.
4. Evaluate the solution/conclusion and the plan used to produce it.

Analysis

1. Identify purpose of the analysis.
2. Identify evidence/clues to look for.
3. Search item by item to find evidence/clues/parts.
4. Identify any pattern among evidence/clues/parts.
5. State findings—with qualifications, as necessary.

Critical Evaluation

1. Identify purpose of evaluation.
2. Identify criteria to be used.
3. Search for evidence related to criteria.
4. Match evidence related to criteria.
5. Judge degree of match of evidence to criteria.
6. State final judgment.

Investigation

1. Identify what is already known/accepted.
   • Identify credible sources.
   • Collect relevant information from sources.
2. Identify contradictions or omissions or confusions.
3. Identify information needed to resolve contradictions, etc.
   • Identify credible sources.
   • Collect relevant information.
4. Present solutions to or findings about contradictions/confusions.

Hypothesis Making and Testing

1. Observe or define a problematic situation or event.
2. Generate a possible explanation (hypothesis).
3. Predict what evidence would exist (or what would be true) if the hypothesis were true (if . . . then).
4. Find that evidence as well as any evidence that contradicts the hypothesis.
5. Evaluate the accuracy, authenticity, sufficiency, and strength of the evidence.
6. State findings about the accuracy of the hypothesized explanation.

Invention

1. Identify the purpose of the invention.
2. Determine the standards to be met by the invention.
3. Create a rough sketch or plan or simple model.
4. Prepare a prototype, draft, or pilot.
5. Try it out.
6. Evaluate its performance against designated standards.
7. Revise it and repeat steps 4–7 until it works.

Experiment

1. Identify a phenomenon or hypothesis.
2. Clarify the variables involved.
3. Plan an experiment that tests identified variables in their effect(s) on the observed phenomenon or hypothesis.
4. Carry out the experiment, ensuring objectivity, control of all variables, and precision.
5. State the results of the experiment.

continued

Figure 2.7 *Continued*

Conceptualization

1. Identify examples of the target "concept."
2. Identify key attributes of all examples.
3. Categorize attributes of all examples.
4. Prepare a diagram or model relating all categories together.
5. Check the concept model by looking for these attributes in other examples and nonexamples.
6. Modify the concept model to accommodate additional concept examples encountered.

writing a report, etc.), we can plan lessons in terms of the *cognitive* operations that constitute the steps in the procedure by which a particular knowledge-producing strategy is carried out.

How might such a strategy-based sequence of learning activities proceed? As an example, take an activity (or a series of activities) organized around the hypothesis-making and testing strategy. This strategy is a widely used knowledge-producing strategy in and out of school. Classroom learning organized around a procedure for carrying out this strategy would engage students in the following:

- Observing or studying an event (e.g., an incident described in a story, a proffered solution to a given problem, a historical happening, etc.), perhaps to identify its causes
- Brainstorming possible explanations (hypotheses) for what happened and why
- For each hypothesized explanation, predicting what would have had to happen or exist if it were true (or would occur if the same circumstances arose again)
- For each hypothesized explanation, predicting what would have had to happen or exist if it were *not* true (or would *not* occur if the same circumstances arose again)
- Identifying the kinds of evidence that, if it existed, would confirm the accuracy of each prediction
- Determining where and how such evidence could be found or produced
- Finding or producing the needed evidence as well as identifying any unanticipated evidence that turns up
- Evaluating the accuracy, strength, authenticity, and sufficiency of the evidence—both positive and negative for each hypothesis considered

- Stating findings about the apparent accuracy or truthfulness of each hypothesis examined

As students engage in and complete these tasks, they essentially move through a strategy of hypothesis making and testing to produce knowledge about the event being examined. In carrying out these tasks, students, of course, employ a variety of higher-order cognitive operations—some rather simple (such as distinguishing relevant from irrelevant evidence) and some rather complex (such as evaluating the accuracy, strength, and sufficiency of that evidence). By using this strategy to structure the students' study, we provide numerous and sustained opportunities for them to engage in different kinds of complex thinking in any subject matter.

Any of the knowledge-producing strategies outlined in Figure 2.7 may be employed to organize a thoughtful lesson or a sequence of thoughtful lessons. Of all these, however, problem solving is the most powerful, for two reasons. First, learning, itself, is problem solving.[32] When we treat any learning as resolving a knowledge or skill gap or deficit, teaching then becomes facilitating student movement through the cognitive operations that constitute the steps in problem solving to close this gap or deficit.

Second, problem solving can employ any of the other strategies outlined in Figure 2.7 as a solution plan or strategy. In other words, to solve a scientific problem, students may employ the strategy of experimenting—monitoring, evaluating, and adjusting that strategy as they move toward a conclusion. To solve a problem about the impact of the African slave trade on Africans, students may employ a hypothesis-making and testing strategy—again, monitoring, evaluating and modifying the strategy as they proceed toward a solution. All of the knowledge-producing strategies listed here can be employed in problem solving to develop new knowledge. Thus, not only is problem solving a knowledge-producing strategy in its own right but it is also a framework for employing and executing other knowledge-producing strategies. Organizing learning around problem solving allows students to practice and, with our assistance, to improve problem solving as well as a host of other useful knowledge-producing strategies in the context of real learning.

In moving through an activity or series of activities organized around the steps that constitute problem solving or any other knowledge-producing strategy, students can engage in each task individually, with a partner, in small groups, or as a whole class, as warranted by their experience, the task, and the materials to be used. If this is the first or second time students have engaged in this strategy, some explicit and continuing direction and supervision will undoubtedly be necessary. This can be accomplished by modeling and explaining the various tasks as they are encountered, directing students through them in step-by-step fashion and explaining why and how each task can best be carried out. However, as students become familiar with the overall procedure as a result of such instruction, teacher direction can give way to more indirect guidance and scaffolding.

By organizing lessons and units around the use of various knowledge-producing strategies like those described in Figure 2.7, we can ensure that students are given sustained opportunities to engage in increasingly complex thinking as a normal, natural part of their learning. Use of such strategies for this purpose also provides numerous natural opportunities for providing students with the instructive assistance they need to sharpen their expertise in the thinking they need to improve.[33]

PROVIDING THINKING OPPORTUNITIES: A SUMMARY

If students are to improve the quality of their thinking, they obviously need repeated opportunities to engage in the kinds of thinking to be improved. We can provide some thinking opportunities by the methods we use in our teaching—methods such as providing wait time, exhortation and asking questions. But students need more than these contrived, outside-initiated thinking occasions. More authentic *opportunities* for thinking are needed—opportunities that grow out of student efforts to develop meaningful learning or to achieve other worthwhile goals. These opportunities must be frequent and repeated. Students must see them as meaningful and worthwhile opportunities to engage in the kind of thinking that we and they are seeking to improve. Such opportunities can be embedded in what students are learning about as well as in the kinds of activities by which content is processed.

Opportunities for Thinking

As classroom teachers, we can ensure the existence of genuine student thinking opportunities by employing some or all of the techniques presented in this chapter:

- Framing learning with thoughtful questions
- Provoking puzzlement or dissonance
- Engaging students in knowledge-producing activities
- Structuring learning around knowledge-producing strategies

This chapter has explained what each of these tasks entails and provided some ways to carry it out. Each can be used to initiate thoughtful learning in any classroom. However, none of these is sufficient by itself to provide all the opportunities and context for learning and thinking that are necessary to improve the quality of student thinking. Educators seeking to create thoughtful classrooms should construct and conduct lessons, courses, and curricula that employ most, if not all, of these techniques. We can, for instance, initiate a unit with a thoughtful question and then guide student efforts to answer it by organizing their study as problem solving in which they employ a number of knowledge-producing strategies and activities. Framing learning like this maximizes the chances of students encountering occasions for thinking that *they* turn into opportunities to think. When this occurs, we then have opportunities to provide the guidance and instruction so necessary for improving the quality of their thinking.

Implications for Using These Techniques

Employing these techniques has several implications of significance for the classroom. For example, all of these techniques require a richness and depth of subject-matter content not often found in traditional survey courses. They require considerable time. Use of these techniques also requires additional efforts to sustain the student engagement the techniques trigger. Acknowledging these in no way argues against use of these techniques, but rather merely points out their practical ramifications.

Constructing knowledge through active engagement in higher-order thinking requires use of considerable subject-matter content. To engage students, this content must not only be perceived by them as of interest or worth but it must also be varied in form and presentation mode. Moreover, this content should be rich in detail and in connections to other bodies of information in other subjects as well as to the everyday life experiences of students. It should also be rich in levels of complexity and implications.[34] A body of content—about a topic, theme, subject, concept, or cognitive procedure—can be enriched by ensuring that it consists, as appropriate, of the following:

Details

Details of these details

Examples

Details of examples

Counterexamples

Details of counterexamples

Analogous instances or examples with details about each

Various points of view about these details and examples

Points of view (elaborative, reinforcing, and critical) about these various points of view

Implied as well as explicit (physical, substantive, symbolic, casual, functional, spatial, and other) connections or relationships to other similar or related phenomena here and now and in other times, places, cultures, situations, and/or individuals

Causes and effects, alternatives and consequences, and constraints and enabling features

Different representations of the data (written narratives, pictures, diagrams, etc.)

Explicit as well as implicit similarities to and differences from other related phenomena, here and now and in other places, times, cultures, and contexts	Multiple representations and sources
	Various interpretations and explanations
Primary source data related to this content or from which it is derived	

The more of these kinds of information provided on any topic or subject, the greater the possibility that students can produce significant interconnections, insights, and meanings by processing it. Such content allows greater possibilities for generating big ideas and clearer, deeper understandings, as well. It also makes imperative the need for thinking. Content consisting of these kinds of ingredients—whether subject matter, big ideas or cognitive processes—is exactly what Perkins calls the generative data that should constitute a thoughtful curriculum.[35]

Another implication of the use of these techniques involves time. It takes time to process large amounts of data to produce or construct valid concepts, generalizations, conclusions and other types of learning. Students need time to plan how they will process the content they are using, to locate and process additional information, to test hypotheses, to search for connections, to evaluate data as well as inferences, and to construct and evaluate arguments justifying their claims, assertions, and discoveries. They need time to devote repeatedly to the kinds of thinking that need improving. And they need time to present and demonstrate the knowledge that they are building.

Furthermore, use of these techniques does not guarantee student engagement in the kind of thinking they are intended to trigger. In most instances, continuing interpersonal mediation or interaction—teacher to student, student to student, and student to teacher—is required to initiate student engagement in thinking. That engagement is sustained by making the students feel they are succeeding in their attempts and making progress along the way. Providing encouragement is essential for anyone who hopes to maintain a thoughtful classroom by keeping students engaged in the thinking opportunities provided for them. The next chapter explains and demonstrates what can be done to encourage and support the student thinking triggered and required by the techniques presented in this chapter.

ENDNOTES

1. Grant Wiggins, "Creating a Thought-Provoking Curriculum," *American Educator* 11 4 (Winter 1987): 10–17.

2. L. S. Vygotsky, *Mind in Society: The Development of Higher Psychological Process* (Cambridge, MA: Harvard University Press, 1987), p. 117.

3. Wiggins, "Creating a Thought-Provoking Curriculum," pp. 10–17; Fred M. Newmann, "Can Depth Replace Coverage in the High School Curriculum?" *Phi Delta Kappan 70* 5 (January 1988): 345–348; David Perkins, "Thinking-Centered Learning," *Educational Leadership 51* 4 (December 1993–January 1994): 84–85.

4. Perkins, "Thinking-Centered Learning," pp. 84–85; D. N. Perkins, "Educating for Insight," *Educational Leadership 49* 2 (October 1991): 4–8.

5. Wiggins, "Creating a Thought-Provoking Curriculum," p. 12.

6. Grant Wiggins, "The Futility of Trying to Teach Everything of Importance," *Educational Leadership 47* 3 (November 1989): 57.

7. David Perkins, *Smart Schools* (New York: The Free Press, 1992), p. 169.

8. Perkins, "Thinking-Centered Learning," p. 84.

9. Perkins, *Smart Schools*, p. 93; David Perkins and Tina Blythe, "Putting Understanding Up Front," *Educational Leadership 5* 15 (February 1994): 6; Vito Perrone, "How to Engage Students in Learning," *Educational Leadership 51* 5 (February 1994): 12–13; Chris Unger, "What Teaching for Understanding Looks Like," *Educational Leadership 51* 5 (February 1994): 8–10.

10. Newmann, "Can Depth Replace Coverage," p. 348; Robert Marzano, *A Different Kind of Classroom* (Alexandria, VA: Association for Supervision and Curriculum Development, 1992), pp. 53, 142–144; Selma Wassermann and Meguido Zola, *Promoting Thinking in Your Classroom* (Wheaton, MD: Association for Childhood Education International, 1984).

11. John Seeley Brown, Allan Collins, and Paul Duguid, "Situated Cognition and the Culture of Learning," *Educational Researcher 18* 1 (January-February 1989): 32–42; Barbara Means, Carol Chelemer, and Michael S. Knapp (Eds.), *Teaching Advanced Skills to At-Risk Students* (San Francisco: Jossey-Bass, 1991), pp. 10–12.

12. Wiggins, "Creating a Thought-Provoking Curriculum," *passim.*

13. Tom Clancy, quoted in "Clancy Doesn't Think Women Belong in Combat," *U.S.A. Today*, August 9, 1991, p. 2D.

14. Peter C. Ellsworth and Vincent G. Sindt, "Helping 'Aha' to Happen: The Contributions of Irving Sigel," *Educational Leadership 51* 5 (February 1994): 42.

15. Rebecca Simmons, "The Horse Before the Cart? Assessing for Understanding," *Educational Leadership 51* 5 (February 1994): 22.

16. As quoted in Deborah Viadero, "Why Textbooks Often Baffle Students," *Education Week* (May 25, 1994): 31–32.

17. Wiggins, "Creating a Thought-Provoking Curriculum," p. 16.

18. Means, Chelemer, and Knapp, *Teaching Advanced Skills*, pp. 10–12.

19. Wiggins, "Creating a Thought-Provoking Curriculum," p. 11.

20. *Ibid.*

21. *Tampa (Florida) Tribune*, October 19, 1991. Reprinted by permission.

22. Michael Gartner, editor of *Daily Tribune (Ames, Iowa)*, quoted in *U.S.A. Today*, April 14, 1994, p. 11A.

23. Jerome Bruner, *The Process of Education* (Cambridge, MA: Harvard University Press, 1963); Jerome Bruner, *Toward A Theory of Instruction* (Cambridge, MA: Harvard University Press, 1966).

24. Rexford G. Brown, *Schools of Thought* (San Francisco: Jossey Bass, 1991), p. 6.

25. John Bransford, "Instruction That Facilitates Problem Solving, "presentation at Conference on Thinking and Learning, sponsored by Association for Supervision and Curriculum Development, San Antonio, February 26, 1993; Marzano, *A Different Kind of Classroom*, pp. 130, 142–144; Wassermann and Zola, *Promoting Thinking, passim*.; Wiggins, "The Futility of Trying to Teach Everything of Importance," *passim*.

26. Perkins, "Educating for Insight," p. 5; Perkins, *Smart Schools*, pp. 45, 75–80, 186, 232; Perkins and Blythe, "Putting Understanding Up Front," pp. 5–6.

27. Allan Collins, Jan Hawkins, and Sharon M. Carver, "A Cognitive Apprenticeship for Disadvantaged Students," in Means, Chelemer, and Knapp, pp. 266, 240; Newmann, "Can Depth Replace Coverage," pp. 345–348.

28. Lilian G. Katz and Sylvia C. Chard, *Engaging Children's Minds: The Project Approach* (Norwood, NJ: Ablex, 1989/1992).

29. Bransford, "Instruction That Facilitates," *passim*; Cognition and Technology Group at Vanderbilt, "Anchored Instruction and Situated Cognition Revisited," 1993, in press; Marzano, *A Different Kind of Classroom*, pp. 13, 25–26; Lynn Olson, "Progressive Era Concept Now Breaks Mold: NASDC Schools Explore 'Project Learning,' " *Education Week 12* 21 (February 17, 1993); 6–7.

30. Carol Meyer, "What's the Difference between Authentic and Performance Assessment?" *Educational Leadership 49* 8 (May 1992): 40.

31. Bransford, "Instruction That Facilitates," *passim*; Brown, Collins, and Duguid, "Situated Cognition," pp. 32–42; Marzano, *A Different Kind of Classroom*, p. 130; Olson, "Progressive Era Concept," p. 6; Wassermann and Zola, *Promoting Thinking, passim*.

32. John R. Anderson, *The Architecture of Cognition* (Cambridge, MA: Harvard University Press, 1983); Norman Frederickson, "Implications of Cognitive Theory for Instruction in Problem Solving," *Review of Educational Research, 54* 3 (Fall 1984): 363–407; John R. Hayes, *The Complete Problem Solver* (Philadelphia: The Franklin Institute Press, 1981).

33. John D. Bransford and Barry S. Stein, *The IDEAL Problem Solver* (New York: W. H. Freeman, 1984). William Stepien and Shelagh Gallagher, "Problem-Based Learning: As Authentic as It Gets," *Educational Leadership 50* 7 (April 1993): 25–28.

34. Jere Brophy, "Probing the Subtleties of Subject-Matter Learning," *Educational Leadership 49* 7 (April 1992): 4–8; Mary Bryson and Marlene Scardamalia, "Teaching Writing to Students at Risk for Academic Failure," in Means, Chelemer, and Knapp, pp. 141–167; Newmann, "Can Depth Replace Coverage," pp. 345–348; Perkins, *Smart Schools, passim*.; Richard S. Prawat, "The Value of Ideas: The Immersion Approach to the Development of Thinking," *Educational Researcher 70* 2 (August–September 1993): 5–16; Wiggins, "Creating a Thought-Provoking Curriculum," pp. 10–17.

35. Perkins, *Smart Schools*, p. 93.

3

Encouraging
Student Thinking

Thoughtful classrooms, at their best, provide repeated opportunities to engage in higher-order thinking. Unfortunately, however, *a great many* students avoid taking continuing advantage of such opportunities. Simply presenting students with thinking opportunities does not ensure that they will respond by sustaining engagement in the thinking tasks these opportunities present. Encouraging students to engage in the thinking operations embedded in these opportunities—and to sustain this engagement—is a second major task involved in providing a thoughtful classroom.[1] This chapter explains what can be done to encourage students to seize and sustain engagement in the thinking opportunities presented in thoughtful classrooms and to do so willingly and even with enthusiasm.

Encouraging student thinking means much more than simply exhorting students with pleas such as "Think!" "Think again!" or "Now, think harder!" or with admonitions such as "You can do it if you just try!" To encourage means to embolden, to give one courage to try doing something perceived as too difficult or unpleasant by providing something that makes the task easier than imagined and that gives one reason to believe the effort invested will produce some measure of success.

Encouraging student thinking involves, in part, making thinking an authentic part of what regularly goes on in class (as described in Chapter 2).[2] Under such conditions, thinking is encouraged by being recognized as a normal class activity in which all students engage and are expected to engage. But, as teachers, we can and need to do more to encourage thinking if we wish students to engage in it willingly and to sustain their engagement

63

over an extended period of time. To accomplish this, we can, in effect, "grease" student thinking by providing some occasional boost or creating conditions that make thinking move along (or appear to move along) more easily. For instance, breaking a complex problem into several smaller, less complex, subproblems encourages efforts to solve the initial problem by making it appear easier than at first imagined and by offering chances of incremental successes along the way. Also, letting our students know we are available for help if needed can also be encouraging enough for them to "give it a try." Encouragement involves more than inspirational prodding when effortful thinking, which higher-order thinking certainly is for most students, is concerned.

We can provide the kinds of encouragement most students need to engage in the sustained thinking typical of thoughtful classrooms by taking at least three kinds of actions:

1. Provide classroom conditions that encourage student thinking.
2. Actively initiate and keep student thinking going.
3. Create and maintain a sense of community in learning.

Any of us—regardless of the grade level, subject, or kinds of students we teach, supervise, or otherwise assist—can employ a variety of techniques to carry out these tasks. The following pages present descriptions and explanations of why these actions are important and how to carry them out.

PROVIDING CLASSROOM CONDITIONS THAT ENCOURAGE STUDENT THINKING

Several classroom conditions must exist for students to feel encouraged to take full and productive advantage of opportunities to engage in sustained, increasingly complex thinking. As presented in Figure 3.1, these conditions include:

1. Classroom arrangements that facilitate student interaction
2. Time for students to think
3. Use, by students as well as by the teacher, of the language of thinking
4. Sustained attention to what is going on in the classroom
5. Minimizing the negative risks of engaging in thinking
6. Continued modeling of the skills and dispositions of good thinking

These conditions, as permanent features of a classroom, encourage student engagement in thinking in two ways. First, they *permit* higher-order thinking and the mediation or interaction that facilitates it to occur. Second, they make higher-order thinking *easier* to engage in by providing or accenting conditions that embolden students to give it a try. These six conditions make thinking natural and more comfortable to engage in. Here is how each

Figure 3.1 Classroom Conditions That Encourage Student Thinking

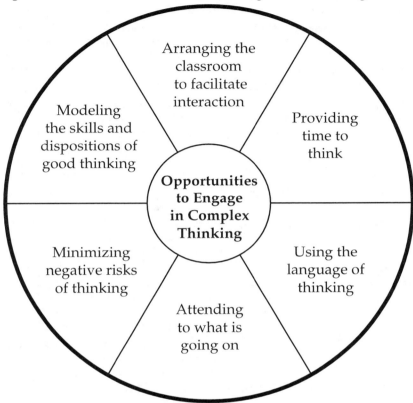

contributes to encouraging student thinking and what can be done to make it a classroom reality.

Arrange Classrooms to Facilitate Student Interaction

Thinking, especially the development and improvement of complex thinking, benefits immensely from student *interaction*. The articulation, deliberation, and reflection involved in discussion, inquiry, argumentation, and debate provide an opportunity to form, express, and challenge thoughts, as well as *produce* knowledge. In addition, interaction provides opportunities for the modeling of good thinking, for feedback on student thinking, and for opportunities for teacher or peer assistance in thinking. All of these activities can encourage student thinking.

Thinking is also facilitated when it is distributed among many individuals. Prior substantive knowledge and experience as well as procedural knowledge and skills can then be shared, appropriated, and built on to help all individuals as well as the entire group go beyond what they already know or believe. Such conditions can lead to more sophisticated and better-grounded insights and more proficient execution of the thinking operations in which they seek to engage.[3] However, this verbal and cognitive interaction is handicapped by the theater-style seating that typifies many traditional school classrooms, especially those in secondary schools. Such classroom seating arrangements neither invite nor make easily possible the kinds of interactions that prove so useful in developing thinking.

To increase the possibilities of student-to-student as well as student-teacher-student interaction:

1. Arrange classroom furniture so students face each other. Student desks (or tables and chairs) can be arranged in clusters facing each other, in a U-shape or in the form of a hollow square. These seating arrangements can be enhanced by moving the teacher's desk to a more unobtrusive position, perhaps to the rear of the room where it can serve as a work station rather than podium. Such a move generally puts students closer to the chalkboards, thus making them available for students to use while engaged in brainstorming or other appropriate learning tasks. Moving the desk from the front of the classroom also provides more space for student grouping.

2. Take advantage of movable student furniture. Arrange students (or allow them to arrange themselves) into groups of various sizes as learning activities require—in collaborative learning groups, in pairs, in focus groups (described later), and in other combinations where face-to-face interaction or active engagement with data can be easily undertaken.

3. Provide rich material resources relevant to what is being studied. These may include sample texts, reference books, literary works, maps, models, model-building materials, educational games, construction materials, computer terminals, as well as audio, video, and other multimedia materials. Having an abundance of this material available for immediate use helps to reinforce one essential feature of thoughtful learning: Information and knowledge claims are fodder for the mind, to be *used* when needed in thinking rather than collected earlier and stored in one's mind for some undetermined use later.

4. Ensure that the classroom communicates an atmosphere of thoughtfulness by the kinds of materials displayed on the walls, hung from light fixtures, affixed to bulletin boards, and/or displayed on tables or in bookcases. Elegant or multiple solutions to math problems, photographs or drawings of experiments, conceptual maps, and other products of student learning can be exhibited, as can cartoons about thinking and thinking problems clipped from magazines and journals as well as those produced by students.

Figure 3.2 Riddles and Puzzles for a Thoughtful Classroom

Item 1
When outsiders first came to Tobuk, they found two kinds of people there. The Amok always lied. All the other natives always told the truth. One day an outsider met three natives. She asked the first if she were Amok. The first native answered the question. The second native then reported that the first native denied being Amok. The third native then said that the first native really was Amok. How any of these natives were Amok?

Item 2
In $y = 3x^2 + 5x - 2$
      If
$x = 0$ then $y = -2$
      So
if $x = 1$ then $y = ?$

Item 3
These are trikes: 606   718   246   011
These are not: 56   618   441   306
What are trikes?

Item 4
Two cyclists start at the same time from opposite ends of a 100-mile-long road. Each bicycle moves at a speed of 40 miles per hour. At the moment they start, a fly leaves one of the bicycles and starts flying back and forth between the two cyclists until they meet. If the fly travels at 60 miles an hour, how many miles does it fly before the cyclists meet?

Item 5
If one greyhound can jump over a ditch 2 yards wide, how wide a ditch can 6 greyhounds jump across?

Item 6
I spring to the saddle, and Joris and he;
I galloped, Dirck galloped, we galloped all three.
What is the same of "he"?

Item 7
One rabbit eats 2 pounds of food in a week. There are 52 weeks in a year. How much food would 5 rabbits eat in a week?

Item 8
Message (in code):   Dpnf up Mpoepo bu podf.
The same (translated):   Come to London at once.
What is the secret letter for "x" in this code?

continued

Figure 3.2 *Continued*

Item 9
What will be the day
after the day after tomorrow,
if the day before the day
before yesterday was Wednesday?

Item 10
Marc, Ana, Julia, and Daniel decide to have a checkers tournament at school. They want to be sure that each of them gets a chance to play each of the others one time. They ask you to make a schedule for the tournament. Here is the information you need to make a plan that works.

- They want to finish the tournament in one week. They can play from Monday to Friday.
- They will play only at lunchtime. There is enough time during lunch period to play one game of checkers.
- The students have two checkers sets, so two games can be going on at once.
- Mark can't play checkers on the days he is a lunch helper (Mondays and Wednesdays).
- Each player must play every other player once.

Make a schedule for the tournament.

Sources: Items 1 and 2: Adapted from Barry K. Beyer, *Practical Strategies for the Teaching of Thinking* (Boston: Allyn and Bacon, 1987), p. 14. Item 3: Jack Censer, Department of History, George Mason University, Fairfax, VA. Item 4: Scott Morris, "Games," *Omni* (October 1981): 206. Reprinted by permission of OMNI, © 1981, OMNI Publications International, Ltd. Item 5: Carl Bereiter, "How to Keep Thinking Skills from Going the Way of All Frills," *Educational Leadership* 42 1 (September 1984): 77. Copyright © 1985 by ASCD. Reprinted by permission. All rights reserved. Items 6 and 8: Reproduced by permission of the publisher, F. E. Peacock Publishers Inc., Itasca, Illinois. From Bruce Hudgins, *Learning and Thinking*, 1977 copyright, p. 181. Items 7 and 9: Barry K. Beyer, "Workshop on Teaching Thinking," no date. Item 10: Debra Viadero, "Teaching to the Test," *Education Week* 13 39 (July 13, 1994): 22. Reprinted with permission from *Educational Week.*

Riddles and puzzles, such as those in Figure 3.2, can also be displayed for students to solve and discuss. Student-made puzzles and riddles can be interspersed with these, as can posters illustrating various heuristics of good thinking, such as "Look before you leap" or "Check your work!"

Mobiles of acronyms for important thinking skills—such as Edward deBono's now famous PMI (Plus [Positive], Minus [Negative], Interesting) or OPV (Other Point of View)—can be suspended from overhead light fixtures. Additionally, quotations such as those in Figure 3.3 can be displayed on large posters. These can be discussed as occasions warrant and can be altered, added to, or replaced by more appropriate ones contributed or found by the students as the year goes on. These and similar statements and acronyms provoke and inform good thinking. Public display of these kinds

Figure 3.3 Statements about Thinking for Classroom Display

The human mind is our most fundamental resource.
  —*John F. Kennedy*

Learning without thought is labor lost;
Thought without learning is perilous.
  —*Confucius*

For every complex question, there's a simple answer—
and it's wrong!
  —*H. L. Menken*

I am my choices.
  —*Jean Paul Sartre*

Thinking always ahead, thinking of always trying to do more,
brings a state of mind in which nothing is impossible.
  —*Henry Ford*

If you think small, you'll stay small.
  —*Ray Kroc*

The thicker the skull, the sharper the hint must be to penetrate it.
  —*Anonymous*

I think, therefore I am.
  —*Descartes*

I am, therefore I think.
  —*Anonymous*

Questions are the creative acts of intelligence.
  —*Frank Kingdon*

How can I know what I think till I see (or hear) what I say?
  —*Graham Wallas*

People are like tacks. They can go only as far as their heads allow them.
  —*Anonymous*

People of action are, after all, only the unconscious instruments of thought.
  —*Heinrich Heine* (adapted)

Thinking spoken here!
  —*Anonymous*

Just a minute, let me think!
  —*Reuven Feuerstein*

Getting more out of your brain gets you more out of life.
  —*Washington Post* (9/13/95)

Don't just think—think BIG!
  —*Anonymous*

---

of items communicates to students that a major business of the classroom is thinking and that it is okay to think in this place!

The physical setting in which teaching and learning occur has considerable effect on the way in which both are carried out. Classrooms arranged, organized, and used as described here help to provide an atmosphere that legitimizes thinking. They also invite and enable student engagement and interaction with each other as well as with information, data, and resources needed to do both. Such classrooms create the kind of physical setting best suited to maintaining the other conditions that constitute a thoughtful classroom. It also encourages and facilitates the student and teacher behaviors and activities that typify higher-order thinking in action.

Provide Time for Students to Think

It takes *time* to successfully execute tasks that involve thinking: time to recall information, formulate and test hypotheses, conclude, and generalize; time to make good decisions; time to resolve complex problems; time to invent or elaborate concepts; and time to critically analyze and evaluate information and assertions. In order for students to execute such thinking and improve the ways they go about carrying it out, they need time to process, reflect, and recall. They need time to brainstorm and to evaluate options in making decisions, and they need time to make, carry out, and revise plans for projects or research. Thoughtful classrooms provide the time students need to undertake the thinking tasks in which they are asked to engage.

One particular area of classroom activity where we, as educators, need to be especially concerned about providing time is in seeking student answers to questions. This accounts for the emphasis in recent years on *wait time*. According to researcher Mary Budd Rowe, most teachers allow, on average, only 1.3 seconds for students to respond to a question—hardly enough time to even start to think, let alone to carry out any significant thinking at all. However, when students are allowed more time—even as little as 3 or 4 seconds—in which to ponder, recall, or otherwise mentally process information before responding to a question, they have more time to engage in thinking. When given this amount of time, students more often respond in the form of sentences rather than in single words or phrases, provide supporting evidence or justification and examples, and make more complex statements. Experts assert that these more elaborate responses indicate that thinking other than rote memory has occurred.[4]

To foster and encourage student thinking, then, we can provide the wait time necessary for it to occur. Some experienced teachers refer to this as Wait Time One and Wait Time Two. *Wait Time One* is the silence between a question and the acceptance or voicing of a response. We need to allow and insist on a period of silence after we have asked a question so students have time to think. *Wait Time Two* is the period of silence that *follows* a student response during which the teacher and students thoughtfully consider the given response. Each of these wait times should last at least 3 to 4 seconds, sometimes longer, if the task is very complicated.

Time for thinking needs to be deliberately built into all complex learning tasks, as well. Activities that require the production of new insights, interpretations, critiques, explanations, concepts, or theories require considerable time for students to execute the mental activity needed to carry out these operations. Where such tasks are to be done collaboratively by a number of students, even more time must be allowed for the silence that accompanies individual mental processing and for the verbal interaction that facilitates complex cognitive manipulation of information and thoughts. Thinking time is absolutely essential to create or maintain a thoughtful classroom. Without it, little, if any, student thinking of consequence is likely to occur.

Use the Language of Thinking as a Regular Part of Classroom Discourse

One of the marks of good thinking and effective communicating is the use of clear, precise language. This is especially important in talking about the cognitive states and actions related to thinking. Consistent teacher and student use of the language of thinking helps students improve the quality—and products—of their thinking.[5]

Rather than use the word *think* as noun or verb in classroom discourse, we, as teachers, and our students should use words that denote clearly and specifically the kinds of cognitive operations, products, and states of mind to which we are referring. For instance, when we wish students to choose from alternatives, we should say, "Decide what to do," rather than, "What do you think we should do?" Using the precise language of thinking is important because the word *think* means so many things (believe, wonder, guess, hypothesize, know, decide, predict, etc.) that it fails to communicate clearly any *specific* kind of thinking, thinking product, or mental state. When someone asks, "What do you think?" it is difficult to know whether he or she means, "What do I guess or hypothesize or suspect?" or "What do I believe?" or "What do I know for certain?" or "What do I wish were true?" When someone says, "I think the answer is thus and so," it is unclear whether the person means to say he or she believes or knows for a fact it is true or guesses or even hopes that is what the answer is. The word *think,* as commonly used, simply does not communicate with the precision or clarity required to aid either effective thinking or understanding.

Researchers and expert practitioners attest to the importance of precise word usage in increasing the quality of one's thinking and its products.[6]

Words serve as vehicles for mentally processing information and articulating thoughts, as well as tools or aids to these cognitive processes called *thinking*. The words used as verbs in directions or questions actually signal listeners or readers as to what they need to do mentally to respond as the speaker or questioner intends. Students use these words to guide their own cognitive performances by employing them as cues to recall the appropriate cognitive procedures required to execute a specific cognitive task. They then use what has been recalled to structure and carry out that task.[7] Simply asking students to think fails to provide the signals or cues students need to respond or behave appropriately.

In terms of classroom practice, the language of thinking must be an integral part of student and teacher discourse. Both teacher and students should adhere to the following guidelines:

1. Use words that clearly specify the cognitive actions we are taking or wish students to take and the mental states we wish them to attain or demonstrate. According to researchers David R. Olson and Janet Wilde Astington we should use words that describe precisely the cognitive actions or conditions we wish to engage in, produce, or have someone else engage in.[8] Instead of saying, "What do you *think* will happen if . . . ?" it is more productive to say, "What do you *predict* will happen if . . . ?" Instead of asking, "What did you *find out*?" it is more appropriate to ask, "What *conclusions* did you reach?" or "What *hypotheses* did you make?" (if conclusions or hypotheses are what you are seeking). When we want students to take something apart to identify its parts and their interconnections, we should ask them to *analyze* rather than to ask what they "think about it" or to "examine" it.

2. Use the language of thinking strategies. When we engage in these strategies or when we want students to engage in these strategies, we ought to use the cognitive terms that denote the various operations being or to be performed.[9] In directing or discussing decision making, this means using the language of decision making: *goals, criteria, alternatives, options, consequences, outcomes, choices, costs, risks,* and so on. In directing or discussing problem solving, this means using terms associated with this kind of thinking: *problem, hypothesis, plan, conclusion,* and so on.

3. Use the language of reasoning. As students process information to infer meaning, relationships, and other kinds of knowledge, it is important to use the words that denote the various facets of reasoning in which they are to engage or are engaging. Words such as *criteria, evidence, claim, deduce, infer,* and *assumption* as well as words like *because of, consequently,* and *therefore* signal important mental moves in reasoning and in reporting the results of reasoning.[10]

Consistent and appropriate use of the language of thinking not only makes thinking a more conscious part of the classroom but also facilitates the execution of student and teacher thinking.[11] Moreover, the careful use and understanding of mental state words also helps the teacher and students understand the *intended* meanings of each other's statements.[12]

This last point is crucial to understanding the importance of the language of thinking and its role in the classroom. Researchers Olson and Astington stress the value of words as cues to employing cognitive operations appropriate to an assigned task. They also stress the value of specific *thinking* words as signals to the *stance* that speakers and writers take toward their own assertions, the degree of certainty they attach to the content of their assertions, and the extent to which they share that point of view.[13] When someone says, "I believe it is so," he or she usually means, "I have some evidence that indicates this is so but I am not certain it is so." But when that same person says, "It is so," he or she means, "I am certain this is true." Because of the multiple meanings assigned to the word *thinking*, simply saying "I think this is so" makes such a distinction virtually impossible. The ability to see through the content of a statement to the intent behind it, as revealed in the words used and the context in which it is asserted, is basic to the ability to engage effectively in critical and other types of complex thinking. Careful and appropriate efforts to incorporate the language of thinking into regular classroom talk is a key to developing this ability, to providing a classroom environment that encourages thinking, and thus to improving student thinking.

Reference to published glossaries or descriptions of thinking skills can clarify the appropriate terminology to use in describing various cognitive operations. Consistent use of these terms can enable teachers and students to employ a common language of thinking throughout a school or school system, thus facilitating student learning and application of these operations across subjects and grade levels.[14]

Ensure That Students Actively Attend to What Is Said in the Classroom

Attending to what others say and do, peers as well as teacher, is not only respectful but necessary if one is to participate constructively in and benefit from what is occurring in a class. Listening and observing are essential for any thoughtful classroom. We, as teachers, and our students must insist on both behaviors as conditions of membership in such classrooms.

Listening means more than being silent or simply looking at a speaker. It means concentrating on what is being said in an effort to comprehend it thoroughly as well as to understand the grounds and reasoning, from the point of view of the speaker, by which such assertions could be justified.

Such concentration is often evidenced by leaning toward the speaker, by thoughtfully tilting the head, by maintaining eye contact with the speaker, by nodding or otherwise signaling understanding or support, by furrowing the brow when in thoughtful puzzlement, by providing additional support or elaboration, and by asking questions for clarification. When listeners assist a speaker in trying to say what he or she intends to say or when they use ideas or information just asserted, they also reveal they have been listening or observing attentively.[15]

A number of things can be done to provide a learning setting that facilitates listening and that, at the same time, helps students develop the inclination and skills of doing so on their own. One of the most useful tactics for this purpose is that of *focus groups*. As adapted from the work of Sidney B. Simon and his colleagues, focus groups are usually student triads in which each student is given one to three minutes to report on something or to present and justify some idea or information. During this time, the other members of the focus group listen attentively to what is being said.[16] The recommended rules for engaging in a focus group are:

1. Listeners maintain eye contact with the speaker.
2. Listeners cannot interrupt the speaker.
3. Listeners can give nonverbal signs of understanding or confusion, if necessary.
4. If the speaker "runs down," listeners may ask questions to elicit examples or elaboration of what is being said, to draw the speaker out or to lead him or her to clarify or elaborate what he or she is trying to say, or to encourage him or her to go on.

Whenever it appears useful for students to share information—for example, as a result of doing research, or of participating in a small group activity and then returning to a larger group—all students in the class can divide into focus groups. Membership in a group may be self-selected, assigned by the teacher, determined by "counting off" so that each group has three members, or assigned to triads according to the kinds of tasks they are to report on. The task focus groups should be homogeneous if the goal is to go deeper into the topic the students are working on. However, if the goal is to share the results of an individual or previous group inquiry, the focus group should be heterogeneous.

In conducting focus groups, each member of a group should be "on focus" for a specified time. After one has completed his or her statement, the others in the triad can paraphrase or summarize—as a "perception" check—what they believe the speaker has said and the speaker can then correct misinterpretations or elaborate. The others can also ask questions for clarification. After all members of the group have been "on focus," all members can (1) question each other for further clarifications, (2) offer information that counters or supports points made, and/or (3) engage in a deliberation to arrive at some consensus or synthesis. The culminating activity, for example, might consist of comparing and contrasting what has been presented by each member to develop a synthesis in the form of a summary, hypothesis, or conclusion. This activity might also consist of judging the strong or weak points of each position taken or analyzing critically the kinds of information presented. A short written summary in which each student completes all or several of the following sentence stems can conclude the entire activity:

I learned . . . .

I believe . . . because . . . .

I wonder . . . .

I wish . . . .

When shared with other members of the triad or with the class as a whole, these learning summaries can lead to further probing, clarification, or elaboration of the topics on which the groups have focused.[17]

Focus groups are especially useful because they guarantee that each class member will be heard and his or her message clarified before being challenged or disputed. They allow the reticent or shy equal time to be heard, free from the intimidating interruptions of overly enthusiastic or louder students. They also prove useful in helping students develop their abilities and inclinations to attend and listen seriously to what is being said by others. Using this technique early in the school year is one way to get students accustomed to the kind of listening that is essential for the functioning of thoughtful classrooms. This skill can then be transferred to large group discussions by reminding students about their applicability and earlier use in the focus groups.

Good listening is more useful than many students imagine. Indeed, as odd as it may seem, listeners can help speakers to articulate more clearly and even to understand something better than they did before they spoke. Speakers also benefit from listeners who follow up a presentation by asking for clarification, more details, examples, definitions, underlying assumptions, and elaboration. Paraphrasing what has been said also helps the speaker generate, on the spot, additional information or reasoning perhaps not included in the initial remarks.[18] By drawing out a speaker's unarticulated knowledge or vaguely formed thoughts or thinking processes, listeners can contribute significantly to the advancement of the class toward its learning goals and to the construction of new knowledge.

Minimize the Negative Risks of Engaging in Complex Thinking

Constructing new knowledge by inferring relationships or hypotheses, formulating conclusions, making predictions, and engaging in other forms of complex thinking is risky business. This is especially true for many students. After all, they are being taught by someone who has more years of experience and education and who *obviously* knows more than they do! Also, until perhaps now, finding the *right* answer rather than developing a reasoned, defensible proposition may have been the essence of their learning game. Students engaging in higher-order thinking and the discussions and deliberations surrounding it run the risk of embarrassing themselves, as well as antagonizing friends and peers by challenging their thinking or demonstrating skills that violate established peer-group norms. No wonder many students find it difficult and are often reluctant to participate without considerable hesitancy or self-restraint in the complex thinking that is the central mode of learning in thoughtful classrooms!

No one wants to be wrong, especially after investing considerable effort in producing a piece of "new" knowledge. Moreover, in many classrooms, it has even become increasingly risky (among one's peers) to be right too often or to be skilled at doing something. Such students frequently risk being teased, mocked, and ostracized. Minimizing the risks inherent in engaging actively in thoughtful learning thus becomes a major responsibility of teachers. However, this task must be shared with the entire class as well, because it takes both teacher and students to create the type of classroom atmosphere needed to produce an environment where risk taking by thinking is protected and made safe.[19]

Some risk in thinking is inevitable, of course, and, indeed, desirable. An element of risking by going beyond where one now is, is what often drives or motivates many students. Thus, the goal is not to eliminate risking itself, even if this could be done; instead, the task of the teacher and class is to make risk taking a positive and safe endeavor.[20] To accomplish this goal, experienced teachers have found the following suggestions useful:

- Keep the focus on the substantive content of assertions and propositions offered by the students.
- Actively solicit, accept, and welcome divergent, varied, unusual assertions and viewpoints.
- Do not permit class members to be critical of, direct jokes at, or otherwise harass any student for the assertions he or she may offer or for being unable to offer appropriate support for them.
- Do not dismiss unusual or obviously incorrect hypotheses or inferences as wrong, but consider them in light of the evidence and reasoning offered. Allow the students—preferably the authors of such

statements—to modify or withdraw such hypotheses or inferences or come up with more appropriate substitutes.

- When an assertion offered by a student turns out, after critical analysis, to be inaccurate, lacking in support, or otherwise flawed, turn the results into a positive move.
- Stress the value of considering what often appear as "way out," unconventional ideas as a way of setting the parameters of what would be the "best" claim and use these criteria to zoom in on developing that claim.
- Share with students the risks we have taken in carrying out complex thinking tasks, how we coped with such risk taking, and what we learned by so doing. Invite students to share similar cognitive risk-taking experiences with the class.
- Encourage questions of and challenges to our own hypotheses, assertions, and claims and openly alter these if evidence and reason warrant.
- Reward the validated products of high-risk thinking undertaken by students by displaying them, sharing them with the class and school, or giving them other suitable attention or commendations.

The following suggestions show how students, too, can contribute to minimizing the negative risks inherent in engaging in complex higher-order thinking:

- Protect other students from personal criticism by enforcing class rules against sniping and by helping others articulate what they mean.
- Offer evidence related to classmates' assertions and endorse those aspects of their assertions with which one agrees.
- Offer nonjudgmental responses to each other's assertions, followed by discussion and evaluation of relevant evidence and reasoning.
- Ask questions of each other and of the teacher.
- Engage directly with other students in dialogue and deliberation as well as initiate deliberation with the teacher.
- Volunteer alternatives to and predict the consequences of conventional or commonly made assertions.
- Offer positive feedback to other students in response to their assertions or reasoning.
- Express interest in assertions and reasoning offered by one's peers or comment about the personal value of such assertions.[21]

By minimizing the negative risks inherent in higher-order thinking, both teacher and students provide more opportunities to engage in such thinking as well as the encouragement to do so. Probably no words better describe this facet of a thinker-friendly thoughtful classroom than does the slogan "Safety First!" Although it may be trite, this slogan highlights an important and necessary condition for learning and for maintaining effective, thoughtful classrooms. Attending to this slogan is a must for anyone who seeks to develop the higher-level thinking of students.

Model the Behaviors and Dispositions of Good Thinking

Most of us are aware of the adage, "Do as I say, not as I do." Most of us are also aware, however, of what youngsters do when they see a marked difference between what their mentors—whether peers, elders, or teachers—say and what they do. Students *do* what they see their mentors *do*. Therefore, we must make conscious, deliberate efforts, as teachers, always to demonstrate or exhibit the kinds of thinking behaviors and dispositions, or habits of mind, that we want our students to develop.[22] By so doing, we legitimatize these as natural and normal classroom behaviors. We also establish these behaviors as legitimate expectations and standards for the kinds of thinking to be exhibited by *everyone* in the classroom.

The power of behaving as we want others to behave—modeling—has been well documented.[23] In order for teachers to impress on students the value of good thinking habits and behaviors, we need to exhibit them constantly in the presence of the students and in our private lives, as well. To encourage student thinking, we must adhere to the following principles in our daily teaching and interactions with students and with other adults:

- Wait before responding to questions and take the time to ponder or reflect. Explain to the students what we are doing and why, perhaps by saying, "Now, let me reflect on that a minute, so I can make my explanation clear" or something similar.
- Give reasons and evidence in support of conclusions, claims, or opinions that we voice. Habitually following such claims with an explanation introduced by "for the reasons that" or "because" will alert the students to what we are doing, and may hopefully become habit forming for them, too.
- Cite credible sources for the information we use and present the credentials of the authorities we cite for information or knowledge claims we present.
- Make clear to students the assumptions or limitations that underlie our assertions.
- Ask aloud questions about our own thinking or conclusions, while we are engaged in developing and presenting them
- Articulate options we are considering when in the position of making decisions and explore aloud the short- and long-range consequences of each.

- Acknowledge the difficulty of "knowing for sure" or of being absolutely sure or definitive about most problems or topics.
- Acknowledge that our opinions or conclusions are from our own points of view and explain how they might look from several other points of view.
- Reflect on or articulate aloud how we construct our responses to student questions, and how we come up with a hypothesis or produce a generalization.
- Plan aloud when considering how best to carry out a task or when having the students carry out a task.
- Acknowledge that we do not have enough information to respond accurately or that more information is required and tell what can be done to locate it.
- Deliberately articulate a concern for finding evidence counter to conclusions or claims voiced. Publicly express and evaluate this evidence, altering these claims if the evidence warrants.
- Make our reasoning explicit when articulating arguments or conclusions we have arrived at or developed.
- Listen attentively to student responses and ask clarifying questions or pose possible examples, not in a tone or manner of quizzing for what students know, but for understanding what they are saying in a "Do you mean this?" way.

These, of course, are not the only thinking behaviors worth exhibiting in the presence of students—or in our daily lives, for that matter. There are many others that should be exhibited as well, including those that exemplify the following habits of mind identified by experts as dispositions essential to good thinking:[24]

Curiosity

Skepticism

Tolerance for uncertainty

Open-mindedness, especially to unconventional ideas

Inquisitiveness

Fair-mindedness (actively seeking evidence counter to a claim before accepting the claim as true)

Seeking and using precision

Suspending judgment

Seeking to be well informed

Willingness to change one's mind when evidence and reason warrant

Objectivity

Persistence in carrying out a task

Flexibility

Critically appraising the process and products of one's own thinking

In addition to consistently demonstrating these dispositions, it is also essential to exhibit the kinds of higher-order thinking that we seek to have our students improve. As we do so, we should, at least initially, make clear to the students what we are doing and why. As educators, we should exemplify in our own behaviors the application of various problem-solving and decision-making heuristics and strategies, as well as argument analysis and construction, critical thinking, conceptualizing, drawing conclusions, and so on.[25] The point, is that to create and maintain an atmosphere of thoughtfulness in our classrooms, we must be thoughtful ourselves. If we want students to exhibit the behaviors and habits of thoughtfulness, we must give these behaviors and dispositions value by continuously putting them in front of students as a natural part of our behavior. Demonstrating, exhibiting, and modeling the dispositions and behaviors of good thinking will help us accomplish this goal.

Establishing and maintaining the conditions described here are crucial to the establishment and maintenance of an effective, thoughtful, thinker-friendly classroom because these conditions encourage student engagement in thinking and make it safe, as well. In doing so the challenge is not to choose which of these conditions is to be incorporated in a classroom; rather, the task is to incorporate *all* of these conditions in our classroom. Each provides a different but essential kind of encouragement to student thinking. Using the language of thinking will not assist students very much if they are not in a position to interact and are not given time to think. Giving them time to think will be of little use if they do not attend and listen to what is being thought about. Every one of these conditions contributes to encouraging student thinking. All must be present to have the most thoughtful classroom possible.

Something else is also important in this regard: the clear communication to students of what is expected of them in this environment. Thinking classrooms are characterized by *high expectations* of what all students, regardless of ability, can do intellectually; *high standards* of how well they should do it; and a *high degree of effort* expected and given to accomplishing it. We must take every opportunity and means available to make sure students and parents are aware of and understand the value of these conditions of learning. Only when these are public and shared by students and teachers will what goes on in a thoughtful classroom lead to significant improvements in student thinking and learning.

INITIATING AND KEEPING STUDENT THINKING GOING

Although creating and maintaining the *conditions* that encourage engaging in new or difficult higher-order thinking is important, the existence of these conditions alone still does not guarantee student engagement in such thinking. As teachers, we must take additional steps to ensure that students take advantage of these conditions to initiate such thinking and sustain it. We must, by our actions and behaviors, exploit these conditions to get and keep our students engaged in the thinking operations we want them to apply and improve.

As Costa[26] has pointed out, we can encourage our students' initial engagement in thinking by the way we introduce thinking tasks and respond to student comments. We can also sustain and even direct their engagement in thinking by participating with them in the thinking tasks in which they are engaged and by helping them to keep the focus on truth and proof as we proceed.

Initiating Student Thinking

Encouraging students to seize an opportunity that requires the execution of some kind of higher-order thinking involves helping them to establish the level of thinking in which they are to engage. It also demands that we set the parameters of the thinking product to be developed. We can initiate student engagement in thinking by the way we lead or move the students into or prepare them for the learning activities or tasks in which this thinking is embedded. To this end, we can do the following:

- In giving directions or asking questions, use language that clearly communicates the kind of cognitive action to be taken and/or the product to be produced. (Example: "*Evaluate* this book [document, essay, map, proof, experiment] to determine how *accurate* it is. Then present your *conclusion* as a well-organized *argument*.") As pointed out earlier, use of language that denotes various types or aspects of thinking cues students to the kinds of mental operation(s) in which they are to engage and the kind of products to be produced.
- Have or help students make explicit their prior knowledge about the thinking operation(s) to be engaged in and/or the product to be developed and tie it to the assigned task. (Example: "What mental operation seems most appropriate at this point?" or "What mental

operation does this situation [task] appear to call for?"Follow with: "What criteria have we already identified that might be applicable to a book [document, essay, map, proof, experiment] like this? Why?"[27]

- Ask lead-off questions that engage students in complex information-*using* tasks rather than in tasks that require collecting, remembering, or reporting information. (Example: "Was the United States more or less democratic in 1860 than in 1776?") Such thoughtful questions require use of several different higher-order cognitive operations as well as location and use of considerable information or data rather than simply remembering or reporting data as an end in itself.

Responding to Students

In a thoughtful classroom, the responses to student assertions, questions, or comments most effective for improving student thinking are those that continue student thinking of the kind needed to carry out the thinking that we seek to improve. Our cognitive purposes in responding to student comments or responses ought to be to *open* student thinking, to *keep it going*, and, if necessary, to *guide it* to increasingly sophisticated levels of complexity. The substantive purpose of our responding is to help students build, bit by bit, the complex subject-matter insights and understanding they are developing through engaging in such thinking. Among the most effective kinds of responses that can be made for these purposes are the following:

- Remain silent. Allow wait time for all students to ponder what was just said and for the speaker to reconsider the accuracy or soundness of his or her assertion and to offer evidence in its support. Students often interpret teacher silence as a signal that "more is needed," thus prompting their more elaborate follow-up justification or explanation. Silence also offers other students an opportunity and invitation to ask the speaker to clarify a statement, to offer support, to elaborate, or even to challenge the speaker's claim(s).
- Signal acceptance of student assertions by paraphrasing (or by having other students paraphrase), by a friendly facial expression, by writing the response on the chalkboard, or by using what was said as the basis for another question that carries the inquiry forward toward the development of new learning. Such acceptance also leaves the door open for further explanation, elaboration, justification, or questioning.
- Draw out and have students clarify fuzzy or ill-articulated assertions by requesting from the speaker or other volunteers clarity in language, definitions of vague or multimeaning terms, or more details, evidence, or examples.

- Probe or seek elaboration of what was said by asking the speaker or others for details (or details about details), examples and nonexamples, analogies, comparisons, additional arguments and counterarguments, or other points of view.
- Prompt or ask students to ask questions of the data, of each other, and of teachers. It will help them understand better what they are trying to learn about and how to go about doing so most efficiently and effectively. Student reluctance to initiate questions often results from fear of generating more work for themselves or from lack of interest in the subject. There are obvious remedies for both of these conditions. But it also results from what is referred to as the "habit of timid silence when one does not understand what someone else is talking about."[28] As the truism goes, the only bad question is the unasked question.
- Ask for additional information or evidence or indicate by silence or a quizzical look that evidence and reasoning are needed to justify the assertion(s) just proffered.
- Seek evidence that might negate as well as that which supports an assertion.
- If the time to locate and collect needed information would unnecessarily interrupt the thinking activity in which students are engaged and that thinking is crucial, provide such information.
- Facilitate data acquisition by telling students where to find needed information and how to get it or, if appropriate, make these sources available to them and help them use these sources to find the appropriate data.[29]
- Use information or assertions provided by the students as jumping-off points for going beyond what they have given, incorporating that information or assertion into a new question or direction. (Example: "If what you said were accurate, then what should the British have done?")
- Encourage effort, perhaps by asking a challenging question, introducing a contrary point of view, or giving missing information.[30]
- Ask or direct the students to reflect on and tell how they arrived at an assertion they have offered. In effect, ask them to tell what they did mentally to come up with this assertion.
- Ask students to appraise or evaluate the accuracy and soundness of assertions and claims proposed in the course of class discussion and in materials used by the students.
- Stimulate students to generalize the thinking operation or concept or understanding being developed by involving them in applying it to analogous instances or additional examples.
- Ask questions or give new tasks that alter the level of complexity of the thinking in which the students are engaged. Move students from

analyzing to evaluating to synthesizing, or from hypothesizing (synthesis making) to testing (an act of analysis and evaluation) to concluding (synthesizing again).

All of these responding behaviors maintain student thinking by pushing or inspiring students to continue their thinking. These kinds of responses also guide students toward using particular kinds of high-level, more complex thinking as well as keep them engaged in the subject being investigated, thus helping them elaborate their developing understanding of it.

Participating with Students in Thinking

By engaging with students in the learning tasks that require complex thinking, we can encourage the kinds of thinking that are required as well as offer assistance, when necessary, to those having trouble in carrying it out. We can join the students to brainstorm, search for, and report needed data, and to analyze, evaluate, and synthesize it. We can also volunteer hypotheses and suggest avenues for further investigation. In the course of participating with the students in a thinking or learning task we can also do the following:

- Provide feedback about how students are carrying out a task, suggest alternative ways to do it, and, on occasion, walk a student through a procedure that needs improvement.
- Act as a devil's advocate or gadfly by offering unpopular or unconventional ideas or ideas not yet articulated by the students that challenge or cause students to reevaluate, broaden, or find additional support for the ideas on which they are focusing.
- Reflect aloud with the students in deliberative fashion to identify hidden assumptions, evidence, reasons, implications, consequences, and alternative points of view as well as to establish accuracy and soundness of arguments.
- Suggest that students assist each other, by brainstorming additional ways to do a task, sharing information with others who might also use it, or seeking information from others who have certain knowledge.
- As the need arises, coach students in how to carry out difficult or poorly executed thinking tasks while they are engaged in attempting to carry them out.

This last function is especially important. While participating with students in thinking tasks in which they are engaged, we can also provide the kind of coaching that will help them improve the quality of their thinking. Effective coaches in athletics or theater or music serve as combination cheerleaders, instructors, models, facilitators, disseminators of tricks of the trade, and motivators. So should it be with those of us who coach thinking. We can provide explicit training in a difficult-to-master cognitive operation precisely when students demonstrate a need for improving their performance of that operation. We can alert students to and demonstrate the application of heuristics that make these operations easier to execute. We can guide or scaffold their execution of thinking tasks that they still find difficult to carry out, and model or demonstrate how these operations can be carried out with expertise, economy of effort, and efficiency. And we can push, press, challenge, exhort, and encourage their cognitive efforts, as well.

In many instances, students themselves can fill these same roles. For example, students can model for their peers effective thinking, share information they have uncovered or relevant experiences they have had, and encourage the thinking efforts of their peers. Some students, too, can assist their less adept peers at carrying out difficult thinking tasks, challenge as well as support the thinking of their peers, and provide feedback that enables their peers to clarify or refine their thinking. In a thoughtful classroom, students as well as teachers can coach.

Participating in thinking tasks with the students has numerous advantages for teachers as well as students. It provides a natural opportunity for us, as teachers, to model the behaviors and dispositions that are in need of improving. It also involves us in a satisfying way in the substance of the learning that is going on, thus providing intellectual stimulation that traditional teaching often does not. Indeed, such participant-teaching-coaching facilitates the continued improvement of our own thinking and also leads to new substantive learning, as well. Moreover, such participation allows us to share our own cognitive knowledge and expertise with the students—something that many students greatly appreciate. Finally, engaging as an active member of a thoughtful class provides us with natural openings during actual learning activities to intervene, as needed, with explicit instruction in any cognitive procedure with which a student or group is having trouble.

Keeping the Focus on Truth and Proof

One way to keep thinking going is to keep student efforts focused continuously on seeking accuracy and proof. Thinking becomes a natural and ongoing part of any learning that consists of establishing the truth of what one is trying to learn about and by critically evaluating evidence, reasons, and reasoning offered as proof for such learning. For, truth and proof are determined not by the status of a speaker or the loudness of someone's voice or a "know-it-all" attitude or the fact that something is in print. Instead, they are determined by the quality—accuracy, relevance, and significance—

of the information offered as evidence as well as by the soundness and logic of the reasoning by which the evidence is tied together and to the claims made. It is in the critical examination of the reasoning and evidence offered in support of and in opposition to knowledge claims that "new" insights are uncovered and knowledge and understanding are advanced.

Critical evaluation of information, assertions, reasoning, and evidence does not mean fault finding, nay saying, or making severe judgments. Rather, it means applying criteria to make reasoned judgments about some quality that something should or claims to exhibit.[31] Thoughtful classrooms apply to all knowledge claims the criteria of accuracy (truth) and of soundness (proof) as tests for acceptability and worth. One critically evaluates proposed solutions, sources of information, arguments, evidence, and other phenomena in order to distinguish those worthy of acceptance from those that are irrelevant, vague, erroneous, unreasonable, misleading, or otherwise flawed. It is the same mental operation one applies to making expensive purchases, voting decisions, career choices, and other personal or workplace decisions.

In a thoughtful classroom, students should continuously assess claims, conclusions, and assertions (their own and those of others) in order to determine their accuracy. This is done by assessing the credibility of the sources from which evidence is being drawn and by evaluating the factual accuracy of this evidence itself. Students should also engage and be assisted in assessing the strength of the logic by which evidence is presented in support of any claim. This involves, among other things, assessing arguments for logical consistency, logical flaws, and the type of logical connections posited and for the role played by assumptions.[32] Concern for accuracy and attention to evidence, reasons, and reasoning are central activities in thoughtful classrooms. We can ensure that these remain central in our classrooms by continuously questioning, modeling these behaviors, and ensuring that students provide and assess the information they use. In time, our students will then provide, on their own initiative, evidence and reasoning to back up their assertions, whether they are reminded to do so or they have developed the habit of doing so. By keeping students focused on establishing the truth and proof of whatever they are learning, we can sustain the kinds of thinking that characterize the most effective thoughtful classrooms.

CREATING AND MAINTAINING A SENSE OF COMMUNITY IN LEARNING

A community is a group with a common goal, shared behavioral norms, and a cooperative spirit. A learning community is a group of students—usually a classroom of students—who share a common learning goal and who cooperate with each other to achieve it.[33] Their classroom constitutes, in effect, what Bryson and Scardamalia call a "knowledge-building" culture.[34] The goal this community shares is to develop significant, meaningful insights and understandings about a common topic; to resolve a common problem; to make the best decision possible; or to produce some other agreed-upon kind of new knowledge. Its shared standards include those of truthfulness and soundness. The cooperative spirit reflects an understanding that each student can and does contribute to the advancement of the entire class toward achieving its goals; it expresses itself through collaboration to engage in the thinking and other activities required to achieve their common learning goal.[35]

Learning communities encourage thinking in at least three important ways: (1) The effort required to think is distributed among all members—many heads are, indeed, often better than one! (2) Members can share and benefit from the knowledge, experience, and skills of each other. (3) An atmosphere of mutual support and cooperation exists.[36]

In a class that behaves as a learning community, all members contribute to and share in shaping and carrying out the class learning goals. All recognize and value the integrity and individuality as well as the interdependence of all class members. Individuals work in the best interest of the entire class while simultaneously working to achieve their own goals. All value active participation in the interest of the entire community as well as individual achievement.[37] Although there may be frequent disagreements, they are never person directed, but rather are data and idea oriented, always with advancing class learning goals in mind.

Moreover, in a thinking community, activities and learning are initiated and given purpose by learner interests, concerns, and experience as much as by teacher guidance. As Lipman has noted, students listen attentively to each other, build on one another's ideas, and assist each other in evaluating information and ideas and in drawing and assessing inferences.[38] There is continual exchange, questioning, criticism, elaboration, and revision as all work together to generate and test ideas, sometimes collaborating in the same task and other times dividing the task into parts for which each individual assumes a special responsibility. Both individual inquiry and shared, group deliberation and investigation are important parts of the learning process that goes on in such a class.[39] In a learning community, each student is a teacher, coach, and learner, helping others to think and to learn and receiving help from others in their own thinking and learning.

Building such a sense of community requires use of intraclass grouping, cooperative learning techniques, and flexible seating arrangements.[40] Many of these techniques are already well known, but educator Marian Matthews's[41] recommended guidelines for using these techniques seem especially appropriate for thoughtful classrooms:

- Design projects so all students can interact and contribute equally. Avoid tasks where finding single, "right answers" is the goal.
- Engage students in activities that require sharing of ideas and information, building on each other's knowledge, and combining a variety of skills, backgrounds, and experiences.
- Allow for student interest and autonomy.
- Provide opportunities for and, if needed, instruction in how to seek and give assistance, take responsibility, move a group along in its task, keep on task, and make and monitor plans for carrying out group tasks.
- Group students in flexible ways, sometimes heterogeneously and sometimes homogeneously, depending on the nature of the learning task involved and the extent to which diversity of background, knowledge, and skill can enhance the learning and/or contribute to improving the attitudes, skills, and knowledge of the students.

By using cooperative learning techniques, in accord with Matthews's guidelines and by insisting on the sharing, helping, and building behaviors that typify community efforts, we can unite students in learning that uses and develops their knowledge and skills of thinking. Such learning situations will encourage and stimulate student thinking and make it a natural part of overall classroom learning.

ENCOURAGING STUDENT THINKING: A SUMMARY

For students to take full advantage of the thinking opportunities provided in thoughtful classrooms and to remain engaged in thinking over an extended period of time requires active encouragement by teachers and peers. As described in this chapter, we can provide such encouragement by providing classroom conditions that encourage thinking, actively initiate and keep student thinking going, and conduct our classes as learning/thinking communities. By so doing, we can maintain thinker-friendly as well as thinking-friendly classrooms. Encouraging thinking is just as important to the establishment of thoughtful classrooms as is providing opportunities to engage in such thinking.

Environments for Improving Student Thinking

Thoughtful classrooms provide exactly the kind of learning environment best suited to fostering thinking because they stimulate, nourish, and protect its application and growth. These classrooms are distinguished by continuous student engagement in increasingly higher-order thinking to *produce*, rather than reproduce, knowledge. As indicated in the preceding chapters, thoughtful classrooms emphasize the cooperative construction of knowledge by all students. This evolves through sustained, active process-ing of information, a search for truth and proof, and the building of deeper understandings and concepts than are typically developed in traditional recitation-type classrooms. Active inquiry is what makes a thoughtful class-room thoughtful.

Providing Thoughtful Classrooms

Although structuring or restructuring classrooms to make them more thoughtful can be accomplished in a variety of ways,[42] this goal can be ac-complished by focusing essentially on two tasks: (1) providing frequent, continuing opportunities to engage in the specific kinds of thinking need-ing improvement and (2) encouraging students to take advantage of these opportunities to engage in this thinking. The preceding chapters have ex-plained in detail a number of techniques for carrying out these tasks. By em-ploying these techniques, we can establish classrooms that invite student thinking and make such thinking a continuing, natural, authentic part of classroom learning.

Thoughtful classrooms provide students with continued practice in thinking, so that ultimately their thinking will become more refined and they will become more comfortable in doing it in a variety of contents. And by so doing, these classrooms also present opportunities for us as teachers to provide the kinds of instructive support and assistance needed by most students to make their thinking more efficient, more effective, and thus more productive. In effect, thoughtful classrooms provide the protection, stimulation and support that nourishes the exercise and development of productive student thinking.

Beyond Thoughtful Classrooms

It is important here to note that there is more to improving the quality of student thinking than simply establishing and maintaining thoughtful classrooms. For a few students, of course, active participation in thoughtful classrooms may be just about all that is necessary to improve the quality of their thinking. But for many—indeed, most—students, opportunity and en-couragement are *not* sufficient by themselves to accomplish this goal. These are the students who cannot or will not engage in difficult or demanding thinking because they do not know how to go about it, or they have—as best they can recall—never done it, or they do not believe they can do it and thus fear embarrassment or failure if they attempt it, or they do not wish to in-vest the effort they perceive it will require. These students need consider-ably more than just an occasion and an encouraging boost to engage suc-cessfully in thinking, especially in complex, higher-order thinking. They also need more than simply engaging in thinking—or trying to—to improve the quality of their thinking.[43]

What most students need and all students find helpful in improving their thinking is assistance in focusing consciously on how thinking works and structured support, guidance, and even direct instruction in how to carry out those thinking operations.[44] Although a thoughtful classroom certainly does provide the basic environmental conditions and nutrients for "growing" thinking, other, more direct, efforts at developing high quality thinking are also required. The remaining chapters of this book describe and explain three additional approaches that can be employed to improve the quality of student thinking within the context of a thoughtful classroom.

ENDNOTES

1. Rexford G. Brown, *Schools of Thought* (San Francisco: Jossey-Bass, 1991), p. 9; Fred M. Newmann, "Can Depth Replace Coverage in the High School Curriculum?" *Phi Delta Kappan 70* 5 (January 1988): 347; Martha Stone Wiske, "How Teaching for Understanding Changes the Rules in the Classroom," *Educational Leadership 51* 5 (February 1994): 20–21.

2. Gaia Leinhardt, "What Research on Learning Tells Us about Teaching," *Educational Leadership 49* 7 (April 1992): 20–25; Lauren Resnick, "Literacy in School and Out," *Daedalus 119* 2 (1990): 169–185.

3. Leinhardt, "What Research on Learning Tells Us," pp. 20–25; David Perkins, *Smart Schools* (New York: The Free Press, 1992), pp. 136–144 ; Lauren Resnick, *Education and Learning to Think* (Washington, DC: National Academy Press, 1987).

4. Mary Budd Rowe, "Wait Time and Rewards as Instructional Variables," *Journal of Research in Science Teaching 11* (1974): 81–94; David Perkins, "Creating a Culture of Thinking," *Educational Leadership 51* 3 (November 1993): 98–99.

5. Philip Adey, "Thinking Science," *Teaching Thinking and Problem Solving 12* 3 (May-June 1990): 1–5; Janet W. Astington and David R. Olson, "Metacognitive and Metalinguistic Language: Learning to Talk about Thought," *Applied Psychology: An International Review 39* 1 (1990): 77–87; David R. Olson and Janet W. Astington, "Talking about Text: How Literacy Contributes to Thought," *Journal of Pragmatics 14* (1990): 705–721; Perkins, *Smart Schools,* pp. 107–109.

6. Perkins, *Smart Schools,* pp. 105–107.

7. Beau Fly Jones, MindaRae Amiran, and Michael Katims, "Teaching Cognitive Strategies and Text Structures within Language Arts Programs," in Judith W. Siegal, Susan F. Chipman, and Robert Glaser (Eds.), *Thinking and Learning Skills,* Volume 1 (Hillsdale, NJ: Lawrence Erlbaum, 1985), pp. 261–262; Olson and Astington, "Talking about Text," p. 719.

8. Olson and Astington, "Talking about Text," pp. 705–721; Astington and Olson, "Metacognitive and Metalinguistic Language," pp. 79–83.

9. Jones et al., "Teaching Cognitive Strategies," pp. 261–264; Perkins, *Smart Schools,* pp. 108–109.

10. Perkins, *Smart Schools,* pp. 108–109; Matthew Lipman, *Thinking in Education* (Cambridge: Cambridge University Press, 1991), pp. 30–31, 229–243.

11. Arthur L. Costa, *The School as a Home for the Mind* (Palatine, IL: Skylight Publishing, 1991), pp. 110–115; Astington and Olson, "Metacognitive and Metalinguistic Language," p. 83.

12. Astington and Olson, "Metacognitive and Metalinguistic Language," pp. 77–87; Olson and Astington, "Talking about Text," pp. 705–721.

13. David R. Olson and Janet W. Astington, "Thinking about Thinking," *Educational Psychologist* (in press).

14. Barry K. Beyer, *Developing a Thinking Skills Program* (Boston: Allyn and Bacon, 1988), pp. 317–352; Arthur L. Costa and Barbara Presseisen, "A Glossary of Cognitive Terminology," in Arthur L. Costa (Ed.), *Developing Minds*, Volume 1, rev. ed. (Alexandria, VA: Association for Supervision and Curriculum Development, 1991), pp. 373–377.

15. Roger Dawson, *The Confident Decision Maker* (New York: William Morrow, 1993), pp. 258–259; Bena Kallick, *Changing Schools into Communities for Thinking* (Grand Forks, ND: Center for Teaching and Learning, 1989). p. 6; Rosemarie Liebmann, "How Important Is the Classroom Environment?" *Cogitare* 2 3 (September 1987): 1.

16. Sidney B. Simon, Leland W. Howe, and Howard Kirschenbaum, *Values Clarification: A Handbook of Practical Strategies for Teachers and Students* (New York: Hart Publishing, 1972), pp. 171–173.

17. *Ibid.*, pp. 163–165.

18. Kallick, *Changing Schools*, p. 7.

19. *Ibid.*, p. 5; Liebmann, "How Important Is the Classroom Environment?" p. 1; Robert Marzano, *A Different Kind of Classroom* (Alexandria, VA: Association for Supervision and Curriculum Development, 1992), p. 20; David Perkins and Tina Blythe, "Putting Understanding Up Front," *Educational Leadership* 51 5 (February 1994): 6.

20. Brown, *Schools of Thought*, p. 5; Lipman, *Thinking in Education*, pp. 229–243; Raymond Nickerson, "On Improving Thinking through Instruction," in Ernest Z. Rothkopf (Ed.), *Review of Research in Education*, Volume 15 (Washington, DC: American Educational Research Association, 1988–1989), p. 39.

21. Kallick, *Changing Schools*, pp. 5–6; Liebmann, "How Important Is the Classroom Environment?" p. 1.

22. Costa, *The School as a Home*, p. 9; Fred M. Newmann, "Higher Order Thinking in Teaching Social Studies," *Journal of Curriculum Studies* 22 1 (January-February 1990): 52.

23. Beau Fly Jones, Annmarie S. Palinscar, Donna Sederburg Ogle, and Eileen Glynn Carr (Eds.), *Strategic Teaching and Learning* (Alexandria VA: Association for Supervision and Curriculum Development, 1987), pp. 33–64.

24. Costa, *The School as a Home*, pp. 143–148; Fred M. Newmann, "Higher Order Thinking in the High School Curriculum," *The National Association of Secondary School Principals Bulletin* 72 508 (May 1988): 61; Nickerson, "On Improving Thinking," pp. 21–25; Perkins, *Smart Schools*, p. 116; Grant Wiggins, "Creating a Thought-Provoking Curriculum," *American Educator* 11 4 (Winter 1987): 11; Grant Wiggins, "The Futility of Trying to Teach Everything of Importance," *Educational Leadership* 47 3 (November 1989): 44–59.

25. Perkins, *Smart Schools*, p. 116; Costa, *The School as a Home*, p. 9.

26. Costa, *The School as a Home*, pp. 43–66.

27. Leinhardt, "What Research on Learning Tells Us," p. 22.

28. Wiggins, "The Futility of Trying to Teach Everything," p. 57.

29. Costa, *The School as a Home,* pp. 63–64.

30. Nickerson, "On Improving Thinking," pp. 25–27; Perkins, *Smart Schools*, pp. 98–99; Perkins and Blythe, "Putting Understanding Up Front," p. 6; Wiggins, "Creating a Thought-Provoking Curriculum," p. 14.

31. Barry K. Beyer, *Critical Thinking—What Is It?* (Bloomington, IN: Phi Delta Kappa Educational Foundation, 1995); Matthew Lipman, "Critical Thinking: What Can It Be?" *Educational Leadership 45* 1 (September 1988): 38–43.

32. *Ibid.*

33. Kallick, *Changing Schools, passim;* Lipman, *Thinking in Education, passim.*

34. Mary Bryson and Marlene Scardamalia, "Teaching Writing to Students at Risk for Academic Failure," in Barbara Means, Carol Chelemer, and Michael S. Knapp (Eds.), *Teaching Advanced Skills to At-Risk Students* (San Francisco: Jossey-Bass, 1991), p. 162.

35. Kallick, *Changing Schools, passim*; Lipman, *Thinking in Education, passim*; Richard S. Prawat, "From Individual Differences to Learning Communities," *Educational Leadership 49* 7 (April 1992): 9–13.

36. Bryson and Scardamalia, "Teaching Writing to Students at Risk," pp. 141–167; Costa, *The School as a Home,* pp. 9–10; C. D. Haertel, H. J. Walberg, and E. H. Haertel, "Social-Psychological Environments and Learning: A Quantitative Synthesis," *British Educational Research Journal 7* 1 (1981): 27–36; Kallick, *Changing Schools,* p. 4; Prawat, "From Individual Differences," pp. 9–13.

37. Kallick, *Changing Schools,* p. 4; Liebman, "How Important Is the Classroom Environment?" p. 1.

38. Lipman, *Thinking in Education,* pp. 52–53.

39. *Ibid.,* p. 15; Prawat, "From Individual Differences," p. 12.

40. Perkins, "Creating a Culture of Thinking," p. 98.

41. Marian Matthews, "Gifted Students Talk about Cooperative Learning," *Educational Leadership 50* 2 (October 1992): 50.

42. Barbara Presseisen, Barbara Smey-Richman, and Francine Beyer, "Cognitive Development through Radical Change: Restructuring Classroom Environments for Students at Risk," in J. N. Mangieri and C. C. Block (Eds.), *Creating Powerful Thinking in Teachers and Students: Diverse Perspectives* (Ft. Worth: Harcourt Brace, 1994), pp. 229–266.

43. David Perkins, "Myth and Method in Teaching Thinking," *Teaching Thinking and Problem Solving 9* 2 (March–April 1987): 1–2, 8–9; Michael Pressley and Karen R. Harris, "What We Really Know about Strategy Instruction," *Educational Leadership 48* 1 (September 1990): 31–34; Michael Pressley, Fiona Goodchild, Joan Fleet, Richard Zajchowski, and Ellis D. Evans, "The Challenges of Classroom Strategy Instruction," *Elementary School Journal 89* (1989): 301–342.

44. Robert Mulcahy and Associates, "Cognitive Education Project," *Teaching Thinking and Problem Solving 15* 6 (1993): 1–9; Thomas E. Scruggs and Frederick J. Brigham, "The Challenge of Metacognitive Instruction," *Remedial and Special Education 11* 6 (November–December 1990): 16–18.

PART II

MAKING THINKING VISIBLE AND EXPLICIT

Before repairing or strengthening something that is broken or not working as well as it should, one has to be aware of where and how it is broken or weak. One also has to be aware of how it works when functioning as it should function as well as of alternative ways it might function even better. This axiom also applies to improving thinking. By making our students' thinking visible and explicit, we can become aware of how their thinking actually works, thus establishing a starting point for fixing or improving it. By making the thinking of skilled thinkers visible and explicit, we can demonstrate how "good" thinking works and what our students can do to "fix" or improve their thinking where needed. The chapters in Part II describe and explain techniques for accomplishing these goals.

THE INVISIBLE SUBSTANCE OF THINKING

What is there about thinking that can be made visible and explicit? Plenty. At first glance, thinking appears to be a rather amorphous phenomenon, but it is not. Most of us realize that when we think, something is going on mentally. However, some people view thinking as a bolt out of the blue, as something approaching the miraculous. For them, thinking just somehow happens, but exactly how it happens is unclear. Because thinking is something that occurs inside the head and out of sight, it seems to be invisible and therefore lacking in substance. However, there is substance to thinking. It is by no means an amorphous or empty phenomenon; nor is it magic. Although specialists do not yet know all they would like to about thinking, they do know that thinking and the cognitive acts that constitute it consist, in large part, of the application of knowledge about when, why, and how to carry out various mental operations as well as skill in applying this knowledge. Happily, much of this knowledge and how it can be and is applied can be made visible and explicit.[1]

Cognitive psychologists describe the substance of thinking as consisting of three types of knowledge: procedural, conditional and declarative.[2] *Procedural knowledge*, according to these specialists, consists of the mental procedures, moves, or steps by which a cognitive operation is carried out. For example, one procedure or set of cognitive steps used in making decisions involves the following:[3]

- Identifying a decision-making opportunity
- Determining the criteria that elicit one's "best" choice (decision)
- Identifying alternative choices one could make
- Predicting the consequences of each alternative, if it is chosen, and the probability of each consequence occurring
- Evaluating the predicted consequences of each alternative in terms of the criteria identified earlier and perhaps added now
- Choosing the alternative, which, in terms of its predicted consequences, best meets these criteria

Each cognitive operation, skill, or strategy in which people engage as they think consists of a mental process that can be described as steps in a procedure. Although there may be no single, correct procedure for executing any particular thinking operation, some procedures are clearly more appropriate than others in carrying out any given thinking operation. Certainly, choosing the first course of action that comes to mind without considering a variety of other alternatives and evaluating their predicted consequences is not as appropriate or effective a procedure for making important decisions as is the procedure just described.

Conditional knowledge is knowledge about when, under what conditions, and in combination with what other cognitive operations a particular thinking operation is appropriate to a given task. For example, one place we use decision making is at that point in solving a problem where we select a plan or strategy to solve the problem we have identified. We also use decision making in making purchases, selecting vacation destinations, and other similar choice-making situations. As another example, we engage in classifying information when it is necessary to generate a hypothesis or conclusion. Knowing when—under what conditions—it is appropriate to use a particular cognitive operation is an important part of the expertise we possess with regard to that operation.

Declarative knowledge consists of the rules, heuristics (rules of thumb), or tricks of the cognitive trade or other knowledge that make carrying out a thinking operation most effective and efficient. In decision making, for instance, "Look before you leap"—evaluate the consequences of all possible alternatives before choosing one on which to act—is a heuristic indispensable to effective execution of this thinking operation. People skilled in decision making have generated this rule of thumb and use it to guide them in making effective decisions. The declarative knowledge of each of the various critical thinking skills (e.g., skills such as detecting bias, determining the credibility of a source, or judging the strength of an argument) consists of criteria applied by the skill procedure to determine the extent to which a particular quality is being met. Effective employment of these skills requires knowledge of as well as skilled application of these criteria. Skilled thinkers have devised and know a great deal of declarative knowledge about the various cognitive operations in which they engage.

Improving the quality of thinking occurs when students know and can apply with increasing proficiency these kinds of knowledge about important cognitive operations and *know they know and can do it!* Making this knowledge of thinking visible or explicit is indispensable to achieving these goals.

MAKING THE INVISIBLE VISIBLE AND EXPLICIT

Making one's thinking visible involves making public and observable the procedure one engages in while carrying out a thinking task or operation. It consists of two interrelated actions. First, it involves articulating—putting into words—the mental procedure by which one is executing or has just executed a thinking operation or task. This can be done by producing a description of this procedure, either orally or in writing. Such a description serves as a trail of one's thinking. The more concrete or observable this trail is, the more useful it is as a baseline for improving thinking.

A verbalized but unrecorded narrative of one's thinking is almost as ephemeral as if it were not verbalized at all. It is public for a few fleeting minutes at best, but then lost. When recorded on video or audio tape or transcribed on paper or on a chalkboard, however, a thinking trail can be examined repeatedly by the individual whose thinking it represents as well as by peers and teacher. Analysis of such a permanent thinking trail allows students to become more aware of their own thinking and raise it to a level of consciousness whereby it can be diagnosed and improved.

Making thinking explicit involves making one's thinking as precise, detailed, and complete as possible. This means articulating in as much step-by-step fashion as possible every significant mental move taken to carry out a thinking operation and the heuristics, rules, and cognitive knowledge employed in executing that operation. Novices in complex thinking, as most students are, are as likely to skip useful steps in a thinking procedure or to be ignorant of useful heuristics as they are to make dysfunctional or irrelevant moves in carrying it out. Attempting to articulate every move they make slows their thinking down so they become more conscious of what they are doing and how they are doing it. But once the mental moves or steps in their thinking procedures have been identified and verbalized in detail, the steps can be analyzed to identify gaps or ineffective or otherwise flawed steps.[4] Articulating these steps also helps encode them in memory and makes them more easily retrieved when needed later.[5] The more complete and precise—explicit—these procedures are the greater the possibility one can improve them, modify them in new situations and direct them to better accomplish one's thinking goals. When thinking remains fuzzy or generalized, skilled, self-regulated, intentional thinking is difficult, if not impossible.

Making the normally hidden workings of thinking visible and explicit thus establishes the conditions that must be met in order for any improvement to occur. As Seymour Papert has written, "The ability to articulate the processes of thinking enables us to improve them."[6] Students must become conscious of how they presently go about their own thinking before they can fine-tune or fix it.

If students do not know that something is broken or not working as well as it could, they assume the way it is working is the way it is supposed to be working, for them as for everyone else. If they do not know there are other, more skillful or efficient ways for something to work, they are not even inclined to seek to improve the way they currently carry it out, let alone make any effort to attempt to fix or improve it. As long as thinking remains unarticulated or invisible or fuzzy to students, it remains largely immune to efforts to improve it because such efforts may fail to intervene at the appropriate place with the appropriate remedy. But once thinking becomes visible and explicit, students have a sense of what needs fixing and what can be done to fix it.

TYPES OF THINKING TO MAKE VISIBLE AND EXPLICIT

Three kinds of thinking need to become visible and explicit for students to move toward improving their own thinking: (1) their own thinking, (2) the thinking of their peers, and (3) the thinking of experts or any individuals skilled in the kind of thinking that the students seek or need to improve. By making explicit and observable the procedures and knowledge employed by a student to carry out his or her own thinking, that student becomes conscious of and begins to understand what he or she is doing while thinking. By making explicit the thinking of his or her peers engaged in thinking tasks identical to those engaged in by the student, a student becomes aware of alternative ways of executing these tasks. The student will find that some are just like his or her own, some seem to work better, and some are less effective or even incomprehensible.

Explicit descriptions of the thinking of individuals skilled or expert in executing the thinking operation a student is trying to improve provide additional alternative procedures for carrying out this same thinking operation. Analysis and comparison of one's own thinking with both peer and expert thinking helps students to identify any sources of weaknesses or deficiencies in their own thinking as well as identify alternative procedures that will serve as potential remedies for these flaws. Awareness of these alternatives also help a student understand that any of several procedures or routines can legitimately be used to carry out the same thinking operation, thus moving the student away from a reliance on rote memorization to improve thinking.

In sum, by making explicit how peers and experts execute the cognitive procedures they themselves go through and the heuristics and other knowledge they employ in carrying out their thinking, students can identify things they can do to modify their own thinking.[7] As the students then incorporate newly discovered alternative procedures into their own thinking and revise their own thinking to remedy flaws or make it more efficient, their thinking improves.

TECHNIQUES FOR MAKING THINKING VISIBLE AND EXPLICIT

How can thinking be made visible and explicit? Classroom and experimental research over the past several decades has demonstrated the value of a number of techniques and teaching strategies for achieving this purpose.[8] Each of these focuses on the procedures by which a cognitive operation is or can be carried out. Some, however, produce more explicit descriptions of their thinking than others. It is these that prove most useful in providing initial instruction in a cognitive operation to students who are unfamiliar with it or for whom the operation is difficult. The following chapters describe and demonstrate techniques, first, for helping students make as visible and explicit as possible their own and their peers' thinking and, then, for making visible and explicit to them the thinking of individuals skilled in carrying out thinking tasks. These techniques, modified as necessary to fit the students, may be employed in any subject with students of virtually any ability and grade level.

ENDNOTES

1. Barry K. Beyer, *Developing a Thinking Skills Program* (Boston: Allyn and Bacon, 1988), pp. 125–152, 317–352; Robert J. Marzano, Ronald S. Brandt, Carolyn Sue Hughes, Beau Fly Jones, Barbara Z. Presseisen, Stuart C. Rankin, and Charles Suhar, *Dimensions of Thinking* (Alexandria, VA: Association for Supervision and Curriculum Development, 1988), pp. 48–51.

2. John R. Anderson, *The Architecture of Cognition* (Cambridge, MA: Harvard University Press, 1983); Thomas Andre, "Problem Solving and Education," in Gary D. Phye and Thomas Andre (Eds.), *Cognitive Classroom Learning* (New York: Academic Press, 1986), pp. 169–204; Raymond S. Nickerson, "On Improving Thinking through Instruction," in Ernest Z. Rothkopf (Ed.), *Review of Research in Education*, Volume 15 (Washington, DC: American Educational Research Association, 1988–89), pp. 18–20; David Perkins, "Myth and Method in Teaching Thinking," *Teaching Thinking and Problem Solving 9* 2 (March/April 1987): 1–2, 89.

3. Beyer, *Developing a Thinking Skills Program,* pp. 56–58, 161–165, 332–333; Joe B. Hurst et al., "The Decision Making Process," *Theory and Research in Social Education 11* 3 (Fall 1983): 17–43; Charles H. Kepner and Benjamin B. Tregoe, *The New Rational Manager* (Princeton, NJ: Princeton Research Press, 1981).

4. L. S. Vygotsky, *Thought and Language* (Cambridge, MA: MIT Press, 1962); Janet W. Astington and David R. Olson, "Metacognitive and Metalinguistic Language: Learning to Talk about Thought," *Applied Psychology: An International Review, 39* 1 (1990): 84; see also Luis Moll, *Vygotsky and Education* (Cambridge: Cambridge University Press, 1991).

5. Jack Lochhead, "Teaching Analytic Reasoning Skills through Pair Problem Solving," in Judith W. Segal, Susan F. Chipman, and Robert Glaser (Eds.), *Thinking and Learning Skills: Volume I—Relating Instruction to Research* (Hillsdale, NJ: Lawrence Erlbaum, 1985), p. 116.

6. Seymour Papert, *Mindstorms: Children, Computers and Powerful Ideas* (New York: Basic Books, 1980), p. 158.

7. *Ibid.,* pp. 109–131.

8. Nickerson, "On Improving Thinking," pp. 3–57; Michael Pressley and Karen R. Harris, "What We Really Know about Strategy Instruction," *Educational Leadership 48* 1 (September 1990): 31–33; Barak Rosenshine and Carla Meister, "The Use of Scaffolds for Teaching Higher Level Cognitive Strategies," *Educational Leadership 49* 7 (April 1992): 26–33.

Making Student Thinking Visible and Explicit

Improving one's thinking starts by becoming aware of what it is about thinking that needs improving or could be improved. Making thinking visible and explicit serves this function. Over the past several years, two techniques have become especially useful in helping students (or any inexperienced or unskilled thinkers) to make visible and explicit how they go about carrying out their own thinking. One is metacognitive reflection; the other is thinking aloud. As teachers, we can use either or both to help our students articulate their thinking and thus become conscious of what they know about and how they execute any cognitive operation at any particular moment. By using these techniques, we enable students to establish a baseline from which they can then proceed to revise, modify, correct, and refine their thinking.

METACOGNITIVE REFLECTION

According to Vygotsky and other experts, articulating how one thinks—the procedural, conditional, and declarative knowledge and rules employed to carry out a thinking operation—enables individuals to improve their thinking.[1] We can help students do this by using the technique of metacognitive reflection when they are introduced to and first attempt to carry out any new or especially complex thinking operation.

Metacognitive reflection consists of thinking back on how one carried out a cognitive act that one has just executed. It is an effort to reconstruct, as best one can remember, the mental procedure carried out and any rules or heuristics or other knowledge applied that informed the execution of that thinking procedure. When individuals reflect on the mental procedure they went through to arrive at an answer to a math problem or to arrive at a decision, they are engaged in metacognitive reflection. This process is one of the most useful ways for becoming aware of *how* one thinks.

Metacognitive reflection and *metacognition*, it should be noted, are not synonymous. Metacognitive reflection involves thinking about one's own thinking *after* having engaged in that thinking. Metacognition, on the other hand, is thinking about one's own thinking *before and while* actually engaging in that thinking. Metacognitive reflection seeks to reconstruct a past cognitive act. Metacognition is constructive, for it is that thinking one engages in to direct or manage one's mind while executing a specific thinking task. Metacognition is what one does mentally in planning how to carry out a thinking task. It involves monitoring and evaluating how one is carrying it out, assessing the extent to which it is getting one where one wants to go, and replanning and adjusting one's mental actions to eliminate flaws, remedy errors, or overcome unanticipated obstacles.[2] Metacognition is what reading specialist Ann Brown calls the executive control level of thinking. Skilled thinkers engage in metacognition simultaneously with the task-oriented thinking that they are carrying out.[3] Metacognitive reflection, on the other hand, is an attempt to identify, in retrospect, the elements of one's thinking *after* one has finished doing it.

An Example of Metacognitive Reflection

The best way to understand metacognitive reflection is to do it. Here is one way to do so. Answer this question:

> If you are facing east and then turn left and then make an about face and turn left again, in which direction are you facing?[*]

Write your answer here: _____

Now reflect for a moment on what exactly you did to come up with your answer. What did you do first? Why? Next? Why? Next? Why? Next? Why? . . .

---

*From *Problem Solving and Comprehension* (3rd ed.) (p. 4) by Arthur Whimbey and Jack Lochhead, 1982, Hillsdale, NJ: Lawrence Erlbaum. Copyright 1982 by Lawrence Erlbaum Associates, Inc. Reprinted by permission.

When you have thought out as clearly as you can how you carried out this task, try to put the procedure you used to arrive at your answer into words by explaining it to someone else. What was the very first thing you did after first reading the question? Why did you do that? What did you then do? Why? Next? Why? List below the complete procedure—all the steps—you went through to come up with the answer to the question. Start with the very first thing you did after reading the given question and continue until you had completed the task:

First, I . . .

Then, I . . .

Next, I . . .

Then, I . . .

Next, I . . .

. . .
. . .
. . .

Finally, I . . .

If you completed this task as directed, you just engaged in metacognitive reflection. What you should have written here is a detailed, step-by-step description of the procedure by which you came up with an answer to the question. Perhaps it resembles the description presented in Figure 4.1. This description was written by a young student teacher who had just completed the same task you did. Notice the detail she has provided. If your description is not as detailed and does not provide as much of a step-by-step explanation of how and why you did what you did to generate an answer to the question, reflect again on what you did. Then revise or elaborate your description to provide as much detail as you can about the procedure you used and any rules you followed.

Engaging in metacognitive reflection, as you may have just discovered or reaffirmed, is often quite difficult, especially for those who have not done

Figure 4.1 Student A's Metacognitive Reflection on a Thinking Task
Student A

When I first read the problem I pictured a direction symbol ($W \overset{N}{\underset{S}{-}} E$) in my head. Noting that there were several times I would have to switch directions. I decided to draw a large direction pointer. For me, the best way to actually go through the steps was to have myself face each direction and move according to the instructions. I took the piece of paper that I had drawn $W \overset{N}{\underset{S}{-}} E$ and placed it so I was facing east. The instructions stated I was to turn left so I turned the paper left and was facing north. I had to do an about face next so remembering my drill team days, I turned the paper so I was facing the opposite way, south. then I was to turn left so after turning the paper I was facing east again.

it often or for thinking operations that are quite unfamiliar or rather complex. The product of this reflection may be somewhat incomplete and, indeed, may even contain information extraneous to thinking. It may or may not be terribly accurate. But the act of generating by metacognitive reflection and then producing a description of how one has carried out a particular cognitive operation is extremely useful, for it is the initial step in improving the quality of one's ability to carry out that act of thinking in the future.

How does this occur in practice? Consider your description of how you generated an answer to the sample question. Did you come up with *east,* the correct answer? If so, exactly what did you do to arrive at this answer? What did you have to know to do this? If you did not come up with this answer, can you—by analyzing the procedure you used—figure out why? Did you skip a step? Did you not know something you needed to know to carry out this task effectively? Did you do something that was unnecessary or that threw you off the track? By analyzing this trail of your own thinking, you can spot problems in your thinking and perhaps remedy them so that you can carry out this procedure more effectively another time.

Now analyze the description in Figure 4.1 of how the student teacher executed the same task you did. What did she *do* as she carried out this operation? What did she *know* that made it possible for her to carry out this operation the way she did? What did she do in executing this task that you did not do? Why might she have done this? What did you do that she did not do? Why? How well did it work for you? Is it worth doing again or is some of what she did useful enough for you to incorporate in how you do this operation? How would you carry out this operation again, if you had to?

Figures 4.2 and 4.3 present the products of metacognitive reflection produced by three other student teachers, describing what they believe they did to come up with answers to the same question you answered earlier. Analyze each to find out how these students carried out this task. Notice what these students assert they did. Note, too, what they did differently as well as what they did in common. What do these descriptions reveal about their thinking that you might wish to avoid or do the next time you engage in this same operation?

For example, student B in Figure 4.2 had a problem. She apparently did not realize this, but an observer can readily see it, thus making corrective action possible! Student C, on the other hand, followed directions to the letter. Notice how she manipulated the paper on which she wrote the compass rose to carry out these directions! Finally, note what student D in Figure 4.3 reported doing to carry out this operation. Notice especially that this student's response describes her *second* try, not her first. She apparently did it another way before doing this! Note, finally, that she is the only one of the four who reported checking her work. However, even though she checked her work, she still came up with an incorrect answer—and apparently does not realize it! Furthermore, she identified a problem she had in doing the task—a problem she tried to resolve on her own but did so incorrectly. From what she described, however, we can discover that what went wrong was a knowledge deficit, not a procedural flaw. Knowing what we now know from analyzing this metacognitive trail of her thinking, we can help student D improve the quality of her thinking.

Figure 4.2 Students B and C's Metacognitive Reflection on a Thinking Task

Student B

First I got a mental picture in my mind of N, S, E, + W.
Then I pictured in my mind facing ~~was~~ east
Then I made an about face which made me face West.
Then I turned left which put me facing south.

Student C

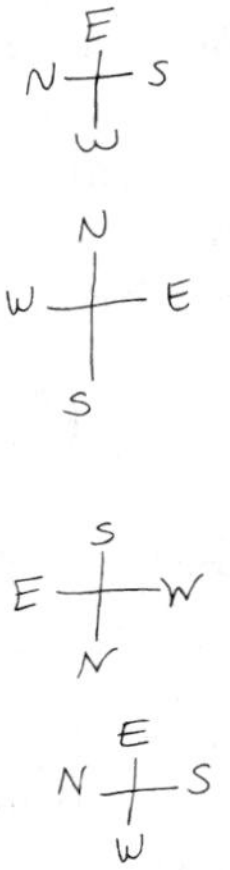

First, I read the question to find out the problem. After reading the entire question, I went back to the beginning. Since the question deals with what direction I am facing, I drew a direction symbol on a piece of paper. W—E (N, S)

I turned the paper so that the East sign was where North should be. This was my direction reference. I re-read the first part of the problem. I rotated the paper 90° to the left to illustrate a left hand turn I was then facing North I then rotated the paper 180° to illustrate an about face movement I was then facing South. Lastly, I rotated the paper 90° to the left, to illustrate a left hand turn. I was facing East again. Since there were no more directions, I had solved the problem. My answer is – East.

Figure 4.3 Student D's Metacognitive Reflection on a Thinking Task
Student D

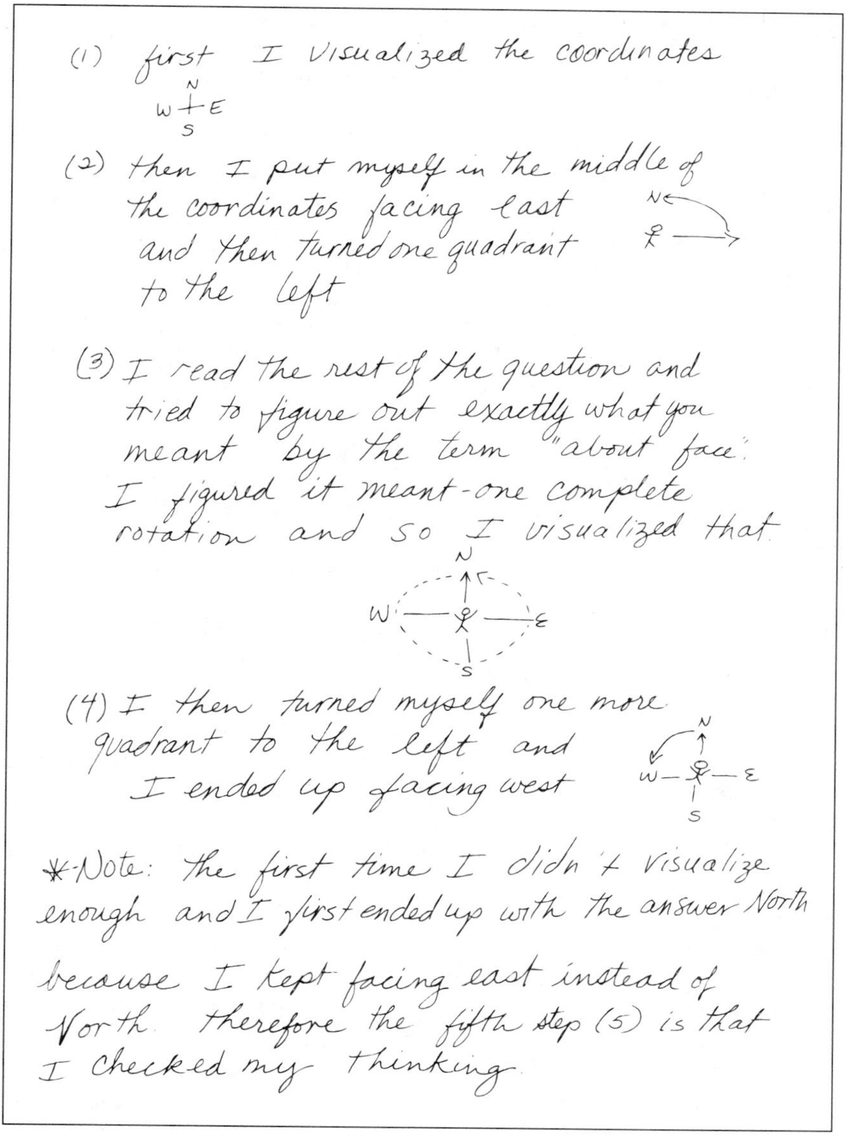

(1) first I visualized the coordinates

$$W \overset{N}{+} E$$
$$S$$

(2) then I put myself in the middle of the coordinates facing east and then turned one quadrant to the left

(3) I read the rest of the question and tried to figure out exactly what you meant by the term "about face". I figured it meant - one complete rotation and so I visualized that

(4) I then turned myself one more quadrant to the left and I ended up facing west

✱-Note: the first time I didn't visualize enough and I first ended up with the answer North because I kept facing east instead of North. therefore the fifth step (5) is that I checked my thinking.

These examples of metacognitive reflection are typical of what happens when using this technique with intermediate grade and secondary school students as well as with adults. They reveal three important implications of this technique for improving student thinking.

First, the four student descriptions presented here (Figures 4.1, 4.2, and 4.3) point out quite clearly that simply articulating how one believes he or she thinks does *not* guarantee good thinking or accurate results. Although the students cited here did describe how they believed they were thinking, two came up with wrong answers. One of these even checked her work! Although metacognitive reflection is a first step in improving student thinking, it is not, by itself, self-correcting.

Second, by articulating what they did to carry out a skill, these students have actually made visible what heretofore was invisible. Having a visible record of one's thinking allows students and teachers to diagnose flaws or gaps in it so they can intervene to correct or close the gaps. As teachers, we can, for example, see that an error may be caused by incorrect information (student D) or by a skipped step (student B). Having spotted these flaws, we can help students identify and adopt ways to correct their errors. Without such a visible, explicit thinking trail, this would be difficult, if not impossible.[4]

Finally, notice that all four of these students used *props* to help them complete the thinking task. Rather than try to remember all the data presented or implied in the given task to keep their place as they carried out the steps, each did something to reduce this load on his or her short-term memory. One drew a large compass rose. Two formed visual images of the directions and of themselves turning through them. One of these two turned the paper (*not* in the direction she reported, incidentally) as a substitute for imagining herself moving. The fourth used a stick figure and drawing to facilitate her thinking.

Other kinds of props are also commonly used in generating an answer to this sample question. Some who complete this task report imagining themselves standing in the middle of the United States, facing the Atlantic coast and then turning left to see Canada, then pivoting left to see the Pacific coast and then the Gulf coast, and then seeing the Atlantic as they turn left again to complete the task. Still others imagine themselves in a place they know faces east. One individual once reported standing at his front door looking out because that is where he could see the sun rise. He had to start with an image he knew that really faced east! A few people calculate the turns in sequence to be 90°, 180°, and 90°, concluding that this adds up to 360°, a complete circle, so they are right back where they started. They never move or imagine themselves moving at all, nor do they refer to compass directions! Occasionally, some individuals simply stand up, face any direction and declare it is east, and then proceed actually to turn themselves as they follow the directions provided in the question. And others simply let their hands do the turning for them!

The importance of using props in executing a thinking operation cannot be overstated. Whether it be a pencil diagram, a visualization, an actual physical move, or some other device, use of a prop facilitates thinking by reducing demand on short-term memory, thus making it more available to handle other data (such as the directions) related to the task. Students should be encouraged, as David Perkins has noted, to use props in carrying out any thinking task or operation.[5] Metacognitive reflection often reveals the great variety of such props that are used successfully.

As the preceding examples show, metacognitive reflection clearly leads to insights that can assist students in improving the quality of their thinking. By enabling them to create or reconstruct a concrete trail of any thinking act, it permits analysis of their thinking for flaws and enables them to become aware of alternative ways to carry it out the next time. At the same time, however, it is just as clear that metacognitive reflection alone does not necessarily accomplish this goal. To get the maximum learning benefit from metacognitive reflection, this technique must be used in conjunction with other, follow-up activities. As educator Arthur Costa has written, teachers or other experienced thinkers must serve as mediators in the course of engaging in these follow-up activities.[6]

Metacognitive Reflection as a Teaching Technique

As the preceding indicates, using metacognitive reflection in the classroom to improve student thinking requires doing more than simply having students reflect on their own thinking. It also involves getting them to articulate as precisely as possible how they carried out that thinking, sharing the results with others who have engaged in the same thinking operation, and considering critically the procedures and cognitive knowledge revealed or implied. Additionally metacognitive reflection involves our intervention or mediation to direct and guide this process as well as to call our students' attention to significant aspects of the thinking that is articulated and to help them generalize what has been uncovered beyond the parameters of the immediate thinking task.

One technique that incorporates all these features is an elaboration of the popular Think-Pair-Share technique. We can use this elaborated technique immediately after our students have engaged in any cognitive operation on which we wish them to focus. It consists of the following four steps, in which students:

1. *Reflect* on what they did mentally to carry out the given cognitive operation.
2. *Tell*—articulate—what they believe they did, in as much step-by-step detail as possible, to execute this operation.
3. *Share* with other students who carried out the same thinking operation what they believe they did in executing the operation.

4. *Consider* carefully what they and others say they did as they carried out this thinking operation.

Figure 4.4 presents a set of directions useful in carrying out this teaching technique.

Each of the four activities that constitute this teaching technique are essential to the effective use of metacognitive reflection about any cognitive skill. First (step 1), students need a minute or two of quiet to reflect on how they carried out the thinking operation that they just completed. The prompts provided in the directions for this activity serve to structure this reflection and may need to be repeated after a minute or so. Remind students that they are to reconstruct their thinking in as much step-by-step detail as possible so that they do not drift off into the subject matter in which they were applying the operation. In doing this, students may wish to list or make notes of some phrases or words that capture the mental moves they recall making.

Figure 4.4 Sample Directions for Using Metacognitive Reflection in the Classroom

---

1. **Reflect**
   Think about—reflect on—exactly what you did mentally to come up with the answer you did. What did you do first? Why? Next? Why? Next? Why? Next? Why? . . .

2. **Tell**
   Now, tell some one else what you believe you did to come up with your answer. Put how you arrived at your answer into words so they will know how you did it. Tell them the very first thing you did. Why did you do that? What did you do next? Why? Next? Why?

3. **Share**
   Share with your classmates who have also completed this same task exactly what you did, step by step, to produce your answer. Tell the first thing you did and why, what you did next and why, and so on, until you have described all you did as completely as you can. Then listen to them tell you, step by step, how they did the task.

4. **Consider**
   You have shared how you believe you did this task with others and listened to how they believe they did it. Now analyze what everyone says they did as well as what you believe you did. How many different procedures for doing this task are reported? Which seem to be especially interesting or effective? How could you use these procedures or any parts of them doing this task again better than you did it before? If you were going to do a task like this one again, how would you go about doing it, step by step?

Next (step 2), the students tell a partner or small group of other students who have also carried out this same thinking operation what they did to carry it out. This step requires each student to articulate as clearly as possible the procedures each employed as he or she reconstructed them. By putting these procedures into words, students clarify what and the sequence of what they presumably did to execute the operation in question. Explaining this to only a few students in a closed group (using the focus group technique described in Chapter 3) provides a private, safer environment for risking than does having to report to the whole class. Trying to explain how one carried out a cognitive task about which one may be rather unclear is oftentimes threatening to students. This small group reporting minimizes any negative aspects of this task.

In carrying out this activity, each partner or group member must receive equal time to state what he or she did as best it can be remembered. Whether one report duplicates another is not as important as is each student articulating as accurately as possible what he or she believes was done to carry out the skill. Again, repeating the need for step-by-step reporting is most helpful. Listeners may ask questions for clarification or elaboration, if they do so with sensitivity, but they should avoid commenting on, judging, or dissecting the procedures described.

Although this step is usually done as an oral activity, especially in the elementary grades, sometimes older students (secondary grades and beyond) who have had considerable experience in reporting orally and discussing the results of reflecting on their own and others' thinking can report in writing how they believe they executed a skill. Writing out the results of student metacognitive reflection has certain advantages as well as drawbacks. A written description leaves a *permanently visible* trail of one's thinking that can then be examined and reexamined, elaborated and clarified, *without* trying to recall repeatedly all that was previously said. Writing out what was believed to have been done, in effect, reduces overload on memory and facilitates deeper and continuing self-analysis of one's thinking.

However, producing a fairly detailed and comprehensive written description is very difficult for many, as seen in student B's example in Figure 4.2. Without practice at articulating one's thinking and without patience in pulling it to the surface, students often seem incapable and even unwilling to write more than a brief, superficial statement or vague or confusing generalizations about what they recall doing. For many students, then, attempting to write out what they recall doing to complete a thinking task proves extremely frustrating and counterproductive.

The graphic organizer in Figure 4.5 can assist students in structuring a written description of how they carried out a thinking task. This is especially effective for students who do not or are reluctant to provide

Figure 4.5 A Graphic Organizer for Guiding Student Written
Metacognitive Reflection

Thinking about Your Thinking
What Did You Do—Step by Step—to Carry Out This Task?

*What is
the very
first thing
you did?
Why?*

*What did
you do
next?
Why?*

*What did
you do
next?*

Why?

Next?

Why?

Next?

Why?

(etc.)

descriptions in as much detail as is needed. By reproducing this form on a regular-size piece of lined or plain writing paper, students can fill it in by responding to the written prompts. The following directions can be given orally to initiate use of this guide:

> Using the organizer provided, write what you did, step by step, to carry out the thinking task you just completed. Be sure you give as much detail as possible, answering each question on the left in a sentence or two to the right. Write exactly what you remember doing each step along the way as you worked through the task to produce your answer. If you can recall why you did each or some steps, tell that, too.

When students have completed the form and reviewed it to add to or modify it, they can then exchange descriptions with other students who have completed the same task and proceed to share their insights. Having secondary school students write such a reflective report and then orally describe to a small group of their peers the procedure described in their written account often leads to the identification of crucial steps they failed to take or to record and occasionally even to self-identification of other thinking errors.

Once students have reported—orally and/or in writing—what they believe they have done and listened to or read what one or more of their peers have done to execute the same thinking operation, volunteers can share with the entire class (step 3) what they believe they did to execute the operation. If no volunteers come forward, we may have to launch this step of the technique by projecting a transparency of a written description of this same operation made by a student in another class or a hypothetical example that we have prepared. As these reports are presented, we should list on the chalkboard, in shortened form, the procedures identified so all students can see them, perhaps dividing the board into two sections headed *steps* and *rules*. It is not necessary or desirable for all students to report. Three to five or so descriptions are usually more than enough to secure a sample of the various procedures probably employed by most students. By asking, "Did anyone do it another way?" we can elicit different procedures rather than repetitions of the first one given.

It is important at this point to assure our students that there is no "right" way to execute a thinking skill. Whatever way they believe they did it is what they should report. Of course, many students will fail to report all they really did mentally to carry out a skill, and a few will not even have done what they claim they did. However, whatever students report doing to execute the skill should be written in the students' own words. Students should also be asked to explain or define any ambiguous or strange words or terms. Descriptions of procedures that duplicate one already listed may be accepted, but rather than writing them out again we can simply check off the steps on the same procedure already listed on the board. The checks acknowledge the second student's contribution yet eliminate the necessity of taking up scarce chalkboard space with a procedure identical to one already on the board. Although we may initially have to prompt such reporting, as our students become familiar with what is expected such prompting becomes less necessary.

Once a variety of procedures are displayed, students should consider (step 4) what has been presented by analyzing and evaluating the reported procedures, rules, and other thinking-related information on display. They can be asked to (1) identify any steps probably taken but unreported, (2) infer any principles or rules that they seem to have been following, and (3) compare the various procedures to each other to identify steps and sequences of steps unique to one as well as steps or rules common to all the reported procedures. Having volunteers paraphrase several promising procedures or apparently important rules to follow is a useful way to conclude the use of this technique. In no case, however, should we conclude this activity with convergence on only one way of carrying out the operation. The purpose of this technique is to open students to the variety of ways a thinking operation can be carried out and to allow them to become aware of how they now do it, gaps, false moves, and all.

Time is a factor in using this technique, as it is in using any teaching technique. As teachers, of course, we can devote as much time to this technique as we wish. However, it is important to note that too little time prevents students from giving the attention to a variety of ways for executing the given cognitive procedure that is needed to clarify it, whereas too much attention may lead to boredom and frustration. The times listed in Figure 4.6 may serve as a general guideline for optimum use of this technique once students have become used to it. More time will be required initially and each of the stages may initially have to be modeled.

Figure 4.6 Approximate Time (in minutes) Suggested for Students

Step	Primary Grades	Intermediate Grades	Middle Grades	High School
Reflecting	½	½–1	1–2	1–2
Telling	½	½–1	½–1	1–2
(Writing)	—	3–4	5–6	6–8
Sharing	2–3	2–3	3–4	3–5
Considering	2–3	3–4	3–5	4–6

Using Metacognitive Reflection in the Classroom

Using this technique of Reflect-Tell-Share-Consider to help students become more aware of and improve their thinking, requires us, as teachers, to concentrate on at least two things. First, we must keep the students focused on the procedural and declarative knowledge that constitutes the thinking operation being examined. Second, we must help students identify especially useful procedures or rules for carrying out this operation and generalize these beyond the data or context in which the operation was performed. These goals can be achieved through the kinds of task directions given as we move students through the various steps of this technique, by the questions we ask in the course of carrying out the technique, and by our comments during the process to call to the students' attention points of significance they might otherwise ignore.

Clear, precise task directions are also essential. The directions presented in Figure 4.4 constitute one such set of directions for employing this technique. These explicitly seek to keep students focused on the procedure by which the operation was executed and to elicit the most detailed, step-by-step descriptions possible.

We can also use questions to keep students focused on the thinking operation being examined as well as to elicit as much precise detail as possible about how they carried it out. This can be accomplished especially well by asking questions that help students articulate reasons why they executed each step as they carried out the skill. Asking "What did you do first? Why? Next? Why? Next? Why?" (and so on) helps students focus on the skill-using procedure in considerable detail. Student responses to "What did you do . . . ?" usually reflect a step in the procedure or routine they believe they used. Responses to "Why?" often reveal principles, guidelines, or other forms of declarative knowledge that, in effect, serve as rules or heuristics for them. Such probes are the heart of this technique.

Variations of this series of probe questions may also be useful with middle- and secondary-level students. For example, a sequence of probes such as the following pushes students to reflect more deeply on their thinking to identify the knowledge they are using as principles or rules to direct it:

1. What was your goal?
2. What did you do first? Why?
3. What did you consider doing next?
   Why?
   What did you actually do?
   Why this?
   (Repeat item 3 over and over until the final product is produced.)

4. How could you have done this differently? When or where would you do it this way? Why?

Not all students can or will respond to these probes, however, especially if we are seeking comments about mental operations used. Young children, youngsters in preschool and primary grades, and students who are academically at risk often lack command of the language needed to report what they believe they mentally did. Most of these students can *show* how they did it, however, and should be invited to do so. "*Show me* what you did first—and tell me why," "*Show me* what you did next. Why?" and so on, effectively stimulate these students or novices of any age to articulate how they believe they carried out a thinking operation. Such students often verbalize physical rather than mental operations, but, through repeated reflection in response to these probes and with increasing experience, they gradually begin to articulate some of the more mental aspects of thinking.

We teachers should feel free to interject comments as students share, and especially as they consider the cognitive procedures presented, in order to clarify, highlight, or help generalize significant procedural operations or knowledge. For it is at this point in using this technique that students can become aware of alternative ways to carry out the procedure in question. Interestingly, in sharing and considering how various class members believe they carried out the same operation, some students become aware of moves they did not make or heuristics that others followed that would have enabled them to carry out the operation easier and with better results. They then adopt these moves or heuristics in subsequent use of this operation, without explicitly indicating they have done or will do so. They simply are attracted by what they hear or see that appears to make their own efforts easier and more efficient.[7]

Many times, however, students do not fully understand the value or significance of ways of executing a cognitive operation that differ from the procedures they used. This is where our comments or intervention as teachers become especially important. While students consider the results of their metacognitive reflection, we can interject comments as well as questions that call their attention to alternative procedures for executing a skill, especially useful heuristics or significant mental moves made by others in carrying out these operations. Moreover, students in the early stages of learning or perfecting a cognitive skill do not always recognize gaps, flaws or errors in their own thinking (as illustrated by students B and D in Figures 4.2 and 4.3). When such errors or gaps appear, we need to intervene and either point these out or ask a student to compare his or her thinking procedure with those provided by other students to "discover" these errors or gaps for themselves. Or, they or other students can simply point out an omission or error they have noticed, explain how it flaws the procedure described, and suggest remedies.

Students just learning a new or difficult skill also rarely recognize the significance or utility of a particularly useful step in a thinking procedure or of knowledge that was used as a heuristic to guide the application of that step in carrying out a new thinking operation. They thus benefit immensely from having this pointed out to them. For example, novices rarely recognize the important role played by the props used by various individuals in executing thinking operations, nor do they spontaneously generalize the idea of props to other thinking operations. However, when we or a perceptive peer points it out to them, they usually readily see the value of props. Most then feel free to use props in the future, and they quickly add them to their thinking repertoire.

Thus, in guiding students through the sharing and considering phases of metacognitive reflection as a teaching technique, we must be alert to the need to call student attention to gaps, errors, flaws, and dysfunctional moves in the procedures they assert they have followed. We must also point out the value of useful heuristics or specific mental steps reported and help students generalize or transfer their insights beyond the context of the immediate thinking task being examined. By such timely interventions, we can highlight and elaborate procedural knowledge that might otherwise be ignored or undervalued by the students.

We can employ any number of variations of this technique without losing its essential elements or diluting its usefulness and impact on learning. Steps 1 through 3, for example, can be carried out by students individually at their own paces, with a partner or small group. Only Step 4—analyzing and considering procedures presented earlier (on posters or written on the chalkboard)—need be conducted as a teacher-directed activity. Although the activities of reflecting, telling, and sharing are essential preparation for this final activity, the mediation that we and our students collectively offer in this final analysis of the various procedures presented is what clinches and makes explicit what students learn as a result.[8]

Strengths and Limitations

Why is the technique of metacognitive reflection as described here so effective in improving student thinking? Simply put, using this technique makes students more conscious of how they think, and being conscious of how one carries out a thinking operation serves two important purposes. First, the oral or written trail of thinking produced by this technique allows students and teachers to analyze and evaluate it to identify strong moves and useful heuristics as well as gaps, flaws, and dysfunctional procedural moves or knowledge. Second, identification of these, in turn, permits later filling in of such gaps, remedying flaws, and adopting more appropriate moves or rules. It allows us to make thinking more efficient, expert, and productive. Raising thinking operations to a level of consciousness also makes students more likely to purposefully access these operations later when there is a recognized need to use them, rather than simply just waiting for something to mentally happen. Because a procedure for executing the operation has become a conscious part of the students' thinking repertoire, it can be more easily recalled and carried out with some degree of confidence. Metacognitive reflection is an extremely useful way of helping student thinking become more *intentional* rather than simply being a "happy accident."

This technique has both strengths and limitations. Foremost among its strengths is the fact that it starts with the students themselves, by assuming they can carry out the operation in some way, even if they do it poorly. Thus, it enables learning to begin where the students are. What they articulate by way of executing the operation provides a platform on which to build. Moreover, by hearing and seeing how others do it, students realize that there are other people who think the same way they do—for good or ill—and so what they do may not be so strange or odd or hopeless. This technique also helps students realize that there is more than one way to carry out an operation successfully and that there may be better, more efficient moves they could incorporate into how they think.

On the other hand, metacognitive reflection as a teaching technique is sometimes handicapped by the inability of some youngsters to recapture or articulate clearly how they executed a thinking operation. Likewise, some students are unwilling to analyze critically their own thinking, and some are inclined to hang on to what they believe they did rather than to modify it by considering demonstrably more effective ways of doing it.

Moreover, there is always present in any metacognitive reflection the tendency to slip from a focus on the thinking operation being examined to the content or subject matter to which the procedure was applied. Although focus on content is not undesirable per se, it is a handicap at this point in learning about a new thinking operation because it is virtually impossible for students to learn about a cognitive operation when discussing only subject matter. This can be controlled by being aware of this problem and by keeping students focused by task directions, questions, and comments on the cognitive procedures being considered.

Finally, there is inherent in this approach a tendency to present or designate or focus on one procedure or routine as *the* correct or only way to carry out the given cognitive operation. This is not only inappropriate but untrue. There are a variety of routines by which different kinds of experts effectively carry out any given thinking operation. We need to ensure that students become aware of several of these in the course of their learning about any specific thinking operation. This can be done by eliciting, displaying, and discussing these varied procedures. Awareness of all these limitations should encourage patience and sensitivity in the use of this technique as well as attention to precision of language and accuracy in articulating and reporting how students describe their thinking.

THINKING ALOUD

Thinking aloud is exactly what its name indicates—verbalizing a mental process one is going through. Like metacognitive reflection, thinking aloud is a way of making one's own thinking visible and explicit. Unlike metacognitive reflection, however, thinking aloud occurs *while* that thinking is occurring, not afterward. Consequently, thinking aloud produces a running account or description of a cognitive act as it is happening, rather than a reconstruction from memory of a cognitive act after it has been completed. Specialists claim that the act of thinking aloud makes a person more conscious of how he or she thinks as well as more aware of the content of that thinking. When recorded (and sometimes simply when it is heard), a "think aloud" serves as a visible or public trail of one's thinking. It can then be examined and analyzed to identify the knowledge and the procedures—or gaps and flaws in these procedures and knowledge—employed to carry out this thinking.[9]

An Example of Thinking Aloud

Thinking aloud consists of producing a move-by-move or step-by-step narrative of what one is doing mentally as he or she executes a thinking task. The most useful think aloud, for purposes of helping students improve their thinking, is one in which students make explicit *how* they think. They verbalize the *mental moves* or steps they are considering taking, about to take, and actually engaged in taking, and the *reasons* for taking these moves as they make them. Trails of such thinking are similar in many ways to accounts of thinking produced by metacognitive reflection, but they tend to be—with practice—more explicit and thorough.

Suppose we asked some intermediate-grade students to think aloud as they individually evaluated the following account[10] in their social studies text to determine if it showed any bias:

Farming used to be a pleasant way of life but now it's terrible. The price we get for what we grow is outrageously low. The soil is thin and rocky. Our sons took factory jobs because they refused to farm. We'd like to sell, but only a crazy person would buy a farm. Nobody wants to be a farmer. Soon there will be no farms left.

After introducing these students to the meaning of the word *bias* (a slanted or one-sided opinion or point of view), we provided examples of bias (e.g., a persistent preference for things chocolate instead of trying other kinds of desserts or candy, a die-hard sports fan's account of his team's defeat as the fault of the officiating). Then we asked half of the students to tell a partner out loud how they were thinking while they carried out the assigned task. Figure 4.7 presents a transcript of the kind of "think aloud" that was produced by one of these students who went through this process and received some prompting in thinking aloud.

Note that this think aloud reports *how* this student is thinking as well as *what* she is thinking. She verbalizes some of the mental moves she is taking as well as the substantive insights generated by those moves. For instance, she starts by thinking about her goal: "I am to see if this is bias—has bias." She then tries to recall the meaning of bias and reports why she is doing this: "I need to know so I can figure out if this shows bias." Unable to recall any clues to bias, she decides to "read it first" and again reports her reason for doing so. Then she starts reading, reporting some words that catch her attention. She infers a tentative connection among these words (she does not verbalize this move although she does report the inference she makes) and

---

*Rather than use a variety of thinking operations to illustrate the various teaching techniques presented here and on subsequent pages, the same skill—analyzing to detect bias—is used throughout. This consistent use of one skill allows you to focus on the teaching technique or strategy described rather than on the nature of the skill itself, thus minimizing any potential distraction engendered by constantly shifting skill examples. The purpose here is not to explicate the attributes of various thinking operations, as worthwhile as such an effort might be, but to become familiar with the various techniques for teaching them. All the teaching techniques explained and illustrated in these pages can be used as described herein with any thinking operation, from remembering to decision making, from detecting bias to judging the credibility of a source to problem solving, and so on. Information on the internal workings of various higher-order cognitive operations like these is readily available in other sources, including: Barry K. Beyer, *Developing a Thinking Skills Program* (Boston: Allyn and Bacon, 1988), pp. 125–151, 312–352; Barry K. Beyer, *Practical Strategies for the Teaching of Thinking* (Boston: Allyn and Bacon, in press); Robert Marzano et al., *Dimensions of Thinking* (Alexandria, VA: Association for Supervision and Curriculum Development, 1988); and Robin Fogarty and James Bellanca, *Teach Them Thinking* (Palatine, IL: I.R.I. Group, 1986). See also Barry K. Beyer, *What Every Teacher Should Know about Thinking Skills* (Boston: Allyn and Bacon, forthcoming).

Figure 4.7 Transcript of a Student Thinking Aloud (Prompted)

STUDENT A

Bias. That's my job. I am to see if this is bias—has bias. What's bias? I need to know so I can figure out if this shows bias.

Slanted. Bias is slanted—being one-sided. Bias.

So, how do I do that? How do I know if something has bias?

I don't know.

So, I'll read it first. Why? To get, like, a sense of it. I mean, I don't know how to decide if something is biased so I'm thinking if I . . . if I just skim it, I may get ideas.

So, I'm reading . . . "a pleasant way" . . . "terrible" . . . "prices . . . low" . . . "soil's thin and rocky."

Hmmm. These words . . . I see these words . . . "terrible, . . . outrageously low, . . . thin and rocky. . . ." What? I'm thinking about these words. They make farming sound hard—bad. Not good. I think I see something here. These words make me think . . . this is awful one-sided.

I'm going back and start again to see if this is so. Now let me see—"terrible . . . out-rageously low . . . thin . . . rocky." Bad-sounding words. Nothing good about farm-ing so far.

These words really do say the same thing. They make farming look, like, in a bad light.

I'm going on . . . The sons refusing to farm sounds bad, too. It's so bad, people want out.

Yeah. No one wants to be a farmer. . . . Only crazies. . . . They can't even sell their farm.

I'm done reading. So I'm thinking about all I've read. Yes. This person is saying farming is bad. Everything here seems to add up to farming is bad.

Isn't there anything good about it? Why are so many people still farmers? I'm skimming this again but I don't see anything here about, like, anything good about farming. Just "pleasant."

Nothing else, though.

Everything here—except the "pleasant"—adds up to bad . . . bad . . . bad. Those words—the bad soil—these ideas—the sons leaving the farm—no one buying—these all make a bad picture of farming. And soon there won't be any farms left. That's awful. Who will grow the food?

Except for "pleasant," this is really one-sided. I think. If bias is being one-sided, I'll risk it—yes, this is bias! This is a bias against farming.

then reports her decision to go back "to see if this is so." From there, she mixes verbalizing *how* she is thinking with some *reasons* for engaging in these mental moves as well as the results of that thinking until she completes the task to her satisfaction.

As this example reveals, a useful student think aloud reveals some of the key mental moves a student believes he or she is making and the reasons for them as well as the substantive results of that thinking. Of course, it may not produce as visible and explicit a trail of thinking as is ideally desirable, but it does make explicit some of the student's thinking procedure. Furthermore, the particular think aloud in Figure 4.7 reveals a sort of rule of thumb that student A has devised for what to do if one does not know what to look for in completing a task such as this. This rule might be phrased as "When you don't know, read on and something might strike you that will be helpful!" Careful review and analysis of this think aloud can clarify and make even more explicit the thinking procedure and heuristics she employed to detect bias in this selection. Analysis of her think aloud by other students may also enable her to make her thinking even more visible and explicit.

Thinking Aloud as a Teaching Technique

We can engage students in thinking aloud in either of two ways: on their own, without any guidance or prompting by anyone else, or with the assistance of a second person (teacher or peer) who has the role of keeping the student on task and talking. An analysis and comparison of think alouds generated by each method shows clearly which is the more useful and productive for articulating and consequently for initiating the improvement of the quality of student thinking.

The think aloud of student A (presented in Figure 4.7) typifies those often generated with the prompting of someone experienced in helping students produce such accounts. As the preceding analysis has already shown, this think aloud presents a fairly visible and explicit trail of a student's thought process employed in carrying out the assigned thinking task. This *prompted thinking aloud* is, in fact, fairly representative of the most explicit think alouds that middle school students with some experience in thinking aloud can produce while executing a higher-order thinking task new to them and with continuing outside prompting.

Think alouds of students B through E presented (in Figure 4.8) are typical of those produced by fifth-grade social studies students while doing the same thinking task as student A, but the former are *without* any guidance or prompting. These students simply report aloud what they are supposedly thinking in response to the same initial directions as given to student A. Their

Figure 4.8 Transcripts of Students Thinking Aloud (Unprompted)

STUDENT B

Is this biased?

Who wrote this?

Farming, it used to be pleasant.

But not now. No one likes it.

Is this bias? . . . I don't think so. . . . Looks straight to me.

STUDENT C

Bias. Like a Penguins nut. It's only the Penguins, no matter what. Can't stand the Flyers!

I'm supposed to see if this shows bias. Okay.

Okay. How do I, like, know if it's biased? These first sentences don't sound—umm—very nice. Like farming is terrible . . . prices awful low.

Not fun being a farmer, I guess.

"Only a crazy person would buy a farm?" My uncle is a farmer and he just bought the little farm next to his. Man, this is weird.

"Nobody wants to be a farmer?" Not true. This, like, really makes farming sound bad. But it's not true. I remember my grandfather telling me how he loved the farm—the outdoors and being on his own and . . . I don't think my uncle would agree with this either. Not everyone thinks farming is bad!

But this one sure does. Yeah, I think this is pretty one-sided.

STUDENT D

One-sided huh? Bias is one-sided.

Well, that means being a *for* or *against*. So what I do is look for things *for* or *against* something. Then I'll know.

Ah, "pleasant"—that's a *for*. "Terrible"—*against*. "Outrageously low"—*against*. "Thin and rocky" soil—*against*. "They refused to farm"—*against*. "Only a crazy person would buy"—*against*. "

Now, what have I got? Almost all *againsts*. Looks pretty one-sided to me. This sure looks like a bias to me—a bias against farming.

continued

Figure 4.8 *Continued*

STUDENT E

Bias . . . Bias . . . Bias . . . I'm looking for bias. . . .

Bias . . . One-sided. Slanted. Okay.

How can you tell bias? . . . I don't know. Maybe if I just read it.

Hmmm, this is about farming. It's terrible. Prices are low. Bad soil.

Must be a farmer . . . and wife . . . writing this—"Our sons." You have to be crazy to buy a farm? No one wants to farm?

Well, what am I trying to do? Find any bias? Well, if bias is—what did he say— being one-sided, then this must be bias. These people sure seem against farming!

Almost everything here is against farming. Farming is terrible. The prices are outrageous. The soil is bad. No one stays a farmer. Farms aren't worth buying.

Yes. This is really one-sided. I guess that makes bias. Right?

---

think aloud narratives typify the range of think alouds produced by middle school students (and even much older students) with limited experience thinking aloud while executing a complex thinking task presumed to be new to them *without* any en route prompting. The differences between these unprompted think alouds and the prompted think aloud underscores the usefulness of a prompted thinking aloud in making thinking visible and explicit.

Think alouds of students B and C record little, if any, explicit trail of the thinking these students are engaged in. Student B's account is virtually useless as a thinking narrative because it fails to articulate any task-oriented thinking other than the posing of two questions presumably stimulated by the reading selection the student was analyzing. The think aloud of student C, however, initially verbalizes several thinking operations, those of defining the task and the term *bias*. But from there on, this think aloud leaves a trail of associative thinking and personalized reflection related to the topic of the selection being analyzed. Although it does provide some useful insights to student C's thinking, it does not provide a clear or explicit trail of that thinking, at least in terms of *how* this student is executing the operation of analyzing or evaluating for bias. Unfortunately, unguided, unprompted thinking aloud, especially with younger students or students inexperienced in doing so, produces many think alouds similar to these.

Think alouds of students D and E, however, do make some thinking visible. Both articulate, but without being terribly explicit, an occasional step in the thinking procedure being employed. Student D, for instance, reports an interesting heuristic for evaluating for bias and one that bears further discussion with its author and his peers. But this account fails to report exactly what was done mentally to come up with the terms noted and why these terms and not others were selected. Student D seems to have spoken only occasionally as he carried out the task and then verbalized his conclusions rather than described or noted the thinking moves in which he was engaging.

The think aloud of student E is clearly the most descriptive thinking procedure of the four. However, even it is sketchy and leaves much to be inferred by later analysis. This student does verbalize some thinking acts: "Maybe if I just read it." and "What am I trying to do?") She also reports thinking about the definition as a criterion for judging the extent of bias in the selection being studied ("If bias is . . . onesided, then . . . ") and having noticed a pattern in the evidence ("Almost everything here is against farming"). Like the think aloud of student D, this think aloud is more explicit about the thinking going on than those of students B and C—but not so explicit as to leave an especially complete, highly visible thinking trail.

In contrast to these four think alouds, the think aloud of student A verbalizes considerable thinking, both in terms of cognitive actions being taken or about to be taken and in terms of reasons why some of these mental actions were taken. Several of these remarks were volunteered, as the task directions required. Others, however, were clearly made in response to *prompting*. For example, she states her goal in evaluating the given selection as she starts her analysis. But as she gets into the task, she verbalizes her thinking primarily in response to a listener's questions, which she repeats each time, before verbalizing her thinking: "What? I'm thinking about these words." But, as she proceeds, she voluntarily reports, "I'm going on . . . " and still later says, "I'm done reading. So I'm thinking . . . ." The prompting helps her produce a more visible and detailed account of her thinking than she otherwise was providing by probing for what she is doing and the reasons for it. Prompting also reminds her of the task—to report what thinking she is engaging in while she is engaging in it.

What all these think alouds reveal is that although a few students do or can think aloud on their own rather explicitly as they carry out a thinking operation, most do not. Most students, unless experienced or prompted in thinking aloud, do not report aloud much, if any, of what they are doing mentally while they are thinking. They just think instead and, on occasion, report aloud the results of their thinking. If left to themselves, the think alouds most students produce are so sketchy, fragmented, and off track that the major cognitive moves they make can only be inferred by close after-the-fact analysis and often with only the reflective input of the students who produced them. Certainly, if students are to develop think alouds that make their thinking as visible and explicit as possible and of the quality needed for them to "see" their thinking in some detail, some sort of guidance or prompting is necessary as they produce them.

Using Prompted Thinking Aloud in the Classroom

Using prompted think alouds to make student thinking visible and explicit consists of carrying out two tasks. First, students must produce or generate think alouds. They must engage in a specific *prompted* thinking activity, thinking aloud as they proceed, and record their narrative or have it recorded. Second, each resulting think aloud must be analyzed by the student who produced it, by other students who engaged in the same thinking activity, and by teachers or teachers' aides experienced in such analysis. Although these two tasks are not always easy to do well, the technique of using prompted think alouds has proven very effective in improving student thinking when employed carefully by teachers and students experienced in their use.[11]

Prompted thinking aloud can be produced in at least three ways. One approach is to pair students. One member of each pair carries out the assigned skill-using task and thinks aloud as he or she does so; the other prompts the process and perhaps records, either in writing or on tape, what the "thinker" says. Another approach is for a student volunteer to think aloud while carrying out the assigned skill-using task with the teacher prompting in front of the class as a whole. In this approach, class members follow along, noting significant moves made by the volunteer and instances they want to ask about when he or she is finished. Finally, teachers or aides can use this technique in working individually with students in diagnostic or remedial situations out of class or even in class while other members of the class are otherwise engaged.

Regardless of which of these approaches are used, there are two aspects of engaging students in prompted thinking aloud that need to be addressed in order to make this technique work effectively in a classroom. First, what the thinker says as she or he talks aloud must be recorded or transcribed for later use. Unless this is done, what the student has said is soon forgotten, misquoted, misconstrued, or subject to argument. Transcribing or recording a think aloud in writing or on audio or video tape will eliminate most of these problems. Recording a think aloud narrative as it is verbalized allows the student who did the thinking, as well as other students in the class, to conduct a later intensive, repeated analysis of the thinking revealed. Particularly clear and elegant recorded narratives can also be used in classes and later years as models or examples of the thinking aloud procedure.

Second, since the direction given to student thinking aloud very much shapes the quality of the verbalization of that thinking, the kind of direction or prompting provided should result in the most detailed and thorough *thinking* narratives possible. Unprompted thinking aloud permits the thinker to talk, or not talk, he or she desires and allows him or her to say whatever comes to mind during the time allotted for completing the task (as is illustrated by the four examples in Figure 4.8). The results are usually less than satisfactory. Unprompted students often stray from the assigned task, go minutes without saying anything while still very much doing the task, and fail to articulate how they come up with the substantive connections, inferences, hypotheses, and conclusions they produce while thinking.

Prompting student thinking aloud, however, can minimize the possibility of these problems from occurring and thus help the thinker verbalize more completely what he or she is doing while thinking. The task of a prompter, whether student or teacher, is twofold. He or she must periodically use questions and requests such as "What are you doing/thinking now?" "Why do you say that?" "Tell me what you are thinking now," and "Tell me what made you think of that" to encourage the thinker to verbalize as much as possible of his or her mental activity. Prompters should also ensure that the "thinker" maintains a steady stream of verbalizing while thinking. Specialists recommend that no silence longer than 3 to 4 seconds should be allowed.[12] Through careful and continuous prompting such as this, thinking aloud usually produces a rather thorough verbalization of what one does in carrying out a cognitive task or skill.

Having observers—who may or may not simultaneously be prompters—record in writing or by audio or video recorders, what the student thinker does *physically* as well as what he or she says, provides an even more useful trail of thinking. Many thinkers, especially good thinkers, distribute their thinking efforts by using aids or devices that reduce the demands on short-term memory and leave it freer to process without trying to retain all the details of directions or data.[13] They make marginal notes, underline or otherwise mark passages, connect related phrases or ideas by lines, make diagrams, and so on. Suppose, for example, the nonverbal actions taken by student A in carrying out her thinking task had been included in the transcript (in Figure 4.7) of her thinking aloud. The complete transcript of thinking performance might then look like this excerpt from it:

Actions	*Verbalization*
Points to *terrible, outrageous* with pencil.	I think I see something here. These words make me think . . . this is awful one-sided.
Circles words mentioned. Moves pencil back to first sentence. Circles *thin* and *rocky*.	I'm going back and start again. . . . Now let me see—"terrible . . . outrageously low . . . thin . . . rocky." Bad-sounding words. Nothing good about farming so far.

Actions	*Verbalization*
Connects circled words with lines.	These words really do say the same thing. They make farming look, like, in a bad light.
Points to lines and circled words.	. . . Everything here—except the "pleasant"—adds up to bad . . . bad . . . bad.
Circles these phrases.	Those words—the bad soil—these ideas—the sons leaving the farm—
Makes line connecting all circled words.	no one buying—these all make a bad picture of farming.

Such physical moves aided this student in her thinking and undoubtedly helped develop the pattern or relationship she articulated upon concluding the task. This student was, in effect, using her pencil to make visible some emerging connections in what she was reading. She was thinking with her pencil as well as with her mind! Observing and recording nonverbal moves made by someone thinking aloud thus provides evidence of this added dimension of thinking. Adding the observed nonverbal actions of a thinker to a transcript of his or her thinking aloud provides an even more comprehensive and visible record of that thinking.

When a thinker is recorded on video tape, no special effort by an observer is needed because the thinker's actions can be picked up by the camera and recorded. Obviously, the use of video recorders for this purpose is a cumbersome and awkward undertaking, especially when using this technique as a part of a whole class activity, but it is not at all impractical when using it in a diagnostic, tutorial, or remedial situation. Regardless of how nonverbal actions of the thinker are recorded, however, the value of knowing about them later should not be underestimated. Clearly, there is often more to thinking than simply mental processing. Observing, prompting, and recording someone thinking aloud are more likely to make thinking more explicit and nonmental "thinking" more apparent than is unprompted, unobserved, or unrecorded thinking.

Prompters must observe one important caution in any thinking aloud activity. They must not, under any circumstances, prompt the individual who is thinking aloud to go in any specific direction by suggesting that he or she look at something or even take a specific thinking action. The prompter should not do the thinking for the thinker. He or she can keep the thinker on task by asking, "Why do you think/say that?" or "How is that related to what you're supposed to be doing?" or some similar challenge. But in no case should the observer or listener attempt to guide the thinking of the person who is thinking aloud.[14] The purpose of prompting is to achieve a complete and explicit verbalization of how one thinks on his or her own, not with outside help. Improving thinking starts with and follows the production of this explicit, baseline record.

The act of verbalizing one's thinking can sometimes actually help a student become more conscious of problems or flaws in his or her thinking while engaged in that thinking. Indeed, this does sometimes occur as students occasionally say, "I don't mean that," after saying something or, "I just don't know what to do next" or "Oh-oh. I forgot to carry the 2." But its real value lies in producing a record of one's thinking that, recorded, can then be submitted to further analysis. A thinker's effort to explain how or why he or she thought what was thought makes his or her thinking even more explicit and enables students to gain even further insights into their thinking.

Strengths and Limitations of Prompted Thinking Aloud

As difficult as it often is to do well while carrying out a complex thinking skill—especially an unfamiliar one—prompted thinking aloud has proven to be an especially useful initial step in improving the quality of thinking. Educators Arthur Whimbey and Jack Lochhead, in fact, have developed an entire skill-teaching strategy built around this technique (described in Chapters 8 and 9). According to them, prompted thinking aloud makes students more conscious of their own thinking and leads to a sense of control over it. It also helps students spot flaws in their thinking, notice skipped steps or erroneous assumptions or inferences, and become more careful, precise thinkers. And it helps them identify some of the moves or heuristics that are essential to effective use of a particular skill.[15] Finally, analysis of the prompted think aloud narratives of others allows students to become aware of other, sometimes more effective or efficient ways of carrying out a particular cognitive operation.[16] This not only broadens their repertoire of thinking tools but it also allows them to replace, often without teacher direction or even awareness, ineffective cognitive procedures with more effective ones. Both results lead to improved student thinking.

Thinking aloud does have its limitations. It is often difficult for students, especially younger ones and some of those considered to be academically at risk, to verbalize their thinking as they do it. This difficulty is often compounded when thinking aloud without much experience at it while carrying out an unfamiliar and/or complex cognitive operation. Task content that is unfamiliar or difficult to comprehend further affects this process in a negative way. We can minimize these problems by our or student peer modeling of the technique and student practice doing it without regard initially as to whether or not it focuses explicitly on process rather than on content. However, for some students, thinking aloud just does not work well at all.

Even where thinking aloud is done well, without appropriate prompting, it usually produces rather incomplete thinking trails. Students thinking aloud rarely report voluntarily, or sometimes even with prompting, all they do as they think. Sometimes, their thinking occurs too fast for them to "capture it." Sometimes, they are simply unaware of how they are thinking. Many simply skip mentioning procedural steps. Others lack the language to label what they may feel they are doing cognitively. Some report physical actions related to thinking, whereas others do not. Many verbalize feelings and extraneous or totally irrelevant information. Often, students stop thinking about their thinking altogether as they get absorbed in listening to or concentrating on the substantive task in which they are engaged. And sometimes, they simply give up in frustration at trying to do both when one task is difficult enough for them.

Although careful prompting helps to minimize these pitfalls, it creates others. Prompting, after all, is an intrusion into one's thinking. Listening and responding to a prompter slows thinking down and sometimes disrupts it. Moreover, as already noted, prompters sometimes try to inject their line of thinking into the process (e.g., "Wouldn't it help to look for more loaded words?"). Occasionally, prompters try to outthink their partners and to push their own thinking onto them, especially when the latter appear to be stuck or going down a "wrong" trail. When this occurs, it undermines the validity of the think aloud. Ensuring that inappropriate prompting does not occur requires experienced student prompters and continuing monitoring of paired thinking aloud activities.

Like metacognitive reflection, then, thinking aloud has its limitations as well as its advantages as a technique for making student thinking explicit. When done poorly and without adequate prompting and recording, thinking aloud may confuse rather than enlighten, frustrate rather than engage. When done well, however, prompted thinking aloud and the subsequent analysis and sharing can help significantly to make student thinking visible and explicit. And by so doing, it provides a take-off point for helping students on their way toward improving the quality of their thinking.

ANALYZING TRAILS OF STUDENT THINKING

The follow-up analysis of an account of a student's thinking is extremely important to the successful classroom use of both metacognitive reflection and prompted thinking aloud. A thorough analysis can make more visible and explicit the thinking implicit in even a fragmented, poorly done account of student thinking, whereas a superficial analysis may add nothing of value to even the most explicit record of such thinking. What we teachers do with think alouds or reports of metacognitive reflection once students have produced them determines their ultimate utility for teaching and learning.

A record or description of a student's thinking can be analyzed in any number of productive ways. Students working in pairs can analyze each other's thinking description. Or an individual student may analyze his or her own recorded or written narrative alone or with our assistance or that of a teacher's aide, intern, or peer tutor trained in conducting such analysis. Or an entire class might analyze a written transcript or an audio recording of a volunteer think aloud, under the direction of the teacher or of the student who produced it.

Regardless of who conducts the analyzing, this analysis must search for statements or actions that explicitly describe or from which we can infer the following:

- A thinking skill, operation, or step in a thinking procedure
- The purpose or goal that is sought by employing a thinking operation or step in a thinking procedure
- The reason why this thinking operation or thinking step is (was) being employed
- The different thinking operations students considered when they were faced with the choice of "what to do next" or how to do it
- Reasons for rejecting any thinking operations considered at any specific point where a choice could be or was made
- Any rules, principles or self-made rules (heuristics) seemingly followed to select or execute a specific thinking operation
- The sequence in which the various thinking operations or steps were employed
- The extent to which the operations employed carried the student toward achieving the thinking or learning goal

At one level, this search can be accomplished simply by noting statements that explicitly denote a cognitive action, consideration, or reason for taking such an action (e.g., "So I'll read first . . . to get, like, a sense of it") At another level, one must read between the lines in the thinking trail to infer cognitive moves being made (e.g., inferring what student A believes it is about the definition of *bias* that will contribute to her ability to "figure out if this shows bias"). Analyzing the trail of a student's thinking requires identifying both explicit and implied (or inferred) thinking actions and reasoning.

In sum, the analysis of a description of a student's thinking procedure should focus on identifying what was done mentally—step by step or move by move—to execute the operation being employed and the reasons for undertaking these steps and not others. Such an analysis of the prompted think aloud of student A, for example, enabled this fifth-grade student and her peers to identify the following as the procedure she used in analyzing the given written selection for evidence of bias:

- Stating the purpose or goal: to detect bias
- Trying to decide what to look for as indicators of bias
- Skimming to identify possible evidence of bias
- Rereading to search for more evidence like this evidence
- Summing up the indicators to identify a pattern in the evidence found
- Comparing the evidence found with the definition of bias
- Stating the finding

Such an explicit description of a student's act of thinking makes students sharply aware of how they now think—which is the first step in improving their own thinking.

There is a third level of analysis of a thinking description that can also help students understand their own thinking. This involves a search for gaps, errors, missteps, or procedural alternatives apparently not considered as the thinking proceeded. By identifying these, we not only assist students in explicating even further their own thinking but we also help them generate specific moves they could employ the next time they engage in a similar thinking task.

One way to accomplish this latter level of analysis is by comparing thinking narratives of the same thinking task. By considering what others did and how they did it and how that is similar to or different from how someone else did it, a student can become explicitly aware of cognitive moves that could be taken to make their thinking more effective. Group or class comparing of descriptions of student thinking and sharing of alternative ways of thinking can make specific thinking operations exceptionally visible and explicit. This is exactly what many students who are just beginning to grapple with a new or difficult thinking skill needed in order to improve their thinking.

Although we teachers can analyze any student's thinking narrative and explain our findings to them, it is more useful for students to engage in this analysis themselves. By so doing, they make their thinking even more explicit. Of course, we can and should provide assistance as needed, and their peers can also assist as well. Supervised practice in conducting these analyses can gradually provide the experience most students require to become able to provide this assistance as well as to better analyze and understand their own thinking.

One of the most useful products of an analysis of a think aloud or product of metacognitive reflection is a written description—in the form of a checklist of steps or a flowchart—of how the thinking procedure described was carried out. The most useful final product, however, is a checklist or flowchart describing, step by step, how this same operation might be executed more effectively in the future. This latter can be devised after students compare their thinking narratives with each other or to someone else's way of executing the same task. Procedural checklists or outlines generated by these analyses can be revised as a result of further class sharing or group analysis and as a result of continued use and reanalysis. General discussion of common flaws in carrying out the particular skill being applied can make thinking analysis exceptionally productive for many students, especially those just beginning to grapple with a new, difficult, or complex cognitive skill by making how they (try to) do it increasingly visible and explicit.

MAKING STUDENT THINKING VISIBLE AND EXPLICIT: A SUMMARY

One of the first steps in improving student thinking is for students to become aware of how they now think. Once they know this, they (or more experienced observers) can spot gaps or flaws in their thinking, which can then be remedied. Assisting students in making their own thinking visible and explicit accomplishes the former. By coming to see or hear how they carry out in as much detail as possible any particular thinking operation, students become more aware of how they think. Both metacognitive reflection and prompted thinking aloud—and the subsequent sharing, analysis and discussion of the narratives of their thinking—can enable students to do this. Sharing with others what they have verbalized about their thinking also helps students assess it for procedural adequacy and appropriateness, economy of effort, and effectiveness. By hearing or seeing how others execute the same thinking operation as they do, students can often spot things they, too, do but had been unclear about. At times, it can also enable them to identify alternative, often more effective, procedures for carrying out the same cognitive operation.

Metacognitive reflection and prompted thinking aloud are the most practical techniques we can use to assist students in carrying out these tasks. They are important tasks as well, for understanding how one thinks is essential to improving it. The next chapter explains techniques for making explicit and visible to students the thinking of those people who are expert or skilled at executing any thinking task. Students can then use these descriptions to identify what it is these thinkers do that they, themselves, can do to improve the quality of their thinking.

ENDNOTES

1. L. S. Vygotsky cited by Janet W. Astington and David R. Olson, "Metacognitive and Metalinguistic Language: Learning to Talk about Thought," *Applied Psychology: An International Review, 39* 1 (1990): 84; see also J. Larkin, J. McDermott, D. P. Simon, and H. S. Simon, "Expert and Novice Performance in Solving Physics Problems," *Science 208* (1980): 1335–1342; D. N. Perkins and G. Salomon, "Are Cognitive

Skills Context Bound?" *Educational Researcher 18* 1 (January 1989): 16–25; Luis Moll, *Vygotsky and Education* (Cambridge: Cambridge University Press, 1991).

2. Raymond S. Nickerson, David N. Perkins, and Edward E. Smith, *The Teaching of Thinking* (Hillsdale, NJ: Lawrence Erlbaum, 1985), pp. 100–109; Scott G. Paris and Peter Winograd, "Promoting Metacognition and Motivation of Exceptional Children," *Remedial and Special Education 11* 6 (November/December 1990): 7–15; Robert J. Sternberg, "How Can We Teach Intelligence?" *Educational Leadership 42* 1 (September 1984): 38–50.

3. Ann L. Brown, Joseph C. Campione, and Jeanne D. Day, "Learning to Learn: On Training Students to Learn from Texts," *Educational Researcher 10* 2 (February 1981): 14–21.

4. Allan Collins, Jan Hawkins, and Sharon M. Carver, "A Cognitive Apprenticeship for Disadvantaged Students," in Barbara Means, Carol Chelemer, and Michael S. Knapp (Eds.), *Teaching Advanced Skills to At-Risk Students* (San Francisco: Jossey-Bass, 1991), pp. 222–223; Grant Wiggins, "Creating a Thought-Provoking Curriculum," *American Educator 11* 4 (Winter 1987): 14.

5. David Perkins, "Mindware: The New Science of Learnable Intelligence," paper presented at the Fourth Annual International Conference on Thinking, San Juan, Puerto Rico, August 1989.

6. Arthur L. Costa, *The School as a Home for the Mind* (Palatine, IL: Skylight Publishing, 1991), pp. 89–90.

7. Perkins, "Mindware," *passim.*

8. Collins et al., "A Cognitive Apprenticeship," pp. 222–223; Wiggins, "Creating a Thought-Provoking Curriculum," p. 14.

9. Jack Lochhead, "Teaching Analytic Reasoning Skills through Pair-Problem Solving," in Judith W. Segal, Susan F. Chipman, and Robert Glaser (Eds.), *Thinking and Learning Skills: Volume 1—Relating Instruction to Research* (Hillsdale, NJ: Lawrence Erlbaum, 1985), pp. 122–124.

10. Adapted from Barry K. Beyer, Jean Craven, Mary McFarland, and Walter Parker, *World Regions* (New York: Macmillan/McGraw-Hill, 1993), p. 242.

11. Lochhead, "Teaching Analytic Reasoning," p. 116; Nickerson, Perkins, and Smith, *The Teaching of Thinking,* pp. 206–209; Arthur Whimbey, "Teaching Sequential Thought: The Cognitive Skills Approach," *Phi Delta Kappan 59* 4 (December 1977): 255–259; Arthur Whimbey and Jack Lochhead, *Problem Solving and Comprehension* (5th ed.) (Hillsdale, NJ: Lawrence Erlbaum, 1991), pp. 22–35.

12. Whimbey and Lochhead, *Problem Solving and Comprehension,* pp. 22–35.

13. David Perkins, *Smart Schools* (New York: The Free Press, 1992).

14. Whimbey and Lochhead, *Problem Solving and Comprehension,* pp. 28–29.

15. Lochhead, "Teaching Analytic Reasoning"; Whimbey and Lochhead, *Problem Solving and Comprehension,* pp. 22–35.

16. Richard T. Hutchinson, "Teaching Problem Solving to Developmental Adults: A Pilot Project," in Judith W. Segal, Susan F. Chipman, and Robert Glaser, (Eds.), *Thinking and Learning Skills: Volume 1—Relating Instruction to Research* (Hillsdale, NJ: Lawrence Erlbaum, 1985), pp. 499–514; Whimbey and Lochhead, *Problem Solving and Comprehension,* pp. 25–27.

5

Making the Thinking of Experts Visible and Explicit

Observing and analyzing how expert thinkers—individuals skilled in carrying out a specific thinking operation—execute that operation helps students improve their thinking in at least two ways. First, it makes students aware of alternative procedures for thinking. Second, it alerts them to procedures that may be much more effective and efficient than those they now use. Understanding how skilled thinkers execute a difficult thinking operation enables students to take specific, purposeful steps toward improving their own thinking.

Two techniques have proven extremely useful for presenting explicit descriptions of expert thinking to students: (1) modeling and (2) comparing student thinking to that of someone experienced in and skilled at carrying out that same kind of thinking. Both techniques make visible and explicit the thinking of skilled thinkers. Either or both of these techniques can be used to familiarize students with and help them understand useful procedures for executing the kind of thinking with which they may be having difficulty. By comparing their own existing procedures for carrying out a particular cognitive operation to those of "experts," students can identify flaws or gaps in their thinking. They can also identify powerful new or revised cognitive strategies to incorporate into their own thinking repertoires.

MODELING

Without question, modeling is the most powerful of all techniques for familiarizing novices with how to carry out a cognitive operation that is new or puzzling to them. Simply put, *modeling* is the act of providing an example to be imitated by others. In terms of thinking, modeling means presenting how—in a step-by-step, rule-by-rule fashion—to carry out a specific cognitive procedure so students can then replicate the procedure on their own. Of all the techniques for making the covert or invisible cognitive procedures of skilled thinkers visible and explicit to students, modeling is by far the most effective.[1]

Although often described as "demonstrating," there is more to modeling than just showing how to do something. Properly done, modeling consists essentially of two actions: (1) *executing*, or carrying out, a cognitive operation in a step-by-step fashion as the students observe and listen, while (2) simultaneously *explaining* the major moves (rules and/or steps) in the procedure being modeled. Modeling thus involves more than simply walking students through steps in a cognitive procedure. It also involves telling the students at each major point along the way the options available at that point in the procedure and the reasons why selecting one particular option at that point is important to the effective execution of the procedure.[2]

Execution of the procedure *is* important, but without the accompanying *explanation* of why what is being done is being done *when* it is being done, students often do not become aware of the steps that are unique or essential to the execution of the procedure, the sequence in which these steps can best be performed, the role of each step in carrying the operation forward, how the steps relate to one another, and the reasons for carrying out each step. Modeling makes all these features of a cognitive operation *explicit* while actually allowing students to see with their very eyes what the procedure looks like when it is executed skillfully.

An Example of Modeling

How does modeling work in actual practice? Suppose we were to model the cognitive skill of evaluating to detect bias for a middle school social studies class. Figures 5.1 and 5.2 present two items we would provide for students during the lesson. Figure 5.1 is an excerpt from a historical document of which we have made copies for the students as well as a transparency for use on the overhead projector.[3] Figure 5.2, which can be displayed in large letters on poster paper, lists simplified steps in the skill procedure to be modeled. At that point in a lesson on the impact of the industrial revolution where we want the students to use the excerpt we have prepared, we can introduce and model the skill of evaluating for bias. Here is a sample

Figure 5.1 Student Material Used in Example of Modeling

Some of the lords of the loom employ thousands of miserable creatures [i]n the cotton-spinning work. [T]he poor creatures are doomed to toil day after day fourteen hours in each day in an average heat of eighty-two degrees. Can any man with a heart in his body refrain from cursing a system that produces such slavery and such cruelty?

[T]hese poor creatures have no cool room to retreat to, not a moment to wipe off the sweat, and not a breath of air. The door of the place wherein they work, *is locked except* at tea-time. If any spinner be found with his *window open,* he is to pay a fine.

[F]or a large part of the time the abominable stink of gas assist[s] in the murderous effects of the heat [w]hich the unfortunate creatures have to inhale. [C]hildren are rendered decrepit and deformed and thousands upon thousands of them [die] before the age of sixteen.

Adapted from William Cobbett, "Such Slavery, Such Cruelty." *Political Register 52* (November 20, 1824).

Figure 5.2 Steps in a Procedure of Evaluating for Bias

1. Define bias.
2. Identify or recall clues to bias.
3. Search piece by piece to find clues.
4. Identify any pattern in the clues.
5. Judge the match between the pattern and the definition of the bias.

annotated transcript of this lesson. It picks up at that point in the lesson where we begin to introduce this skill to the students by modeling it:

Teacher Talk	*Teacher Actions*
. . . To identify some effects of Great Britain's industrial revolution, we can use documents like the one you have in front of you (Figure 5.1). But before we believe everything it says, we ought to see if it is an accurate, balanced account or not. It could be biased. A *bias* is a one-sided or slanted view or statement. Any written or oral statement could contain or reveal bias and thus not be the complete truth.	Writes the word *bias* on chalkboard. Writes *one-sided or slanted statement* after *bias*.

This document (Figure 5.1) was written in England about 1820. Skim your copy a minute and then I'll show you how to evaluate it to see if it shows bias.

Projects a transparency of Figure 5.1.

(Silence as students read.)

Well, let me show you how to evaluate this to see if it reveals any bias. Watch and follow along. One useful way to detect bias in a written account is to use a procedure like I am going to use.

Affixes large poster (Figure 5.2) to corner of chalkboard, next to projection screen.

You can follow these steps to detect—to evaluate for—bias:

Points to steps as each is read aloud.

1. Define bias.
2. Identify or recall clues to bias.
3. Search piece by piece to find evidence of these clues.
4. Identify any pattern in the evidence we find.
5. Judge the match between the pattern (if we find one) and the definition of bias.

Now let me show you one way skillful thinkers do this so you can do it, too. First, I have to decide on and define my purpose. I am going to analyze and then evaluate this document to see if it has any bias. Why do I need to define bias? Because I need to know what to look for as I analyze this document.

Points to Step 1 on poster and to definition on chalkboard.

Defining what I am looking for—in this case, bias—helps me to recall or identify the clues to look for. If I know what I need to look for, my analysis will be easier than if I do not. You know, analyzing is like being a detective. A detective faced with a burglary has to look through all kinds of stuff to solve the crime, but he or she looks only for clues or evidence related to burglaries—not for anything related to kidnapping,

Writes the word clues on chalkboard.

murder, forgery, or other kinds of crimes.

Like a detective, I have to search through a lot of information here to find out if this author is guilty of committing the crime of giving us a biased report instead of a balanced or completely truthful one. Knowing that I am searching for a slanted or one-sided view means I need only hunt for clues to a slanted view. I can forget about looking for anything else—like spelling. Right? Okay!

Points to definition again.

Underlines *clues* on chalkboard.

Now, I have to come up with the clues to look for. What are some clues to bias? If I didn't know any, I guess I would have to ask someone or look them up somewhere. Do you know any clues to bias?

Points to Step 2 on poster.

Pauses and accepts any correct clues offered by volunteers.

I believe I learned some other clues once. I remember that some kinds of words are clues to bias: I call them *loaded words*—words that sound good or sound bad. Like *toil*. Someone could describe work as work or even labor and I wouldn't mind, but *toil*? I wouldn't like to do that! Toil gives work a bad image. It sounds hard! It has a negative tone to it. If I found lots of negative-sounding words like *toil*, I would suspect I had found a bias *against* something. If I found all good-sounding words, I might have found a bias *for* something! A bias can be slanted either for or against, positive or negative.

Writes *loaded words* under *clues* on chalkboard.

I remember another kind of clue to bias I could look for—exaggerations or over-generalizations—words or phrases such as *never* or *all the time* or *always*. It's rare when something *never* or *always* happens! I'll bet in English class, you call

Writes *exaggerations* under *loaded words* in *clue* column.

exaggerations like this *hyperbole*. Well, hyperbole is a clue to bias if we find a lot of it!

I could hunt for other clues if I could think of any, too, but I can't right now, so looking for these two can get me started.

So, now I need to read this account piece by piece—in a written document, this means line by line or phrase by-phrase—to see if I can find any of these clues—any loaded words or exaggerations. I could look for both at once but that might confuse me. So I will look only for loaded words on my first time through. Then I'll reread it to see if I can find any evidence of the other kind of clue: exaggerations.

Here I go, looking for loaded words. . . . Hmmm. . . . Ah, *miserable creatures*— there's some loaded words! What would be some less loaded, more neutral words? *Workers*, sure. *Employees*, yes, Good. Oh, I missed one—*lords of the loom*. That's loaded, too. It could have been *employer*, right? I'll circle these words to help me keep track of them. They're clues—maybe! I'm hunting for loaded words, remember. If I keep recalling the kind of clues that I am searching for, it will keep me focused on what I need to find. Here are some more: *poor creatures* and *doomed*! Doomed? Why not *destined* or *appointed*, maybe, but *doomed*? That sounds so negative! Aha! And here we have the word we talked about earlier: *toil*. *Work*, maybe, but *toil*, never! Sounds like our class motto!

What other loaded words are here?

Points to Step 3 on poster.

Points to *loaded words* under *clues* on chalkboard.

Runs pencil along first several lines on transparency while reading to self.

Accepts any correct student suggestions.

Circles words noted on transparency.

Points to *loaded words* under *clues* on chalkboard.

Runs pencil along lines of document on transparency, circling loaded words on the transparency as they are encountered.

(Continues in this manner to the end of the document, pointing out and circling each loaded word noted, accepting student contributions as any are offered, and then rereading to look for examples of exaggeration, accepting student-identified examples, if offered.)

Hey! Look at this: "Can any man with a heart . . . ..?" That's an odd question. It answers itself. It's called a rhetorical question. It's a no-win question. It tells me what the answer is supposed to be if I'm at all a man with a heart. Who wants to be—who is—without a heart? I just *can't* be against the answer it suggests. I have to curse this factory system, if I have a heart! Rhetorical questions tell you the authors' point of view. Here, it's negative—against factories.

On transparency, circles last sentence in first paragraph, beginning with Can. *Reads first part aloud.*

You know, sometimes as you analyze something, you discover things you hadn't thought of as clues to what you are looking for. Sometimes new clues just pop up as you are analyzing, like now. Rhetorical questions could be good clues to bias. Whenever you find them with other evidence of bias, you may really have bias! We've got another kind of clue to look for!

Writes rhetorical question under exaggeration in clues column on chalkboard.

Are there other rhetorical questions here? Hmmm. . . . I don't see any. So— let's stop here.

Runs pencil along lines of document on transparency.

When I have collected all the kinds of evidence I can find, I need to see if it makes a pattern. Do we have lots of evidence? Does the evidence we found point in the same direction? (Pause) A few bits of evidence—loaded words or exaggerations or rhetorical questions— by themselves may not indicate any-

Points to Step 4 on poster.

thing. I need to see if we have a lot and if all are on the same side. (Pause) I'm looking to see if they are all negative or all positive or mixed. Is there a pattern here? I believe so! All these loaded words, exaggerations, and the rhetorical question seem to fit together pretty well. They are very negative—very anti-factory owner. The evidence here seems very anti-factory. That's the pattern I see.

Points at circled words and examples of exaggerations on transparency.

Draws line connecting *loaded words* with *exaggerations* and *rhetorical question* on chalkboard.

So, is there evidence of bias here? I need to compare what my clues tell me to the definition of bias. This will help me judge or evaluate the evidence I have found. Let's see—a biased account is one-sided and slanted. Hmmm. I sure have lots of one-sidedness here! It looks to me as if this account shows bias. I'd say this account is slanted against factories and factory owners—it's sympathetic to the workers. I don't find much good here about working in factories. (Pauses)

Points to Step 5 on poster.

Points to definition on chalkboard.

I'm reviewing this judgment. Yes, I'm satisfied that there is strong evidence of bias here. I figured this out by analyzing this document for bias—by taking it apart, piece by piece, to find evidence of clues to bias. Then I evaluated it.

Points to Step 3 on poster.

Points to Step 2 and then to list under *clues* on chalkboard.

We should evaluate for bias whenever we are presented with an account about anything, whether it is written or spoken—like a newspaper article or a speech—or even visual—like a video documentary or show. What other times would it be useful to look for bias?

Accepts volunteered responses.

Now, let's review what I did to evaluate for bias. First, I . . .

Points to steps on poster and points to different students to read each aloud (or to paraphrase each).

Modeling as a Teaching Technique

Three features of modeling as an instructional technique stand out in this example. First, note the kinds of information we provide about the cognitive operation being modeled while simultaneously walking students, step by step, through the procedure. Although we focus on and organize the modeling around the procedure itself, we also present information about all three kinds of attributes of this operation.

Procedural knowledge—information about what to do and the sequence for doing it—constitutes the bulk of our explanation. For instance, in launching this lesson by stating five major steps in detecting bias we introduce students to a procedure for executing this skill. Thereafter, we state each step as we take it (e.g., "First, I have to decide on and define my purpose. I am going to analyze and then evaluate this document to see if it has any bias"). At the same time, we reinforce this statement by pointing to this step on the poster. Each time we present procedural information, we point it out on the poster or write it on the chalkboard. This stating and pointing out or writing of procedural knowledge continues to the conclusion of our modeling and constitutes the basic framework of our modeling.

We also provide *declarative* knowledge in the form of hints, procedural rules, or rules of thumb that facilitate the execution of the operation. In this example, the information about the clues to look for—the criteria that something must meet to be considered bias—exemplifies this kind of cognitive knowledge. Without knowing what (criteria, features, parts, components, etc.) to look for, students find it virtually impossible to carry out analytical and evaluative operations such as this one. Not all cognitive operations, however, require knowledge of criteria or clues.

In addition, other statements in the sample transcript provide *conditional* knowledge—information about when and under what circumstances the procedure should be employed and how it might work under different circumstances. For instance, consider the statement, "But before we believe everything [a document] says, we ought to see if it is an accurate, balanced account or not." This remark presents a condition under which this thinking operation should be performed. Becoming skilled at executing a cognitive operation requires knowledge of when and where to employ it and why the various steps that constitute the skill-using procedure are employed. To be most useful to students, any modeling of a cognitive operation must provide conditional as well as declarative and procedural information about the operation being demonstrated.

Second, note that in this example of modeling, the cognitive procedure modeled does not represent the only procedure by which experts carry out this operation. Nor does it present exactly all that skilled thinkers know about this operation or all they do when carrying it out. Individuals skilled in carrying out a cognitive operation know much more about that operation and how to execute it than novices need to know or do. For this reason, initial modeling of a new or especially difficult thinking operation does not need to—indeed, should not—include all the knowledge or procedural steps relevant to that operation. Such information would be neither meaningful to nor understood by anyone to whom the operation is strange and perceived as complex. It would, in effect, be overload! Moreover, to provide such information and to enact it would require too much time, resulting in loss of student attention and almost certain boredom. Instead, the initial modeling of a cognitive operation should focus only on a limited number of key steps in the procedure and provide only the knowledge essential for carrying out these steps. Subordinate, alternative, and optional steps or procedures and additional knowledge can be developed or provided later, as students become comfortable in carrying out the cognitive operation itself.

Finally, note that in this example, we use visual aids to support the modeling. Having a step-by-step description of the procedure being modeled available to the students throughout the lesson—in this case, a poster showing the steps—permits them to have an overview of what is about to occur before it starts. By providing an overview of the complete procedure before starting the demonstration, a teacher provides a procedural context that can serve as a learning map—something that field-dependent students seem to benefit from immensely. Providing such a visual also allows students to see where each step fits into the overall procedure and where it is leading as it is executed. Keeping such an aid visible at all times also allows students to concentrate on *how* the operation is being performed without having to try to recall each step from memory along the way. This visual aid thus serves as a temporary prop for student learning and minimizes the demands on students' memories at this crucial point in learning.

Using Modeling in the Classroom

When is it appropriate to model a thinking operation? The obvious answer is whenever we, as teachers, realize or believe our students do not know how to do it but are going to have to use it. The modeling can be preplanned and presented before student application of the operation, or it may be provided more spontaneously at any point where students, in attempting to execute the skill on their own, demonstrate their inabilities to do so. The former approach involves deliberate lesson planning and scheduling. The latter requires that we, as teachers, be prepared to stop a lesson in progress and, at a moment's notice, shift into modeling the required operation. This latter approach is not uncommon in many classrooms. Who among us has not, in the middle of some student task, noticed that students are having difficulties in carrying it out and then proceed to interrupt them with, "Stop. Everyone hold it! Listen up! You're having trouble with this! Let me show you an easier way to do it!" Such an approach requires that we be knowledgeable about and comfortable in using the operation to the degree we can provide what is becoming known as "just-in-time" teaching.

Some teachers, of course, often feel it advisable to model a cognitive skill *before* permitting students to try carrying out that operation. In some instances, this may be appropriate. However, this approach may actually undermine our efforts to help our students understand the operation being modeled, because it decontextualizes the skill. In such a situation, students lack an experiential referent for what it feels like or why it is even worth trying. As a result, the modeling "hits them cold" and they find it difficult to attend to it. When this occurs, modeling fails to serve its intended purpose.

Experience indicates that it is often more useful to model a new cognitive operation after, rather than before, students have had a try at doing it on their own as best they can. As frustrating as this may be for some students—and for those of us feeling the pressure to "cover" the course—such a trial effort allows students to apply what they already know about doing the operation, to get a feel for doing it even if imperfect, and to become aware of the particular problems they may be having in trying to execute it. It also gives students a general sense of what is involved in carrying—or trying to carry—it out. The result is greater student attention to the modeling of the skill that follows—modeling that presents the operation in an authentic context, meaningful to them. Scheduling modeling to follow—or even interrupt—initial student attempts to execute the operation on their own stimulates and focuses their attention and assists them in better understanding exactly what is being modeled.

Although modeling is a useful technique in and of itself, it cannot be employed in isolation of other techniques and be expected to be useful. Seeing an operation modeled is only one step in learning that operation. Internalizing the model must occur and this can be accomplished only by student efforts to apply the model—to attempt to replicate or approximate it—immediately following the demonstration.[4] In terms of the example presented earlier, for instance, the next thing to occur in this class would be for students to try to replicate the model as they carry out the same skill, (i.e., (evaluating to detect bias) on a similar account in the same content area with our assistance as necessary and with the list of procedural steps in full view.

Strengths and Limitations

How does modeling "teach" thinking? First, it presents students with an explicit procedure for executing a thinking operation. Second, it calls their attention to the key or significant mental moves in this procedure. Third, modeling provides reasons, or a rationale, for carrying out the key moves demonstrated. Finally, and most important, modeling gives students a visual and mental image of how the operation modeled ought to work in practice. This image serves as a pattern or blueprint students can attempt to duplicate or approximate as they try to carry it out when given the opportunity to do so. In effect, modeling creates a performance routine for learners to imitate or follow in carrying out the operation modeled.[5]

Any thinking operation or skill can be modeled. It need not be by a teacher—a student who has demonstrated some proficiency in the skill may also model it. In some cases, videotaped demonstrations may be available or written protocols or samples of the procedure may be used. But in whatever way the modeling is presented, it must include the two essential features of modeling—an *execution* of a procedure for carrying out the operation being demonstrated with an accompanying *explanation* of the key steps and rules (and criteria, if a critical thinking skill).

In spite of its value as an instructional technique, modeling does have disadvantages. It can go awry. Modeling complex thinking operations may take considerable time during which students are passive onlookers rather than active participants—something that often leads to student inattention and boredom, thus interfering with, rather than facilitating, learning. Moreover, if done by an individual who is not knowledgeable about the operation being modeled, the procedure presented may be so garbled, idiosyncratic, inaccurate, or misleading that it confuses rather than enlightens, frustrates rather than clarifies. If presented as the *only* way to carry out a cognitive procedure, modeling denies the fact that the same cognitive operation can be and often is carried out in a variety of different but quite effective ways by people of different levels of experience and different knowledge backgrounds. And when students are not allowed to apply what they have seen modeled *immediately* after the modeling has been completed, its effectiveness is considerably lessened.

Awareness of these pitfalls, however, allows us to minimize their ill effects and, in some cases, eliminate them altogether. To make students active participants in rather than passive observers of modeling, we can invite their participation in the demonstration itself. They can be encouraged or asked to volunteer what the next step is in the procedure being demonstrated, which they can do simply by reading or paraphrasing the appropriate step from the list of steps posted at the beginning of the demonstration. Students can also contribute examples of clues or evidence being sought when critical thinking operations are being modeled. Such opportunities to contribute to the modeling of an operation allow those students who may have some ideas of how to do it to voice their ideas. It involves them more actively in what is going on, thus ensuring their continuing attention. It also allows them to begin to take ownership of the procedure being modeled as they use the language that denotes the cognitive operation and knowledge of which it consists. Effective modeling need not be exclusively a monologue!

There are two important cautions to be observed in the use of modeling cognitive operations. First, in modeling a cognitive operation, *what* is modeled is as important as *how* that modeling is carried out. The cognitive procedure modeled must represent an efficient and effective—indeed, expert— way to carry out the operation, and the skill knowledge presented must be accurate and meaningful to the students. It is difficult, if not impossible, for anyone unfamiliar with or unskilled in how to carry out a thinking operation or procedure to model it intelligibly and accurately to those who know little or nothing about it. Because we, as teachers, often assume or are accorded the role of "expert thinkers," we must ensure our own expertise in and understanding of skilled, effective ways to carry out any thinking skill *before* trying to model it for our students. We do not serve students well by trying to articulate and model a cognitive operation in or with which we are inexpert or unfamiliar.

Second, modeling ought not to be prescriptive. A model of how to execute a particular cognitive operation should *not* be presented as the only way to carry it out. Rather, it should rather, clearly indicate that what is being modeled is *one effective way* to carry out the skill. It is important to acknowledge that different individuals may execute the task differently, but still skillfully. Students should be made to feel free to deviate from the modeled procedure if they have a more effective procedure or to modify it to accommodate their prior experience and knowledge.

Interestingly, students rarely imitate a model completely. Some, of course, do try to repeat the modeled procedure without deviation, because they simply have no idea of any other way of doing it. However, many students add their own steps, combine several, drop some, or otherwise modify the procedure modeled. These latter students tend to use the model as a springboard or reference point rather than as a blueprint to be slavishly followed.[6] Having seen a model alerts students to what the skill looks and feels like in action, and how it ought to work for them. However, they may attempt to replicate it, adapt it, or elaborate it when they initially try to carry out the skill.

Any of these behaviors may be a satisfactory follow-up as students begin to incorporate the cognitive operation into their own thinking. And this is exactly the intent of modeling!

COMPARING TO AN EXPERT

Comparing to an expert is related to modeling. In general, it engages students in analyzing and comparing a cognitive procedure used by someone skilled in that procedure to the way they carried out the identical cognitive operation. By repeated analysis and comparison of "expert" and self-generated procedures for executing the same thinking operation, students can gradually identify and develop more effective procedures for carrying out that operation and begin to generalize it to a variety of application contexts.[7]

The central feature of this cognitive teaching technique is a description of an expert executing the same thinking operation that students are trying to improve or learn. This description—usually written—presents a step-by-step procedure used by the expert. The following description exemplifies such an expert description. It was prepared by educators Arthur Whimbey and Jack Lochhead, leading proponents of this technique.[*] It explains how a skilled thinker went about solving this problem:

> If the circle below is taller than the square and the cross is shorter than the square, put a *K* in the circle. However, if this is not the case, put a *T* in the second tallest figure.

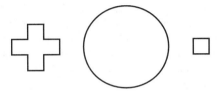

In reading, below, how the expert carried out this task, note that quotation marks indicate he was reading aloud from the problem statement. The absence of quotation marks indicates what (the expert) says he was doing or thinking:

> "If the circle below is taller than the square and the cross is shorter than the square, put a *K* in the circle."
>
> Let me start again.
>
> "If the circle below" . . . I'll put my finger on the circle . . . "is taller than the square" . . . Yes, the circle is taller than the square.
>
> "And the cross is shorter than the square" . . . I'll move my finger from the cross to the square and compare them . . . this part is false . . . the cross is not shorter than the square.
>
> "Put a *K* in the circle."

So I shouldn't put a *K* in the circle. Part of the statement is false. I would only write *K* if both the first part and the second part were true.

I should read the whole sentence again and see if my conclusion is correct.

"If the circle is taller than the square" . . . Yes . . . "and the cross is shorter than the square" . . . No . . . "Put a *K* in the circle" . . . I didn't. That's correct.

I'll continue to the next part of the problem.

"However, if this is not the case" . . . and it isn't the case . . . "put a *T* in the second tallest figure."

The second tallest figure is the cross, so I'll put a *T* in the cross.

In this example, an expert's thinking is presented as a transcript or protocol of someone who is good at solving problems like this one. It reports literally what this individual thinks and does while working through a thinking task as well as what the expert says when reading or rereading the problem statement. By studying this description, we can identify the mental steps in the procedure employed to carry out the cognitive operation being executed and the heuristics—rules of thumb—being applied by the expert. By comparing this expert's thinking procedure to how they carry out this same task, students can identify gaps or errors (if any exist) in the procedures they employed, and perhaps, identify—and even later adopt—what the expert did that might make their own thinking work better.

An Example of Comparing to an Expert

What exactly occurs when students compare their thinking to that of a skilled or "expert" thinker? We can answer this question in several ways. One way is simply to do it—that is, compare how we carry out a given thinking procedure to how an expert executes that same procedure.

To do this, (1) evaluate the statement on farming that appears on the next page to determine whether or not it is biased. When finished (2), reflect on what you did mentally to make this judgment and list in step-by-step fashion on a sheet of paper what you did—and why—to arrive at your judgment. Then (3) analyze the description in Figure 5.3 of how an expert evaluated this same statement for bias and compare the procedure and heuristics you believe you employed to the procedure and rules he employed. Finally, (4) when you have finished doing this, write out as a checklist on another sheet of paper the sequence of mental steps you would employ if you were to apply—in as efficiently a way as possible—this same skill (evaluating to detect bias) to another paragraph or extended statement such as a newspaper editorial or a political speech.

Figure 5.3 An Expert's Protocol for Thinking Aloud While Evaluating for Bias: Example A

A

Let me see, I have to see if this thing is biased—or at least if it shows bias. So . . . hmmm. What is bias exactly? (Looks up at overhead light and frowns.)

I know. Bias is a slanted point of view. It's one-sided. A biased story doesn't tell the whole story! (Smiles with sense of satisfaction.)

So, how do I know if something shows bias? (pause) What do I know indicates bias? (Stares at chalkboard.) Oh, I remember now. Loaded words in place of neutral-sounding words, *toil* instead of *work,* maybe, or *idol* instead of *statue.* Anyway, bad- or good-sounding words. (pause) And overstatements—exaggerations—extremes, like *never, always,* and so on. What else? (pause) Oh, these will do for starters.

So, I'll go on. Maybe I'll spot other things later. For now, I'll keep these things in mind as I read this. I'll read each sentence so I don't miss anything.

(Starts reading.) Puts check mark above *pleasant,* then above *terrible.* (pauses) Hmmm. Some loaded words here. I'll go on. I'm looking for loaded words like these and . . . (Continues reading.) Aha! (Puts check mark above *outrageously.*) I *do* have loaded words here—and not good ones, either. (Circles *terrible* and *outrageously.*)

Are there others? (Reads on, moving a pencil along each line as it is read.) *Thin* and *rocky*? These aren't loaded words but they tell what the soil is like. Not good. I'll put brackets around these so I can find them later. (Encloses each in brackets.) So (reads on) . . . the sons don't farm. Not good either . . . Aha! "Only a *crazy* person!" Now there's a loaded word if I ever saw one! (Circles *crazy.*)

(Continues reading, then stops.)

"Nobody wants to be a framer" "Nobody?" Well, that's an exaggeration, I think. (Underlines sentence beginning with *Nobody.*) Hmmm. This is an exaggeration, too (underlines final sentence). These two sentences are really exaggerations. There will always be farmers—there *have* to be! If no one buys this farm, these people will still be farmers!

So, I'm done reading. What do I have? (Draws line connecting the three circled words.) I have some bad-sounding words. They all make farming look bad. (pauses) I can connect these, too. (Draws line connecting underlined sentences.) These exaggerations don't make it sound very good either. And I still have that line about (rereads) "The soil is thin and rocky." That sure makes farming sound bad.

Bias is one-sided. Isn't there anything here to show how farming is good—pleasant? (Scans paragraph, moving pencil quickly over the lines.) Nope. I don't see anything else. My clues say farming is not so good.

So, I think I've got some bias here. Whoever wrote this is presenting only the bad parts of farming. It's one-sided. It's anti-farming! The bias here is against farming. (Writes *Bias—farming is bad* under paragraph.)

Another way to identify what is involved in comparing to an expert is to observe what occurs as students compare their thinking to that of an expert in a classroom setting. To do this, assume for a moment that we wish to use the technique of comparing to an expert in introducing middle school social studies students to the critical thinking skill of evaluating for bias. To the best of our knowledge, these students have never yet employed this skill in our class or in any class in our school. Fortunately, however, they are familiar with the technique of comparing their thinking to that of an expert, for we have used it before in our efforts to improve other skills.

We launch this activity by asking our students, working individually or in pairs, to evaluate a short statement we are about to use in our study to determine whether or not it reveals any bias. After defining or getting the students to define as accurately as possible what bias means, we then distribute copies of the following statement[8] and let them proceed with the designated task:

> *Farming used to be a pleasant way of life but now it's terrible. The price we get for what we grow is outrageously low. The soil is thin and rocky. Our sons took factory jobs because they refused to farm. We'd like to sell, but only a crazy person would buy a farm. Nobody wants to be farmer. Soon there will be no farms left.*

Upon completing their task or after devoting a reasonable amount of time to trying to do so, several volunteers report their results to the entire class. Then we ask the students to reflect on how they executed this task, listing as best they can the key steps they went through to complete it. A wide variety of lists are produced—some will be brief and vague, several somewhat more detailed, some will articulate several cognitive steps, but many will report primarily content considered rather than cognitive processes. Some degree of frustration may begin to surface at this point, but we tell them "not to worry" because we have something that will help them.

At this point, we introduce and distribute a description (Figure 5.3) of how someone skilled at detecting bias executed this same task using this same statement. We direct them to work with a partner to analyze what this "expert" did, step by step, to carry out this operation and then to compare that with what they did. As they proceed, we find some students numbering what they identify as steps in the expert's procedure, others underlining presumed steps and circling reasons the "expert" gave for taking these steps, and still others coding these elements of thinking in some fashion. To those having difficulty getting started, we provide a hint or two to get them going. After several minutes, we remind them they are also to compare what they did to determine if this statement is biased to how the expert did it and they turn to searching for procedural steps similar to and different from theirs. Discussion at this point may be quite lively and animated.

If our students seem anxious to share what they are finding, we invite volunteers to do so. Some may report how they initially executed the skill of evaluating for bias while others report how they believe the expert did it. Some may report what they and the expert did in common while others report what they perceive as differences between the procedures followed. Several may volunteer procedural moves they or the expert made that seemed especially useful. One or two may even indicate moves they made that did not prove helpful at all. By our questions and comments, we keep their focus on the thinking operation of evaluating for bias.

Finally, after several minutes of such dialogue, we direct the students to work as individuals or with their partners to produce a written step-by-step checklist and list of rules that they could give to students in one of our other classes (which is several days behind them in getting through our study) to help them carry out the thinking skill of evaluating for bias. Again, the students share, consider, compare, and revise their checklists. In our next class, we shall post these lists and provide time for the students to examine each. They will then again revise their own lists before they use the revised checklists to apply this thinking skill again and compare how they did it to how another expert executed it on the same data they will use.

Comparing to an Expert as a Teaching Technique

Descriptions of how an expert executes a cognitive operation can be used in a number of ways. The most commonly used approach consists of a three-step procedure in which students:

1. Articulate how they carried out or would carry out a cognitive skill or operation.
2. Analyze the procedure used by an expert in carrying out that same cognitive operation in the same content or situation.
3. Compare the two procedures to determine the similarities and differences between what the expert did and what they did in executing the operation.

Repeated use of this procedure, in different contexts, as Whimbey and Lochhead have demonstrated, helps students become more conscious of how they are thinking as well as more careful, precise, accurate, and deliberate in executing the cognitive skills they are learning.[9] One way to carry out this technique is as follows:

Step 1.   Students, individually or in pairs, verbalize a procedure by which they just carried out, are carrying out, or plan to carry out a specific cognitive task, skill, or operation. This can be done through metacognitive reflection or thinking aloud, as described in Chapter 4. An alternative is that several students work together to create a thinking plan for carrying out this task or skill in a given context. Regardless of which approach is used, students should produce a step-by-step written account of their procedure for carrying out the operation. In so doing, they need to be as clear as possible about the steps they want to or would go through, the sequence in which they did or would carry them out, and the reasons for carrying out each step as they did or would.

Step 2.   Students, again individually or in pairs, analyze a description of the procedure used by someone expert in carrying out this same cognitive operation to complete the same task as they did (or will). To do so, they take apart the expert's procedure to identify (1) each step in the procedure, (2) the reason(s) for carrying out each step as it was carried out, and (3) the ways by which the steps are linked together, their sequence and interrelationship.

Step 3.   Students then compare the procedure(s) they used to the procedure used by the expert. Their primary goal is to identify anything the expert did that they did not do, as well as to identify what they may have done that the expert did not do, and the reasons (if any are given) for why each of these moves were made as they were. Once these differences have been identified and evaluated for their efficiency and utility in carrying out the intended cognitive task, students can determine which of the identified steps seem to have been most appropriate and useful.

We can repeat this procedure as many times as we wish in order for students to begin to refine their understanding of the thinking operation being applied. However, the content or material used in at least the first several follow-up applications should be similar to those of the initial application. This way, the students can concentrate on their thinking without having to grapple with new kinds of content or material. We can intersperse the steps in the procedure with class discussion of what the students have just completed doing—as in the example of the class activity just presented—or we can simply move among them as they work in pairs through the entire procedure repeatedly without any class discussion at all. As the students articulate their thinking, analyze that of the expert, and compare both, they gradually come to identify some flaws in their thinking procedures. They will then adopt and integrate into their thinking whatever of the expert's procedure that, to them, make sense and give promise of helping to them carry out the skill more efficiently and effectively in the future.

Using Comparing to an Expert in the Classroom

Engaging students in comparing how they carry out a thinking operation with how an expert executes the identical operation entails at least two major tasks for us, as teachers. First, we need to find or create suitable descriptions of the skilled execution of any cognitive operation we wish our students to improve. Second, we need to employ this technique in a learning context that best enables students to reap the maximum learning benefit from its use.

Preparing Descriptions of Expert Thinking.   Securing or producing expert descriptions of how a particular cognitive operation is carried out is not easy. Few, if any, expert descriptions appropriate to any complex thinking operation are readily available (other than those devised by Whimbey and Lochhead for verbal reasoning, analogy analysis and analogy making, solving mathematical word problems, and analyzing trends and patterns). And virtually none is available using subject matter our students are most likely to be using in our classes.[10] However, with practice, skill, and the assistance of knowledgeable colleagues, we can produce our own.

Before suggesting how this can be done, however, the term *expert* needs clarification. There are experts and then there are experts. When we refer here to experts in the execution or demonstration of a thinking operation or procedure, we mean individuals *skilled* in carrying out or performing these procedures, not to researchers who study thinking or people who specialize in teaching it. *Experts*, as used here in modeling or comparing to an expert, means *individuals*—perhaps teachers, academicians, business people, crafts people, or other adults or even students—who are skilled at carrying out a particular thinking procedure. An expert is anyone whose execution of a cognitive procedure reveals an expertise in doing so that clearly demonstrates the key elements and rules that constitute an effective and efficient—mathematicians say "elegant"—procedure for doing it.

Probably the best way to develop an expert description of how a given thinking operation is performed is to sit with an "expert" (another teacher or a student who has earlier demonstrated expertise at executing the kind of thinking on which we wish to focus) and record in detail what that person does and says as he or she thinks aloud to carry out the skill. This is the way the earlier example was reportedly developed by Whimbey and Lochhead.[11] Another way, almost as effective, is to have students or colleagues who demonstrate some degree of expertise at carrying out this operation write out or tape record their metacognitive reflections on how they did it. The results would be something like the accounts presented below in Figure 5.5 and Figures 4.7 and 4.8 in Chapter 4.

Still another way to prepare an expert description is personally to execute a thinking operation, tape recording ourselves thinking aloud as we do it. Or we could later reconstruct the thinking that we did in carrying out the skill. We actually do something like this last technique when we model problem-solving procedures and demonstrate proofs. What we produce can be converted into written explanations relatively easily.

Yet another way to prepare such thinking descriptions is to imagine ourselves carrying out the skill to complete a specific task and recording the mental and related moves made during the imagined process. The first two methods are likely to produce rather accurate and useful descriptions. The others, however, without considerable editing and elaboration, often turn out to be less accurate or complete than needed. Frankly, this is because sometimes—unless we are experienced in this technique—we do not really know how to execute skillfully a given cognitive operation or use language that clearly communicates to our students what we believe we did.

A description of an "expert" executing a specific thinking operation need not be like that in Figure 5.3. An expert description may also be a reflective account of what the person recalls doing as he or she carried out a specific cognitive procedure. Or, it may be presented as a stream of consciousness record of an expert's thinking aloud as he or she carries out the skill. Or, it may be a third-person narrative describing how a skilled thinker was observed carrying out the skill. Or it may be a summary of steps to take presented as directions to follow with explanations as necessary. In all instances, the description conveys what occurred in the expert's mind and often what the expert may have done physically and verbally to carry out the cognitive operation being performed (such as rereading a problem statement or making a diagram or counting on his or her fingers or writing something down).

In addition to the expert thinking descriptions presented earlier in Figure 5.3, Figures 5.4 through 5.8 present examples of these other types of descriptions of how an expert executes a thinking operation. In each instance, the "expert" evaluated the above statement on farming to determine if it contained bias.

Expert description A (Figure 5.3) is generally similar to the Whimbey-Lochhead expert account provided earlier, in that it incorporates into the description thinking-related actions as well as the expert's thinking. Protocols like these can be produced by observing what experts did and recording their oral account of what they were thinking and doing while carrying out the operation. Producing protocols such as this has been a major technique used for years by cognitive and writing researchers to develop better insights into how people solve problems, make decisions, and compose. Use of protocols like this one makes readers feel as if they are actually observing and listening to the expert in action.

Figure 5.4 (Example B) presents an edited account of this same expert thinking aloud as he moved through the execution of this same thinking skill. It does not include all his actions, but instead incorporates some

Figure 5.4 Example B of An Expert's Protocol for Thinking Aloud While Evaluating for Bias

---

B

Let me see, I have to see if this thing is biased—or at least if it shows bias. So . . . hmmm. What is bias exactly?

I know. Bias is a one-sided point of view. A biased story doesn't tell the whole story!

So, how do I know if something shows bias? (pause) What do I know indicates bias? I have to have something to look for—some clues or indicators. Oh, I remember now. Loaded words in place of neutral words. *Toil* instead of *work,* maybe, or *idol* instead of *statue.* Anyway, bad- or good-sounding words may indicate a bias. Overstatements! Right! Exaggerations. Extremes, like *never* and *always.* They may indicate bias, too! What else? Oh, sure. Giving only one side of the story— that shows bias, too! What else? Oh, these will do for starters.

I can't remember anything else that might be a clue, so I'll go on. Maybe I'll spot other things later. For now, I'll keep these three things in mind as I read this. I need to go slowly and read each sentence or line so I don't miss anything. So—onward! (Reads) *Pleasant?* A loaded word. Sounds good. Oh, *terrible.* Another loaded word. Sounds bad. *Outrageous.* Two bads. I'll circle these two. They both make farming look bad.

Are there more words like these? No— just thin soil and rocky. These are facts, but not good-sounding ones. I'll put a box around these because there may be more later like these. Now, I'll go on. Here's another loaded word—*crazy.* I'll circle it. *Only* a crazy person? That sounds exaggerated. Wouldn't anyone else, not even someone who likes the outdoors? I'll underline this sentence—it overstates the case, I think. And *nobody?* Wow. That *is* an exaggeration for sure. Underline this one! Oh, underline this one too—*no farms* sure is an exaggeration. There'll always be some farms, I think.

I'm done. So what do I have—some loaded words that seem negative about farming—some facts that say it's not very good—some sentences that really exaggerate the bad and sound negative, only a *crazy.* . . . *nobody* . . . *no farms.* . . . These all seem to paint a bad picture of farming. And there's nothing good said about it.

It looks to me that this is rather one-sided. It's all bad sounding, too. Sure looks like bias here. I think this is against farming. That's the bias!

---

actions into the thinking described as he decides to carry them out. It also makes explicit additional thinking in which the expert engaged. Accounts like this can be produced by having the expert read and reflect on what he or she was thinking at those points in the original where that thinking was not verbalized.

Example C in Figure 5.5 represents a reflective account of how the expert engaged in this same task, produced as if written *after* the task had

Figure 5.5 Example C of An Expert's Protocol for Evaluating for Bias: A Reflective Account

---

C

Let me see, I had to see if this thing is biased—or at least if it shows signs of bias. So . . . hmmm. I tried to remember what bias is, exactly.

Then I thought, well bias is a slanted point of view. It's one-sided. A biased story doesn't tell the whole story!

So, how could I tell if something shows bias? Well, I thought, what do I know indicates bias? I have to have something to look for—some clues or something. Then, I remembered: loaded words in place of neutral sounding words. Like *toil* instead of *work* or *idol* instead of *statue.* Anyway, bad- or good-sounding words may indicate a bias. I thought of overstatements! Exaggerations. Extremes, like *never, always,* and so on. They may indicate bias, too. Then I remembered that giving only one side of the story shows bias, too!

I couldn't remember anything else that might be a clue. So, I went on. I figured maybe I'd spot other things later. I decided for now I would just keep these three things in mind as I read.

I needed to go slowly and read each sentence or line so I wouldn't miss anything. So I did. I found *pleasant* and thought it seemed to be a loaded word. Sounded good to me. Then I came onto *terrible,* another loaded word. Sounded bad to me. Then *outrageous.* Two bads, I thought. I circled these two—*terrible* and *outrageous*—because they both made farming look not so good.

Then I asked myself: Are there more words like these? I saw "thin soil and rocky." these are facts, but not good-sounding ones. I put brackets around these because I figured there may be more facts later, like these. Then I went on. I found another loaded word—*crazy.* I circled it. Then "only a *crazy* person." That sounded exaggerated. I thought, wouldn't anyone else, not even someone who likes the outdoors? I underlined that sentence—because it really overstates things. Then *nobody* popped up. I felt that this word definitely was an exaggeration for sure. So I underlined it too. I underlined this one, too—*no farms*—because it sure is an exaggeration. There'll always be some farms for sure, I think.

Then I stopped. What I had was some loaded words that seemed negative about farming, some facts that said it's not very good, and some sentences that really exaggerated and sounded negative: only a *crazy* . . . *nobody* . . . *no farms.* They all seemed to paint a bad picture of farming. And there's nothing good said about it.

So, it looked to me like this is rather one-sided and bad sounding, too. The whole thing sure looked like bias to me. So I thought, this is against farming. That's the bias!

---

been completed. This is an example of metacognitive reflection, an attempt by the expert to reconstruct the mental actions just taken while carrying out the skill-using task. Note that in this case, the expert explains the reasons

Figure 5.6 An Observer's Account of an Expert Thinking Aloud While Evaluating for Bias: Example D

D

First, she recalls what bias is. *Bias,* she remembers, is a one-sided or slanted presentation.

Next, she recalls some common clues to bias. These clues may include, she remembers, repeated use of:

- Loaded or emotionally charged words, such as *toil* instead of *work,* for example
- Exaggerations, especially *always* or *never*
- Information limited to one side of the issue

She writes in the margin the words *loaded, exagg* (for exaggeration) and *one-sided* and leaves a little space under each to write any examples of these clues she might find as she reads the information to be analyzed.

Then she examines the information presented piece by piece or, in this case, line by line and sentence by sentence, to see if she can find any of these or even other clues to bias.

As she reads the first sentence, she notices a word that seems strong and positive—*pleasant*—and then a negative-sounding word, *terrible.* In the next sentence, she sees that prices were *outrageously* low, another negative, or bad, word. Two bad-sounding words, she notes. So she writes them under *loaded* in the margin and puts a *B* by each—for "bad."

She continues on to the next sentences and sees something about farm conditions—thin and rocky soil. She sees nothing else about farm conditions mentioned and asks herself, "Is there nothing good or favorable about it?" Nothing here, it seems to her—and she writes *thin* and *rocky soil* in the margin under *one-sided.*

Continuing to the next sentences, she reads along and then picks up on, "Only a crazy person would buy this farm." A bad-sounding word, *crazy,* she decides, a negatively loaded word like the words *outrageously* and *terrible* she came across earlier. She adds *crazy* to the words under *loaded* and puts a *B* by it.

Seeing *only* alerts her to what looks like an exaggeration. No one else, maybe another farmer, she wonders? She concludes that *only* seems a bit too overstated to be accurate—but she doesn't write it in the clue list in the margin because she isn't sure it's really an exaggeration!

And then in the next line she sees, "*Nobody* wants to be a framer." This *is* an exaggeration, she decides, and writes *nobody* under *exagg.* in the margin. Then she wonders if *only* in the preceding sentences really isn't an exaggeration. She rereads that sentence and decides it is. So she writes *only* under *nobody* under *exagg.* in the margin.

Figure 5.6 *Continued*

In reading the final sentence, she sees *"no farms left"* and asks herself, "No farms—none at all?" That she decides it is really an exaggeration. There will always have to be some farmers somewhere, she believes. So she writes *no farms* under the list of words under *exagg.* in the margin.

Now she stops and looks at her list of clues in the margin. She looks for a pattern in the clues. Do they all point in the same direction? she asks herself. She looks at each set of clues in turn to see if they do. There are several negative words, some bad aspects of farms, and some exaggerations that make farming sound bad. Nothing is written about any good features of farming—nothing to show its pleasant side like it once seems to have been. So, she concludes, this statement is really very one-sided.

Finally, she reports her findings by saying, "This paragraph is biased against farming, and I've got evidence to prove it!"

---

for making certain mental moves. Note also how the expert recounts using a pencil as a prop to aid in thinking.

Figure 5.6 (Example D) presents an instance of how the expert executed the skill of evaluating to detect bias written as a third-person narrative. Notice that it presents a step-by-step explanation of what the expert thought, wrote, and read as he executed the skill using the given data. Had it been written by the expert in the first person, as a reflective account, this description could have been presented as a product of metacognitive reflection on the part of the expert himself (similar to the form of the skill-using description presented in Figure 4.3).

In Example E, Figure 5.7, the expert's execution of the task has been reduced to a set of directions that can be followed by anyone seeking to execute this same operation. Like the preceding examples, it includes the cognitive steps in an expert's procedure as well as examples of how these steps work when one is carrying out the skill. It also provides explanations of the heuristics the expert followed to guide his execution of the procedure. This format resembles, in effect, an elaborate checklist of steps in a skilled procedure for carrying out a cognitive operation. As such, for some students, this type of expert description is the easiest—though least informative and perhaps least interesting—"expert" description to employ.

As shown in Figure 5.8, such a list of expert step-by-step directions can be reduced in complexity by eliminating the explanations for each of the steps listed. While such a procedural checklist is easier to follow than the more elaborated version shown in Figure 5.7, it does not communicate the conditional or declarative knowledge presented in the latter format and necessary for understanding what is behind each step in the process. Such a

Figure 5.7 An Expert Procedure for Evaluating for Bias: Example E

E

Step 1   Recall the definition of bias.

Bias is a slanted, one-sided view or presentation.

Step 2   Recall some clues to bias. These include but are not limited to:

- Loaded or emotionally charged words, words with great feeling such as *toil* instead of *work*
- exaggerations or overgeneralizations (hyperbole)
- one-sided presentations

Step 3   Examine the information piece by piece—in this case, line by line or sentence by sentence—to find evidence of these clues, remembering the clues to look for as you read.

In the first sentence, there are two loaded words—*pleasant* and *terrible*. In the next, there is another, *outrageous*. Two of these three seem negative. They put farming in a bad light. Circle these two so you can find them later.

The third sentence gives facts—thin and rocky soil. Not loaded but still negative.

The next two sentences give more facts—the sons dislike farming and don't do it. All these facts paint a bad picture of farming. You can put a box around these facts and around "thin and rocky soil" so you can find them later if you need them. The next sentence has another loaded word—*crazy*. Only crazy people would want to farm? Not a very positive way to view farming.

The next two sentences sort of exaggerate things. *Nobody* wants to farm. Not anyone? Ever? and "soon there will be *no* farms left?" Not any—anywhere? That's probably pretty impossible. There'll be some somewhere! You can underline these sentences to indicate they are exaggerations.

Step 4   Now, review the evidence you have marked, looking for a repetition or pattern in what it says.

There are negative-sounding words, facts, and exaggerations that make farming look bad. What does all this add up to? The evidence is all one-sided, a very negative view of farming. All the clues add up to be anti-farming.

Step 5   State what you find.

This written account shows bias. The bias is against farming.

Figure 5.8 Directions for Evaluating for Bias: Example F

F

Step 1   Recall the definition of bias.

Step 2   Recall some criteria or clues to bias.

Step 3   Examine the information piece by piece—in this case, line by line or sentence by sentence—to find evidence of these clues.

Step 4   Now, review the evidence you have marked, looking for a repetition or pattern in what it says.

Step 5   Judge how closely the evidence and pattern found, if any, match the definition/criteria of bias.

---

bare-bones checklist is thus not useful at the early stages of learning a new cognitive skill. However, it does prove helpful when used to scaffold student practice of the skill when it is being used *after* an initial, more explicit introduction to it (see Chapter 6 for examples).

Other formats for presenting expert skill-using procedures may also prove effective with this teaching technique.[12] It should be noted, however, that those like examples A, B, C, and D—which tend to be rather extended, wordy descriptions—require students to infer or discover the exact steps and heuristics as well as the declarative knowledge (in the examples here, the indicators of bias) that constitute the skill being executed. In example E, on the other hand, because of its brevity and straightforwardness, the procedural steps and declarative knowledge are made quite clear. Furthermore, although descriptions A, B, C, and D present how an expert carried or is carrying out the cognitive skill, they do not communicate directly to a reader or give assurance that what is done is what *should* be done or can best be done to carry out the demonstrated operation. Readers have to remain aware that the speaker or doer is, in fact, skilled at executing this procedure, and so the procedure described is one they can imitate if they want expert results, too. By labeling the major procedural moves *steps*, however, examples E and F signal communicates expert authority and correctness. In effect, such a description says, "This is an expert (effective) way to do this, so if you do it this way, you will be successful." Many students prefer format D, even though formats A, B, and C are more complete, more personalized, and engage students more actively in an analysis that helps them better understand and internalize the procedure presented.

Indeed, different kinds of expert thinking descriptions may be appropriate for different kinds of students. Those with reading difficulties may require heavily edited or revised and brief transcripts, rather than lengthier transcripts such as Examples A through D. Students who have some experience in executing a skill may benefit most from descriptions like Example E that are less detailed than those provided to students just beginning to deal with a new thinking operation. In fact, it may be advisable to prepare an expert's description in several different forms to accommodate such student differences.

It may also be highly desirable, if time permits, to prepare and provide descriptions of how several different "experts" execute the same thinking operation on the same content material. Use of all of these by students would go a long way toward helping them to understand the variety of ways skilled thinkers execute the same thinking operation and thus keep us and our students from converging on one procedure and one procedure only for executing a given kind of thinking.

In sum, regardless of the type of expert description devised it is important that the following criteria are met:

1. The individual generating what is to serve as an expert thinking description is, indeed, skilled in executing the cognitive procedure that the description purports to describe.
2. The procedure is, indeed, the cognitive operation that it purports to be.
3. The procedure described is clear, complete, and not idiosyncratic or vague or disorganized.
4. The procedure is applied to the same problem, data, or content the students will or did use.

Producing and using descriptions of cognitive procedures that meet these criteria is essential to any effort to use this technique to improving student thinking.

Making the Technique Work.   Thankfully, employing this technique in our classrooms is much easier than producing it. To maximize its effectiveness, this technique of comparing to an expert should be used in conjunction with two other techniques, both related to metacognition. Prior to referring to an expert's description of a given cognitive procedure, the students should attempt to carry it out themselves, as best they can, and record how they did it. They can do this by using either of the techniques described in the preceding chapter—metacognitive reflection or thinking aloud. In order to make a meaningful comparison, students need something to which to compare the expert's procedure—their own procedure, as incomplete, flawed, or skilled as it may be. Having a rather detailed, step-by-step record of how they carried out the given skill gives the students a basis for making useful comparisons. As an alternative, students, either individually or with a partner, may write out a procedure they would use if given a task to perform using the cognitive operation in question.

Once students have completed their analysis of the expert's procedure and compared it to theirs, they then should write a list or draw a flowchart of the step-by-step procedure they would use the *next* time they execute the cognitive operation on which they are focusing. This plan may be a revised description of the procedure they initially employed, a replica of the procedure used by the expert, or some combination of the two. If working alone, students may then also benefit from sharing their planned procedures with a partner or in a group. If working with a partner, this planning can be jointly done and represent the best thinking of both members of a pair.

Ideally, the final result of any comparing to an expert is a planned procedure for engaging in a thinking operation. Such a procedure should be built on how each student has carried out the thinking operation on his or her own as well as incorporating or adapting how an expert carried it out in the same context. In the process by which students have constructed this planned thinking procedure, they will have become aware of, talked about, or reflected on various steps in the procedures they have examined, and begun consciously to integrate and internalize them.

In sum, the most productive way to employ comparing to an expert is for students to (1) try doing a skill; then (2) engage in the three-step procedure of (a) articulating how they did it, (b) analyzing how an expert did it, and (c) comparing how they did it to how the expert did it; and then (3) provide a step-by-step plan for employing this skill again. Once a new plan exists, students should carry it out using new content, and repeat the entire process several more times until they no longer need expert models to guide them in executing the skill.

Strengths and Limitations

Comparing to an expert has proven useful in helping students improve their abilities in mathematical computation, in verbal and mathematical reasoning, in solving mathematical word problems, in pattern and trend analysis, and in other tasks that are rather limited in the amount of written data provided.[13] Where extensive verbal data are involved, however, the expert descriptions often become cumbersome in length and unduly complex in content, and thus extremely difficult to create or for students to attend to and use effectively.

Yet, comparing to an expert has proven to be a very useful technique for improving student thinking. Because it involves students in reflecting on their own thinking as they engage in articulating and then comparing their thinking to that of an expert, it offers some of the same benefits as does the technique of metacognitive reflection. Comparing to an expert starts with where the students are and helps them become conscious of the explicit cognitive steps they execute in carrying out a given cognitive skill. And, like modeling, use of an expert's description familiarizes students with an effective, efficient, and modeled procedure for carrying out the same skill. Unlike the technique of metacognitive reflection, however, this compare-to-an-expert technique provides students with an authoritative alternative model for how to do it. And unlike modeling, where students are encouraged to replicate the modeled skill-using procedure in their follow-up use of the thinking skill, comparing to an expert gives students options. They may ignore, adapt, or replicate the modeled expert procedure provided, much as they do in carrying out a thinking skill again after reflecting on how they did it the first time. Throughout the use of this technique, students engage in active intellectual involvement as they employ, articulate, analyze, and plan their thinking. Done well, comparing to an expert proves to be a powerful technique for helping students to make visible and explicit their own thinking.

The fact that this teaching technique has major limitations must be obvious. Like modeling, it may give the erroneous impression that the procedure modeled is the only or the "correct" way in which to execute a particular skill, when, in fact, it is only one way to carry it out. We, as teachers, must be especially careful to make clear to students that while the procedures employed by "experts" are very effective in carrying out a thinking operation, different experts may do it differently. There are a variety of ways to execute a thinking task, including those employed by students skilled in doing so.

The compare to-an-expert technique relies heavily on students' reading abilities. This is a problem for many because the students for whom this approach may be most beneficial are often poor readers or do not attend to detail when they read. Moreover, this technique (except when using expert descriptions like examples D, E, and F) requires students to infer or ferret out from the expert description the key steps in the skill procedure and reasons why they are useful. Unfortunately, this is something that requires effort, practice, and knowledge that some students do not have or wish to use in many classrooms.

Furthermore, finding or creating authentic expert thinking descriptions is extremely difficult. For best results, we must locate a credible expert who can provide or generate a clear description of a cognitive procedure we wish to help students improve. Generally, we should be cautious about using our own unexamined, self-generated procedures because they may not turn out to be as skillful, accurate, or clear as they need to be to facilitate student learning. A second opinion is always advisable in creating one's own expert skill procedure descriptions—so, too, is a liberal application of self-criticism in judging the accuracy of the final product and its degree of congruency to how other "experts" carry out the skill in question. Finally, in editing or altering expert descriptions into different formats, we must know enough about the skill procedure being described to identify and clearly present its essential procedural and other components.

MAKING THINKING VISIBLE AND EXPLICIT: A SUMMARY

The four cognitive teaching techniques described in Chapters 4 and 5—metacognitive reflection, thinking aloud, modeling, and comparing to an expert—perform two major functions that benefit students immensely. They raise student thinking to a level of consciousness that makes it amenable not only to self-correction and modification but also to deliberate and purposeful application in the future. They also provide models of how the operation should work when executed with skill and expertise. These models can then serve as mental maps (routines or programs) to follow when students next attempt to carry out that operation on their own.[14]

Making thinking visible and explicit also benefits students by increasing their awareness of alternative procedures for carrying out any particular thinking skill—an awareness that most students lack.[15] Gifted students welcome alternative procedures for carrying out these skills because knowledge of such procedures increases their thinking repertoire. These students are quick to personalize or elaborate these procedures as they incorporate aspects of them into their own ways of carrying out a thinking operation.[16] Average students often recognize some of the procedures as more effective than theirs and adopt, adapt, or combine aspects of one or more of them to generate a new systematic procedure of their own. Students who are at risk, or those completely unfamiliar with any procedure for carrying out an unfamiliar thinking operation, welcome the articulation of specific thinking procedures that will enable them to complete thinking tasks they find otherwise extremely difficult or impossible to complete on their own.[17]

We, as teachers, also benefit from making thinking visible and explicit. By articulating how we think and by coming to understand the thinking procedures of our students, we can sharpen our own thinking. Making the thinking that occurs in our classrooms visible and explicit also improves the quality of our teaching. It sensitizes us to the differences in how individuals think, provides numerous opportunities for diagnosing student thinking and learning, and allows us to provide more appropriate remediation of flawed thinking or inadequate learning.

Most importantly, making student thinking, as well as that of experts, visible and explicit provides the foundation for improving the quality of that thinking. For once specific thinking procedures have been articulated, we can help students identify the differences in the thinking procedures both they and experts employ to carry out the same thinking operation. This, then, allows our students to intentionally modify any of their flawed or inefficient thinking procedures by adapting or adopting other more obviously skillful and effective ones. The chapters in Part III explain techniques that can be employed to accomplish this goal.

ENDNOTES

1. Jere Brophy, "Probing the Subtleties of Subject-Matter Teaching," *Educational Leadership 49* 7 (April 1992): 5; Mary Bryson and Marlene Scardamalia, "Teaching Writing to Students at Risk for Academic Failure," in Barbara Means, Carol Chelemer, and Michael S. Knapp, (Eds.), *Teaching Advanced Skills to At-Risk Students* (San Francisco: Jossey-Bass, 1991), pp. 141–167; Means, Chelemer, and Knapp, "Introduction," *Teaching Advanced Skills,* p. 14; Michael I. Posner and Steven W. Keele, "Skill Learning," in Robert M. W. Travers (Ed.), *Second Handbook of Research on Teaching* (Chicago: Rand McNally College Publishing, 1973), pp. 805–831; Michael Pressley and Karen R. Harris, "What We Really Know about Strategy Instruction," *Educational Leadership 48* 1 (September 1990): 32–33; Barak V. Rosenshine and Carla Meister, "The Use of Scaffolds for Teaching Higher Level Cognitive Strategies," *Educational Leadership 49* 7 (April 1992): 27–28.

2. Bonnie B. Armbruster, Richard C. Anderson, and V. Cindy Mall, "Preparing Teachers of Literacy," *Educational Leadership 49* 3 (November 1991): 21–24; Allan Collins, Jan Hawkins, and Sharon M. Carver, "A Cognitive Apprenticeship for Disadvantaged Students," in Means, Chelemer, and Knapp, *Teaching Advanced Skills,* p. 209; Raymond Nickerson, "On Improving Thinking through Instruction," in Ernest Z. Rothkopf (Ed.), *Review of Research in Education,* Volume 15 (Washington, DC: American Educational Research Association, 1988–89), pp. 18–26.

3. Adapted from William Cobbett, "Such Slavery, Such Cruelty," *Political Register 52* (November 20, 1824).

4. Nickerson, "On Improving Thinking," pp. 18–26; David Perkins, "Myth and Method in Teaching Thinking," *Teaching Thinking and Problem Solving 9* 2 (March/April 1987): 1–2, 8–9

5. Posner and Keele, "Skill Learning," pp. 805–831; Rosenshine and Meister, "The Use of Scaffolds," pp. 26–28.

6. Pressley and Harris, "What We Really Know," pp. 31–33; Thomas E. Scruggs and Frederick J. Brigham, "The Challenge of Metacognitive Instruction," *Remedial and Special Education 11* 6 (November/December 1990): 16–18.

7. Jack Lochhead, "Teaching Analytic Reasoning Skills through Pair Problem Solving," in Judith W. Segal, Susan F. Chipman, and Robert Glaser (Eds.), *Thinking and Learning Skills: Volume I—Relating Instruction to Research* (Hillsdale, NJ: Lawrence Erlbaum, 1985), pp. 109–131; Arthur Whimbey and Jack Lochhead, *Problem Solving and Comprehension* 3rd ed. (Hillsdale, NJ: Lawrence Erlbaum, 1982), pp. 11–29 (5th edition: 1991).

8. Adapted from Barry K. Beyer, Jean Craven, Mary McFarland, and Walter Parker, *World Regions* (New York: Macmillan/McGraw-Hill School Publishing, 1993), p. 242.

9. Whimbey and Lochhead, *Problem Solving and Comprehension*, pp. 18, 20, 21, 23, 26–27.

10. *Ibid.*

11. *Ibid.*

12. *Ibid.*

13. *Ibid.*; Raymond S. Nickerson, David N. Perkins, and Edward Smith, *The Teaching of Thinking* (Hillsdale, NJ: Lawrence Erlbaum, 1985), pp. 206–209; Grant Wiggins, "Creating a Thought-Provoking Curriculum," *American Educator 11* 4 (Winter 1987): 14.

14. Pressley and Harris, "What We Really Know," pp. 31–34.

15. *Ibid.*

16. Thomas E. Scruggs and Frederick J. Brigham, "The Challenges of Metacognitive Instruction," *Remedial and Special Education 11* 6 (November/December 1990): 16–18.

17. Robert Mulcahy and Associates, "Cognitive Education Project," *Teaching Thinking and Problem Solving 15* 6 (1993): 1–9.

PART III

GUIDING AND SUPPORTING STUDENT THINKING

If research and experience indicate anything, it is that making students repeatedly engage in unfamiliar—especially complex, unfamiliar—cognitive tasks without any instructive assistance at all does *not* lead to improved thinking. If anything, in fact, it often leads to a disinclination to engage in such thinking "ever again!" On the other hand, research and experience also indicate that the quality of student thinking does improve when students are consciously aware of what it is they are trying to improve about their thinking and when they receive continuing assistance and support in attempting to make specific improvements. Making thinking visible and explicit is a first step in bringing about this improvement. Supporting and guiding frequent practice and refinement of the cognitive operations being improved is the next. Suggestions for providing this guidance and support constitute the focus of Part III.

The significant words here are *guidance* and *support*. These words are not intended to mean simply providing encouragement or "warm fuzzies" or "smiling faces" or praise. As used here, they are intended to mean the kinds of instructive assistance that buttress, prompt, steer, and frame student efforts to carry out a cognitive operation—especially one they may be quite unsure of or find difficult to execute. Such guidance and support actively assist students in moving through a sequence or combination of the key steps and/or rules that constitute a thinking operation. Many of us, of course, already provide some support and guidance for student thinking by providing hints, suggestions, reminders, obstacle alerts, trouble shooting, feedback and even actual assistance. As valuable as these supports are, however, they are not sufficient, in themselves, to provide the kind of cognitive support and guidance needed by most students tackling a new or complex thinking operation. Improving student thinking requires other kinds of guidance and support, as well.

One kind of guidance and support that is especially helpful to students trying to improve their skill at carrying out a new cognitive operation is that which provides direction, structure, and feedback in how to carry out that operation. Because they are rather unsure of *how* to execute it, novices need prompts that make them aware of *what* to do as well as *when* and *how* to do it. They need to be alerted to one or more productive sequences for carrying out a thinking procedure and guided through such sequence(s). They also need feedback on how well they are doing as they proceed. We can provide this kind of support on a one-to-one basis. But it can also be provided through instructional materials, learning aids, and verbal or visual cues that can be presented to all students in a class simultaneously and from which each can select the particular support needed. Guiding and supporting student thinking involves using a range of devices and techniques that actually *guide* as well as *prompt* students through the execution of a new thinking skill as they practice doing it.

As teachers, we can provide two kinds of helpful guidance and support to students as they practice executing new thinking operations. We can scaffold student practice and we can cue it. *Scaffolds* are somewhat explicit, skeletal frameworks—like checklists—that make a skill-using procedure explicit and to which students can continuously refer as they engage in carrying out the procedure. *Cues* are symbols, words, or other devices—such as a mnemonic or the name of the cognitive operation, for instance—that trigger recall and help organize the subsequent use of already familiar thinking procedures. Students need *both* kinds of guidance and support—scaffolding in their early efforts at applying a newly encountered skill when they are still unsure of how to carry it out, and cueing later, when they have internalized much of this knowledge and may need only to jump-start their memories to get a thinking procedure underway.

As Beau Fly Jones and her colleagues have pointed out, cueing and scaffolding are based on research which demonstrates that (1) use of a name or attribute enhances recall of whatever is stored in memory under that name or attribute and (2) information that is organized, or structured, is easier to learn and apply as well as to recall. Hearing and seeing the name of a thinking skill required to complete a task each time that skill is employed allows students to label what they store in memory about or associate with that skill. When that name or label is later used, it then triggers what is stored in memory under that label. The label thus serves as a cue to help students retrieve that information as well as organize it for storage in memory.[1]

When information about a skill—the procedural, declarative and conditional knowledge associated with it—is organized or structured when originally stored under a particular label or symbol, then use of that label not only triggers that information but helps to produce it in its structured form. So, when students respond to appropriate prompts—whether scaffolds or cues—they can recall relevant skill-using information in a fashion that is already structured. This makes executing the operation so much more effective. Scaffolding and cueing serve these two functions—they aid retrieval of skills from memory directly (as in the case of scaffolds) or indirectly (as in the case of cues) and structure their ensuing execution.

Like metacognitive reflection, modeling, and similar techniques, scaffolds and cues are flexible, temporary teaching and learning aids. They can change in form as well as structure as students become more experienced in carrying out a specific cognitive skill-using task, so as to reflect changes in the students' developing expertise in executing that skill. They also eventually put themselves out of business, so to speak, because their use is usually gradually reduced in frequency as students become increasingly proficient in executing a skill being learned. A very explicit scaffold like a checklist, for example, may be replaced by a less explicit one such as graphic organizer, which, in turn, can be replaced by any of a number of cueing devices. Eventually, no cues or scaffolding at all are required for a newly learned cognitive operation to be skillfully performed.

The two chapters that follow describe specific ways we can scaffold and cue application of any cognitive skill by students at any grade or ability level and in any subject. Each technique is explained, demonstrated or exemplified, and analyzed for its limitations as well as its advantages. By using these techniques and devices, we can provide the kinds of guidance and support that students find most helpful in improving their thinking.

ENDNOTE

1. Beau Fly Jones, Minda Rae Amiran, and Michael Katins, "Teaching Cognitive Strategies and Text Structures Within Language Arts Programs," in Judith W. Segal, Susan F. Chipman, and Robert Glaser (Eds.), *Thinking and Learning Skills: Volume I— Relating Instruction to Research* (Hillsdale, NJ: Lawrence Erlbaum, 1985), pp. 259–270.

6

Scaffolding Student Thinking

Scaffolding thinking consists of supporting student application of a cognitive operation by structuring the execution of that operation with verbal and/or visual prompts. Like a scaffold that holds up and gives form to a building under construction or a renovation, a thinking scaffold is a temporary, adjustable, skeletal structure that gives shape to a cognitive procedure in the process of its execution. It is a device or technique that frames a procedure in such a way that when it—the scaffold—is removed (as it eventually is), the procedure when executed retains the structure shaped by the scaffold. Students just beginning to apply a newly encountered or complex cognitive operation benefit immensely from having their initial attempts to practice that procedure scaffolded until they have internalized the procedure and can execute it on their own without external support.

Instructional techniques or devices that prove most useful as scaffolds for thinking possess two major characteristics. First, they frame or sequence the major steps in a procedure for carrying out the cognitive operation or skill they represent. A scaffold for problem solving, in effect, moves students through the steps in solving a problem. A scaffold for detecting bias moves students, step by step, through a cognitive procedure for carrying out this operation. Second, these devices are used by students *while they are engaged* in executing the cognitive operation being scaffolded. Students must be able to consult and follow the scaffold device as they carry out the skill. Devices or techniques scaffold thinking only if they structure it and are used by students while thinking.

There are at least three teaching techniques or devices that provide the kind of specific, explicit, formative structural scaffolding appropriate for supporting student efforts to apply cognitive operations in the early stages of practice or development.[1] These are procedural checklists, process-structured questions, and graphic organizers. Each of these techniques provides a framework of verbal and/or visual prompts that guides students through the execution of any cognitive operation. By using any of these techniques, we can scaffold initial student efforts to improve their execution of specific cognitive operations while students actually apply these operations and without our having to intervene directly in their learning. Thus, when using scaffolds, we not only provide instructive guidance to all students but we also are freed to provide personalized, individual assistance to those students who may require additional assistance.

PROCEDURAL CHECKLISTS

Procedural checklists provide probably the most explicit and visible scaffolds for executing any cognitive operation. As customarily designed, these checklists present in written, step-by-step fashion, or occasionally even as flowcharts, the mental moves that constitute an effective procedure for carrying out a given thinking operation. Figure 6.1 presents a procedural checklist for the cognitive operation of evaluating to detect bias. This checklist illustrates the features of an effective cognitive procedural checklist: It presents the key steps in the procedure to be executed, arranged in a sequence, briefly stated, in language meaningful to the intended users, and with a space to check off each step as it is completed.[2]

Figure 6.1 A Procedural Checklist for Executing a Cognitive Skill

_____ Recall the definition of *bias.*

_____ Recall or identify clues to bias:
- Loaded words
- Overgeneralization or exaggeration
- One-sided presentation
- Rhetorical questions

_____ Search, piece by piece to find evidence related to these clues.

_____ Identify any pattern in the evidence found.

_____ Judge the extent to which any pattern in the evidence matches the definition of *bias.*

It should be noted that other procedures for carrying out this same cognitive operation could replace those in the checklist format of Figure 6.1. The point of presenting this example here is to illustrate what a procedural checklist looks like, not to present a description of the only way this particular cognitive procedure can be executed. Clearly, the exact procedure presented on any checklist will reflect the source and experience from which it was generated and the nature and skill-using experience of its intended users. Procedural checklists like the one in Figure 6.1 can be produced for any cognitive operation or skill.

Procedural checklists serve three very useful purposes. They make explicit a workable sequence of key steps in a procedure. By so doing, they help to ensure that students do not skip or omit any important step in the procedure—something novices tend to do all too frequently. Checklists also keep the skill-using procedure right in front of the student, allowing the student to devote his or her mental effort to how to carry out the procedure rather than to trying to remember what the procedure is.

This last point is most important. Often, checklists are referred to only after a skilled operation has been performed in order to ensure that all the important steps have been done. However, a checklist—like any useful scaffold—is most useful in scaffolding thinking when used by students *while* they carry out the cognitive procedure presented on it. It serves as a prop as well as a prompt for a student's working (short-term) memory. Instead of having to recall how to carry out the procedure while also processing and remembering the data being processed, a student using a procedural checklist is freed to devote his or her short-term memory almost completely to executing the procedure and to the content being processed. Thus, use of a checklist reduces demand on short-term memory by presenting a visible and explicit routine of what is to be done mentally with or to data. Checklists not only scaffold thinking but reduce cognitive overload.[3]

Checklists can be employed in at least four ways to support student execution of recently introduced or difficult cognitive skills:

1. Checklists may be referred to by students prior to carrying out a skill-using task to rehearse what they plan to do to execute the skill. When used at this point students can paraphrase each step on the checklist, provide a rationale for executing that step, and tell how it relates to other steps in the procedure.
2. While students are carrying out the checklist procedure and checking off each step as they execute it, reference to the checklist helps them keep aware of where they are in the procedure and alert to what is to happen next.
3. Checklists serve as a trouble-shooting aid when students encounter problems in applying a cognitive procedure by allowing them to

retrace their mental steps and modify what they are trying to do, if necessary.

4. Upon conclusion of a skill-using task, a checklist can be reviewed to ensure that students have followed the procedure presented and not done a mentally sloppy job.

Employing a checklist in these ways maximizes its scaffolding effect immeasurably.

Creating Checklists

Checklists can be devised in any of several ways. One is to base them on descriptions of how experts execute a particular cognitive operation. Thus, a simple checklist for detecting bias (see Chapter 5) might well be like the checklist presented in Figure 6.1. Notice that this procedure is essentially a briefer version of the expert directions presented in Figure 5.7 but a somewhat more detailed version of that skill procedure than is presented in Figure 5.8. Descriptions of thinking procedures generated by individuals skilled in executing them or by specialists in teaching thinking may serve as useful sources for creating thinking skill checklists like this one.

Procedural checklists may also be generated by students, with teacher assistance as needed. They may grow naturally out of the concluding segment of a lesson in which a new or difficult thinking operation has been introduced. As these lessons draw to a close and students review and summarize what they have learned up to that point about a particular skill, they can (as individuals, groups, pairs, or an entire class) produce procedural outlines in the form of checklists to be used in subsequent applications of the operation. Figure 6.2, for example, presents a form that can be provided to students after an introductory lesson on detecting bias on which they can enter two different procedures for carrying out the skill. Additional copies of this form could be distributed periodically for students to complete as they modify with experience how they execute this operation in subsequent lessons.

Note that the checklist format of Figure 6.2, without the box labeled "Clues," can be used for any thinking operation checklist. Because detecting bias involves evaluating something against criteria, the box in this example provides a special place on this checklist for highlighting these criteria or clues. This format would be appropriate for any thinking operation—such as judging the quality of an essay or report, determining the credibility of a source, or assessing the strength of an argument—where criteria are applied. For cognitive operations where criteria are not used—such as classifying, comparing, or predicting—checklist boxes like this might be appropriate for noting important heuristics or rules, or they can be omitted altogether.

Figure 6.2 Form for Recording Classroom-Generated Procedural Checklists

SKILL: _____

Procedure A:

____   _____

____   _____

____   _____

____   _____

____   _____

____   _____

Clues to look for:

Procedure B:

____   _____

____   _____

____   _____

____   _____

____   _____

____   _____

As Figure 6.2 indicates, a checklist may include more than one procedure for carrying out a given operation. To acknowledge that there usually are several different but effective procedures for carrying out any thinking operation, several different procedures might be presented—or recorded by students—on a single checklist, especially in the initial stages of trying it. Use of a multiple procedure checklist offers students who are learning a new thinking operation options for executing it and reinforces the feeling that they have some choice in how to carry out the operation. Such multiple procedure checklists often evolve from lessons in which students share the various ways they carried out a thinking skill and revise previously devised checklists as they become more experienced in executing the procedures by which they execute these positions.

Thinking skill procedural checklists may be presented to students in a number of forms. Initially, they can be hand-printed, in large letters, on large sheets of paper and displayed on a classroom wall as cognitive skill-using "prompts." They can be replaced frequently as they are modified by the students based on their experience in applying them. Another possibility is to duplicate them on notebook-size pages to be included in student notebooks for ready reference as needed. Sometimes they can be attached to assignments or tasks that require use of the skill procedure they describe. Other times, they can be forms like that presented in Figure 6.2, to be completed prior to carrying out a task requiring use of a particular thinking operation and then as a device for recording what students have generated about that operation upon completing such a task. Sometimes, it may even be helpful to produce them in the form of small cue cards that students can prop up on a desk or place on a book page when needed.[4]

Using Checklists

To help students use an already prepared checklist to its fullest advantage the first time or two it is used, we can have them:

1. Preview the checklist, read over the steps listed, and put them into their own words or ask questions about any step that is unclear.
2. Carry out the skill-using task, checking off each step in the procedure as they complete it.
3. Upon completing the task, review the checklist to be sure all steps have been executed.

Once our students have used a checklist several times, we should encourage them to modify or revise it to reflect their developing understanding of how to use the procedure it describes and the way in which they are coming to personalize the operation they are executing. To do this, we may replace step 3 above and add a new step 4 as follows:

3. In moving through the process, or upon completing it, note any changes in the procedure actually employed including:
   a. Steps omitted or skipped
   b. New steps executed
   c. Steps combined into single steps
   d. Steps broken down into several substeps
4. Upon completing the skill-using task, revise the checklist, if modified in any way, by writing a completely new checklist to be used the next time this cognitive procedure is to be applied.

This elaborated use of a checklist acknowledges the fact that with experience in applying a cognitive operation, students personalize it and often compress it, collapsing multiple steps into fewer but more efficient and more all-encompassing moves. Such a revision procedure also reduces unthinking reliance on a written checklist. Revising a checklist seems to help students internalize the procedure it describes, by helping them gradually incorporate into their cognitive structures a personally meaningful procedure for using a complex or new cognitive operation. Ideally, the use of a checklist for any thinking operation ought to gradually diminish; this elaboration/revision procedure can lead in this direction.

Checklists prove especially useful in helping students apply unpracticed or forgotten cognitive skills introduced the preceding academic year. They can also be very useful in helping students bridge, or transfer, a skill from one data set or context or subject to another. Students can rely on the procedural checklist for assistance in carrying out the skill while they devote much of their mental effort to coping with the new content or media or subject matter they find themselves using. As they continue to use a thinking skill checklist as a guide whenever that particular operation is used, students can continue to modify it and adapt it. A checklist, like the thinking it describes, should be dynamic and growing rather than remain a static crutch.

Strengths and Limitations

Checklists are very useful in the initial stages of cognitive skill learning, for they provide the visible, explicit details of a procedure that can be followed to execute new skills. They structure or support how students carry out the appropriate procedure; they guide and steer student execution of the operation; they give students a sense of security in carrying out an operation new to them; and they minimize the danger of students becoming attached to flawed or dysfunctional cognitive procedures. They are, in effect, very useful learning props for novices.

Checklists also have their limitations. Because they are purposely brief, they are relatively meaningless to students who have not had some prior opportunity to make the procedure visible and explicit. Unexplained or un-elaborated directions or "steps" fail to provide much of the detail and ex-planation of "how to use" knowledge necessary for individuals unfamiliar with a thinking skill to understand the how and why of each step to be un-dertaken. Thus, they are not useful by themselves as devices for introduc-ing students to new cognitive skills. However, they are excellent techniques to follow up explicit skill introductions, because they can provide in brief form the cognitive procedures that emerge from these introductory skill-using experiences.

Checklists can be abused, too. Once a cognitive procedure is reduced to print, there is a real danger that the printed procedure appears to be the *only correct* way to carry out this procedure. This impression must be guarded against constantly. Providing students with the opportunity to generate their own checklists, providing checklists containing two or more workable procedures, and/or having students regularly revise and modify proce-dural checklists help guard against this possibility.

Procedural checklists should also match the cognitive procedures that emerge from students' initial experience with the operation being de-scribed. It is not productive to model one procedure, have students ap-ply it, allow them to report how they did it, and then distribute a check-list that represents the modeled procedure and ignores how students may actually have modified it in trying to carry it out. Nor is it wise to launch a lesson introducing a new cognitive skill by providing a ready-made checklist on how to do it, for such a checklist does not provide sufficient guidance for successfully carrying out a new operation. Nor does this ap-proach acknowledge the fact that some students may already be quite good at carrying out this operation, but use a quite different (but just as effective) procedure.

Finally, there is a danger that checklists may be used too long in the process of practicing a cognitive skill that needs improving. For many stu-dents, checklists may become a permanent crutch when, in fact, they should be only a temporary aid as the students gradually adapt or modify a proce-dure being developed and begin to internalize it. Again, having students modify and revise checklists as they engage in applying a skill helps to over-come this danger.

In spite of these limitations, however, and because of their advantages, procedural checklists prove to be one of the most effective techniques for scaffolding student thinking, especially in their early efforts to apply that thinking. Procedural checklists, accurately and precisely designed, provide clear, explicit, and visible prompts for carrying out cognitive operations when students are unsure and inexperienced in executing them. Of all the scaffolding techniques, checklists provide the most explicit aid in structur-ing thinking.

PROCESS-STRUCTURED QUESTIONS

Questioning has been one of the most common techniques used over the years to teach thinking. Generally, questions asked by the teacher and text have served and continue to serve a variety of learning functions. Some provide opportunities for students to engage in higher-order thinking by posing thought-provoking situations that require student engagement in interpretation, application, decision making, reasoning, and so on. Others stimulate and encourage thinking by posing engaging topics for study that fairly beg a student response. When asked in certain sequences, questions can even move thinking along and take students from the known to the unknown, from the literal to the interpretive and synthetic, from the specific to the general, or from the concrete to the abstract.[5] The quality of student thinking is obviously enhanced by questions that provide opportunities to think, stimulate thinking, and move thinking and learning along. Such questions clearly require and exercise thinking, if appropriate responses are to be generated. But these questions often fall short of what questions could do to actually support or scaffold complex thinking *per se*.

Questions such as Is this material biased? or Is this accurate? or What are the unstated assumptions here? provide little help to students in carrying out the mental operation required to produce appropriate responses unless they already know something about how to do these things. Such questions scaffold nothing. They may provoke thinking, even encourage it, but they contain little that assists someone who knows nothing about a procedure for producing the response called for. Such questions may be appropriate for students who have begun to demonstrate an ability to answer them, but they are not appropriate for helping beginners launch their use of a skill.[6]

Yet, like well-structured checklists, some questions, too, *can* scaffold thinking. Classroom experimentation and research on questioning suggest that questions *structured according to thinking procedures* actually assist students in understanding, applying and adopting these cognitive procedures.[7] When used as suggested by this research, such questioning proves to be an extremely useful technique for supporting student learning of newly encountered or difficult thinking operations and subject matter.

There are a number of ways to sequence questions that structure or scaffold thinking.[8] One way is by creating questions that call explicitly for execution of each step in a thinking procedure and sequencing these questions so as to move students through the complete procedure by which the thinking operation is executed. Such process-structured questions are, in effect, clusters or sets of questions that lead students sequentially through the essential mental steps of *a specific thinking* operation. For example, a process-structured question cluster for detecting bias might be:

- What is bias?
- What kinds of evidence or clues, if found, would indicate bias?
- What evidence of the clues to bias did you find (in the given material)?
- What pattern did this evidence, if any, make?
- To what degree was (this material) biased?
- What, if any, is the bias?

Question clusters like this steer a student through the major mental steps in a cognitive procedure—in this instance, the procedure of evaluating for bias. They start by asking students to recall or identify a definition of the procedure to be employed as a way of helping students retrieve what they already know about this operation. Students can then develop a mental set that will facilitate the execution of the procedure and that definition will be readily available later to use as the standard against which to assess the evidence found by answering the intervening questions. From there, additional questions reflect an explicit step-by-step procedure for carrying out the operation. By so doing, this technique provides considerable structured support or scaffolding to a student who is just beginning to practice the particular operation being directed by the questions. This kind of process-structured question set is essentially a procedural checklist presented in the form of questions. By responding to each of these questions in turn, students can execute the procedure of detecting bias. Because this type of question cluster is so explicit in indicating what a student should do, it proves to be most useful as a scaffold for activities that apply this operation immediately following the introduction of the skill.

Creating Process-Structured Questions

There are at least two types of process-structured questions that scaffold student thinking effectively. One type (the preceding questions on detecting bias) structures a thinking operation in explicit procedural detail. Another type structures the metacognitive planning and execution of a thinking procedure. A set of questions structuring the execution of the skill of decision making, for example, might be:

1. What do you want to make a decision about?
2. What do you want to accomplish by making this decision?
3. How will you know when you have made the *best* choice?
4. What are all the alternatives you have to choose from?
5. What are the consequences of each alternative—long range as well as short range?
6. What are the pluses and minuses of each consequence?
7. Which alternative is *best*? Why?

Again, these questions are basically a checklist presented as questions. They lead the students step by step through the cognitive procedure of decision making. The answer to each question moves the students toward the final decision they seek to make. These decision-making questions are generic—the can scaffold students through any decision-making task. Similar sets of questions can be produced for any cognitive operation and at any level of complexity, just as checklists can. In fact, one useful way to produce such questions is first to identify an explicit procedure for carrying out the operation to be scaffolded and then to convert each step (or, sometimes, combination of steps) in the procedure to a separate question.

Question clusters can also structure metacognitive thinking *about* a specific thinking operation, as, for example:

1. What is *bias*? What steps could you go through to detect bias in a written statement? To what extent is the attached statement biased and, if it is, what is the bias? What in this statement justifies your evaluation? What steps would you recommend a younger student take to see if this statement showed *bias*?

2. What is *decision making*? What steps could you go through to make a very important decision? Use your list of steps to make a decision about (a given situation, issue or problem). What problems do/did you have with the steps you are going or went through? What changes would you make in your decision-making procedure so it would work better next time you use it? Revise the procedure you went through so it incorporates what you actually did or should have done so you can make the best possible decision next time.

These question clusters ask students to think about the cognitive skill they are employing *before* they apply it, *while* applying it, and after it has been *applied*. Metacognition involves thinking about what one is going to do before doing it and planning how to do it; monitoring and evaluating how well it is being carried out and making appropriate adjustments en route; and assessing the procedure employed when finished, revising it as necessary for later use. Each of these two question sets moves students through this process, although by slightly different questions. Similar sets of questions can be developed to scaffold the application of any cognitive skill or procedure.

Using Process-Structured Questions

Once prepared, process-structured questions can be displayed on large posters around the room for student reference as needed, or reproduced as handouts for student notebooks, or prepared as small cue or prompt cards. They can also be displayed to students on an overhead transparency when needed to carry out a task calling for use of the specific thinking operation. And, like checklists, these question sets can be continuously revised to reflect changes in how the students carry out the operation as their experience in using it increases.

Process-structured questions like those described here can be most useful to students where skill learning is integrated into instruction in subject matter. Having them readily available at the time the appropriate thinking operation needs to be applied reduces overload on memory and allows students to focus on the application of the skill they are applying while referring to the process questions for guidance in recalling what to do next. In the process of using such questions, students can begin to modify them into a personalized procedure. Such revision helps them to internalize *what* they are doing and to gradually take ownership of it.

Strengths and Limitations

Process-structured questions serve as a less didactic alternative to checklists. The most explicitly detailed question clusters provide the most helpful scaffold for students in the initial stages of applying a newly introduced cognitive skill. As students adopt or adapt the procedure structured by these questions, the metacognitive type of process questions can then be used to guide students through a process of articulating their adaptation of the skill-using procedure they have been executing. Emphasis shifts from how to carry out the skill procedure to recalling or planning a procedure and carrying it out.

However, metacognitive questions are generally effective in improving thinking only when employed after questions that structure the cognitive procedure to be improved have been used for some time. By employing these types of question sets in this order, we can provide the kind of support appropriate to where the students are in their understanding of the skill. We can then gradually withdraw such explicit support to the point where a question such as Is this material biased? can elicit application of the cognitive procedure it triggers because of the preceding use of the more detailed process questions. This sequence of process-structured questions serves as surrogate teaching; it provides guidance and support in how to carry out a skill, thus freeing us, as teachers, to provide any individual assistance to students as needed while they are using these questions to complete assigned tasks.

Structured questions, however, suffer from the same limitations as do checklists. Unless gradually made less explicit and eventually withdrawn, they can become thoughtless crutches. Poorly constructed or derived from inaccurate descriptions of the procedures they purport to represent, they can be dysfunctional rather than supportive. Yet, when developed and used as suggested here, they can provide just the kind of guidance and structure students need to improve their competence in executing newly introduced or complex cognitive skills.

Again, it should be noted that not all questions scaffold students through a thinking procedure. This is especially true of the rather commonly used questions based on Bloom's *Taxonomy of Educational Objectives— Handbook I: The Cognitive Domain*. Such questions merely demand that a student engage in a specific or at least an intended cognitive operation, but they do not assist the student at all in executing this operation. Even a series of questions, each at a different level of the taxonomy, suffers from this same limitation. Such questions may move students from simpler to more complex *levels* of understanding, but they do not scaffold any particular thinking operation. Only a series of questions that walk students through the steps in executing a thinking operation provide the kind of question-based scaffolding that guides and supports student thinking.

Other kinds of process-structured questions than those presented here may be derived from what is known about skill learning and teaching. But the two types presented here exemplify some of the possibilities in this regard. They also highlight the importance of *how* questions can *frame* the execution of a thinking skill. Clearly, the ways we direct questions can help students process responses. But how we frame a sequence of questions for students can go even further by providing a degree of instructive guidance in how to carry out a skill that students are seeking to master.

GRAPHIC ORGANIZERS

In general, a graphic organizer is a chart or diagram that arranges the components of something in some way. It may take the form of a web, a pictograph, a series of boxes or columns, a matrix, or any other diagram that displays information in a visually structured manner. Students fill it in by entering the kinds of information indicated by the visual or verbal prompts embedded in the organizer. By providing a structure for the content or information it displays, such an organizer assists students in storing and then retrieving this information as well as making it meaningful and applying it.[9] Graphic organizers are widely used in most subjects to organize information, to represent the meaning of written texts, and to describe subject-matter concepts (see Figure 6.3).

Graphic organizers are also extremely useful for structuring or scaffolding thinking operations. When used for this purpose, however, a graphic organizer presents a visual representation of a thinking *procedure* rather than of a product of thinking. Graphic organizers of thinking *products*, such as concept webs or hamburger paragraphs, may demand thinking to produce them but do little to help that thinking along. A graphic organizer for a thinking *procedure*, on the other hand, is one that requires

Figure 6.3 Graphic Organizers for Comparing and Sequencing

COMPARING

AND

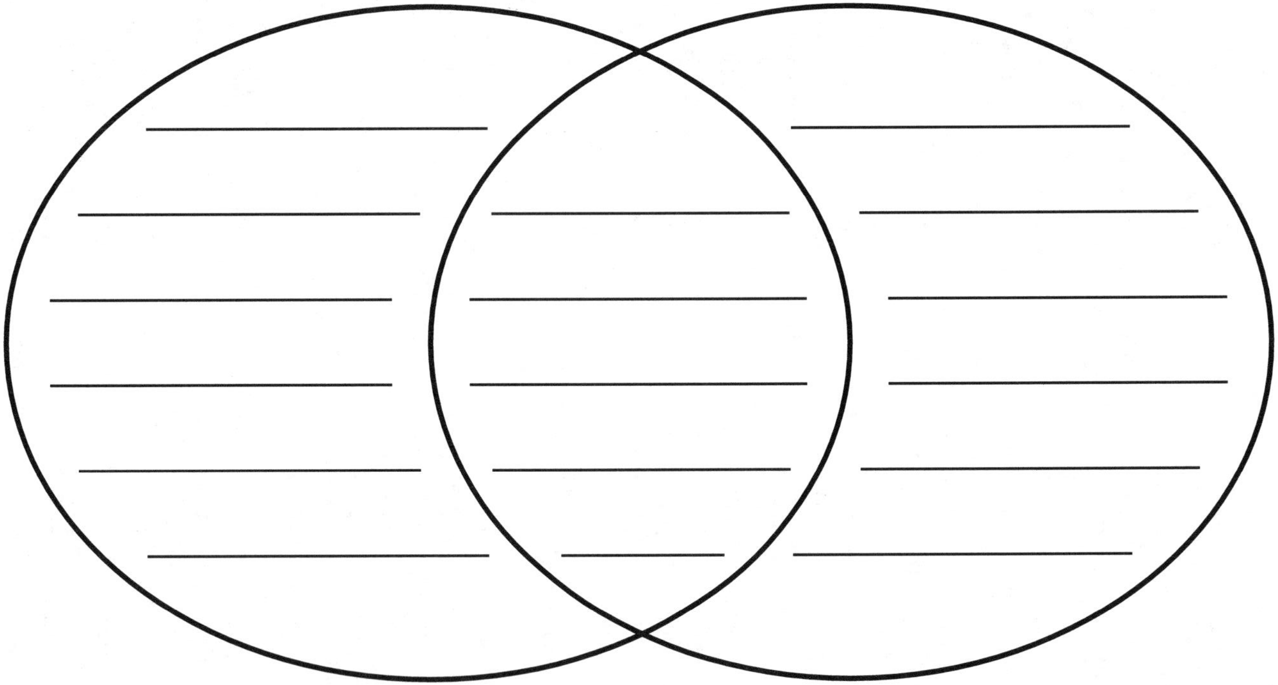

A SEQUENCE FOR: _____

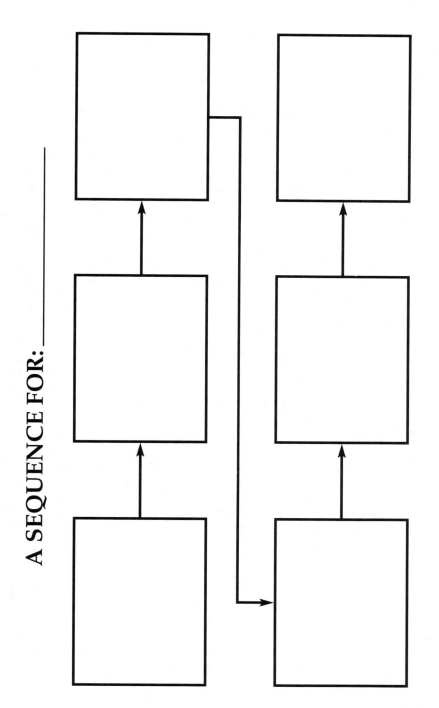

and assists students to move mentally through the steps by which a particular cognitive operation can be effectively carried out. These graphic organizers present visually, but usually less explicitly, what checklists present in verbal fashion—the key steps in a procedure for carrying out a cognitive skill or process. They serve as a nonintrusive prop that moves students through a skill-using procedure in such a way that they do not skip important procedural steps or ignore rules or other skill-related knowledge essential to efficient and effective execution of the procedure.

Graphic organizers have been and can be prepared for use with virtually any cognitive operation. Figure 6.3, for example, presents organizers commonly used in scaffolding elementary school students' execution of the skills of comparing and ordering (sequencing).

To complete the Venn diagram a student must identify two items being compared by entering their names on the lines above the overlapping circles. Then the student must search both items to identify their features or attributes. Those found to be the same in both items are listed on the lines in the center, where the two circles overlap. Features found to be unique to only one item are listed in the circle under that appropriate item label outside the overlap. As students complete this graphic organizer, they literally move through the cognitive operation that constitutes the skill of comparing. The flowchart organizer structures the operation of putting things in order (sequencing). To complete it, students must determine the criteria (as for example, *by size* from smallest to largest) for sequencing some items, objects, or other phenomena, enter that criteria on the top line and then arrange these items in terms of that criteria, by labeling the sequenced boxes in ascending or descending order.

These graphics are simple and uncluttered by written prompts. And, like most simple graphic organizers, they may not be useful for applications of the cognitive procedures represented to complex situations or data. The Venn diagram, for example, is useful for comparing just two items, but comparing multiple items requires a different graphic to move students through the steps in a procedure for accomplishing this task. Figure 6.4 presents one graphic organizer for this more complex operation; it can easily be modified to compare any number of items.

Organizers can be developed for even more complex thinking operations, as well. Figure 6.5 presents a graphic organizer for the procedure of concept making. As students work with data to build a given concept, they enter the appropriate information in the spaces as prompted on the organizer. As they do, they move through the essential steps in the skill of conceptualizing. After first (1) naming the concept they wish to construct and then (2) identifying several examples of the concept, they (3) list (under traits) the key features of these examples. Then they classify the features

Figure 6.4 A Graphic Organizer for Comparing Many Items

COMPARING

Items Compared	Features or Traits Compared					
1.						
2.						
3.						
4.						
All the Same?						
Differences:						

Figure 6.5 A Graphic Organizer for Conceptualizing

BUILDING A CONCEPT OF: _____1_____

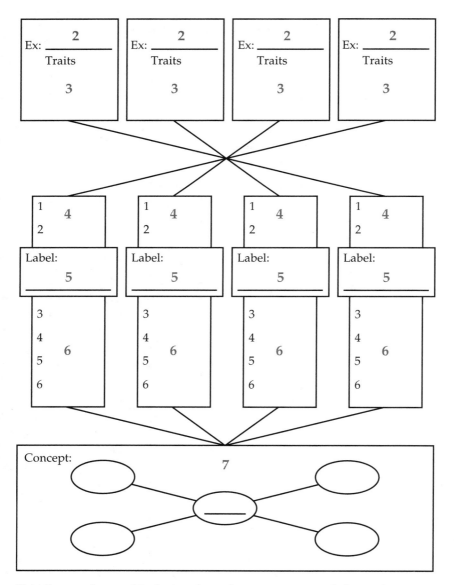

Note: Gray numbers on this chart are for explanatory purposes only (see text).

they have identified into categories or groups of features common to all examples, labeling each category as they do this classifying. Usually, after matching two features (4) and naming how these two traits match, students can write this name as the category label (5). Additional traits from their examples can (6) then be added under the appropriate category labels. Finally, (7) the groups of traits are related to each other in the form of a web to present a visual image of the concept that has thus emerged. *Note:* The numbers 1–7 on the graphic organizer shown in Figure 6.5 are shown here only for explanation purposes.

Note that concept webs like that produced in step 7 of the conceptualizing procedure just described represent the *product* of conceptualizing but not the mental process by which it was arrived at. However, steps 1–6 in this graphic organizer scaffold a cognitive *procedure* for generating this concept. In the box at the bottom of the organizer, the center circle in the web presents the name of the concept, entered on the line. The satellite circles represent four (there could be less or more than four) groups of traits that define the concept—the groups formed by classifying in the tombstone boxes in the center of the organizer. Students can elaborate the web by adding additional circles and lines to represent other key traits or subordinate categories of traits under each key trait, as necessary or desired. What is unique about this skill graphic organizer is that it leads students through the cognitive process required to produce the concept described at the bottom while also providing a place to represent that product. This graphic organizer has proven extremely effective in helping middle and secondary school students execute and improve their skill of conceptualizing while constructing subject-matter concepts of significance in a variety of subjects.

Selecting and Preparing Graphic Organizers

A number of cognitive skill graphic organizers have been described in the professional literature in recent years.[10] Not all, however, focus on a cognitive procedure Many focus on the substantive product of that procedure. Although useful for representing knowledge, these latter organizers are not useful in scaffolding a thinking operation that students are just learning to execute. In selecting as well as in preparing graphic organizers for use in scaffolding thinking, we must thus be very alert to the essential features of graphic organizers appropriate for thinking. A graphic organizer most useful in supporting student execution of a cognitive operation is one that meets the following requisites:

1. It presents in visual form the *key steps* in a procedure for carrying out that operation.

2. It requires student use of any significant rules, heuristics, and declarative knowledge (such as the criteria that distinguish critical thinking operations from each other and from other types of thinking).
3. It should be clear and uncluttered.
4. It should be limited to a page in size.
5. It should provide enough space for students to enter the kind of information needed.
6. In some instances, prompts, in the form of one or two words (as in Figures 6.4 and 6.5, for example) may be included.

Graphic organizers for thinking operations may best be prepared or evaluated by referring to credible descriptions of the cognitive procedures they are intended to structure. In selecting or preparing a graphic organizer for decision making, for example, one should judge its accuracy and adequacy by comparing it to a reputable description of what one does in making a decision. The organizer in Figure 6.6 was developed in just this way. It represents a simplified description of decision-making recommended for intermediate-grade students.[11]

To fill in the decision-making graphic organizer in Figure 6.6, a student must identify and write a brief description of the problem initiating the decision-making opportunity and write in the appropriate place one or more goals to be accomplished by the decision. Then he or she must brainstorm or otherwise generate as many alternatives as possible by which this goal can be accomplished and identify the pros and cons (which are student-friendly terms meaning positive and negative consequences) of each, entering this information into appropriate spaces on the organizer. Then, and only then, does the student choose the best from among all the listed alternatives as his or her decision. This action requires the student to weigh the pros and cons of all the alternatives against each other before settling on a final choice. Finally, by recording the reasons for this choice, the student actually verbalizes the essential criteria the preferred choice has met. This is something that experienced and skilled decision makers do in setting their goals, but that young students find frustratingly difficult in the early stages of improving their decision making.[12]

Graphic organizers can be devised for students at differing levels of experience in a particular cognitive operation. The organizer shown in Figure 6.6 proves useful in helping intermediate or middle-grade youngsters become proficient in the essential steps of rational decision making, but it omits some of the more complicated aspects of this operation as used by experts. When these students demonstrate proficiency in the procedure represented by this organizer (Figure 6.6), however, they can then be introduced to these more complicated parts of the procedure—namely, stating the decision criteria "up front" instead of as a rationale at the end of the process,

Figure 6.6 A Graphic Organizer for Decision Making for Intermediate Grade Students

DECISION MAKING		
Problem:	**Goal(s):**	
Alternatives:	**For:**	**Against:**
Decision:	**Reasons:**	

and specifying various types of consequences such as costs (e.g., time, money, opportunities lost, etc.), impact on self and others, and, where appropriate, risks involved, before evaluating each consequence in terms of these specific criteria.

Figure 6.7 presents a graphic organizer that includes these elaborated elements of decision making. In this organizer, the final section on reasons

Figure 6.7 A Graphic Organizer for Decision Making for Secondary
School Students

DECISION MAKING

Situation/Opportunity:							
Problem:			**Goal/Criteria:**				
Alternatives:		**Consequences/Costs/Etc.:**					**Evaluation:**
Decision:			**Reasons:**				

serves as a check (when compared to the section on "goals/criteria" articulated at the top of the organizer) on the validity of the process and a guard against decision bias. A graphic organizer can also be constructed for an even more sophisticated and explicit description of decision making, too. This would include identifying unanticipated consequences of already identified alternatives, rating the probability of the identified consequences of all alternatives occurring, ranking the alternatives in terms of the evaluation of their identified consequences, evaluating the top three or so alternatives in terms of previously unanticipated risks or costs, and then choosing from these the "best" alternative as the final decision.[13]

Graphic organizers, then, can represent and scaffold the same cognitive operation at different levels of complexity and different degrees of explicitness. Figures 6.8 and 6.9 present two different organizers for the cognitive process of classifying. The organizer in Figure 6.8 is most appropriate for

Figure 6.8 A Graphic Organizer for Classifying for Primary Grade Students

GROUPING

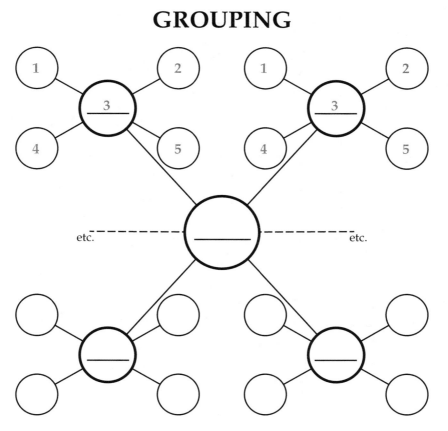

students just beginning to practice sorting or grouping things or information. The organizer in Figure 6.9 is more useful for students who can benefit from the very explicit procedure it structures.

Figure 6.9 A Graphic Organizer for Classifying for Intermediate Grade Students

CLASSIFYING

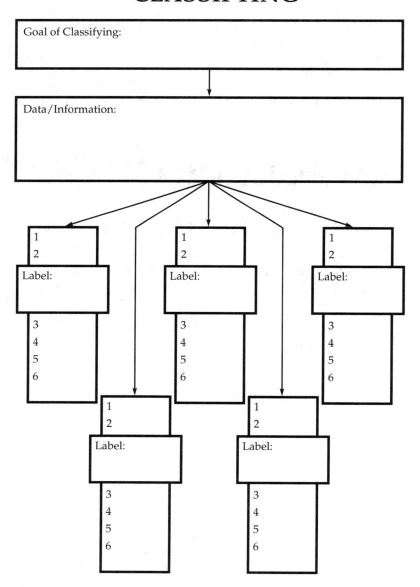

In Figure 6.8 the student classifies given data (perhaps household objects) into at least three groups by listing the objects in any group in the small circles around a large circle; into the latter they put the name (label) they assign to the group. This process may be repeated for each grouping. The organizer is partially structured by numbers, so that students identify and label a group as soon as they have selected two items that, in their judgment, share the same attribute and have entered them in the appropriately numbered circles. They then continue making that grouping using the label as a tool for searching the remaining data for other items that share that attribute. Several of the grouping circles are numberless because, after doing the two top groups, most students understand the process through which they are moving and no longer need them. By not numbering these circles, students are given the freedom to invent groups another way, such as coming up with a group label first and then finding all the items that fit that label, and to add additional circles as appropriate.

This procedure for classifying can be repeated to produce each group. Or students may turn from working on one group to another and back again, as they wish. They can produce subgroups by adding circles and lines to any circle in any cluster. They can conclude by labeling the central circle with the feature shared by all groups and connect lines to it from the group labels, or add circles to connect only two groups, if that is what they arrive at. The procedure for classifying structured in this graphic organizer is one commonly used by individuals who either (1) let the groupings emerge from the data itself or (2) start with specific groups in mind or groups that emerge from a quick survey of the given data or from the task directions.

The organizer in Figure 6.9 guides students through essentially the same procedure, with the learning goal for classifying explicitly requested. This helps delimit the kinds of groupings appropriate, but visually it appears more linear (top to bottom) and more structured. It also provides a place to display the data for the students to classify.

Figures 6.10 and 6.11 present graphic organizers for other cognitive operations found by many students to be difficult. Figure 6.10 presents a graphic organizer for the basic elements of problem solving. It can be used as is, simplified, or made more explicit, depending on the problem-solving experience of the students and the instructional goals to be achieved.

Figure 6.11 presents a graphic organizer for evaluating (judging). It can be employed by students as they judge virtually anything from the adequacy of a proof in math, to the validity of an experiment, the quality of a novel, the leadership of a given individual, the quality of a short essay or term paper, or even the quality of a local athletic team. It may, in fact, be used by students to conduct any kind of evaluation, including evaluating any written, visual or oral communication for bias, stereotyping, credibility, logical fallacies, authenticity, accuracy, strength of an argument, and similar factors that affect the quality of such communications.

Figure 6.10 A Graphic Organizer for Problem Solving

PROBLEM SOLVING

Problem	Information
Ideal state:	Given:
Present state:	
Gap:	Needed, but missing:

Plan to Be Followed (Steps to Be Taken)	✓	Actions Taken to Complete Each Step
1.	—	
2.	—	
3.	—	
4.	—	
5.	—	
6.	—	

Solution	Check

Figure 6.11 A Graphic Organizer for Evaluating

EVALUATING

Purpose/ Goal: To judge _____

Clues or Criteria	✚ Evidence ▬	
_____		
_____		
_____		
_____		
_____		
_____		

Pattern Found:	Judgment:

In using Figure 6.11 to detect bias in a written statement, for example, a student must first record his or her purpose or intent (to judge the extent or degree of bias in a given paragraph, perhaps) and then define bias. Next, he or she must list in the left-hand column, from memory or from some other reliable source, some of the criteria or clues that, if met or found, reveal bias (e.g., loaded words, exaggeration, etc.). Then, the student records in the two columns to the right any evidence in support of (+) or that is contrary to (-) these criteria or additional clues that he or she finds by searching the communication being evaluated. Next, the student must identify and describe any pattern in the evidence found—for example, "All the evidence matches the criteria used" or "Some evidence supports, some contradicts the criteria" or so on. Finally, the student must judge and state the degree of match (if any) between the evidence and all these criteria or clues and the definition of the quality being assessed and then record the final assessment or judgment in the box labeled "Evaluation." By completing this graphic organizer, a student is guided through one very effective procedure for detecting bias, without the need for any further outside direction.

As illustrated by many of the graphic organizers for thinking presented here, it is helpful to students (and sometimes even necessary) to add word prompts to the organizers, especially when students are using them the first several times. Such prompts enable students to make sense of the diagram or chart, if they are unfamiliar with it, and to link it to the procedure as verbalized in previous lessons or activities in which this cognitive procedure was made explicit and visible. Prompts also add to the scaffolding power of an organizer by combining verbal and visual cues to trigger recall of the procedure needed to complete the organizer and, when completed, to store the procedure used in memory for later use. Where detailed step-by-step prompts are not necessary, a simple title for a graphic organizer denoting the cognitive skill with which it is to be used proves useful in triggering and scaffolding the cognitive procedure to be employed. Verbal prompts may be used initially, but as students get accustomed to using organizers, such prompts can eventually be eliminated.

Using Graphic Organizers

Having students use graphic organizers to scaffold their application of new or complex cognitive skills in any grades beyond the primary level and in any body of content generally requires little teacher direction or explanation as long as two conditions have been met:

1. The graphic organizer must clearly (for the user) prompt his or her use of a *recognized* cognitive procedure.
2. The purpose and procedure of completing a graphic organizer must be clear to the students.

Before asking students to use a graphic organizer to scaffold their developing thinking, we should ensure that in its structure and verbal prompts it clearly presents—for students—a cognitive procedure they have already encountered. That is, the organizer should trigger for the student mental actions that have been made visible and explicit in some earlier introduction to the procedure being scaffolded. For, unless students consciously recognize the connection between how they are thinking and the graphic organizer and unless this connection is meaningful and purposeful for them, filling in the organizer is likely to be treated simply as another piece of busy work. Consequently, it is crucial that in selecting or developing graphic organizers, we must be sure they meet the criteria of effective organizers for thinking.

As previously noted, graphic organizers are most effective when used to guide student application of a cognitive operation that has been introduced explicitly in a preceding lesson or activity. If students are already familiar with what graphic organizers are and how to use them, then any specific graphic organizer can simply be distributed to students with instructions to fill it in as they proceed to complete a given skill-using task. The first several times students use a new graphic organizer, however, we should preview the structure of that organizer, calling attention to any prompts presented on it, suggesting the order in which to complete its various sections, and helping students make connections between these sections and prompts and the steps in the skill procedure around which the organizer has been structured. Students may then work, in pairs or individually, to complete the organizer while using the content material provided to them. Once the organizers have been completed, volunteers can report to the class what they had to do to fill in each section of the organizer, tell what each prompt on it meant to them, and report any problems they had in completing it. After any problems have been resolved, students can turn to a discussion of what they wrote on the organizers and continue their subject-matter learning. After a specific graphic organizer has been used several times with this kind of preview and follow-up, it simply can be distributed to students with instructions to use it to complete the assigned skill-using task.

There are other ways, too, to introduce students to graphic organizers as learning aids.[14] One alternative is, after previewing the idea of graphic organizers for scaffolding thinking, to present students with a partially completed organizer. Review what was done up to that point to fill it in and then allow the students—perhaps in pairs—to complete it, providing individual assistance as needed. A follow-up discussion by students can focus on what they had to do to complete the organizer. They could then work together again to complete new copy of the organizer using different data, but data identical to that used in the initial example. What is important in using either of these teaching strategies is that students see how an organizer works, understand its connection to and value in executing the thinking operation which they are practicing, and actually complete one or two on a sort of trial or practice basis. When introduced to students with these purposes in mind, graphic organizers can be more easily used later.

As students gain experience using any particular thinking skill graphic organizer, it may be necessary to revise it to represent any more streamlined or alternative procedure they have evolved for carrying out this particular cognitive operation. As noted earlier, the way one executes a cognitive operation changes with experience. So, periodically constructing a new or modified organizer may be a worthwhile activity for them to undertake. As an alternative, the organizer may be dropped and replaced by another more student-centered scaffolding device such as a checklist, mneumonic, or set of structured questions. Eventually, as in the case of any construction, when the procedure or structure that it supports has been internalized and taken hold, the scaffold must be removed. At this point, students should be able to carry out the skill procedure with only a minimum of prompting, cueing, or other support—or none at all.

Strengths and Limitations

Appropriately designed graphic organizers can serve as useful scaffolds for carrying out cognitive procedures that are relatively new, complex or difficult to execute. They assist students in carrying out a mental procedure by providing visual and often verbal prompts as to what is to be done first, then next, then next, and so on, to the completion of the process. By their visual structure and verbal prompts, they also provide feedback while the students move through the procedure. Furthermore, they provide a complete and continuously available view of the entire operation to be performed so the user can see exactly where he or she is in carrying it out and how what has been or is to be done relates to the whole. Finally, successful student use of these organizers does not require highly developed student reading skills.

There are, however, at least three notes of caution to be pointed out about the use of graphic organizers for scaffolding thinking. First, not every graphic organizer structures a cognitive operation, procedure, or process. Many, like most webs, usually present the *products* of thinking rather than how a thinking product is generated or developed. Thus, care must be taken in constructing or selecting graphic organizers to scaffold thinking to ensure that they actually do clearly articulate a cognitive procedure by which the desired thinking operation is executed. To be effective, a thinking skill graphic organizer must, as it is completed, move students through the key steps of a systematic procedure for carrying out the thinking skill or skills required to complete it.

Second, many skill-teaching graphic organizers, such as the Venn diagram or a flowchart, so visually embed the cognitive moves that constitute the thinking procedure that some students may miss this procedure altogether and view their task as simply an information-finding task. Such organizers fail to do much to improve student thinking. Adding numbers to such organizers, such as the classifying organizer in Figure 6.6, or just a label or title as in the Venn diagram, or even a few word prompts as in many of the other examples presented here, helps to make their structure more explicit. Helping students verbalize the connections between the parts of a graphic organizer and the steps in the skill to be practiced using it also helps make the cognitive procedure more visible.

Finally, it may not be possible to devise a clear or appropriately structured graphic organizer for every cognitive procedure of significance. Some thinking procedures may not be explicit enough to allow us to create visuals that walk students through them. In constructing organizers for thinking, we must be careful to ascertain that the structure of any organizer we design reinforces, replicates, or enacts a very explicit, step-by-step procedure for carrying out a specific cognitive operation or combination of operations. To do this requires, first, identifying the cognitive procedure to be executed and then developing a graphic that moves users through each step in the procedure, without providing any detailed directions or commands to the students as to what to do. If an appropriate organizer cannot be devised, other scaffolding techniques should be employed.

These cautions should not be ignored. Not only can poorly designed graphic organizers for scaffolding thinking be dysfunctional to students but also for us. Use of such devices may lull us into believing that our students are improving their thinking when they very well may not be. While these concerns are relevant to any technique that purports to present students with explicit procedures for thinking, they are especially germane for graphic organizers where these procedures are deliberately embedded in visual structures rather than presented verbally. Yet, in spite of these limitations, accurate and well-crafted graphic organizers remain one of the most productive tools for scaffolding student application of newly introduced cognitive operations. They can be an invaluable device for helping students become more effective thinkers.

SCAFFOLDING THINKING: A SUMMARY

The devices described here—procedural checklists, process-structured questions, and graphic organizers—scaffold thinking by providing explicit and readily visible prompts for each of the key steps in a cognitive procedure. They help students carry out whatever operation they represent by moving them through these steps as they respond to prompts to provide the requested information. These devices are most useful to students when used to guide them through those applications of a new cognitive skill during the times they attempt to apply it immediately following their introduction to the skill.

Scaffolding devices can be used in at least three different ways to assist students in improving their execution of any cognitive skill. Students can use them to provide an overview of what they are about to do in using a skill before they actually start to use it. They can refer to them to ensure they "touched all the bases" immediately after they have completed executing an operation. Most importantly, however, students can use them while they are actually executing a skill. When used in this third way, scaffolds steer students through an effective procedure for carrying out the cognitive operation embedded in the scaffold and allow them to concentrate on carrying out the procedure rather than on trying to remember what to do next.

Scaffolding devices feed forward skill-using information and/or provide skill feedback to students in a number of ways. They help students recall what they know about each prompted step in a given procedure and thus get thinking started. They also keep students focused on the procedure to be followed, allow them to keep their place in the procedure, and permit them to go through all the steps without putting undue demands on short-term memory. This frees students to focus almost exclusively on the content of the task at hand and any nonprocedural directions associated with the task. Having such scaffolds available while carrying out a thinking operation allows students to refer to it continuously as they complete the skill-using task and, as they do, to begin to internalize the procedure.[15]

Like all teaching techniques, the use of scaffolding has its limitations, too. Although to be useful, scaffolds for thinking must represent skilled procedures for carrying out a designated thinking operation and be detailed or explicit enough to articulate the key steps in that procedure, there is the danger that they may not do so. Checklists, questions, and graphic organizers can scaffold thinking, but not just any checklist, set of questions, or organizer will do so. We must take special efforts to ensure that any of these devices we design or employ do accurately represent the cognitive procedure they purport to represent and are explicit enough to make visible the key steps in that procedure.

Scaffolding devices, moreover, are not especially useful in supporting thinking unless they tap prior knowledge of the thinking procedure they represent. Unless students are familiar with what is meant by the prompts presented in these devices, they usually do not understand what the prompt means or how to carry out what it is supposed to prompt. This prior knowledge, of course, is a product of a preceding effort to make the procedure visible to the students using some of the techniques described in Part II. The effectiveness of scaffolding in guiding thinking depends on the prior skill-related knowledge of the students. If there is little or none, these devices prove largely ineffective insofar as improving thinking is concerned.

Acknowledging these limitations in no way diminishes the potential value of scaffolding as a technique for guiding student application of newly learned thinking operations. Rather, it underscores the importance of the context in which scaffolds should be used. Ensuring that these devices articulate the skill operation they purport to structure and provide enough detail to assist students in carrying out that operation are conditions essential for their effectiveness. These conditions can be ensured if the guidelines presented here are followed.

Scaffolding, of course, is only one type of guidance and support we can provide students as they practice newly encountered thinking operations. And they are only temporary in nature. Eventually, they must be dropped and replaced by less explicit supports (cues). The following chapter describes techniques useful for providing this type of guidance for improving the quality of student thinking.

ENDNOTES

1. Beau Fly Jones, Minda Rae Amiran, and Michael Katims, "Teaching Cognitive Strategies and Text Structures Within Language Arts Programs," in Judith W. Segal, Susan F. Chipman, and Robert Glaser (Eds.), *Thinking and Learning Skills: Volume I—Relating Instruction to Research* (Hillsdale, NJ: Lawrence Erlbaum, 1985), pp. 259–290; Jay McTighe and Frank T. Lyman, Jr., "Cueing Thinking in the Classroom: The Promise of Theory Embedded Tools," *Educational Leadership* 45 7 (April 1988): 18–24; Michael Pressley and Karen Harris, "What We Really Know about Strategy Instruction," *Educational Leadership* 48 1 (September 1990): 31–34; Barak Rosenshine and Carla Meister, "The Use of Scaffolds for Teaching Higher-Level Cognitive Strategies," *Educational Leadership* 49 7 (April 1992): 26–33.

2. Carl Bereiter and Marlene Scardamalia, "Reconstruction of Cognitive Skills." Paper presented at the annual meeting of the American Research Association, New Orleans, April 1984.

3. David Perkins, *Smart Schools* (New York: The Free Press, 1992).

4. Bereiter and Scardamalia, "Reconstruction of Cognitive Skills," *passim.*

5. Meredith D. Gall, "The Use of Questions in Teaching," *Review of Educational Research* 40 5 (December 1970): 707–721; Norris M. Sanders, *Classroom Questions: What Kinds?* (New York: Harper and Row, 1966); Philip N. Winne, "Experiments Relating Teachers Use of Higher Cognitive Questions to Student Achievement," *Review of Educational Research* 49 1 (Winter 1979): 13–50.

6. J. T. Dillon, "Do Your Questions Promote or Prevent Thinking?" *Learning* 11 3 (October 1982): 56–57; J. T. Dillon, "The Multi-Disciplinary Study of Questioning," *Journal of Educational Psychology,* 74 2 (April 1982): 147–165.

7. Rosenshine and Meister, "The Use of Scaffolds," pp. 26–33; Hilda Taba, S. Levine, and F. F. Elzey, *Thinking in Elementary School Children* (San Francisco: U.S.

Office of Education Department of Health, Education and Welfare Cooperative Research Project No. 1574, San Francisco State College, 1964); William W. Wilen, *Questioning Skills for Teachers* (Washington, DC: National Education Association, 1982).

8. Rosenshine and Meister, "The Use of Scaffolds," pp. 26–33.

9. Jones, Amiran, and Katims, "Teaching Cognitive Strategies," pp. 261–264; McTighe and Lyman, "Cueing Thinking in the Classroom," pp. 18–24; Bonnie B. Armbruster, "Using Graphic Organizers in Social Studies," *Ginn Occasional Papers: Writings in Social Studies* No. 22 (Lexington, MA: Ginn, 1985).

10. Armbruster, "Using Graphic Organizers"; Beau Fly Jones, Jean Pierce, and Barbara Hunter, "Teaching Students to Construct Graphic Representations," *Educational Leadership 46* 4 (December 1988–January 1989): 20–25; McTighe and Lyman, "Cueing Thinking in the Classroom," pp. 18–24.

11. Barry K. Beyer, *Developing a Thinking Skills Program* (Boston: Allyn and Bacon, 1988), pp. 161–165, 332–333.

12. McTighe and Lyman, "Cueing Thinking in the Classroom," p. 23.

13. Joe B. Hurst, Mark Kinney, and Steven J. Weiss, "The Decision-Making Process," *Theory and Research in Social Education 11* 3 (Fall 1983): 17–43; Charles H. Kepner and Benjamin B. Trego, *The New Rational Manager* (Princeton, NJ: Princeton Research Press, 1981).

14. Jones, Amiran, and Katims, "Teaching Cognitive Strategies," p. 262; Jones, Pierce, and Hunter, "Teaching Students to Construct Graphic Representations," pp. 24–25; Rosenshine and Meister, "The Use of Scaffolds," pp. 26–28.

15. McTighe and Lyman, "Cueing Thinking in the Classroom," pp. 18–24.

7

Cueing Student Thinking

A cue is a prompt that reminds one of what to do or say next. Just as in a play or television production where a prompter or cue card may provide key words or phrases to help a performer recall what is to be said or done next, so in teaching thinking a teacher or even instructional materials may provide cues to prompt students to recall what to do next in carrying out a thinking operation. Cueing the application of specific thinking operations assists students in carrying out these operations and moves them toward becoming more independent, autonomous thinkers.[1]

Research and exemplary classroom practice have demonstrated a variety of effective cues for improving student thinking. These include previewing, rehearsal, incomplete activities or examples, cued directions and questions, mnemonics, and symbols. Although much less explicit than the scaffolding techniques described in the preceding chapter, these techniques can trigger student recall of what to do to carry out a cognitive skill and, indirectly, enable students to execute that operation. Cueing serves as an effective technique for supporting and guiding student thinking when scaffolding techniques such as checklists and graphic organizers are no longer necessary but when some guidance is still required to ensure students use the appropriate operation at the appropriate time. This chapter describes and gives examples of these cueing techniques.

PREVIEWING

Helping students preview what they know about what they are about to do is one of the most useful techniques for cueing student thinking. By reflecting on what one is going to talk about or the nature of an activity one is about to engage in, previewing gets one prepared to actually do it. As a technique for cueing thinking, previewing helps students locate in long-term memory what they know about a skilled operation about to be performed and to pull it up into short-term memory ready for use.[2] This helps students develop the mental set, or readiness, for successful execution of that thinking.

Previewing, in effect, engages students in verbalizing what they know about a cognitive skill they are *about* to carry out. Initially, as teachers, we can guide them in providing this information by asking a series of specific questions. As students become accustomed to the approach of previewing, however, they voluntarily provide this information on their own initiative or in response to a single general question such as, What do you (we) know about (the name of the cognitive skill we are about to carry out)? and eventually, to an even more general request such as, Preview this skill for us, please.

Previewing a cognitive skill seeks four kinds of information about that skill: (1) the name or label by which the skill is commonly known; (2) synonyms, if any, for this name; (3) several examples of where or when students may or could have recently employed the skill or where it could be appropriately employed in class or out; and (4) an accurate but tentative working definition of the skill. We can launch a preview simply by naming and then writing on the chalkboard the name commonly used to denote the skill. But students, too, can initiate a preview by volunteering a name for the skill when they recognize that is the operation they are about to carry out and on which the class is to focus. Once the name of the skill is before the class, we can elicit the remaining information needed by asking a series of questions or otherwise prompting appropriate student responses.

Articulating synonyms and examples of a skill serves multiple purposes. Since most cognitive skills are generally known by several names (e.g., classifying is also referred to as sorting, grouping, and categorizing), students need to know and associate all these labels with the same operation. By noting the various labels by which a skill is denoted, we can facilitate student recall and transfer of this skill whenever any of these labels is given. Of course, not all synonyms for a specific skill need to be introduced in the early grades, especially when some of them are rather technical. For example, sorting and grouping serve as useful labels for classifying until the intermediate grades, when classifying and categorizing can be added to them. But obviously, the more synonyms students associate with a specific skill, the easier it will be for them to recognize that skill when it is referred to later by any of its names. Giving instances or examples of the skill helps to jar memory of the skill procedure and proves especially useful when students may not understand or recall the label(s) by which it is being called.

Classroom experience with previewing suggests that in the first several lessons where a new skill is being applied, this skill information should usually be elicited or presented in the order recommended here. Although the definition is clearly the most important information in previewing, holding it until the close of the preview allows students to generate it out of the synonyms and examples already articulated. More precise and accurate—certainly more relevant and workable—definitions usually result. Once the class has established and refined a meaningful, accurate definition after several opportunities to apply the operation, then, of course, the order in which the information is provided is less important. What is important, however, in any effort to preview a cognitive operation is to elicit or give its name or label, synonyms for these, examples of the operation in use, and an accurate definition of the operation.

Figure 7.1 presents an example of one way to assist students in previewing a cognitive skill. It is a transcript of a lesson in which middle school students were about to apply the skill of detecting bias after having been introduced to it just several days earlier. Note that all four of the previously mentioned elements appear in this preview. This teacher encouraged student participation, based on what her students recalled from an earlier introduction to the skill, but, at times, she provided information, too. Previewing is not a time to beat around the bush or embarrass students into struggling to remember what they may or may not know! This preview, because it launches the first lesson on this skill following an introductory lesson on it, took about the maximum time—two to four minutes—that should be devoted to this task.

Efforts to preview this skill in subsequent lessons require even less time as students become more accustomed to executing the skill. After carrying out a new skill several times, students can preview it by mentioning the skill name, one or two synonyms (if any are known), one or two examples where it has been applied previously in class, and an accurate definition. Eventually, the preview may be even shorter—several synonyms to serve as cues, perhaps, and a definition. Since the major purpose of previewing is to cue retrieval and use of what students already know about a skill, less and less attention need be paid to this as students become more experienced in carrying out that skill.

In conducting a preview of a recently introduced thinking procedure, we must guard against letting the preview become the entire lesson itself. Its purpose, remember, is to trigger what students know about what they are going to do, not to relearn or reteach the skill all over again. Not all possible

Figure 7.1 Transcript of a Class Previewing a Thinking Skill

Teacher	*Students*
So, you think we should see if this is biased? Great!	
Okay. Let's analyze it to see if we can detect bias. (Writes *detecting bias* on chalkboard.)	
What is *bias*?	Bias is a prejudiced view of something.
Is that it? Any clearer definition? No? (Pauses, then circles *bias* on the board and writes *prejudiced view?* under it.)	
We'll get a clearer definition in a minute.	
Any words or phrases that mean about the same as detecting bias?	One-sided?
Any others?	
No?	
Okay. Good—a bias is a one-sided view. Very good.	
Now, What do we mean by *detecting* bias? (Underlines *detecting bias* on chalkboard.)	Finding if there is any bias?
Yes. Detecting bias is judging if there is any bias—evaluating to see if we can find any evidence of bias. (Writes *finding evidence of* under *detecting bias.*) Okay?	
Where or when is it useful to try to detect bias—in our class—in school—outside of school?	When teachers or students give their opinions and in reading textbooks, in watching videos, viewing TV news, listening to political speeches, etc.
Why search for bias?	To see if what someone says is really true?

Figure 7.1 *Continued*

Teacher	Students
	Yeah—to find what's real.
Now, what does bias mean? Let's get a clearer definition. A bias is. . . .	Slanted—something that is tipped in favor or against something.
Great! (Writes *a slanted view* after *detecting bias* on chalkboard and erases *prejudiced view.*	
Now that we know what skill we are going to use . . .	
(class continues)	

synonyms need be noted in every preview and two examples of the skill in use will usually be sufficient. On the other hand, a workable definition should always be verbalized. If students fail to volunteer these, we should not hesitate to provide them. Learning more about the skill and elaborating it are what follows a preview, not a function of a preview itself.

Previewing proves useful in guiding and supporting student thinking on at least two different occasions in the course of improving student thinking. It is especially helpful in initiating students' efforts to apply a new or difficult cognitive operation the first half dozen or so times they are called on to engage in it *after* they have been formally introduced to it. For instance, following a lesson in which students have been introduced to detecting bias, we can begin each of the several lessons where we want students to practice detecting bias by having them preview this operation to recall what they can remember about it. We can also engage students in previewing a thinking skill when, after not having done it for some time, they are faced with having to do it but appear vague about it. In both kinds of instances, previewing assists students in tapping their memories to initiate recall of what they already know about this operation, which is the first step in establishing a plan or routine for carrying it out.

By previewing, we can help students search their memories for whatever they know—or believe they know—about a thinking operation *before* they have to apply it. Such a search not only helps them recall what the skill is about but, more importantly, it also puts them in a position to recall quickly any procedure for carrying out that operation they might have already stored in memory. Articulating such a procedure can be accomplished by another technique for cueing thinking—a technique known as rehearsal.

REHEARSAL

Rehearsal cues thinking by engaging students in recalling and articulating a *procedure* for carrying out a cognitive operation they are about to execute. This does not mean actually carrying out a cognitive skill step by step. Instead, rehearsal of a thinking operation or skill consists of verbalizing what one *will* or *could do*, as specifically as possible, to execute it, just before actually executing it. Rehearsal in this sense is analogous to skimming over the main points to be included in an argument we are about to make or a talk we are about to give so as not to omit them when we make our actual presentation. Rehearsing a cognitive operation in this way helps students bring up into short-term memory and establish the cognitive procedure they intend to apply. In essence, it "feeds forward" into the task to be undertaken by providing a readily accessible routine for executing the operation required to carry it out.

Rehearsal of a cognitive operation involves essentially two operations. First, it involves recalling the key procedural elements of a skill—the mental steps and/or the rules and criteria by which the skill is operationalized. Second, it involves presenting these elements—as in stating the steps in the procedure, or producing a flowchart of this procedure, or writing out a checklist of steps. It can be done by students, individually, in pairs or, as a class, as a prelude to actually applying the operation being rehearsed. Whatever approach is used should require a minimum of time, not more than two to three minutes or so, for the main purpose of rehearsal is to assist students in recalling and running quickly through what they are about to do next.

When used to guide and support student application of a newly encountered cognitive operation, rehearsal is best employed in combination with and following previewing. It builds on the knowledge students have recalled about the skill to be performed—its name, synonyms for it, examples of where it has been or could be applied, and a practical, working definition—by prompting recall in some detail of a procedure and/or rules for carrying out that procedure. As students articulate the steps or elements in this procedure, they basically articulate a plan for carrying out the steps they can follow to execute it.

Immediately after concluding a preview of a cognitive skill to be performed, students can be asked how they would carry it out—that is, what steps they might go through or rules they would apply (or both) to execute it. This activity may be done in any of several ways. It might consist of asking students simply to state from memory some key steps in the procedure or some useful heuristics they can follow. It might consist of having them produce from memory a written procedural checklist or process-structured questions to follow in carrying out the planned operation, or of paraphrasing a checklist or questions developed at the conclusion of the preceding lesson on the skill. It might involve explaining some mneumonic that they learned or developed earlier for using the operation. Regardless of which of these techniques is used, any rehearsal should seek as explicit a description of the procedure about to be enacted as is appropriate to the stage where students are in their use of the new skill. Normally, more explicit rehearsals are most desirable in the early stages of skill practice, whereas less detailed rehearsals are sufficient for later stages of practice.

Figure 7.2 provides an example of students rehearsing a cognitive skill just prior to carrying it out. This is a continuation of the transcript presented in Figure 7.1 (a middle school class preparing to engage in applying the skill of analyzing to detect bias). Here, the teacher follows her preview of detecting bias by prompting students to recall and verbalize a procedure they can use to carry out this operation. Since this particular skill, detecting bias, is a critical thinking operation, students are asked in this rehearsal to recall the criteria (sometimes called clues) that can be used to identify a bias as well as one or more procedures for making this judgment. Because the opportunity to apply this skill is the first opportunity to practice it since its introduction two days previously, the rehearsal goes slowly—and perhaps painfully. But after several minutes, a procedure and several criteria are recalled and articulated, and the teacher then moves the class on to carrying out the skill. This segment of the lesson took about three minutes to complete, which is about normal for initial efforts to rehearse a cognitive operation that has only been examined and tried once before, at least in a classroom setting.

Since executing a new cognitive operation should be the focus of any instructional effort to improve student skill in carrying it out, rehearsing it should not take up much time. Normally, it can be accomplished in two to three minutes, at least initially. In subsequent lessons where students are to apply this same skill, rehearsal can be accomplished in less time, as students better understand the skill and access the required procedural information more easily and quickly. What we should seek here is recall of the major steps in one or two procedures for executing the skill to be applied. There is no need for students to verbalize all the nuances about employing the skill. Nor is it appropriate in rehearsing a skill to turn the rehearsal into an attempt to teach students new information about how to carry it out.

Rehearsal, even more so than previewing, obviously requires prior student knowledge of procedures for carrying out the skill being rehearsed as well as some prior experience on their part in actually carrying it out. Students cannot rehearse something of which they are not aware. However, when based on prior experience, rehearsal proves extremely effective in aiding student recall of a skill about to be applied, in developing their readiness to carry it out, and, indeed, even in building student confidence in their abilities to carry it out successfully.

Figure 7.2 Transcript of a Class Rehearsing a Thinking Skill

Teacher	Students
Now that we know what skill we are going to use, what do we do to carry it out? What do we *do* to detect bias?	Look for clues on one-sidedness or slant. Look for bad words.
How can we go about doing that—what can we do first?	Think up what we can look for that will tell us *bias!*
Why?	Why what? I know. Because if we know what to look for, like Sherlock Holmes did, it makes it easier to do this.
Right. Knowing some clues to look for means we don't have to take account of everything we come across. It makes our search more efficient. We won't waste time.	No sweat!
So—what are some clues to bias?	I remember now—bad-sounding words—or all good-sounding ones!
(Writes these under clues on board and puts a box around them.)	. . . giving only one side . . .
Any other clues? (Pauses)	
How about exaggeration—overgeneral-ization—hyperbole? What are those?	Oh, all people are happy.
Why is that an example of exaggeration?	Well, some somewhere probably aren't—Democrats maybe or people in Bosnia or my friend whose father just died.
(Writes exaggeration under clues on chalkboard.)	
Any other clues? No? We'll probably come across more later on.	

Figure 7.2 *Continued*

Teacher	*Students*
So—what can we do next?	Read each sentence to hunt for one clue at a time, just like we did last time. Loaded words are easiest, I think.
	Yes, and then we can go back and read each sentence again hunting for another one.
Another one what?	Clue—like exaggerations.
	Oh, then we can add up the clues we find to see if they show only one side or a real slant.
Okay, that's a good start. Is there another procedure we could follow to detect bias?	
Well, you could just skim the material to see if any thing jumped out at you and said BIAS! Right? There are other clues in addition to those you mentioned.	
Yes, Peter?	Or, we could just decide it is biased—'cause you wouldn't give it to us otherwise. Then we just hunt for how much is all on one side—or if there are two sides or more.
Thanks, Peter! Well, now, let's see, to find bias, we can (pointing at students who contributed the above):	Tell some clues to look for.
How?	Look for them by reading each sentence.
That's one way. Ready? Let's try it—let's evaluate this to see if there is any bias.	See where all clues we find point.

INCOMPLETE ACTIVITIES AND EXAMPLES

At times, giving students a partially completed activity or prompt requiring use of a specific cognitive operation provides all the support that is needed to enable them to carry out the operation with some degree of completeness and success. Again, such a technique, as do all cueing techniques or devices, presupposes some prior knowledge and experience on the part of the student about the procedure to be carried out as well as about the information being used. But students can use a cognitive task already started for them as a basis for recalling how to carry out the remainder of the operation. This technique seems especially useful if a cognitive procedure tends to be the repeated application of one or two rules or criteria rather than a sequential execution of a number of discrete cognitive operations.

Although there is little in the research literature on the use of partly completed examples, classroom teachers have used them for years to guide and support student practice of many cognitive skills. Figure 7.3, for example, presents a partly completed example for the skill of outlining. Here, an incomplete outline is presented partially filled in. Student examination of what has already been done to the outline—the selection of items, their placement in a hierarchy of content relationships with details and examples subsumed under major categories—helps them repeat this process as they select items from above the outline to continue building this same pattern. This device works especially well when students work in pairs to complete it.

Virtually any skill-using activity can be presented to students in the form of an incomplete activity guide, with some of the steps in the procedure already partially carried out. Students can use what has already been completed as prompts, if necessary, for carrying out these same steps again or related steps to complete the task. These partly completed activity guides may take any of a number of forms. Cognitive skill-using activities, such as those depicted in Figure 7.3, suggests one type. Providing partially completed cognitive procedure checklists or questions may also be useful as incomplete prompts. Partially filled-in graphic organizers may also serve this purpose well. In this case, several entries on an organizer provide guidance for how to follow the prompts to carry out the embedded procedure. Incomplete narratives describing the execution of a cognitive skill may also be useful in structuring student execution of the skill procedures being described. In similar fashion, incomplete think aloud descriptions of a skill-using task may also prove to be effective in initiating and structuring the application of a given cognitive operation.

Regardless of the type of device used, the essential feature of this type of cueing technique is the degree of implicitness with which the skill procedure that the students are practicing is embedded in it. Because of this, completion of the activity or example requires students to actively recall

Figure 7.3 An Incomplete Example of the Skill of Outlining

From a Presentation on Teaching Thinking:

~~skills~~	~~teaching techniques~~	~~nature of thinking~~
seeking and giving reasons	classifying	teaching strategies
~~making a topic sentence~~	reflecting on how I did it	conceptualizing
initiating transfer	teaching thinking	modeling
~~detecting bias~~	dispositions	~~metacognition~~
~~processes or strategies~~	~~using precise language~~	~~decision making~~
~~providing guided practice~~	~~rehearsing~~	using graphic organizers
		introduction

Outline of the Presentation

I. Nature of thinking

    A. <u>Processes or strategies</u>

        1. Decision making

        2. _____

    B. Skills

        1. _____

        2. <u>Making a topic sentence</u>

        3. Detecting bias

    C. _____

        1. Using precise language

        2. _____

    D. Metacogniton

II. _____

    A. Teaching techniques

        1. _____

        2. _____

        3. Rehearsing

        4. _____

    B. _____

        1. _____

        2. Providing guided practice

        3. _____

what they already know about how to carry it out. Although responding to cueing techniques such as this one involves considerable student mental effort, they provide helpful support for student thinking.

CUED DIRECTIONS AND QUESTIONS

Directions and questions can also be employed to cue the kind of thinking required to follow or answer them. This can be done by using the name or label of the cognitive operation to be performed in the directions or questions that launch the activity. Instead of asking, "What do you think caused the water to rise in this experiment?" we can cue the kind of thinking we really want the students to engage in by saying, "What do you *hypothesize* caused the water to rise in this experiment?" or "Make a *hypothesis* that explains why the water rose in this experiment." Instead of asking, "What do these three facts tell you about revolutions?" a teacher who seeks to cue the thinking operation required ought to ask, "What *conclusion* can you draw about revolutions based on these three facts?" Instead of saying, "Tell me this same thing in your own words," we ought to say, "*Translate* this for me." Using the word or phrase that specifically denotes the thinking operation to be performed helps students recall what they need to do to answer the question. The skill name, however, must already be associated by the students with that operation, and the procedure for executing it must have already been stored in their memories in a structured way. The name of the skill serves to cue both recall and, through recall, an organized execution of a previously learned skill.[3]

A cognitive skill cue can be any form of the word commonly used to denote that skill, or synonyms for it, or even words commonly associated with it. For example, one can cue predicting by saying:

Predict what the weather will be like tomorrow.

or

What do you *predict* tomorrow's weather will be like?

or

Make a *prediction* about tomorrow's weather.

One can cue the procedure for evaluating to detect bias in similar ways:

Is this document *biased?*

or

Is there any evidence of *bias* in this?

> or

What, if any, *bias* can you detect in this source?

Whether the skill name appears as a verb or a noun does not seem to matter. In each case, it is clear to the listener that a response calls for a very specific cognitive operation, as long as the word used accurately denotes that operation.

Sometimes, a cognitive operation is commonly denoted by more than one name or label. Unless students learn all the names by which a given operation is commonly known, they are not likely to realize that all these names denote the same cognitive operation. This happens in the case of the skill of classifying, as noted earlier, and predicting (which is also commonly referred to as forecasting, foretelling, and even hypothesizing). In order for these words for predicting to prompt or cue that cognitive operation in the future, they should be learned by students early on as synonyms for predicting and used continuously by teacher and students as alternative labels for this operation. This same principle applies to all thinking operations that are commonly denoted by more than one name or label.

Often, words other than the name of a cognitive operation are so closely associated with a particular operation that they, too, can serve as cues for the application of that skill. In comparing, for instance, students look for similarities and differences or what is alike and what differs. These terms can prompt use of comparing just as effectively as can the use of the skill name. "Tell how these items are alike and how they differ" is as effective a cue to comparing as "Compare these items," but only when teachers help students deliberately make this association early on in practicing this skill. Not all cognitive operations are known by a variety of synonyms or labels or employ special catchwords in their execution, but for those that do, linking these to the skill operation early on builds a network of multiple cues that sharply enhances their access.

Cued questions and directions prove helpful to students in recalling an organized procedure for responding when they have already learned such a procedure attached to the cue used. But such questions or directions often fail to provide the support in carrying out the procedure that many students need, even if after they have been practicing the operation for some time assisted by procedural checklists or graphic organizers. A more structured kind of cueing may thus be most helpful in bridging the gap between scaffolding and single cues.

Educator Allan O. Kownslar has suggested a type of cued question that fills this need.[4] This type of cued question actually consists of three questions, as is illustrated by these four examples:

1. What is *bias*? What, if any, *bias* can you detect in (the given material)? What evidence or clues prove your response to the preceding question is correct?
2. What is *classifying*? *Classify* the given information in order to identify the major features of the nation shown. Then explain how you made the *groupings* you made.
3. What is meant by *analyzing*? *Analyze* the following paragraph to identify its major *parts* and how they *relate to each other*. Then explain why your *analysis* is valid.
4. What is *decision making*? *Decide* which book you are going to report on next month. Tell us, in as much detail as you can, exactly what you did to arrive at your *decision*.

Questions or directions structured in this fashion incorporate more cues (*italicized* in these examples) than single-cued questions. In this format, (1) they ask the student to recall what he or she knows about the operation to be performed, then (2) to execute the operation based on this knowledge, and finally (3) to articulate the reasons for or the procedure used to arrive at the response given to the second question in the set. Cues are embedded in at least two of the three questions or statements in each cluster.

By asking first for a definition, these question clusters or sets prompt recall of what is already known about the operation to be performed and help get students ready to carry it out. After executing the skill, the student is asked to verbalize the procedure, criteria or evidence used in order to generate feedback for assessing the quality of their execution of the cued operation. Such multiple-cue questions or directions thus provide more procedural prompting than do questions or directions containing only a single cue. Of course, they still provide much less scaffolding than techniques such as checklists, process-structured questions, or graphic organizers.

Figure 7.4 presents a list of cued cluster questions and directions for prompting critical thinking in any of a variety of contexts. It is adapted from Kownslar's original list. These questions can be used to trigger most of the major cognitive operations that constitute critical thinking as described by Ennis, Lipman, Paul, and other experts in this field.[5] Although prepared for secondary-level students, they can be easily rewritten for use at the intermediate level, as well.

Once students have practiced explicit procedures for carrying out the operation triggered by one of these question sets, that question set can be used to cue application of that operation to any type of written text, from newspaper accounts to original documents and textbooks, as well as to speeches, lectures, video presentations, or other types of presentations. If all students in a class possessed a copy of this list in their notebooks or on a laminated card, teachers could assign learning activities by number or students could select from this list those question sets appropriate to their

Figure 7.4 Cued Questions for Critical Thinking

1. What is (a) a verifiable fact, (b) a reasoned opinion, and (c) a value claim? What verifiable facts can you find in this information or source? What reasoned opinions are presented here? What value claims? How can you tell what each is?

2. What is the main difference between relevant and irrelevant information, claims, or reasons? What claims, reasons, or statements did you find in this material relevant to the main topic of your inquiry (or to the main topic of the material)? Irrelevant to the main topic? How did you tell whether each was relevant or irrelevant?

3. What is *bias?* What, if any, bias did you detect in this information or source(s)? How did you arrive at this evaluation?

4. What is an *unstated assumption?* What unstated assumptions are there in this material? What did you do, specifically, to find these unstated assumptions?

5. What is meant by *ambiguous* and *equivocal?* What, if any, ambiguous or equivocal claims are made in this material? What are the reasons for your response?

6. What is a *credible source?* What criteria must a source meet to be considered credible? How credible is the source of this material? What did you do to determine its credibility?

7. What is a *point of view?* What is the point of view presented in these material? How do you know that this really is the point of view of this material?

8. What is the main difference between a warranted and an unwarranted claim? What, if any, warranted claims are presented in this material? What unwarranted claims are presented? How did you tell if these claims are warranted or unwarranted?

9. What makes a *strong* argument strong? How strong is the argument made in this material? What did you do to arrive at this judgment?

10. What is meant by *accuracy?* How accurate is the given information? What did you do to determine what is accurate or inaccurate?

Adapted from Allan O. Kownslar, "What's Worth Having Students Think Critically About?" *Social Education* 49 4 (April 1985): 305. Adapted by permission of the author.

own purposes when thinking critically about some text or other form of communication.

It is important to remember that verbal cues are effective only when students already know fairly well how to carry out that thinking and when they perceive what is intended as the cue. Unless students have learned earlier that a word denotes a specific cognitive procedure, they are not likely to respond to that word by retrieving and using that procedure. So, what we intend to use as cues must be taught and learned in the early stages of learning a cognitive operation for them to have any beneficial effect.

There are several ways to accomplish this. In introducing a new or complex cognitive operation to students, we should ensure that students hear and see and thereafter use interchangeably the terms commonly used to denote that operation. In subsequent lessons—both at the beginning and the conclusion of each—these synonyms should be previewed and used, and new ones added as appropriate. By continuously hearing, seeing, and appropriately using the various synonyms for the cognitive operations being developed, students are more likely to link these to specific operations and to perceive them as cues in the future. Using the language of thinking, as pointed out in Part I, contributes significantly to enhancing student abilities to engage in effective thinking.

Labeling is another way to establish a link between potential skill cues and the mental operation they are intended to prompt. Labeling is similar to cueing, but it normally occurs *after* a thinking act has occurred. For example, when a student has reported, "It is probably going to rain tomorrow," the teacher might respond with, "That's an interesting *prediction* (and might even go on to ask, "What did you do to come up with that *prediction*?"). Use of the skill label helps students associate what they just did mentally with that name; it also helps them store what they did under that label in memory. Use of this label later acts as a cue by triggering recall of what is stored in memory under that label—the skill procedure—and allowing the student to employ that procedure to carry out the operation that was cued. Cueing is a technique to employ after students know something about how to carry out a new cognitive operation. However, foundation needs to be established in the initial stages of learning each cognitive operation and thereafter.

Cued questions and directions, then, perform useful functions in facilitating student thinking. Cueing not only seeks to trigger what a student is to do by way of response but, depending on how students have organized the procedural knowledge stored under the cue, it may also serve as a prompt as to how to do it. Not all phrases or words intended as cues turn out to be cues for some students, but if they have been linked to the appropriate cognitive operation early on, they do. Carefully crafted cued questions and directions contain within themselves hints for guiding and supporting student use of specific thinking skills.

MNEMONICS

Mnemonics can also be used to cue cognitive skills. A mnemonic is a device—such as a rhyme, saying, set of initials, or word—that helps us store things in and recall things from memory. How many of us still repeat to ourselves the rhyme "Thirty days hath September . . . " when trying to remember the number of days in a given month? Those of us who teach math often tell our students to **P**lease **E**xcuse **M**y **D**ear **A**unt **S**ally as a way of recalling the order of the basic math operations of parentheses, exponents, multiply, divide, add, and subtract. Social studies teachers among us often urge students to use HOMES as a way of recalling the names of the Great Lakes. Those of us who teach science often have students use **M**y **V**ery **E**ducated **M**other **J**ust **S**erved **U**s **N**ine **P**ickles as a device for remembering the planets in order outward from the sun. Such techniques prove extremely useful as aids to remembering information. They can be just as useful in remembering the steps or procedural components of thinking skills, as well.

One of the most popular and widely recognized mnemonics associated with thinking skills is Edward deBono's PMI. This mnemonic stands for Plus, Minus, Interesting. Whenever we hear a new or strange idea, deBono claims, we should PMI it before embracing or rejecting it.[6] We should determine its *good* (plus) features or implications, its *bad* ones (minuses), and finally those things about it that are simply *interesting*. Applying PMI in various situations prevents individuals from jumping to conclusions and also permits them to think their way all around an idea or statement rather than seeing only one part of it.

Useful one-word mnemonics, called acronyms, can be derived from the initial letters of the steps in many cognitive procedures. When students associate these words with the steps of an operation, they are especially useful as aids to structuring as well as remembering how to carry out that operation. Figure 7.5 presents some acronyms for selected thinking operations devised by teachers in the course of helping their students master these operations. Students, too, can generate acronyms and, not surprisingly, research indicates that student-devised mnemonics prove more helpful as memory aids than do those suggested by others.[7]

Classroom research and experimentation indicate that students of all ages and abilities can learn, use, and even create mnemonics as aids to their thinking.[8] Where the mnemonic identifies a recognized sequence of essential steps in a skill-using procedure, it helps students in the early stages of learning that procedure store the procedure in memory in a structured way, thus facilitating its later recall. And when used then as cues to prompt recall, these mnemonics not only aid retrieval of those steps but also help students recall them in a sequence organized for effective use.

To be most useful, a thinking skill mnemonic should itself be easy to remember and should trigger with minimum effort a specific skill-using procedure. Mnemonics that best meet these criteria are those that are short, preferably a single word or set of initials. Where possible, they should bear a direct and easily associated relationship to the cognitive procedure they seek to prompt, as DECIDE does to a skilled procedure for decision

Figure 7.5 Thinking Skill Acronyms

Classifying	*Analyzing*
Gather data	**A**gree on purpose
Read it	**P**ick clues to look for
One and another like it	**A**nalyze piece by piece
Use a label for both	**R**elate clues to each other
Place others here	**T**ell what you find
Subdivide or combine	

Synthesis	*Summarizing*
Get data	**S**kim
Arrange in groups	**H**ighlight main ideas
Tell the label of each	**O**mit details/examples
Hook groups together	**R**emove repetition
Establish connections between groups	**T**ell the summary
Report the connections	

Sequencing	*Decision Making*
Scan	**D**efine goal
Compare to each other	**E**numerate alternatives
Arrange in ascending/descending	**C**onsequences
order	**I**n order, rank
Tell sequence	**D**ecide
	Execute

I am indebted to the many teachers with whom I have worked over the years for sharing their thinking mnemonics, including Mary Lane, Marilyn Pugh, and Anne Thornett.

making. Each key letter should easily elaborate into a meaningful step in the skill procedure. The steps in the skill should be expressed in as few words as possible, one or two words being preferable to lengthy phrases. Thinking skill mnemonics should be meaningful or catchy and elaborate readily into an easily understood skill procedure. Not all words or phrases or combinations of initials meet these criteria.

Thinking mnemonics, like other cueing techniques and devices, are not substitutes for a deep understanding of how to carry out a thinking operation. However, they are an important aid en route to automatizing that operation and making it a permanent part of one's cognitive tool chest. Over-reliance on a mnemonic, unchanged throughout all phases of skill learning, may turn out to be dysfunctional as students many times modify initial procedures by adding steps and heuristics and sometimes compressing several steps into a broader operation that includes all of them. Thus, mnemonics should change—or be discarded—as students become experienced and more proficient in carrying out a skill.

SYMBOLS

Not all cues need be verbal. Symbols may also serve to prompt different kinds of thinking. Maryland educator Frank T. Lyman and his colleagues have developed a number of such symbols for this purpose (see Figure 7.6). After students have learned what these symbols represent, the symbols can prompt use of the various cognitive operations.

Lyman recommends the use of thinking symbols as part of a matrix for generating different kinds of questions about content. In the matrix, the symbols and their meanings are placed on the left, and various topics (e.g., elements of a novel, story, historical period, event, etc.) are entered across the top. Where a symbol intersects with a topic, that symbol can then be used to cue student invention of a question on that topic that calls for the kind of thinking represented by the symbol. For example, where the symbol for *differences* intersects the topic *triangles*, students might generate a question such as, "In what ways does an isosceles triangle differ from an obtuse triangle?" According to Lyman, these "Think Trix" can also be used to help students generate responses to written questions or to label examples of oral or written discourse. When these symbols are mounted on a classroom wall, converted to a laminated desktop card for use by each student, or placed on a large cue card propped up on the teacher's desk, they are readily accessible to everyone in a class for these purposes.

Using symbols to prompt thinking has a variety of other useful classroom uses. They can be incorporated into the margins of textbooks or activity books, worksheets, computer programs, games, and simulations to trigger the use of specific thinking skills that students have learned to associate with them. They can be enlarged and posted on a bulletin board or hung as mobiles from classroom light fixtures so we or our students can point to them to cue the particular cognitive operations called for by a particular task or question.

Figure 7.7 presents additional symbols that might be added to those developed by Lyman for use as described here. We and our students might also generate still others. Since such symbols are not language bound, they may prove to be especially useful for prompting different kinds of thinking for English-as-a-second-language students or for students with language disorders. Like any of the cues or prompts presented in this chapter, though, in order for them to actually cue a particular type of thinking, students must, in the early stages of practicing or learning those operations, have identified these with the type of cognitive operation they are intended to cue.

Figure 7.6 Think Trix Symbols for Cueing Thinking

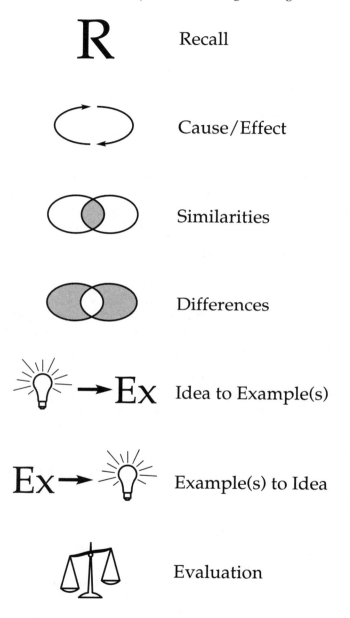

R   Recall

           Cause/Effect

           Similarities

           Differences

           Idea to Example(s)

           Example(s) to Idea

           Evaluation

Source: Frank T. Lyman, Jr. Reprinted by permission (*See also:* Frank T. Lyman, Jr., "The Think Trix: A Classroom Tool for Thinking in Response to Reading," in Joan Develin Coley (Ed.), *Reading: Issues and Practices.* Western Maryland College; Yearbook of The Maryland Reading Association Council, 1987, pp. 15–18.)

Figure 7.7 More Symbols for Cueing Thinking

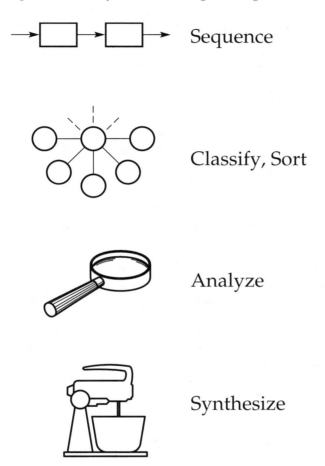

Sequence

Classify, Sort

Analyze

Synthesize

CUEING STUDENT THINKING: A SUMMARY

Cueing student thinking is one way of providing the guidance and support students find helpful in improving the quality of their thinking. Although many techniques or devices may exist for providing such assistance, use of previewing, rehearsal, incomplete examples, cued questions and directions, symbols, and mnemonics prove to be the most widely used and helpful to students. Any of these devices or techniques can be employed, with appropriate modifications, for guiding the execution of any cognitive operation by students of any ability, in any grade level.

Cueing proves useful in supporting student thinking primarily because it serves to trigger thinking. It aids students in retrieving from memory what they know about the operation cued. It also allows skill-using procedures, if originally stored in memory in a structured way, to be retrieved and used in carrying out the operation. Cueing, then, is a powerful aid to guiding as well as initiating student thinking. While it requires a minimum of intervention on our part, it requires considerable student knowledge of the thinking operation being cued. Use of this technique is a valuable bridge between scaffolding during the early stages of skill practice and final student-directed and autonomous skill use.

The major limitation of the cueing techniques described here—except for previewing when it incorporates very explicit scaffolding techniques such as checklists—is that students must have some prior knowledge of the skill to be cued. What this means for efforts to improve student thinking is that what we plan to eventually use as a cue should be provided to students early in the process of improving their execution of a new or difficult procedure. From the time students are first introduced to a cognitive operation—through modeling, metacognitive reflection, and similar techniques—they should be made familiar with common synonyms for the operation being introduced as well as its common technical label. If this practice is repeated in the early stages of learning and practicing a thinking operation, then any of these words can serve to cue the execution of that skill later on. Use of cueing techniques is also important in helping students to transfer a skill to settings in which they have not heretofore used it. This applies also to any symbol or mnemonic intended to serve later as a cue or prompt to using a specific skill. These, too, must be introduced to the students in early encounters with learning how to carry out the skill so they will later associate it with the procedure it is intended to trigger. Cues can only cue what has already been stored in memory that is associated with that cue!

GUIDING AND SUPPORTING STUDENT THINKING: A SUMMARY

Scaffolding and cueing thinking build on what students already know or have learned about a thinking operation by assisting them to recall and apply an explicit procedure for carrying out that operation. To scaffold thinking, we can employ such techniques as procedural checklists, process-structured questions and directions, and graphic organizers. To cue thinking, we can engage students in responding to previewing, rehearsal, completing incomplete skill-using activities or examples, cued questions and directions, visual symbols, and mnemonics. All these techniques provide the kinds of guidance and support that enable students to recall newly encountered or difficult thinking operations as they practice and become increasingly proficient in applying them.

Scaffolding and Cueing Compared.   The scaffolding and cueing techniques and devices presented share a number of features. All prompt recall of a cognitive procedure and, to some degree, of steps by which that procedure can be carried out and thus guide its execution. Yet, cueing and scaffolding differ considerably, too. Cueing assists in retrieving from memory what one already knows about whatever is related to the cue. Scaffolding assists by providing explicit, observable structures and prompts that, in effect, "walk" students through the steps of a cognitive procedure. Cueing relies on memory to provide the procedure. A scaffolding device makes an actual procedure visible and relatively explicit while it is being applied, thus allowing the student to refer to it for guidance as to what to do while applying the procedure[9]

In sum, scaffolding and cueing techniques and devices differ considerably in the degree of explicitness with which they guide and support student thinking. And therein is the crucial distinction between the two. Scaffolds place less demand on memory than do cues. Cues rely heavily on how the cued information is originally stored and structured in student memory. Scaffolds provide structure external to the students; cues tap information students are expected already to possess. It is possible to use scaffolding devices to steer students through the execution of a cognitive operation even though they may lack an understanding of what they are doing or why. Responding effectively to a cognitive cue, however, requires such understanding. Scaffolds are useful for what they help students *do.* Cues are useful for what they help students *remember* to do.

From Scaffolding to Cueing to Doing.   Because of the way they prompt and structure thinking, the techniques and devices best used to scaffold and cue thinking are most appropriately employed at different stages of the skill-learning process. Scaffolding, because of the degree to which it makes thinking visible and explicit, is most appropriately used in the early stages of practice when students are unfamiliar with the steps in a cognitive procedure and uncertain of exactly how to carry them out. Cueing, on the other hand, because it provides less detailed or explicit prompts to thinking, is most appropriately used in the later stages of skill learning when students are more familiar with the effective skill-using procedure and need only a general prompt to initiate its recall and execution.

In assisting students to improve their skill at executing a new thinking procedure, we can first employ a scaffolding technique, such as a procedural checklist, then gradually replace it with successively less explicitly structured techniques such as a graphic organizer, cued directions and questions, and, finally, a mnemonic. Specialists refer to this as *fading*—reducing the degree of support provided to assist students in executing a skill. Figure 7.8 arranges the scaffolding and cueing techniques presented in Chapters 6 and

Figure 7.8 Scaffolding and Cueing Techniques Arranged by Degree of Support Provided

SCAFFOLDING ... TO ... CUEING ... TO ... DOING

Procedural Checklists

or

Process-Structured Questions

Graphic Organizers

Previewing

Rehearsal

Incomplete Examples/Activities

Cued Directions/Questions

Mnemonics

Symbols

MOST	Support	LEAST
EXPLICIT	Provided	EXPLICIT

7 in a sequence that moves from the most explicit scaffolds to the least explicit cues.

We can use scaffolding and cueing techniques like those described here to support and guide student application of virtually any thinking operations or skills in any subject. All the scaffolding and cueing techniques presented in Part III support student efforts to learn *how to carry out* a thinking skill because they prompt, with varying degrees of explicitness, the key steps in a procedure for executing it. By becoming conscious of and eventually internalizing these procedures through scaffolded, cued, and guided practice and attention to executing them, students improve their proficiency in thinking. The chapters that follow in Part IV explain and demonstrate how to integrate these techniques with each other and with subject-matter instruction to provide the instruction and practice that helps students improve their thinking while simultaneously using it to achieve subject-matter learning goals.

ENDNOTES

1. Beau Fly Jones, Minda Rae Amiran, and Michael Katkins, "Teaching Cognitive Strategies and Text Structures Within Language Arts Programs," in Judith W. Segal, Susan F. Chipman, and Robert Glaser, (Eds.), *Thinking and Learning: Volume I—Relating Instruction to Research* (Hillsdale, NJ: Lawrence Erlbaum, 1985), pp. 261–262; Jay McTighe and Frank T. Lyman, Jr., "Cueing Thinking in the Classroom: The Promise of Theory Embedded Tools," *Educational Leadership 45* 7 (April 1988): 18–24; Barak Rosenshine and Carla Meister, "The Use of Scaffolds for Teaching Higher-Level Cognitive Strategies," *Educational Leadership 49* 7 (April 1992): pp. 26–33.

2. John R. Anderson, *The Architecture of Cognition* (Cambridge, MA: Harvard University Press, 1983), pp. 171–260.

3. David R. Olson and Janet W. Astington, "Talking about Text: How Literacy Contributes to Thought," *Journal of Pragmatics 14* (1990): 705–721.

4. Allan O. Kownslar, "What's Worth Having Students Think Critically About?" *Social Education 49* 4 (April 1985): 304–307.

5. Robert Ennis, "A Concept of Critical Thinking," *Review of Educational Research 32* 1 (Winter 1962): 81–111; Matthew Lipman, "Critical Thinking: What Can It Be?" *Educational Leadership 46* 1 (September 1988): 38–43; Richard W. Paul, *Critical Thinking: What Every Person Needs to Survive in a Rapidly Changing World* (2nd ed., rev.) (Rohnert Park, CA: The Center for Critical Thinking and Moral Critique, 1992).

6. Edward deBono, "The Direct Teaching of Thinking as a Skill," *Phi Delta Kappan 64* 10 (June 1983): 703–708.

7. Francis S. Bellezza, "Mnemonic Devices: Classification, Characteristics and Criteria," *Review of Educational Research 51* 2 (Summer 1981): 247–275.

8. *Ibid.*

9. Rosenshine and Meister, "The Use of Scaffolds," p. 29.

PART **IV**

INTEGRATING INSTRUCTION IN THINKING AND SUBJECT MATTER

Where we direct our efforts to improve student thinking—in which classrooms or course(s)—and how we organize our teaching to do it are as important as the techniques we employ. The preceding pages of this book have dealt primarily with the latter, but we must also attend to the former. Just where in our crowded classes, courses, and curricula can we focus our major efforts on improving the quality of our students' thinking? Where *should* we? How can we organize our teaching to ensure that these efforts will be successful?

Answering these questions requires us to confront three related but distinct issues. First, should our major efforts to improve thinking be institutionalized as special courses on thinking or somehow combined with subject-matter teaching in regularly offered academic courses? Second, how should we organize the various techniques available for improving student thinking to bring about the improvement we seek? And third, if we wish truly to integrate instruction in thinking with instruction in subject matter, then where and how should we provide the kind of instruction that genuinely improves student thinking while continuing simultaneously to provide instruction in subject matter? The chapters in Part IV address these issues.

WHERE TO PROVIDE INSTRUCTION IN THINKING

Where to provide instruction designed to improve the quality of student thinking, in one sense, is a grade-level question. At which grade level(s) should we provide such instruction? The answer—agreed upon by virtually all experts—is at *all* grades, from preschool onward.

Thinking develops gradually as students have repeated experiences to engage in it. But, as explained in more detail in Chapter 9, not everyone develops similar degrees of proficiency in all kinds of thinking at the same rate. Nor do all people achieve the potential levels of proficiency of which they are capable, on their own, without a broad range of repeated experiences, considerable mediation, and continuing instruction in doing it. How do we, as teachers, ensure that students engage in these experiences and receive appropriate mediation and instruction? Specialists agree that systematic instruction in different types of thinking and in the important and complex operations of which thinking consists should begin in the earliest years of formal schooling—in preschool and kindergarten years, if possible—and continue through secondary school and even college. Although the types of mediation and instruction most appropriate to improving thinking obviously differ for different students in different grade levels, for best results such instruction should be continuous and closely articulated across all grade levels. The recommendations and suggestions presented in these pages assume the acceptance and implementation of this approach.

Where to provide instruction, in another sense, is a class, course, and subject-matter question. In what kinds of classes, courses, or subjects is systematic instruction in thinking likely to be most productive in improving the quality of student thinking?

In general, the most commonly perceived options for resolving this issue are either "content-free" skill(s) courses or subject-matter courses. For secondary schools, this choice becomes one of either specially designed skills courses or academic subject-matter courses already being offered. For elementary schools, this becomes a choice between specially designed content-free skills units, pull-out skills classes, or skill-learning lessons mixed into the various subject matters already taught in regular elementary grade classrooms. However, at both levels there is another option, too—some combination of special, content-free skill course(s) or units *and* existing subject-matter courses or units. It may even be possible to create an additional option by combining several of these options!

Once the initial choice is made as to where to focus concerted systematic efforts to improve student thinking—probably in subject-matter courses or subject-matter segments of elementary school classes, as will soon be evident from what follows here—a new issue and more options arise. The issue then becomes *which* subjects or subject-matter courses: primary-grade subjects and intermediate/secondary courses, academic subject-matter courses only, only electives, only those required of all students, or some combination of all these? Related to this issue is another: *Where,* in the courses finally selected, do we concentrate or distribute our thinking instruction? Do we present skill instruction in these courses in introductory or periodic units separate from or preparatory to subject-matter study, or do we integrate this instruction into and distribute it rather regularly throughout subject-matter study? There are, indeed, a number of significant issues, each with a range of options, embedded in the overall question of where to teach thinking! Pointing this out is not intended to complexify the problem nor to deter us from dealing with these issues. Rather, it seeks only to alert us to the dimensions and implications of this overall issue. *Where,* indeed, should we concentrate our instructional efforts to improve student thinking? Why? Chapter 8 addresses these questions.

ORGANIZING INSTRUCTION TO IMPROVE THINKING

The subject matter about which students think as they work to improve the quality of their thinking clearly contributes significantly to achieving this goal. But so, too, do the techniques and approaches employed to facilitate and produce such improvement. The preceding parts of this book have described a variety of techniques useful for this purpose and explained how to carry them out. However, improving student thinking involves more than simply employing one or more of these whenever it seems necessary to do so. These techniques produce improved thinking only when they are organized in ways that move students from unskilled execution of a thinking operation to its skillful, independent execution.

Developing proficiency in any kind of thinking requires becoming conscious of, understanding, and being able to apply automatically at one's own direction, with skill and in a variety of contexts, procedures by which that thinking can be effectively carried out. Improving the quality of student thinking is thus not a matter of employing the skill-teaching techniques described here as "one-shot" crutches or remedial devices. Rather, it is a matter of providing the continuous, systematic instruction, direction, guidance, and support that assists students in becoming increasingly self-directed and expert in how they execute their thinking. Each of the techniques described in these pages can contribute toward providing this kind of instruction, but it is only when we combine and employ them in purposeful sequences that they contribute to achieving this goal.

A variety of such strategic combinations of skill-teaching techniques have been devised for classroom use; others can be readily envisioned. But these strategies are not simply random combinations of arbitrarily selected techniques. The success of any single skill-teaching technique in improving thinking frequently rests on what students learn as a result of the prior use of other teaching techniques. For example, rehearsing how to execute a thinking skill prior to applying it is an extremely effective technique for moving students toward effective self-directed thinking, but only when students already understand the skill being rehearsed well enough to articulate its essential rules and procedural components. Scaffolding devices do not lead to improved thinking unless students are already aware of what they need to do mentally to complete or work their ways through them. Producing and employing appropriate strategic combinations of the teaching techniques described here is as essential to improving student thinking as is understanding how these can be skillfully applied. Chapter 9 describes some of the most effective combinations of selected techniques and presents guidelines for producing them.

INTEGRATING THINKING INTO SUBJECT MATTER

Having clarified where in our curricula to concentrate our efforts to improve the quality of student thinking and how best to combine skill-teaching techniques to achieve this goal, a crucial issue still remains: How do we actually incorporate the use of these techniques with subject-matter teaching and learning activities and techniques in a way that facilitates improvement in both thinking and subject-matter learning to the highest degree possible? Where and how in any subject-matter course or unit—like science, for example—will instruction in any particular type of thinking or thinking operation be introduced, practiced, generalized to transfer, and applied autonomously to advance both improved thinking and significant subject-matter learning? In a way, this almost takes us back to the original issue, because the basic options here are in content-free units within subject-matter courses or throughout subject-matter study in lessons where the specific thinking operation is being employed by students to accomplish the subject-matter learning task at hand, or some combination of both.

Another way to look at this issue is to cast it as a series of questions: Do we teach thinking in the service of improving subject-matter learning with the latter as our major goal? Or, do we teach subject matter in the service of improving thinking as our major goal? Or, do we seek *both* goals? In other words, do we immerse students in subject matter so they simply have to think better? Or, do we infuse instruction in thinking into subject matter so students can improve their thinking and improve their subject-matter learning at the same time? Or, do we in some way combine or integrate these approaches into yet a third approach? Chapter 10 provides suggestions for dealing with and resolving these concerns.

Dealing with all these issues and answering the questions raised here are crucial to the success of any effective effort to improve student thinking, for *where* we focus and *how we organize* these efforts have considerable impact on the results we can reasonably expect to achieve. This issue is a complex combination of several related issues, each with a number of options. Once a choice is made to resolve one of these issues, another related issue confronts us with new options to consider. Integrating thinking into school curricula is a much more complicated issue than may first appear. Resolving it requires us to deal thoughtfully with both *where* and *how*. The following chapters address these issues and questions.

8

The Thinking/
Subject-Matter
Connection

At least two places in our curricula have been traditionally suggested—and, on occasion, have served—as appropriate settings for systematic instructional efforts to improve student thinking. One is separate, stand-alone courses devoted exclusively to the study and practice of selected types of thinking and thinking skills. The other is existing subject-matter courses. In the former, cognitive skills are studied as an end in themselves and are the primary focus of teaching and learning. In the latter, cognitive operations are used for achieving subject-matter learning objectives and receive attention usually in the course of achieving these subject-matter objectives. In thinking skills courses, thinking skills are commonly introduced and practiced as discrete entities using fragmented, decontextualized, and often diverse subjects or topics selected from a variety of subject matters and/or real-life experience or both. In subject-matter courses where thinking is also "taught," thinking skills receive varying degrees of attention in the course of developing subject-matter learning and understanding, and occasionally as separate units that initiate a course. Numerous examples of both approaches probably exist in practice today. However, educators have long debated which of these is *more* productive in improving the quality of student thinking and learning.

This debate is more complicated than might at first be imagined, for it actually involves consideration of two major issues. The first to be confronted is in what kind(s) of course(s) to situate systematic efforts to improve student thinking. Once this has been resolved, another issue arises: Where in the course(s) selected do we provide the kind of instruction in thinking we wish to employ? This chapter deals with both of these questions. On the one hand, considering the arguments for the various options available for answering these questions allows us to examine or reexamine what we now do to identify perhaps a potentially better option and reasons for adopting it. On the other hand, considering these arguments may instead allow us to develop a clear rationale for the approach we already employ or choose to adopt—a rationale that can provide clear guidance for employing the approaches to teaching thinking we deem most appropriate to the needs of our students.

SEPARATE THINKING SKILLS COURSES OR SUBJECT-MATTER COURSES?

Providing instruction in thinking and thinking skills in separate skills courses or doing so in subject-matter courses both have their proponents and critics, their strengths as well as their limitations. In judging their value, however, each option must be judged in terms of the extent to which employing it is most likely to lead to the kind and degree of *improvement in thinking* sought. Only if the quality of student thinking is improved as much as possible will the quality of student subject-matter learning be improved. Just which approach is more likely to accomplish this goal?

Separate Thinking Courses

Consider, first, the case for concentrating efforts to improve student thinking in discrete courses whose exclusive *subject* is thinking. This approach reflects a belief in the need to attend consciously and explicitly to the kinds of thinking being "learned" or improved, unencumbered by concerns for anything else, including subject matter or content. Improving complex thinking especially requires considerable explicit attention initially to the cognitive, mental procedures and related conditional and declarative knowledge being employed when carrying out such thinking as well as attention to considerable practice of these procedures.[1]

Subject matter of a high degree of intrinsic interest or to which there is a high degree of emotive attachment, subject matter that is strange or unfamiliar or only superficially understood, and subject matter that is highly abstract or complex *do* interfere with students' attending to *how* they think about that subject matter.[2] In any competition with subject matter and process, students seem to focus on subject matter, primarily because it is more tangible and easier to articulate than are the hidden, often obscure mental processes in which they are engaging. Consequently, many specialists assert that major efforts to improve thinking must be carried on in special thinking courses where attention can be given *exclusively* to the thinking that is going on.[3]

Clearly, the major advantage of a separate thinking skills course is the opportunity it provides for continued, explicit attention to the procedures by which the cognitive operations to be improved are executed, without concern for the quality of the substantive learning generated by use of these thinking operations. In such courses, cognitive operations are the *prime* (usually the *only*), subject of study. Teacher and students concentrate exclusively on how these operations work and how to carry them out, to improve the degree of expertise and facility with which students apply them. Little, if any, serious attention is given to what subject-matter knowledge may be developed or learned through exercising these operations. In thinking courses, students think about their own and others' thinking, and receive direct instruction in how to improve their thinking. In many cases, they do not worry much about what they are thinking about, insofar as the subject matter is concerned.

Several of the most powerful and popular thinking skills programs available today consist of just such discrete skills courses. These include Reuven Feuerstein's Instrumental Enrichment (IE) and Edward deBono's CORT (for Cognitive Research Trust). Both are especially popular in middle and junior high schools.[4] Some specialists also recommend and teach courses devoted exclusively to critical thinking at the college and university levels as well as at pre-college levels (including elementary schools) and defend them ardently as the most effective and efficient way to hone student thinking.[5]

Yet separate thinking courses suffer from many disadvantages. One is time. Most school curricula are bulging with courses in a wide variety of subjects. In order to offer special courses on thinking, or to add them, educators have to take time from other subjects, all deemed essential. This is done when, in fact, we as teachers of these subjects, even now complain that we do not have the time needed by our students to achieve the established or expected goals and meet the content standards in these existing courses. As useful as separate courses on thinking might be, finding time for them is often extremely difficult, if not impossible.

There is a more serious disadvantage of separate thinking courses, however. It deals with how such courses are usually taught. The problem is not so much the explicit focus on cognitive operations as it is that what is "taught" as thinking is usually fragmented and decontextualized.[6] In many instances, a variety of skills, often unrelated to each other, are studied each as a discrete entity, practiced repetitively and separately, and then dropped in favor of another discrete skill. In such courses, the content and subject matter to which the skills are applied is usually a collection of unrelated subjects or topics. Skills are introduced and applied outside the context of situations or problems that naturally require use of the skill and knowledge. What often results is that such skill learning becomes a mechanistic, episodic enterprise—one in which students work at improving skilled performances in routine, unthinking fashion without understanding why they are doing what they are doing or understanding or even much caring about what is learned or accomplished in the process.[7] This ignores the important role that subject matter and context play in thinking.

Subject-Matter Courses

The alternative to devoting efforts to improving the quality of student thinking by creating and offering separate courses in thinking is to concentrate these efforts in already existing subject-matter courses. Courses that combine instruction in thinking and subject matter do so partly out of convenience—subject-matter courses already exist and good thinking is required to succeed in most of them—as well as out of a belief in the relative importance of thinking vis-à-vis subject-matter learning. But they also do so out of recognition of the role academic content and its study in depth play in thinking and out of the transformative relationship that exists between thinking and subject matter.[8]

Integrating instruction in thinking with content instruction in subject-matter courses is based on the assumption that skilled thinking is not an end in itself. Rather, it is desirable because thinking is a tool or means for accomplishing larger, more significant substantive goals, such as being able to solve diverse problems, make good decisions, and develop deeper knowledge or understanding in various subjects.[9] Consequently, thinking should be improved for what more proficient thinking can do for accomplishing these and other goals. Thus, school-based efforts at improving the quality of student thinking should do so in the service of these goals rather than in competition with or isolation from them. Given the curricular conditions found in most schools today, whether we elect to offer separate skills courses or not, it is most useful to provide instruction in thinking in the subject-matter courses where it is to be used rather than in content-free fragmented, decontextualized, drill and practice settings.

Cognitive skills—mental operations—are neither employed nor learned naturally in subject-matter-free or content-free contexts. One has to think about something when thinking. Conversely, to make sense out of information or experience, one has to process it mentally by thinking about or with it. Cognitive skills cannot be taught without using content and experience of some kind to demonstrate and exercise these skills. Conversely, content cannot be taught or learned without using some mental skills to process it. One has to think about *something* to think! One has to *do* something mentally with content to understand. Cognitive processes and subject-matter content are thus inextricably interwoven.[10] Improving one's mastery of either involves the use of both. No matter *where* we decide to direct our serious efforts to improve the quality of student thinking, we have to use content of some kind.

The role of subject-matter content in thinking and improving thinking simply cannot be ignored. And of all the contents one could use as an arena or vehicle for developing or using thinking, academic or other curricular subject matter is the most useful. Not only are such subject matters the focus of already existing school courses, but changing standards of student achievement in such courses increasingly emphasize and require the use of complex, higher-order thinking. This is just the kind of thinking in which students seem terribly deficient or inexpert and where instruction and improvement are most needed. So, many specialists assert, why not "teach" thinking in subject-matter courses that already exist and where students already need to use it?[11]

Numerous cognitive and subject-matter specialists have repeatedly pointed out that academic subject matter offers the most productive of all content arenas for developing thinking.[12] One thinks, in and about a range of contents, including content drawn from life experiences and personal knowledge accumulated over the years as well as in and with academic subject matter. Knowledge drawn from all these contents is used in thinking; however, many specialists claim that academic content is the most important and powerful in improving thinking.

Learning about and with certain academic subject matters—history, science, mathematics, and language, for instance—provide natural, *authentic* contexts for improving one's skills at applying complex thinking operations.[13] Subject-matter content piques thinking.[14] Achieving subject-matter learning goals—even if those goals are extrinsic to the students—stimulates engagement in thinking and gives purpose to applying thinking operations and to improving one's proficiency in doing so. Subject-matter content also informs thinking by giving direction to what kind of thinking operations are needed, by providing knowledge relevant to the execution of these operations, and by organizing information as it is manipulated.[15] This content, in sum, *enables* thinking. Furthermore, subject matter legitimatizes and authenticates thinking. Learning subject matter gives thinking utility. For these reasons, many specialists, such as researcher Lauren Resnick, assert that subject-matter instruction *must* serve as the occasion for efforts to improve and extend student thinking.[16]

Proponents of integrating instruction in thinking with academic subject-matter instruction take this position for yet another important reason.

Students who "learn" thinking skills in separate thinking skills courses are not likely to employ these operations on their own initiative or with much skill beyond these skill courses.[17] There are at least two fundamental reasons for this. First, much, if not most thinking seems to be domain specific. Not only does the way we use various cognitive operations vary depending on the subject matter to or with which we are applying these operations, but our knowledge of these subject matters shapes how, when and why we use them.[18] Second, cognitive skills do not automatically transfer readily to unfamiliar subject-matter contexts. When students are not familiar with the subject matter of a thinking situation that confronts them, they seem to be unwilling and often unable to initiate and apply thinking operations applied previously in other subject-matter contexts. In such cases, the successful application of thinking operations requires mediation, guidance, and even instruction by others somewhat expert in those operations in these new contexts.[19] So, it is often asserted, why not provide instruction in thinking in the academic disciplines or school subjects where it is needed in the first place?

Finally, instruction in thinking in subject-matter courses benefits from greater student interest in improving their thinking than exists in "content-free" skills courses. Once students recognize a need to engage in a particular kind of thinking and realize they are unable to do so skillfully, they are more motivated to want and more receptive to receiving instruction or structured assistance in how to do it better. Situating systematic efforts to improve thinking in subject-matter courses, where many different kinds and levels of thinking are required for success, seeks to capitalize on this situation. By engaging students in subject-matter learning tasks that require the application of increasingly complex thinking, we actually create opportunities for students to become aware of their limitations in thinking. This awareness, combined with the recognized need to accomplish the subject-matter learning objectives, then gives us opportunities to provide the kinds of instructional assistance and support in thinking that students need and welcome. Just as thinking is natural to subject-matter learning, instruction in thinking is natural to instruction in subject-matter courses.

Skills Courses Combined with Subject-Matter Courses

Interestingly, whether or not to teach thinking in subject matter may be a moot point. In fact, the skills course versus subject-matter course dilemma is what critical thinking specialist John Chaffee calls a "classic false dilemma."[20] These approaches are not in opposition to each other, he asserts; rather, they compliment each other. Each provides essential elements for improving student thinking. Both approaches are useful and needed.

Cognitive research and research on instruction indicate that learning or trying to improve execution of a new or complex cognitive operation benefits immensely from initially focusing explicitly and directly on that operation.[21] This is exactly the kind of skill learning provided in direct instruction and in well-conducted separate thinking skills courses. And, this is exactly what novices in any difficult or complex thinking operation need to understand and carry out that operation with later facility and ease. However, unless these operations are also applied—with appropriate instruction, support, and mediation—in contexts where they are expected to be used, what is presented in the skills-only course simply may not and usually does not transfer to these other settings.[22] Focus on a cognitive skill is necessary but not sufficient for improving thinking in a range or variety of subject-matter contexts.

Recognizing this limitation of skills-only courses is important. However, it is important also to note that it is not the focus on skills that is the reason for this limitation. Skills courses are limited in their effectiveness by the kinds of subject matter or content used as vehicles for skill practice in these courses. They are limited also by the failure of many skills courses to apply skills in the depth needed in the various academic subjects to enable students to develop the proficiency needed to use these skills effectively in these subjects.[23] No matter how good skills courses are at providing initial instruction in a skill, they do not offer the subject-matter background or continuing and in-depth immersion in that subject matter needed to develop the domain-specific thinking needed to succeed in subsequent subject-matter study.

However, providing initial focus directly on a cognitive skill followed or overlapped by continuing, extended, explicit attention to application of the skill in a variety of subject matters in which the skill is employed contributes immensely to improving student thinking. Without such follow-up application with continuing attention to skill procedures, mediation, and reflection, however, skill courses normally are not likely to improve the quality of thinking for most students. *Stand-alone, special thinking skills classes or courses, unless linked directly and purposefully to systematic follow-up instruction in subject-matter courses, are not sufficient for accomplishing this goal.*

Acknowledging this limitation, many specialists in thinking advocate the importance of tying instruction in thinking in special skills courses to continuing follow-up application, elaboration, and transfer of these skills in subject-matter or content courses.[24] Some, such as Matthew Lipman, an acknowledged leader in the teaching of critical thinking at the elementary and high school levels, have even developed courses that continue instruction in regular academic subject-matter courses in thinking operations introduced earlier in specialized skills courses.[25] Most specialists agree that efforts to improve student thinking require instruction in thinking in the subject-matter courses and the work, social, and civic contexts where such thinking is repeatedly needed and employed in the daily lives of students and adults. Separate thinking skills courses, as conventionally taught, do not appear, *in and by themselves,* to provide sufficient experience and learning to generate lasting improvement in the quality of student thinking. Yet they can provide an absolutely essential feature of effective initial skill learning by focusing on how to carry out a cognitive operation unencumbered by complex or unfamiliar subject matter.

Thus, a third option emerges. Separate thinking courses can be combined with continuing follow-up instruction in that thinking in various subject-matter courses. Can such course sequences be created and taught? Of course. We can readily conceive, for example, of an extremely valuable course in decision making at the beginning of the middle school or junior high school years. These students are at the point in their lives where they need desperately to be skillful decision makers. A special course in a systematic process of decision making that includes a focus on procedures for carrying out each major step in this process can prove immensely useful to accelerating student proficiency in this skill. When followed by systematic application, elaboration, and transfer in an ever-increasing range of contexts in the subject-matter courses taken over the next few years, such instruction can move students toward a high degree of self-directed autonomy in the application of this skill far beyond the confines of its skills-only course introduction.

The same kind of approach offers considerable promise for developing a similar degree of proficiency in critical thinking for senior high school students, as well. A course in critical thinking—required of all students and taught by all high school faculty and staff—could be required of all students entering high school. The skills introduced and practiced in this course could then be applied, elaborated, and transferred in all the academic subject-matter courses subsequently taken. Employing this approach gives every promise of improving considerably the quality of student thinking and student learning.

The obstacles to institutionalizing course sequences such as these are often seemingly so overwhelming and so frustrating as to discourage efforts to do so. Because school curricula are already overstuffed, introducing new skill courses is often considered to be virtually impossible. Coordinating appropriate follow-up instruction in thinking by teachers in academic courses is complicated by scheduling conflicts as well as by intergrade and intersubject rivalries. And assigning primary skill teaching responsibilities to only one or a few teachers of special skills courses appears to absolve other teachers of any responsibility for also providing instruction that builds appropriately on these earlier efforts. Indeed, the act of having skills courses, regardless of any intended follow-up in other courses, often leads many teachers to believe it is not their job to "reteach" what someone else "should have taught" or that there is little they can do to help students think better if "they haven't done so by now." Although these handicaps can be overcome, the difficulties in doing so often appear insurmountable.

Conclusion

So, where does this leave us? As useful as they may be in providing the kinds of focus in thinking needed to improve it, separate courses in thinking, *by themselves*, are simply not enough for improving the quality of student thinking over the long haul. This is because they neglect to tie thinking in sufficient depth to the academic subject areas and other contexts where skilled, complex thinking is required and because transfer is difficult without continuing instruction in follow-up subject-matter courses. Efforts to improve the quality of student thinking will most likely prove more productive when thinking instruction is tied closely with continuing skill instruction and learning in subject matter. This means we should either (1) combine special courses in thinking with continuing follow-up systematic instruction in thinking integrated into subsequent subject-matter courses or (2) integrate instruction in thinking with instruction in subject matter courses right from the start. In either case, we cannot avoid integrating instruction in thinking with instruction in subject-matter courses if we really wish to improve the quality of student thinking.

For these reasons, providing systematic instruction in thinking in already existing subject-matter courses where such thinking is required anyway may seem the most productive approach at the moment. Doing so is the recommendation here. *To best improve the quality of student thinking in our schools, thinking should be as much a subject of instruction in subject-matter courses as is the content on which these courses focus.* Even if we elect to initiate instruction in thinking with a special thinking skills course, we must still integrate thinking skill instruction into subsequent subject-matter courses.

INFUSION OR IMMERSION IN SUBJECT-MATTER COURSES?

If the decision as to *where* to provide instruction in thinking is to do so in subject-matter courses, as is recommended here, then another question arises: *How* should such instruction be provided in these courses? Specialists suggest two different responses to this question: infusion and immersion. Although meanings given to these terms vary, both refer to the degree to and ways in which thinking and instruction in thinking are related to the use of and instruction in the subject-matter content of a course. A brief delineation of the nature of each approach will clarify the essential differences between them and the value of each for improving student thinking.

The Infusion Approach

Critical thinking expert Robert Ennis, as well as several other specialists in teaching thinking, defines *infusion* as "deep, thoughtful" instruction in subject-matter content in which the general principles of thinking are made *explicit*.[26] According to critical thinking specialist Robert Swartz, infusion involves more than "getting thinking going." It also involves direct teacher intervention to help students keep it going and enable it to "go better," and this includes direct instruction in the cognitive skills needed to engage successfully in complex thinking in whatever subject it is being applied.[27]

In infusion, subject-matter learning and content provide the occasion, context, purpose, and vehicle for deliberate, continuing, systematic, and explicit efforts to apply and to improve student thinking. In this approach, cognitive skills are taught on a "need to use" basis or, as cognitive psychologist John Bransford says, "just in time," in the context of their application to subject matter, to achieve specific subject-matter learning goals.[28] Its purpose, Swartz asserts, is to make students become more expert in the kinds of thinking needed in their daily lives in and out of school, as well as in developing knowledge from and understanding about the academic and other subjects they study in school. In infusion, deliberate sustained attention is given to both subject-matter learning and improving thinking.[29]

Where subject-matter learning is infused with instruction in thinking, learning may commence either with subject-matter tasks or instruction in about-to-be needed but at present poorly executed cognitive operations. Whenever we, as teachers, sense that students cannot apply effectively and with ease or confidence a cognitive operation needed to accomplish a subject-matter objective, we help the students step back from the content being processed and discussed to focus explicitly on the operation in question. We can do this in at least two ways. We can preplan lessons or a series of lessons that introduce and provide some practice in a new skill. Or we can simply stop a planned subject-matter lesson to concentrate instead on explicit attention to the skill in question—a sort of, "Look! Let me show you how to do this!" approach. Although continuing to use the content being studied, we thus help students make visible and explicit *how* they are applying the thinking operation they are employing. Then subject-matter study resumes. As students continue to apply this thinking operation to subject matter in the course, we scaffold, cue, and otherwise mediate their efforts to practice doing so until they demonstrate the ability to employ the operation with appropriate expertise and success. Subject-matter learning continues but always in conjunction with the explicit attention to various thinking operations, as needed.

A major advantage of infusing thinking instruction into subject-matter learning is that cognitive operations receive acknowledged instructive attention in the context of subject-matter learning goals where they are informed by the content to which they are being purposefully applied. Learning subject matter thus provides the occasion and purpose, and content provides the vehicle, for focusing on a cognitive operation. Student motivation to attend to improving their skills at carrying out that operation is thus sharply enhanced because skilled execution of that operation pays off in the subject-matter knowledge developed through increased expertise in applying this operation—or at least in the higher score expected on the test which is expected to end the unit of study! Subject-matter learning and skill development thus progress, hand in hand, with each supporting the other.[30] As researcher Raymond Nickerson has noted, "Study of a discipline that focuses explicitly on principles of reasoning can improve thinking in general."[31]

Attending systematically to thinking skills in a subject-matter course does not inhibit subject-matter learning. Rather, students continue to learn subject matter even while focusing on the cognitive procedures by which they manipulate that subject matter when the subject matter is the content of the conversation. That is, as students apply a cognitive operation to subject-matter data to develop new insights, connections, hypotheses, conclusions, or generalizations, and use that content or refer to it in articulating, explaining, and justifying how they did what they did mentally, they internalize the subject matter and understandings used or developed in their learning.

For example, as a result of explaining and discussing how they went about detecting bias in the accounts presented in Chapter 4, many students later recalled vividly the contents of these accounts as well as the essential features of the cognitive procedures and heuristics articulated. Research indicates that explicit attention to cognitive skill development in subject-matter study enhances the quality of subject-matter learning as well as of thinking.[32] Clearly, this dual outcome is an advantage of infusing instruction in thinking in subject-matter teaching.

Yet infusion is not without its drawbacks. Interrupting a focus on subject matter to focus on *how* to carry out an explicit thinking procedure cuts into content coverage—whether it be in breadth or depth of content being studied. This creates problems of conscience, if not actual administrative or assessment problems, for many of us. Thus, we often resist attending explicitly to thinking, even though we realize that coverage is futile when students lack the skills required to learn from such coverage.

Attending explicitly and directly to thinking in a subject-matter course also requires that we, as teachers, know more than many of us appear to know about the procedural, conditional, and declarative knowledge of various cognitive skills and how best to "teach" these. It requires, too, that both we and our students engage consciously in what historian educator Ted Fenton has called "the simultaneous pursuit of multiple objectives" while teaching and learning. This is no easy task, especially where we are unsure of the content or the cognitive skills—or both—that we are supposed to be teaching. For many of us—teachers as well as our students—focusing on one thing at a time, whether it be thinking skills or content, seems to be easier.

On balance, however, the advantages of infusion far outweigh the disadvantages. Infusion assumes that skill learning is an important substantive goal of instruction in subject matter and, in many cases, every bit as worthwhile and of more lasting value as the subject matter being learned. Integrating the two recognizes the interactive nature of both, gives functional meaning to each, and enhances the learning of both. As educator Richard Prawatt points out, attending to improving thinking by focusing explicitly on how students think and can think better need not be at the expense of what it is that students do think.[33]

The Immersion Approach

Immersion is usually offered as an alternative to infusion. According to Ennis, immersion is thought-provoking subject-matter instruction in which the principles of complex thinking are *not* made explicit.[34] In this approach to integrating thinking and subject matter, teaching and learning emphasize and concentrate on developing subject-matter insights, knowledge, and understanding. Although thinking is obviously needed to accomplish these goals, it is not a subject of explicit, systematic attention. Students are *expected* to think. Indeed, they are *made* to think by the subject-matter learning demands imposed on them, some of which they may generate themselves. Proponents of immersion believe it is the challenge or struggle to carry out thinking and repeated opportunities to exercise it that lead to more skilled thinking.[35] For them, the measure of success of this approach to improving thinking is the kind of knowledge learned, its depth, complexity, and degree of "thoughtfulness."

There is one major advantage to *insisting* that students think (and "think harder") without devoting any significant class time to helping them make explicit how they do it and how it can be done more skillfully. And that is that virtually full class attention can be devoted to subject matter, whether it is being studied in breadth or depth. Such an approach is especially appealing to those of us who value subject-matter or content learning above all other kinds of learning. These individuals would most likely agree with Matthew Arnold's observation that "it is a very great thing to be able to think as you like, but after all, an important question remains: *what* you think!"[36] For them, content learning is or should be the primary goal of schooling. The development of thinking, they believe, occurs naturally in the pursuit of this goal and incidental to it. Any attention to the explicit teaching of thinking in any subject-matter course they feel, would detract students considerably from the attention required for subject-matter learning. Indeed, many of these individuals may agree with Richard Prawatt's observation that "a focus on thinking skills may actually direct attention away from important curricular issues"—and this when improving student thinking itself *is*, in fact, one of those very issues![37]

From the point of view of educators who consider improving student thinking an important learning goal, immersion as an approach to improving student thinking has serious disadvantages. One is that little, if any, serious or sustained attention is given to making explicit and providing continuing practice in many of the higher-order thinking skills required to accomplish assigned subject-matter learning goals. The assumption that if students are made to engage in complex thinking in an academic subject, they all will do so skillfully and successfully, runs counter to the reality of most classrooms.[38] For many students, the immersion approach to thinking feels like drowning. This is a serious weakness in this approach to integrating thinking in subject-matter learning and limits its potential as a major approach to improving student thinking.

There is little doubt about the importance of developing subject-matter knowledge as one major goal of schooling. But to believe that it is or should be the only goal of education or that subject-matter study alone is sufficient to develop such knowledge is naive. To achieve this goal, skilled execution of complex thinking such as problem solving, analytical and critical thinking, and decision making are all required.[39] As Nickerson points out, domain knowledge alone does not guarantee effective thinking about a domain. Although necessary for deeper and effective thinking, such knowledge is not sufficient by itself to sustain or carry out that thinking.[40]

Indeed, subject-matter knowledge can actually serve as a barrier to thinking and learning, as Bena Kallick and others have noted.[41] When what is believed to be true as knowledge is considered immutable fact, it can prevent us from developing new meanings from content as conditions change, as relevant new information becomes available, and as our proficiency in thinking elicits new insights. Subject-matter learning, thus, can actually inhibit thinking. It is only through integration of the two—instruction in both content and thinking—as well as of skilled processing of content that we transcend the limitations of knowledge as well as create it.

Thus, it is erroneous to assume that subject-matter in the form of understandings, concepts, and generalizations, are the only intellectual tools used in learning.[42] Cognitive skills and principles related to cognitive processing also are important intellectual tools. Both content and subject-matter knowledge on the one hand and skilled thinking on the other are necessary to develop the knowledge we seek as the goals of classroom learning.

Students need to focus on, reflect on, and discuss *how* they come to know what they know as well as what it is they believe they know.[43]

Conclusion

Developing or learning subject-matter related knowledge *cannot* be considered the only goal of schooling, no matter how important it is. For subject-matter learning to occur, skilled use of a wide variety of cognitive operations is also essential. This means that improving thinking must be considered a goal of schooling as important as knowledge development.[44] While enhancing understanding of subject matter should be an explicit goal of cognitive skill training, as Resnick asserts, developing expertise in carrying out the cognitive skills needed to accomplish this goal must also be an explicit goal of schooling. These two goals are mutually supportive of each other. Achieving both is essential for either to be accomplished to the fullest possible extent.

Moreover, thinking and knowledge have important affective dimensions. A significant feature of subject-matter learning, for example, is the attitude or disposition of suspending judgment. Another is being willing to change an opinion where evidence and reason warrant. Yet another is seeking and giving evidence to justify a claim. Attitudes *toward* knowledge and knowledge claims are an important result of and conditioner of knowing. It is not surprising to note that these dispositions, are also dimensions of effective thinking.[45] Schools long have considered the development of attitudes, dispositions, and the values from which they derive to be major goals of instruction, and these are just a few of the attitudes that serve as such goals. Schooling legitimately seeks a variety of major learning goals in the form of skills, values, and attitudes in addition to knowledge, which, because they are closely interrelated, are important. Integrating instruction in thinking with instruction in subject matter enables rather than inhibits the achievement of all these goals.

Infusion Then Immersion

Infusion and immersion vary considerably in the emphasis and time given to thinking in subject-matter courses as well as in the kinds of thinking instruction provided. However, as in the case of the skill course/content course "dilemma," the infusion/immersion dilemma is actually another "false dilemma." The choice among these options is not an either/or choice. The choice is *when* to employ each, rather than which of the two approaches to employ. Both offer important advantages as ways to improve thinking and subject-matter learning.

For maximum learning of subject matter as well as maximum improvement in the quality of student thinking, *both infusion and immersion approaches to teaching thinking should characterize an instructional program in subject-matter courses.* Initial instruction in any cognitive skill or operation in a subject-matter course should be provided through the infusion approach. New or difficult operations should receive explicit introductory emphasis using subject-matter content with which students are familiar, and then be practiced with scaffolding and mediation thereafter as they are applied to new subject matters in continued subject-matter learning. At a point where students demonstrate the ability to employ these operations on their own, the immersion approach becomes appropriate and natural. We can continue to "teach" cognitive operations by cueing. Only rarely thereafter is brief review or extended mediation required as our students probe deeper into subject matter. In integrating efforts to improve thinking and develop subject-matter learning, we can use both approaches—first infusion, then immersion—in every course. If we do, students will then increase their proficiency and confidence in using the thinking operations being emphasized to develop deeper and more complex understandings about the subject matter they study.

INTEGRATING THINKING IN SUBJECT MATTER: A SUMMARY

Where is the most productive and appropriate place in school curricula to direct instructional efforts at improving the quality of student thinking? Simply and directly put, it is in required academic subjects—such as English (literature, writing and grammar) mathematics, social studies/history, and the sciences, certainly, and in other important subject areas such as health, fine arts, industrial arts, and other subjects if possible. These are subject matters usually required of or taken by most students, are drawn from disciplines that facilitate, inform, and demand complex thinking, and focus on developing subject-matter learning of value to all students. Moreover, all the major types of thinking play a continuing and significant role in making meaning and developing understanding in these subjects. The underlying rationale for integrating instruction in thinking with instruction in subject-matter learning in this manner stresses that (1) developing expertise in thinking is as major a goal of schooling as is subject-matter learning and deserves as well as requires explicit attention in the curriculum, and (2) proficient thinking should serve subject-matter learning goals, just as subject-matter learning should serve as a vehicle for improving thinking.[46]

Integrating Thinking and Subject Matter: K–12. For maximum impact, integrating instruction in thinking and in subject matter must be at least a K–12 effort. It must start in the earliest primary grades—even in preschool years—

and continue through the secondary grades and even into the postsecondary level of education. Improving student proficiency in thinking, as well as the confidence born of repeated success in so doing, requires considerable time. This is so for two major reasons. First, there are many kinds of thinking to be mastered—including problem solving, decision making, and critical thinking—and each consists of a myriad of frequently complex cognitive operations as well as related procedural knowledge and supporting dispositions, attitudes, and habits of mind. Second, elaborating and generalizing these cognitive operations beyond the settings in which they are first encountered to the wide range of increasingly complex subject matters and other contexts in which they can be productively used, takes years of mediated instruction, practice, and reflective analysis. *Purposeful efforts to improve student thinking must be a continuing, systematic effort across all grade levels and in virtually all subjects, beginning when students first enter school.*

Integrating Thinking and Subject Matter in Practice.   Integrating instruction in thinking with subject-matter instruction, in practice, moves students through all types of thinking instruction described in the preceding chapters. This ranges from making a thinking procedure visible and explicit when introducing thinking through scaffolded and cued practice to transfer and to autonomous use—all in the continuing pursuit of subject-matter learning. Each of these types of thinking instruction can and should be provided in the subject matter of the course in which this instruction is taking place. Even though the focus of an introductory thinking skill lesson may be on the skill, course subject matter can still be used as a vehicle for helping students articulate procedures for executing that skill. In doing so, students will learn about subject matter as well as about the skill.

The initial practice lessons that follow a lesson introducing a thinking operation represent the infusion approach, as defined by Ennis and described by Swartz—a series of lessons in which students practice applying the skill with gradually decreasing teacher support and guidance. In these lessons, attention is given to both subject-matter learning and to the execution of the skill. From this point on, students engage repeatedly in applying the skill, perhaps initially on our cue but soon completely on their own initiative and under their autonomous direction, to develop subject-matter knowledge and understanding. In these lessons, students gradually come to employ the cognitive skill without assistance as a natural, implicit part of completing subject-matter study. Such a combination of thinking and subject matter typifies the immersion approach defined by Ennis and described by Prawat.

Learning to execute complex thinking skillfully must be as much a goal of schooling as is developing subject-matter knowledge and understanding.[47] Achieving one requires achieving the other, because thinking and subject matter interact. Neither can be well developed or employed in the absence of the other. So, integrating instruction in thinking in subject-matter courses rather than confining it to separate thinking courses is precisely where such instruction should be situated if student thinking is to be improved to the degree it can and should be. And, *infusing* instruction in thinking with instruction in subject matter and then *immersing* thinking in subject-matter learning prove the best possible ways of carrying out this integration of thinking and subject matter. The following chapters explain what we can do specifically to bring about this integration.

ENDNOTES

1. See, for example, Reuven Feuerstein, *Instrumental Enrichment* (Baltimore: University Park Press, 1980).

2. Michael I. Posner and Steven W. Keele, "Skill Learning," in Robert M. W. Travers (Ed.), *Second Handbook of Research on Teaching* (Chicago: Rand McNally College Publishing, 1973), pp. 808–810; Arthur Whimbey, "The Key to Higher Order Thinking Is Precise Processing," *Educational Leadership 42* 1 (September 1984): 66–70.

3. See, for example, Edward deBono, "The Direct Teaching of Thinking as a Skill, " *Phi Delta Kappan 64* 10 (June 1983): 703–708.

4. Edward deBono, *CORT Thinking* (New York: Pergamon Press, 1973/1983); John Edwards, "Measuring the Effects of the Direct Teaching of Thinking Skills," *Human Intelligence Newsletter 9* 3 (Fall 1988): 9–10; Feuerstein, *Instrumental Enrichment, passim.*

5. John Chaffee, "A Classic False Dilemma: Teaching vs. Infusing Critical Thinking," *Educational Vision 2* 2 (1994): 8–9.

6. John D. Bransford and Barry S. Stein, *The IDEAL Problem Solver* (rev. ed.) (New York: W. H. Freeman, 1984/1992), p. 197.

7. John D. Bransford et al., *MOST Environments for Accelerating Literacy Development.* Paper prepared for delivery at the NATO Advanced Study Institute on the Psychological and Educational Foundations of Technology-Based Learning Environments. July 26-August 2, Kolymbari, Crete; David Perkins, Presentation at ASCD Conference on "Thinking and Learning: How Cognitive Science Will Transform the Next Generation of Schools," February 25, 1993, San Antonio.

8. Hilda Taba, "Learning by Discovery: Psychological and Educational Rationale." *Elementary School Journal 63* 6 (March 1963): 311.

9. Raymond Nickerson,"On Improving Thinking through Instruction," in Ernest Z. Rothkopf (Ed.), *Review of Research in Education,* Volume 15 (Washington, DC: American Educational Research Association, 1988–89), p. 31; David Perkins, *Smart Schools* (New York: The Free Press, 1992); David Perkins and Tina Blythe, "Putting Thinking Up Front," *Educational Leadership 51* 5 (February 1994): 4–7; Lauren Resnick and Leopold E. Klopfer (Eds.), *Toward the Thinking Curriculum* (Alexandria, VA: Association for Supervision and Curriculum Development, 1989).

10. Nickerson, "On Improving Thinking," p. 31; Taba, "Learning by Discovery," p. 311.

11. Resnick and Klopfer, *Toward the Thinking Curriculum, passim.*; Richard S. Prawat, "The Value of Ideas: The Immersion Approach to the Development of Thinking," *Educational Researcher 70* 2 (March 1991): 3–30.

12. Bransford et al., *MOST*, p. 4; Allan Collins, Jan Hawkins, and Sharon M. Carver, "A Cognitive Apprenticeship for Disadvantaged Students," in Barbara Means, Carol Chelemer, and Michael S. Knapp (Eds.), *Teaching Advanced Skills to At-Risk Students* (San Francisco: Jossey-Bass, 1991), pp. 220–221; Nickerson, "On Improving Thinking," pp. 28–31; Perkins, *Smart Schools, passim.*; Resnick and Klopfer, *Toward the Thinking Curriculum, passim.*

13. Ann Brown and Annmarie Palinscar, *Coherence and Causality in Science Readings.* Paper presented at the American Educational Research Association Annual Meeting, March 1989; John Seeley Brown, Allan Collins, and Paul Duguid, "Situated Cognition and the Culture of Learning," *Educational Researcher 18* 1 (January-February 1989): 36; Robert J. Marzano, *A Different Kind of Classroom* (Washington, DC: Association for Supervision and Curriculum Development, 1992), pp. 31–32; Nickerson, "On Improving Thinking," pp. 3–57; Prawat, "The Value of Ideas," p. 9; Robert Swartz, "How to Infuse Thinking," *Cogitare V* 3 (Spring 1991): 1, 7.

14. Nickerson, "On Improving Thinking," p. 14.

15. Prawat, "The Value of Ideas," pp. 3–30.

16. Resnick in Resnick and Klopfer, *Toward the Thinking Curriculum, p. 28.*

17. D. N. Perkins and Gavriel Salomon, "Are Cognitive Skills Context Bound?" *Educational Researcher 18* 1 (January–February 1989): 16–25.

18. Brown, Collins, and Duguid, "Situated Cognition," pp. 36–37; Nickerson, "On Improving Thinking," p. 14; Robert Glaser, "Education and Thinking: The Role of Knowledge," *American Psychologist 39* 2 (February 1984): 93–104; Lauren Resnick, *Education and Learning to Think* (Washington, DC: National Academy Press, 1987).

19. D. N. Perkins and Gavriel Salomon, "Teaching for Transfer," *Educational Leadership 46* 1 (September 1988): 22–32.

20. Chafee, "A Classic False Dilemma," pp. 8–9.

21. deBono, "The Direct Teaching," *passim.*; Edwards, "Measuring the Effects," pp. 9–10; Nickerson, "On the Improving Thinking," pp. 3–57; Posner and Keele, "Skill Learning," pp. 805–831.

22. Perkins and Salomon, "Teaching for Transfer," pp. 16–25.

23. Nickerson, "On Improving Thinking," pp. 3–57.

24. Chafee, "A Classic False Dilemma," p. 8.

25. Matthew Lipman, *Thinking in Education* (New York: Cambridge University Press, 1991), p. 180.

26. Robert H. Ennis, "Critical Thinking and Subject Specificity: Clarification and Needed Research," *Educational Researcher* 18 3 (April 1989): 5.

27. Swartz, "How to Infuse Thinking," pp. 1, 7.

28. John Bransford, Presentation at ASCD Conference on "Thinking and Learning: How Cognitive Science Will Transform the Next Generation of Schools," February 25, 1993, San Antonio.

29. Prawat, "The Value of Ideas," p. 4.

30. Nickerson, "On Improving Thinking," p. 31.

31. *Ibid.*, p. 17.

32. See, for example, Thomas H. Estes, "Reading in the Social Studies—A Review of Research Since 1950," in James Laffery (Ed.), *Reading in the Content Areas* (Newark, DE: International Reading Association, 1972), pp. 178–183; Nickerson, "On Improving Thinking," p. 17.

33. Prawat, "The Value of Ideas," p. 5.

34. Ennis, "Critical Thinking," p. 5.

35. Prawat, "The Value of Ideas," p. 5.

36. Quoted in John Bartlett, *Familiar Quotations* (15th ed.) (Boston: Little, Brown, 1980), p. 18.

37. Prawat, "The Value of Ideas," p. 5.

38. Perkins, *Smart Schools,* pp. 145–148.

39. *Ibid.*

40. Nickerson, "On Improving Thinking," p. 14.

41. Bena Kallick, *Changing Schools into Communities for Thinking* (Grand Forks, ND: Center for Teaching and Learning, 1989), p. 9.

42. Prawat, "The Value of Ideas," p. 5.

43. Lipman, *Thinking in Education,* pp. 180, 223–224.

44. Resnick, in Resnick and Klopfer, *Toward the Thinking Curriculum,* p. 28.

45. Robert H. Ennis, "A Logical Basis for Measuring Critical Thinking Skills," *Educational Leadership* 43 2 (October 1985): 46; David R. Krathwohl et al., *Taxonomy of Educational Objectives—Handbook II: Affective Domain* (New York: David McKay, 1964), pp. 181–185.

46. Prawat, "The Value of Ideas," p. 5; Resnick, in Resnick and Klopfer, *Toward the Thinking Curriculum, passim.*

47. Prawat, "The Value of Ideas," p. 5.

9

Organizing Skill-Teaching Techniques for Improving Thinking

Infusing and then eventually immersing instruction in thinking into instruction in subject matter can contribute significantly to improving the quality of student thinking. Even more significant in accomplishing this goal, however, is the kind of direction, guidance, and support we provide to students—and the ways we organize them—to bring about the kinds of improvement sought. We can, of course, use any of the skill-teaching techniques described in the preceding pages for this purpose. But using these at random or in isolation from each other—while temporarily perhaps facilitating thinking—does little to produce the permanent improvement in that thinking, which is our goal.

Improving thinking differs considerably from facilitating thinking. *Facilitating* thinking means making it easier to execute or engage in. It is usually a one-time intervention to help someone overcome a temporary obstacle to the completion of a specific thinking task or to ease someone through an unfamiliar thinking procedure. *Improving* thinking, on the other hand, means enabling thinking to work better in the long run than it does now. Improving student thinking means *moving* youngsters toward achieving and maintaining the highest levels of skilled, independent, self-directed thinking of which they are capable.

Improving thinking, then, requires not a one-time intervention but a continuing, systematic effort. Only by *combining* into strategies the techniques selected from among those presented in the preceding pages and sequencing their use appropriately can we provide the kinds of continuing direction, guidance, and support that enable students to improve their thinking permanently. This chapter describes such strategic combinations as well as a framework for employing them in our classrooms. When we organize and apply the teaching techniques described here to reinforce and facilitate the natural process by which skilled thinking performances develop, we not only ensure the improvement of student thinking but accelerate this improvement, as well.

HOW SKILLFUL THINKING DEVELOPS

Thinking is a complex phenomenon. Any act of thinking consists of executing a variety of thinking operations, each of which often consists of executing a number of other subordinate mental operations. Improved thinking results as students become increasingly skilled in executing the various procedures and applying the rules that must be employed to carry out all these operations effectively. Developing proficiency in executing these thinking operations takes reflection, time, instruction, and practice. For best results, the reflection, instruction, and practice must be a continuing activity, mediated and structured in ways that provide direction, guidance, support, and feedback related to the *thinking* being practiced.[1]

Research indicates that individuals execute any thinking operation differently at various points en route to achieving the highest levels of proficiency in that operation that they can attain. Typically, individuals initially exhibit a very halting, fragmented, error-prone, and effortful execution of a new thinking operation. We move only gradually toward the rapid, efficient, self-directed and automatized execution that marks the skilled performance of that operation characteristic of a high degree of proficiency or expertise.[2] Figure 9.1 outlines how University of California professor Hubert L. Dreyfus has described this process.[3]

According to Dreyfus, as well as Benjamin Bloom, Robbie Case, and other researchers, virtually all people are capable of moving through this process at their own paces, although for many, it is a slow and often unfulfilled progression. Most people, in fact, fail to move through all phases in most thinking. Indeed, even as adults, many individuals get only as far as being what Dreyfus calls competent users of the most complicated operations by the time they reach their senior years. Many youngsters and even college students are at even earlier levels of this progression in many, if not most, higher-order cognitive operations.[4]

Figure 9.1 How Skilled Performances Develop

Novice	We fragment a thinking procedure into its various steps, apply them with little regard for the context in which we are executing them, judge the results by how well we followed the rules and "covered" the steps, and show little concern for the substantive results obtained.
Advanced Beginner	We begin to integrate the pieces of the procedure, tie it to a specific situation or context, and focus on rules, but proceed in a slow, often uncoordinated, laborious manner, referring occasionally to personal experience and content cues.
Competent User	We begin to elaborate the procedure, detaching it from any specific context or task, engage in rule-guided actions, recognize important parts on which to focus, plan in a detached way, and begin to feel responsible for and concerned about the results or products of our thinking.
Proficient Performer	We recognize present contexts as similar to earlier encountered ones, *spontaneously* recall appropriate thinking procedures to employ and generate plans for carrying them out, and execute these procedures smoothly and with economy of effort.
Expert	We carry out our thinking rapidly and holographically rather than in step-by-step fashion, moving from abstract to case-specific rules—breaking some rules as the occasion seems to demand and operating on our own rules to an increasing extent as plans simply spring to mind—and act and learn from the results without apparently conscious effort or awareness.

Note: Based on H. L. Dreyfus, "Expert Systems versus Intuitive Enterprise," unpublished paper delivered at George Mason University, Fairfax, VA, May 29, 1984.

Moreover, this progression does not apply uniformly to all thinking for any one individual. An individual may be a novice in one kind of thinking but a competent user or proficient performer in another, while perhaps nearing expertise in a third. This will depend on the occasions he or she has had in the past to engage in that thinking, the kinds of mediation involved in doing so, the variety of contexts in which that thinking has so far been applied, and the efforts he or she has made to improve that thinking. People vary considerably within as well as among themselves in the level of expertise they achieve and demonstrate in the various kinds of thinking in which they attempt to engage.[5]

Fortunately, however, research also indicates that movement toward increasing expertise in any cognitive operation can be enabled and ensured as well as accelerated by purposeful and continuing instruction and media-tion.[6] We can provide such instruction and mediation in the form of the learning experiences or lessons that employ in various strategic com-binations and sequences selected techniques drawn from the pool of skill-teaching techniques described in this book.

AN INSTRUCTIONAL FRAMEWORK FOR IMPROVING STUDENT THINKING

The kind of instruction that seems best suited to improving student think-ing is that which builds on what students naturally do as they develop in-creasing proficiency in thinking. According to Dreyfus, in moving from novice to expert in the ability to execute any kind of thinking, all people go through three distinctly different phases. In first attempting a new skill, an individual takes it apart to figure out what he or she has to do to make it work, to identify a procedure that will be effective in carrying it out, and then applies this procedure slowly, step by step, to get a "feel" for doing it (the Novice level in Dreyfus's conception). Then, the person practices that procedure over and over again, gradually integrating the various steps and adjusting how the steps are executed until he or she does so increasingly smoothly and automatically (the Advanced Beginner/Competent User lev-els). Eventually, the person applies what is now their own internalized pro-cedure for carrying out the skill in an increasing variety of situations. The individual generalizes or transfers and refines "skill" in executing it beyond the limits of the circumstances or situation in which he or she initially en-countered it (the Proficient Performer/Expert levels). This three-phase process provides an excellent framework for classroom efforts to improve the quality of student thinking.

Figure 9.2 outlines this instructional framework. It provides three types of instruction or learning experiences in any kind of thinking or thinking skill. It begins with (1) an *introduction* to one or more explicit, step-by-step procedures and rules for executing a particular cognitive skill. A series of lessons follow that provide (2) *guided practice* in applying that skill, with the degree of teacher guidance and support gradually decreasing as students demonstrate the ability to carry out the operation with increasing confi-dence and skill on their own. Finally, it seeks also to enable students to (3) generalize or *transfer* their developing expertise in executing the skill to an increasing variety of situations or contexts. This instructional sequence pro-vides for exactly the kinds of learning experiences and instruction that stu-dents of all ability levels benefit immensely from in their efforts to master the elements of good thinking.[7]

The primary function of an introductory lesson in this instructional framework is to make students consciously aware of exactly how a specific

Figure 9.2 An Instructional Framework for Improving Thinking

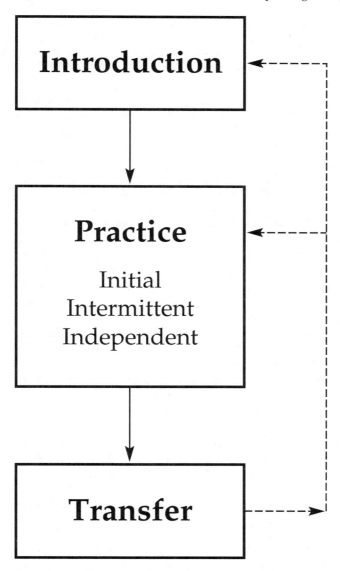

thinking operation or skill can be effectively carried out. To this end, an introductory lesson articulates step-by-step procedures and specific rules by which the students themselves presently carry out the operation as well as how skilled performances of that operation are carried out. Making visible and explicit procedures by which a thinking skill is carried out establishes the foundation for improving performance in that skill that is the goal of the practice that follows.[8]

Effective thinking skill practice is distinguished by varying degrees of teacher-provided structure, guidance, and mediation as students have repeated opportunities to apply the skill. It consists of (1) *initial practice*, that frequent practice immediately following the introductory encounter with a thinking skill to be improved, when students are just beginning to practice applying the new skill; (2) the less frequent *intermittent practice* of the skill that follows as students seek "to get the hang of it;" and (3) subsequent more irregular, self-directed but often cued *independent practice* of the skill in which students direct most of their attention to achieving substantive goals through application of the skill on their own. We can move students through all three kinds of guided practice, in this sequence, in order to help them develop the proficiency needed to be autonomous in their thinking.[9]

This framework also provides explicitly for *transfer*. Since most thinking skills are tied closely to the context or topic in which they are initially encountered and since most students do not normally, on their own, transfer a newly encountered skill to other contexts, it is necessary to help them make this transfer.[10] We can do this in our classrooms by providing continuing practice in generalizing the skill beyond the context in which it was introduced and first practiced. Much of this instruction is a part of the intermittent and independent stages of skill practice.

The primary goal of our efforts to improve student thinking, of course, is to enable students to engage on their own initiative in skillful, self-directed, autonomous application of a thinking operation when and where it is appropriate to do so to accomplish substantive learning or other relevant goals. Thus, we continue to provide numerous, regular, authentic subject-matter opportunities and encouragement to do so beyond the conclusion of a skill practice and transfer schedule. In a sense, our efforts to improve student thinking should never end, although our intervention and mediation in the application of this thinking may become considerably less explicit, frequent, and direct as student proficiency in executing it increases.

Instruction based on this framework has three distinguishing features. It makes *how* to execute a thinking operation—whether it be problem solving, predicting, classifying, judging the strength of an argument, or any other thinking skill—the subject to be learned. It organizes instruction in this operation into a series of different types of lessons, each with a specific function in developing student proficiency in this operation, and arranges these lessons in a specific sequence. The teaching techniques employed in these lessons engage students, increasingly on their own, in applying, analyzing, articulating, and evaluating procedures and rules by which the thinking operation can be skillfully carried out. When conducted properly, such continuing, systematic instruction in a variety of thinking skills can lead to marked improvement in student thinking.[11]

TEACHING STRATEGIES FOR IMPROVING
STUDENT THINKING

A variety of skill-teaching techniques may be employed to assist students in improving their thinking. Figure 9.3 lists these techniques and matches each to the kind of instruction with which it can be best used.

Lessons and learning experiences appropriate to the different phases of skill development described earlier and to the instructional framework derived from it can be created by combining various of these techniques. For example, combining, in sequence, in a single lesson, the techniques of previewing, modeling, and metacognitive reflection produces an effective strategy for introducing a new thinking skill. Combining previewing and rehearsal with a scaffolding technique such as a graphic organizer and with metacognitive reflection produces a strategy for guiding initial follow-up practice of that recently introduced skill. Combining and sequencing in various ways these and other techniques described in the preceding pages enables us to produce a variety of strategies for conducting any of the kinds of daily classroom lessons that will develop further student proficiency in thinking.

Introducing Thinking Skills

Upon first encountering a need to execute a new or unfamiliar thinking operation, students benefit most from trying to identify the mental moves required to carry it out successfully. Some can do this inductively—they

Figure 9.3 Techniques for Improving Student Thinking

Introducing	Initial Frequent Scaffolded Practice	Intermittent Cued Practice to Independent Use and Transfer
By	*Teacher Mediation and Support by:*	*Teacher Prompting by:*
modeling	checklists	previewing
or		rehearsal
comparing to an expert	process questions	incomplete examples
and		and activities
thinking aloud	graphic organizers	cued directions and
or		questions
metacognitive reflection	metacognitive reflection	mnemonics
		symbols

simply try to carry out the skill as best they can to identify what must or can be done to execute it. Then they reflect on what they did to formalize and refine the procedure that emerged. Others prefer to do this deductively— they look for a model, a set of directions, or some other kind of assistance that spells out these moves in step-by-step order so they can follow them when they try to do it. Either way, novices in a skill need to identify and then apply specific steps that can be followed to execute the skill.

It is not surprising, then, that in introducing a thinking operation, making explicit and observable the procedures, rules, and knowledge by which it is carried out is essential to improving student proficiency in executing the operation.[12] This is especially true for youngsters who do not know how to execute a given cognitive operation as well as for virtually all students encountering a complex or difficult operation for the first time. Making visible precisely how any cognitive operation works when used skillfully makes novices aware of effective procedures by which they can execute it and provides a model of how it should work in practice. Accomplishing these goals should be the first thing those of us who are teachers should do when launching any concerted instructional effort to improve student proficiency in a new or difficult thinking operation.

Lessons that best introduce students to a thinking operation are those that build on what novices naturally do as they begin to learn a new skill, by helping them to (1) deconstruct the skill to identify key procedural steps in executing it, (2) articulate and demonstrate how this procedure can be executed, and (3) identify significant rules that may guide its skillful execution. Research, in fact, indicates that these introductory lessons should do the following:

- Make explicit the significant steps in one or more procedure(s) by which that operation is or could skillfully be carried out and the knowledge that informs the application of these procedures.[13]
- Demonstrate how a skilled execution of one or more of these procedures works, thus giving students a model of how the skill works.[14]
- Provide students with immediate opportunity to apply what they have seen, read, or heard about this operation to carry it out themselves as best they can, so they can begin to establish a routine for carrying it out.[15]
- Keep the focus primarily on the cognitive procedure(s) being introduced to minimize or eliminate interference often caused by the use of unfamiliar subject matter or subject matter to which students attach strong feelings.[16]

Skill-introducing lessons that incorporate these features provide the most productive take-off points for the meaningful skill practice and transfer that must follow.[17] The teaching strategies around which we organize these lessons employ techniques that make visible and explicit the thinking of experts and of students, as well as cueing techniques such as previewing or even rehearsal. But these techniques can be combined in different ways to produce different types of skill introductions. Inductive skill-introducing strategies, for example, let students start where they are by executing the skill and teasing how it can be done better out of this experience. Deductive (didactic or directive) skill-introducing strategies provide a given common procedure for all to follow. A developmental lesson combines both approaches. Figure 9.4 outlines four of these strategies. Additional strategies might also be devised by combining in other ways techniques that serve these same purposes.

How do these strategies work in practice? Assume as teachers we wish to introduce in our study of world history or geography the skill of evaluating for bias, and that we elect to use a directive strategy—Strategy A outlined in Figure 9.4—for this purpose. After clearly establishing that the focus of our lesson is to be on a thinking skill, we first *preview* this skill as described in Chapter 7. This involves labeling the skill with its technical name, providing or getting from volunteers several synonyms (if there are

Figure 9.4 Strategies for Introducing Thinking Skills

A **A Directive Strategy**	B **Inductive Strategy I**
1. Preview the skill. 2. Model a procedure for executing it. 3. Review the procedure. 4. Apply the procedure. 5. Reflect on how the procedure was executed. 6. Review and bridge the skill.	1. Preview the skill. 2. Think aloud while applying it. 3. Reflect on the procedure applied. 4. Compare to an expert's procedure. 5. Revise, plan, and share procedures. 6. Repeat 2–5 switching roles. 7. Review and share.
C **Inductive Strategy II**	D **A Developmental Strategy**
1. Preview the skill. 2. Apply the skill. 3. Reflect on and share procedures employed. 4. Apply the skill again. 5. Reflect on and share procedures employed. 6. Review and bridge the skill.	1. Apply the skill. 2. Reflect on and share procedure(s) employed. 3. Model any poorly executed steps or important rules. 4. Apply again (or continue applying) the skill. 5. Reflect on, share, and prepare a checklist for the procedure(s) to be used another time.

any) for its name, and providing or eliciting examples of where or when this skill has been or could be useful to employ in as well as out of school. Then, with the aid of the class if possible, we generate a simple, tentative definition of the skill. By doing this we help the students tap any knowledge they already have of this skill and develop readiness to execute it.

Next, we make explicit and visible a skillful procedure for executing this skill by modeling it. In so doing, we move through the key steps in this procedure to process information students are studying, explaining as we proceed why we are making the cognitive moves that we are. We explain how this procedure proceeds while we actually do it. The example of modeling presented in Chapter 5 illustrates what this might entail.

After our students paraphrase or review the key steps in the procedure we have demonstrated and highlighted, they then apply the skill procedure just modeled to the same kind of data used in modeling it. It is important for them at this point to use data with which they are already familiar or which is very similar to that used in the modeling, because they need to concentrate on applying the procedure of the thinking operation just introduced. They cannot focus well on the skill if they also have to make sense of complicated or unfamiliar information.[18] As they engage in this task, individually or in pairs, the students can refer to the steps and/or rules in the skill procedure articulated in modeling the skill and now displayed on a large poster, the chalkboard, overhead projector, or a handout.

Now, the students get an opportunity to reflect on the skill they have been using and how *they* employed it. As explained in Chapter 4, they reflect on how they executed the operation—in this continuing example, detecting bias—and then report it to or share it with another student. Volunteers then share the procedures they used with the entire class, with our prompting and guidance as necessary, and compare the various procedures reported to each other and to that modeled. They can conclude their metacognitive reflection by identifying key steps and rules in one or several effective procedures for executing this skill.

We close this directive skill-introducing lesson by having students identify the most important steps in the procedure(s) articulated, revise (if necessary) the definition of the skill presented or generated in the introduction to the lesson, and add other examples and synonyms or select one or two of those stated earlier that are especially accurate, given the class experience during the lesson with the skill. Students can also relate the skill to other skills and indicate conditions under which the places where use of this particular skill might be appropriate. This last technique *bridges* or extends the skill beyond the context of this particular lesson to help generalize the conditions under which it might appropriately be employed at other times.

This strategic combination of skill-teaching techniques can be employed to introduce any thinking operation to any students unfamiliar with it, regardless of their grade or ability levels or the subject matter being studied. Depending on the complexity of the skill being introduced, the ability levels of the students and their previous experience in applying the skill—however imperfect it may have been—and our experience in employing the teaching techniques included, lessons employing this strategy may be completed in anywhere from 20 to 45 minutes.

Strategy B in Figure 9.4 is more inductive than Strategy A. After previewing the skill, it involves our students in articulating, as best they can, how they presently execute the skill being introduced and then building on what they already know about it to refine or improve their execution of it. As based on the work of Arthur Whimbey and Jack Lochhead, the initiating technique consists of students working in pairs, one member of which executes the skill while thinking aloud as the other monitors what is being done.[19] After clarifying the mental steps taken, the two students then compare the procedure they have outlined to that used by an expert to execute the same task. Then, after revising their procedure or planning a new way to carry out the skill, the students switch roles and repeat the entire process, applying the same skill to new data, reflecting on what they did and comparing it to how an expert did that same task. The lesson then concludes with students reviewing the procedure(s) they employed, sharing them with their peers, and perhaps even preparing checklists they can use to execute the skill the next time they have occasion to employ it.

As Figure 9.4 indicates, the skill-teaching techniques described in the preceding chapters can also be combined in other ways to devise additional strategies for introducing thinking skills. A number of these strategies have been described in detail elsewhere.[20] Most of these strategies are built around techniques of making the thinking of students and/or of experts visible and explicit, as described in Part II of this book. Any combination of these techniques may be used as described here or with appropriate modifications to introduce unfamiliar or especially complex thinking operations to students.

Guiding and Supporting Practice

The primary purpose of *practice* is to internalize one or more efficient, effective procedures for carrying out a newly encountered or heretofore imperfectly executed thinking operation and to develop the ability to carry it out smoothly, rapidly, efficiently, and effectively. Research indicates that to be most effective, such practice must, at the very least, include the following:

- Build on an awareness—provided in the introductory lesson—of an explicit procedure for carrying out the thinking operation.

- Gradually move from frequent to intermittent practice.[21]
- Provide guidance and support, which are gradually withdrawn until performance is self-directed.[22]
- Gradually shift from focus on the thinking procedure to exclusive attention to the substantive knowledge generated by its application.[23]

As this research indicates, practice in thinking differs considerably from common "skill drill" exercises. The kinds of practice most useful in moving students through the levels that Dreyfus refers to as advanced beginner and competent user are keyed directly to the degree of proficiency in thinking that students exhibit at that point in mastering the skill they are practicing. *Initial* practice—that immediately following an explicit introduction to the thinking that is to be improved—is characterized by frequency, a high degree of guidance and structure, and focus on the explicit thinking procedure being practiced. This type of practice fits most closely into the infusion approach to integrating thinking and subject matter. The *intermittent* practice that follows is characterized by continuing but less frequent application of the skill with less structured and guided support and is more integrated into the subject-matter application of the thinking being practiced. It is, in effect, a transition between the infusion and immersion of thinking in subject-matter instruction. *Independent* practice—continuing, self-directed, but often cued application of this thinking in a variety of contexts—concludes formal instructional practice and is, in fact, typical of the immersion approach to integrating thinking and subject matter. Moving students through these three types of practice in sequence enables them to develop the degree of skill and expertise in thinking required of effective autonomous thinkers and learners.[24]

The techniques for scaffolding and cueing thinking presented in Part III may be employed in several ways to facilitate the kinds of practice presented above. They can be sequenced according to the degree of explicitness by which they structure the thinking operation being practiced, from most to least explicit. They can be combined into classroom teaching strategies to provide purposeful lessons that provide each of the kinds of practice necessary to develop a high degree of proficiency in the thinking operation being practiced.

As indicated in Figure 9.3, different kinds of skill-teaching techniques are appropriate for different kinds of practice. For example, because they are so explicit and detailed, procedural checklists or process-structured questions are most helpful to students during their initial practice of a newly introduced thinking skill. As students become a little more proficient in carrying out this skill, a graphic organizer can then be employed for this same purpose. Cueing techniques such as previewing, rehearsal, partly completed examples, and cued directions or questions can then gradually be substituted for a graphic organizer as students improve in their abilities to apply the skill and as their opportunities to do so become increasingly intermittent. Previewing and metacognitive reflection may also be employed at any time during the first half dozen or so times students need to apply a thinking skill after it has been introduced. Finally, as they demonstrate the ability to employ the skill with little, if any, support or guidance, perhaps mnemonics or even symbols will provide all the support or prompting needed to trigger a skill's application and successful execution. By sequencing the use of these techniques in this fashion, we gradually fade the degree of explicitness in the guidance and support we provide our students as they move to a point where they can carry out the skill satisfactorily on their own.

It should be noted here that it is neither necessary nor desirable to use every one of the scaffolding and cueing techniques described here in the course of guiding student practice of any single thinking skill. It is not helpful to students to use a checklist in one practice lesson for a given skill, a graphic organizer in the next practice of this skill, a partly completed example in the third, and so on. Nor is it helpful to use a checklist and graphic organizer in the same lesson. Such approaches are confusing and counterproductive, to say the least. The techniques enumerated here should be viewed as a catalog or pool of potentially useful skill practice supports. We can choose from them the several best suited to the particular skill to be practiced and employ them in sequence through a number of appropriate practice lessons.

We can, however, provide an even greater degree of structural support and guidance to students, especially in the initial and intermittent stages of practice, by incorporating several cueing and scaffolding techniques into the same lesson. As Figure 9.5 illustrates, these techniques can be combined to create a variety of strategies for this purpose. For example, the PREP strategy combines, in sequence, previewing the skill, rehearsal and execution of the skill, and metacognitive reflection (pondering) on how the skill was executed. Such a strategy can be used to organize a 10- to 20-minute portion of any lesson in which students are to apply a recently introduced thinking skill. The first several times this skill is employed, students may use a procedural checklist to guide their application of the skill. In subsequent practice of this skill, PREP lessons may employ a graphic organizer in place of the checklist as we begin to fade the support being provided to our students and move them toward more self-directed application of the skill.

As students demonstrate an ability to remember what to do to execute the skill as they apply it, we can turn to the PEP strategy to guide its application. As the outline in Figure 9.5 indicates, this strategy modifies the PREP strategy to eliminate use of rehearsal and to employ only cueing rather than

Figure 9.5 Strategies for Guiding and Supporting Student Skill Practice

PREP **Strategy for Scaffolding** **Initial Practice**	**PEP** **Strategy for Cueing** **Intermittent Practice**
1. Preview the skill. 2. Rehearse procedures for executing it. 3. Execute the skill, using a checklist, structured questions, or graphic organizer. 4. Ponder (reflect on) and share the procedure(s) employed.	1. Preview the skill. 2. Execute the skill, using increasingly less explicit cues (partly completed examples to cued questions to mnemonics and symbols). 3. Ponder (reflect on) the procedure(s) employed.

ALL-PURPOSE
Strategy for Practicing
a Thinking Skill

1. Preview the skill.
2. Apply the skill, thinking aloud.
3. Reflect on the procedure employed.
4. Compare to an expert's procedure.
5. Revise and plan the procedure to be used next time.

also employing scaffolding techniques. The specific cueing techniques used can be altered gradually as student proficiency in carrying out the skill continues to improve. Indeed, the "preview" step can gradually be dropped, as can the "ponder" step, until students are simply cued to use the skill by a mnemonic or symbol or general question or eventually simply the skill name or label. This strategy is well suited to moving students through intermittent into independent practice of a thinking skill.

The ALL-PURPOSE practice strategy outlined in Figure 9.5 combines the techniques of thinking aloud, metacognitive reflection, and comparing to an expert. This strategy, based on the work of Whimbey and Lochhead,[25] may be employed to guide students through all stages of practicing any thinking skill. After the skill to be practiced is previewed to develop the students' readiness or mental set for applying the skill they are to practice, pairs of students or individuals can apply it. If students work as pairs, one student in each pair thinks aloud as he or she actually carries out the skill; the other monitors what the partner is doing and keeps him or her on task. After reflecting on the procedure used, the pair compares the procedure used to that used by someone skilled at executing the same task. Then the student pairs revise their skill-using procedure for later use. Depending on the amount of practice needed, students may then repeat steps 2 through 5, reversing roles, and continue repeating this process, changing roles each time. In the initial stage of skill practice, they can use or make procedural checklists, process- structured questions, or even graphic organizers *before* they apply the skill a second or third time and then revise it *after* they have once again compared their skill-using procedure to that of an expert. In the later stages of practice, the application of the skill can be guided, as needed, by rehearsal, rather than by comparing to an expert, then later by cued directions, and eventually perhaps by an appropriate mnemonic. By altering the scaffolding or cueing techniques employed, we can move students through an entire practice schedule as they apply the skill repeatedly over an extended period of time.

Use of these strategies and techniques does not ignore the subject matter to which the structured thinking is being applied. In fact, these techniques actually assist students in generating more significant subject-matter insights than they otherwise might, especially if they are in the early stages of attempting to master a new or difficult thinking skill. However, in all skill practice lessons where these techniques are being employed, students should concentrate on applying, reflecting on, and discussing the skill being practiced *before* processing the subject-matter insights and knowledge developed by applying the skill. This concentrates student attention on the skill and minimizes the interference caused by competing subject matter. It also engages students in analysis of the skill while it is as fresh in their minds as it will ever be. However, as students move from initial to intermittent skill practice, less time need be devoted to analyzing the skill and more to subject matter analysis each time the skill is applied.

Practice of any thinking operation when scaffolded and cued as described here eventually moves students to the point where they can execute that operation on their own with some degree of expertise. They can recall how to carry it out and perform it relatively rapidly, more efficiently, and with less mental effort than they did earlier. However, they still need continuing opportunities to apply this skill in the pursuit of authentic learning objectives as well as to employ the skill in combination with other cognitive operations with which it is normally used to accomplish these objectives. At times, they may even need prompting to recognize these skill-using opportunities.

The techniques described in the previous chapters can be employed to provide the opportunities and cues that characterize this independent practice. As in all three stages of skill teaching, we can employ the knowledge-producing activities, learning strategies, projects, and other techniques described in Chapter 2 to provide these thinking opportunities and do so as a regular part of subject-matter study. For example, if this skill is that of evaluating for bias, we can regularly engage students in using a variety of different sources to gather information. Evaluating these sources for bias would be a natural part of this activity. We can also integrate the skill(s) to be practiced with other appropriate thinking skills by engaging students in problem solving or other knowledge-producing strategies and activities. For secondary school students. this may take the form of activities or tasks that require students to deal with questions such as:

> What evidence do these sources provide to support or refute the hypothesis that (. . . x . . .)?

Such a task requires students to employ a variety of thinking skills, including distinguishing relevant from irrelevant information, separating factual claims from value judgments and reasoned opinions, judging the credibility of the sources used, and determining their accuracy as well as evaluating them for bias.

To help students recognize the opportunities provided in a learning task to apply the skill to be practiced, we may find it necessary to cue use of the skill. We can do this simply by using the name of the skill in any task directions. This means using thoughtful language in all classroom discourse, as described in Chapter 3. Thus, perhaps by asking if a source being used is balanced, or even suggesting that it might be biased, may provide enough of a trigger for students to recognize this as an opportunity to evaluate it more closely for this purpose. Being more direct, if necessary, we can even ask, "Is there any evidence of bias here?" Task directions may actually require students to "Be sure to *evaluate* these sources for *bias* as well as for accuracy, credibility, and relevance (or other important qualities)."

For intermediate-grade students practicing more basic cognitive operations, however, each skill may have to be highlighted by separately cued questions or directions. Such cueing might simply divide the learning task into a sequence of subtasks and then cue the thinking that needs to be done to complete each, as follows:

> Compare the physical features of the main regions of the original 13 American colonies. Then *classify* these features into at least three different groups. What can you *conclude* about the physical geography of these colonies? Then, *predict* two areas of the 13 colonies that would be among the densely populated of the colonies by 1763. Give *evidence* and *reasons* that will *convince* us your prediction will come true.

As students become more skilled at identifying opportunities to employ specific cognitive skills and in making smooth transitions from their use to the appropriate application of other skills, cues will no longer be needed. General task directions or problems will then provide enough context for students to infer the kinds of cognitive operations they will have to engage in to respond to or resolve them.

Providing practice of cognitive operations from their introduction to independent use is not as casual an undertaking as the kind of skill practice conventionally undertaken in many classrooms. There is more to using practice to learn a cognitive skill or improve student performance of it than simply providing opportunities to do it and exhortation to take advantage of these opportunities. Figure 9.6 summarizes the essential features of appropriate practice and lists the skill-teaching techniques most useful in each type of such practice. Throughout skill practice, students require guidance and support in carrying out the skill being practiced, although this assistance often varies in type, amount, frequency, and degree of explicitness. The teaching strategies described here acknowledge these differences by combining appropriate skill-teaching techniques into effective practice lessons for developing student expertise in thinking.

Teaching for Transfer

Improving the quality of student thinking also consists of helping students to generalize a thinking operation beyond the context in which it is originally practiced. The purpose here is twofold. First, teaching for transfer seeks to enable students to execute a skill with ease in a variety of contexts. Second, and more important, it seeks to enable students to recognize those features of *any* context they may encounter in the future that make application of the skill appropriate and understand how these features may affect the skillful execution of the skill. Individuals who can do this demonstrate the level of skill proficiency Dreyfus describes as Proficient Performer, although the basis for this level of performance is established in the preceding levels of skill-using proficiency.

As already noted, a thinking operation is closely tied to the context in which it is initially encountered.[26] The longer students practice it in that same context, of course, the more skilled they become in executing it in that context. However, this does not mean they will transfer its application to or execute it effectively in other appropriate contexts on their own initiative. This is because, in most cases, a thinking skill works somewhat differently in different settings or contexts, including different subject matters and media. For example, what we look for in a film or video to detect bias and how we go about doing so differs somewhat from what we look for in a written account of a scientific experiment to detect bias.

It would seem that practicing a new skill in an ever-widening variety of contexts immediately after it has been explicitly introduced would enable transfer. But this is not so. Shifting contexts for skill practice during the initial stage of practice seriously interferes with student efforts to become more skilled at executing the operation. This is because students are forced to attend to the attributes of the ever-changing contexts in which the skill is being applied while they are, at the same time, trying to attend to the

Figure 9.6 Essential Features of Thinking Skill Practice

	Initial Practice	Intermittent Practice	Independent Practice
Goal	To perform a new thinking operation in a simple setting	To perform a thinking operation increasingly smoothly and efficiently	To perform a thinking operation with proficiency, from memory, in several settings
Duration	2 to 4 weeks following introduction of the operation	3 to ? weeks following conclusion of initial practice	Unlimited and continuing after intermittent practice
Frequency	Every 2 to 3 classes or days to every 3 to 4 classes or days	Every 3 to 4 classes or days gradually extending to once a week	At varied but irregular intervals not exceeding 7 to 8 class days
Features	Immediate feedback Brief application Extended reflection and discussion Consistent context Scaffolded skill support Simpler tasks Focus on skill/ procedure	Feedback Longer application Gradually fading Reflection/ discussion Contexts varied Cued skill support Increasing complexity Increasing focus on subject matter	Limited feedback Occasional skill discussion Contexts varied Cueing faded Focus on subject matter
Techniques	Procedural check-lists Process-structured questions Graphic organizers Previewing	Previewing Rehearsal Partly completed examples Cued questions/ directions Mnemonics	Previewing Cued directions and questions Mnemonics Symbols
	Metacognitive Reflection		

elements of the procedure they are attempting to carry out and about which they are still uncertain. Making students apply a newly introduced thinking procedure in new contexts too soon undercuts their developing expertise in executing it in even one context. Being able to apply a skill well in one context, however, actually makes transfer to additional contexts easier.[27] So, what can we do to teach for transfer?

We can use some of the skill-teaching techniques presented here to deal with this dilemma. First, we can use several of the techniques presented here in all the lessons and strategies described thus far to help students generalize the skill beyond the circumstances or subject in which they are applying it at the moment. For instance, by frequently generating and using synonyms for the technical or common skill name when previewing a skill, as described in Chapter 7, we broaden student awareness of the number of conditions and tasks that can also cue use of the skill. Articulating examples of where and when the skill has been or could be employed—both in previewing it to launch a lesson and in reviewing or bridging it to conclude a lesson—serves this same function. When students reflect on how a skill was executed, they also can be helped to generate principles or general rules for when and how to employ it in other contexts. As they practice applying it in different situations, they can also identify and generalize the features of these situations that make use of that skill appropriate.[28] The strategies and sample lessons presented in this chapter incorporate these techniques.

We can also teach for transfer more directly. For instance, we can treat every new context in which a skill is to be applied as a new skill-learning task and move students through the entire instructional framework presented in Figure 9.2 to become proficient in carrying it out in that context. That is, for each new context encountered, we can introduce the skill and then provide a series of initial, intermittent, and independent skill practices in that same context. We can repeat this sequence of lessons for *each* new context in which we wish the students to be able to apply the skill.

In addition, we can gradually alter the subject matter, media, and situations in which a specific cognitive operation is being practiced or applied to provide guided experience in using that thinking skill in different contexts. It is appropriate to begin doing this during that point in a practice schedule—perhaps midway or toward the end of a series of intermittent practice lessons—where students demonstrate an ability to execute an operation without extensive support. Their application of the operation to a new setting or context can then be initiated by reintroducing the skill in this new context or by a scaffolded practice lesson that serves the same purpose. This "reintroduction" to the skill can then be followed by scaffolded and cued lessons applying the skill in this new setting that provide the types of guided practice outlined earlier.

For example, after students are introduced to the skill of evaluating for bias in a written historical account, we can move them through a practice schedule in this skill using a series of historical accounts until they can apply it rather skillfully without our assistance. We can then introduce them to how this skill works in evaluating accounts of scientific experiments, then coach their practice of this skill with a number of such accounts through a series of initial, intermittent, and perhaps independent practice lessons. Then, we can introduce them to how this same skill can be applied to a documentary film or video and provide scaffolded and cued practice in applying this skill to a series of documentaries. The amount of required practice in each new context will decrease as the number of contexts increases, because students will always be applying essentially the same skill procedure at which they are becoming increasingly proficient. However, some time will have to devoted to learning the specific criteria being applied in each new context and the procedural and contextual nuances inherent in applying this procedure in various contexts.[29]

Some of the strategies presented in Figures 9.4 and 9.5 may be used in developing transfer. In structuring transfer lessons where the new circumstances are similar to the context in which the operation has already been introduced and previously practiced, a PREP strategy may be most useful. But when the new circumstances differ markedly from those surrounding previous applications of the operation, the directive introductory strategy may be most useful, since modeling the operation in this new setting may be especially helpful to the students. Indeed, when students demonstrate an inability to carry out in new circumstances a recently practiced thinking operation, we may even have to jump in and *reintroduce* the operation by treating it as if we were introducing it for the first time. Then we can follow that introduction with guided practice in additional examples of these new circumstances.[30]

Thus, it is important to remember that generalizing any thinking operation to situations or contexts beyond where students initially encountered or practiced it can be addressed in a variety of ways. When we employ the techniques described here continuously over an extended time, their cumulative impact is to broaden the range of contexts in which students can successfully apply a skill and to improve considerably student proficiency in carrying it out.

ORGANIZING SKILL-TEACHING TECHNIQUES FOR IMPROVING THINKING: A SUMMARY

We can improve student thinking by organizing instruction in any thinking operation requiring improvement according to the instructional framework described here. Using selected skill-teaching techniques in the sequences and in the strategic combinations presented here first introduces students to explicit, step-by-step procedures for executing a particular skill. Use of these and other techniques then moves students through a sequence of carefully guided and structured types of practice in applying the skill to its independent use and finally to its generalized, autonomous application in an increasing range of different contexts. When used in the instructional framework presented here, these skill-teaching techniques and strategies can be employed to improve the proficiency of students of all abilities and grade levels in any thinking operation, no matter how difficult this operation may appear.

Employing the teaching techniques and strategies described here works because this instructional framework acknowledges basic conditions regarding cognitive skill acquisition and development. Since students are more likely to learn what they are taught or what they perceive they are being taught rather than what they are not or do not perceive being taught, these strategies keep the focus of learning continuously on explicit cognitive procedure(s) that students are supposed to be improving or "learning."[31] Because improved thinking results from considerable experience, conscious effort, and reflection, instruction provided in this framework guides students through carefully structured, mediated thinking experiences that exhibit these essential features while students engage in that thinking for meaningful purposes.[32] And, because developing proficiency in any thinking operation requires its continued application over an extended period of time and in a variety of contexts, this approach provides the continuing skill-focused instruction required to develop transfer.[33]

Figure 9.3 summarized the skill-teaching techniques that can be used to assist students in improving their thinking and where in the skill-teaching framework they may be most appropriately employed to accomplish this goal. Those most appropriate for introducing a new thinking skill are techniques that make thinking visible and explicit. Those most suitable for aiding students in practicing this skill immediately after it has been introduced are those that provide considerable explicit scaffolding of the thinking procedure(s) to be applied. Those techniques most useful to guiding students through the intermittent practice that follows are those that prompt or cue recall of the skill(s) to employ and of how to execute it (them). Any of these techniques may be employed in guiding transfer, depending on how explicit and structured is the support needed by the students. By combining selected techniques from within each list or across lists, we can create strategies for providing exactly the direction, guidance, and support students need to sharpen their abilities to execute any thinking operation.

To be successful in any serious effort to improve student thinking, we should develop a repertoire of these techniques and strategies and become skilled in employing them in our classrooms. We should be just as capable of employing them spontaneously whenever our students—in the midst of a subject-matter lesson—evidence an inability to carry out an important thinking operation as we are in employing them to organize preplanned skill teaching lessons.

Continued, systematic use of these techniques and strategies will enable students to develop the highest degree of proficiency in thinking of which they are capable. It also ensures and accelerates that development.

Moreover, when these strategies are integrated with instruction in subject matter, such improved thinking can be developed just when students need it to enhance their academic achievement and learning. Chapter 10 describes and explains how to produce such integrated instruction in thinking and subject matter.

ENDNOTES

1. Ann Brown, Joseph C. Campione, and Jeanne D. Day, "Learning to Learn: On Training Students to Learn from Texts," *Educational Researcher 10* 2 (February 1981): 14–21; Walter Doyle, "Academic Work," *Review of Educational Research 53* 2 (Summer 1983): 159–199; Bryce B. Hudgins, *Learning and Thinking* (Itasca, IL: F. E. Peacock, 1977), pp. 92–99; Michael I. Posner and Steven W. Keele, "Skill Learning," in Robert M. W. Travers (Ed.), *Second Handbook of Research on Teaching* (Chicago: Rand McNally College Publishing, 1973), pp. 805–831.

2. Doyle, "Academic Work," pp. 163–173; Hubert L. Dreyfus, "Expert Systems versus Intuitive Enterprise," unpublished paper delivered at George Mason University, May 29, 1984, Fairfax, VA; see also Robbie Case, *Intellectual Development* (Orlando: Academic Press, 1985) and Robbie Case, *The Mind's Staircase* (Hillsdale, NJ: Lawrence Erlbaum, 1992).

3. Dreyfus, "Expert Systems," *passim*.

4. Benjamin Bloom, (Ed.), *Developing Talent in Young People* (New York: Ballantine Books, 1985); Doyle, "Academic Work," pp. 163–173; Dreyfus, "Expert Systems," *passim*; Case, *Intellectual Development*, *passim*; Lauren B. Resnick, "The Science and Art of Curriculum Design," in Jon Schaffarzick and David H. Hampson (Eds.), *Strategies for Curriculum Development* (Berkeley: McCutchan, 1975), p. 44.

5. *Ibid.*

6. Reuven Feuerstein, *Instrumental Enrichment* (Baltimore: University Park Press, 1980).

7. Edward deBono, "The Direct Teaching of Thinking as a Skill," *Phi Delta Kappan 64* 10 (June 1983): 703–708; John Edwards, "Measuring the Effects of the Direct Teaching of Thinking Skills," *Human Intelligence Newsletter 9* 3 (Fall 1988): 9–10; Russell Gersten and Douglas Carmine, "Direct Instruction in Reading Comprehension," *Educational Leadership 41* 7 (April 1986): 70–78.

8. Howard Anderson (Ed.), *Teaching Critical Thinking in Social Studies, 13th Yearbook* (Washington, DC: National Council for the Social Studies, 1942), pp. v–vii; Barry K. Beyer, "Common Sense about Teaching Thinking Skills," *Educational Leadership 41* 3 (November 1983): 44–49; Edward M. Glaser, *An Experiment in the Development of Critical Thinking* (New York: Bureau of Publications, Teachers College, Columbia University, 1941), p. 69; Hudgins, *Learning and Thinking, passim*; Beau Fly Jones, MindaRae Amiran, and Michael Katins, "Teaching Cognitive Strategies and Text Structures Within Language Arts Programs," in Judith W. Segal, Susan F. Chipman, and Robert Glaser (Eds.), *Thinking and Learning Skills: Volume I—Relating Instruction to Research* (Hillsdale, NJ: Lawrence Erlbaum, 1985), pp. 259–296; David Perkins, *Smart Schools* (New York: The Free Press, 1992), pp. 27–30, 195–196; Posner and Keele, "Skill Learning," pp. 805–831; Barak Rosenshine and Carla Meister, "The

Use of Scaffolds for Teaching Higher-Level Cognitive Strategies," *Educational Leadership 49* 7 (April 1992): 26–33; Hilda Taba, "Learning by Discovery," *Elementary School Journal 63* 6 (March 1963): 308–316; Hilda Taba, "Teaching of Thinking," *Elementary English 42* 15 (May 1965): 534.

9. Jere Brophy, "Probing the Subtleties of Subject-matter Teaching," *Educational Leadership 49* 7 (April 1992): 4–8; Mary Bryson and Marlene Scardamalia, "Teaching Writing to Students at Risk for Academic Failure," in Barbara Means, Carol Chelemer, and Michael S. Knapp (Eds.), *Teaching Advanced Skills to At-Risk Students* (San Francisco: Jossey-Bass, 1991), pp. 141–167; Doyle, "Academic Work," pp. 163–173; Robert M. Gagne, *The Conditions of Learning* (3rd ed.) (New York: Holt, Rinehart and Winston, 1985); Hudgins, *Learning and Thinking,* pp. 92–99; Jones, Amiran, and Katims, "Teaching Cognitive Strategies," pp. 259–296; Robert Pasnak, "Teaching Basic Cognitive Operations to At-Risk Students, " *Human Intelligence Newsletter 10* 2 (Spring-Summer 1989): p. 5; Posner and Keele, "Skill Learning," pp. 805–831; Barak V. Rosenshine, "Synthesis of Research on Explicit Teaching," *Educational Leadership 43* 7 (April 1986): 60–69; Jane Stallings, "Effective Strategies for Teaching Basic Skills," in Daisy G. Wallace (Ed.), *Developing Basic Skills Programs in Secondary Schools* (Alexandria, VA: Association for Supervision and Curriculum Development, 1983), pp. 1–19.

10. Perkins, *Smart Schools*, pp. 122–130; David N. Perkins and Gavriel Salomon, "Teaching for Transfer," *Educational Leadership 46* 1 (September 1988): 22–32.

11. deBono, "The Direct Teaching," pp. 703–708; Edwards, "Measuring the Effects," pp. 9–10; Gersten and Carmine, "Direct Instruction," pp. 70–78.

12. Bonnie B. Armbruster, Richard C. Anderson, and V. Cindy Mall, "Preparing Teachers of Literacy," *Educational Leadership 49* 3 (November 1991): 21–24; Allan Collins, John Seeley Brown, and Susan E. Newman, "Cognitive Apprenticeship: Teaching the Crafts of Reading, Writing and Mathematics," *Thinking: The Journal of Philosophy for Children 8* 1 (n.d.): 2–10; David Perkins, "Myth and Method in Teaching Thinking," *Teaching Thinking and Problem Solving 9* 2 (March/April 1987): 1–2, 8–9; Michael Pressley and Karen P. Harris, "What We Really Know about Strategy Instruction," *Educational Leadership 48* 1 (September 1990): 31–34; Rosenshine and Meister, "The Use of Scaffolds," pp. 26–33.

13. Jones, Amiran, and Katins, "Teaching Cognitive Strategies" pp. 259–296; Perkins, *Smart Schools*, pp. 195–196; Posner and Keele, "Skill Learning," pp. 805–831; Rosenshine and Meister, "The Use of Scaffolds," pp. 26–33.

14. Posner and Keele, "Skill Learning," pp. 805–832; Rosenshine and Meister, "The Use of Scaffolds," pp. 26–33.

15. *Ibid.*

16. Anderson, *Teaching Critical Thinking*, pp. v-vii; Glaser, *An Experiment,* p. 69; Beyer, "Common Sense," pp. 44–49; deBono, "The Direct Teaching," pp. 703–708; Hudgins, *Learning and Thinking, passim*; Posner and Keele, "Skill Learning," pp. 805–831; Jon Schaffarzick, "Questions and Requirements for the Comparative Study of Curriculum Development Procedures," in Schaffarzick and Hampson, *Strategies*, pp. 211–256; Taba, "Learning by Discovery," pp. 308–316; Taba, "Teaching of Thinking," p. 534.

17. Posner and Keele, "Skill Learning," pp. 805–831; Barry K. Beyer, *Practical Strategies for the Teaching of Thinking* (Boston: Allyn and Bacon, 1987), pp. 74–76, 124–133.

18. Posner and Keele, "Skill Learning," pp. 805–831.

19. Jack Lochhead, "Teaching Analytic Reasoning Skills through Pair Problem Solving," in Segal, Chipman, and Glaser, *Thinking and Learning Skills*, pp. 109–132; Arthur Whimbey and Jack Lochhead, *Problem Solving and Comprehension* (5th ed.) (Hillsdale, NJ: Lawrence Erlbaum, 1991), pp. 1–28.

20. Beyer, *Practical Strategies*, pp. 87–138; deBono, "The Direct Teaching." pp. 703–708; Robert Sternberg and Janet Davidson, "A Four Pronged Model for Intellectual Development," *Journal of Research and Development in Education* 22 3 (Spring 1989): 26–28; Lochhead, "Teaching Analytic Reasoning," pp. 109–132; Arthur Whimbey, "Teaching Sequential Thought: The Cognitive Skills Approach," *Phi Delta Kappan 59* 4 (December 1977): 255–259.

21. Beyer, *Practical Strategies*, pp. 139–161; Lochhead, "Teaching Analytic Reasoning," pp. 109–131; Perkins, *Smart Schools, passim*; Posner and Keele, "Skill Learning," pp. 805–831; Rosenshine and Meister, "The Use of Scaffolds," pp. 26–33; Whimbey and Lochhead, *Problem Solving*, pp. 21–40.

22. Pressley and Harris, "What We Really Know," pp. 31–34.

23. Perkins, *Smart Schools, passim*; Perkins and Salomon, "Teaching for Transfer," pp. 22–32.

24. Doyle, "Academic Work,"pp. 163–173; Hudgins, *Learning and Thinking*, pp. 22–99; Posner and Keele, "Skill Learning," pp. 805–831.

25. Whimbey and Lochhead, *Problem Solving*, pp. 1–28.

26. Perkins and Salomon, "Teaching for Transfer," pp. 22–32.

27. Hudgins, *Learning and Thinking*, pp. 142–172; Perkins and Salomon, "Teaching for Transfer," pp. 22–32; Posner and Keele, "Skill Learning," pp. 805–831.

28. Perkins, *Smart Schools, passim*; Perkins and Salomon, "Teaching for Transfer," pp. 22–32; Posner and Keele, "Skill Learning," pp. 805–831.

29. Beyer, *Practical Strategies*. pp. 163–190.

30. *Ibid.*, pp. 163–178; Perkins, *Smart Schools, passim*; Pressley and Harris, "What We Really Know," pp. 31–34; Rosenshine and Meister, "The Use of Scaffolds," pp. 26–31; Grant Wiggins, "Creating a Thought-Provoking Curriculum," *American Educator 11* 4 (Winter 1987): 10–17.

31. Frederick J. McDonald, *Research on Teaching and Its Implications for Policy Making* (Princeton, NJ: Educational Testing Service, 1976); Barak V. Rosenshine, "Content, Time and Direct Instruction," in Penelope L. Peterson and Herbert J. Walberg (Eds.), *Research on Teaching* (Berkeley: McCutchan, 1979), p. 39.

32. Posner and Keele, "Skill Learning," pp. 805–831; Raymond Nickerson, "On Improving Thinking through Instruction," in Ernest Z. Rothkopf (Ed.), *Review of Research in Education*, Volume 15 (Washington, DC: American Educational Research Association, 1988–89), pp. 3–57.

33. Hudgins, *Learning and Thinking*, pp. 142–172; Perkins, *Smart Schools*, pp. 122–130; Perkins and Salomon, "Teaching for Transfer," pp. 22–32.

10

Integrating Instruction in Thinking and Subject Matter

Integrating instruction in thinking and subject matter consists of incorporating the teaching of each to facilitate the learning of both. This means incorporating instruction in thinking with instruction in the major school subject matters—math, the sciences, social studies, and language arts and literature, at the very least—in such a way that each contributes to advancing student proficiency in thinking and academic learning. To accomplish this type of integration requires both careful curriculum planning as well as flexibility in teaching.

Integrating thinking and subject-matter learning requires attention to two tasks: incorporating *thinking* into subject matter and incorporating *instruction in thinking* into instruction in subject matter. The two differ considerably. Incorporating *thinking* with subject matter involves identifying the kinds of thinking to be emphasized (e.g., strategies such as problem solving, conceptualizing, and decision making; critical thinking operations such as detecting bias or judging the strength of an argument; microthinking operations such as analysis, evaluation, and synthesis; some combination of all of these) and then making sure that the kinds of subject-matter knowledge to be learned require repeated application of these cognitive operations. Incorporating *instruction in thinking* into subject-matter instruction consists of integrating specific skill-teaching techniques and strategies into the instructional methods and activities used to develop the subject-matter learning desired. This chapter identifies the major tasks that must be undertaken to achieve this goal and suggests some practical ways to carry them out.

INTEGRATING THINKING AND SUBJECT MATTER

Before we can integrate instruction in thinking and subject matter, we must first be clear about the thinking we wish students to improve and where we will try to provide this instruction. This means incorporating the kinds of thinking and thinking skills to be emphasized into the subject-matter learning that we seek, so that they are integral to subject-matter learning rather than extraneous add-ons. Accomplishing this goal involves at least four tasks:

1. Identify the specific types of thinking (problem solving, critical thinking, decision making, etc.) and thinking skills (hypothesis making, evaluating for bias, making conclusions, etc.) to receive instructional emphasis;
2. Identify the procedural, declarative, and conditional knowledge that constitutes the thinking operations selected.
3. Assign the introductory teaching of these selected thinking operations to those subjects and to grade levels that offer the largest number of authentic opportunities for students to apply them.
4. Identify where, in specific courses or units in these subjects, such thinking is required or can be purposefully applied.

Once we have accomplished these tasks, we will be able to plan and offer to our students the kind of instruction, practice, guidance, and support best suited to improve student proficiency in executing the thinking operations selected for emphasis. The following suggestions will facilitate the completion of these tasks.

Identifying Thinking Operations on Which to Focus

Learning any subject matter naturally involves thinking, whether it be memorizing or remembering, problem solving, pattern finding, or any other cognitive operations. However, our teaching does not always provide enough continuing, frequent opportunities to apply the kind(s) of thinking that students may most need to improve. So, probably the best way to determine what thinking to concentrate our instructional efforts on is to identify the important cognitive operations, skills, and strategies with which our students now have difficulty or are likely to have difficulty in the future. We can identify these operations in a variety of ways.

One way to identify thinking operations to be emphasized is simply to note, as we teach, those instances in which students demonstrate frustration, difficulty, or actual mistakes in executing any specific thinking operation or thinking behavior. The greater the number of students demonstrating such difficulties with the same specific operation or behavior, and the greater the frequency with which such difficulties are encountered, the more likely a thinking operation deserves to be a subject of systematic, continuing instruction.

We can also identify thinking operations with which students presumably will have difficulty even before we observe their behaviors during classroom instruction. Our past experiences with students may provide clues to such skills. We can also analyze student performance on standardized tests or other assessments, recommendations of experts in cognition and in cognitive instruction, the instructional materials we will be using, published expectations of future employers or college faculty, and educational reports and studies to assist us in identifying thinking operations suitable for classroom instruction.[1] Cognitive psychologists, for example, find that unless youngsters can classify and seriate by the end of the second grade, they will quite likely always have serious difficulties reading and comprehending. Such findings ought to alert us to the need for early attention to these operations—and the supporting operations of attributing, comparing, and predicting. These five thinking skills, consequently, ought to be a major emphasis of thinking instruction in all subject matters included in preschool and primary grade education.[2] Complaints by employers about the inability of employees to engage successfully in problem solving and by college faculty about undergraduate student unwillingness or inability to engage in sustained analytical and critical thinking surely indicate other thinking operations that need considerable instructional attention in our classrooms.[3]

By searching these sources and using other appropriate diagnostic methods, we can identify literally dozens of thinking skills in which our students may need to improve.[4] But time and the amount of subject matter we teach simply do not permit us to attend explicitly and in continuing fashion to *all* the thinking skills that might be so identified. Thus, we are faced with winnowing a list of cognitive operations we *could* teach to a number in which we actually *can* or *will* provide the kind of continuing systematic instruction through practice to transfer that our students may most require.

Criteria for selecting thinking operations for classroom instruction have been identified by a number of specialists.[5] In general, they recommend that thinking skills earmarked for systematic instruction throughout a curriculum should be those that are:

1. Demonstrably difficult for our students to skillfully execute
2. Naturally and frequently employed in the subject matter(s) in which they are to be taught,

3. Frequently employed or required for success in a number of academic subject-matter courses,
4. Frequently employed or required for success in out-of-school, every day, social, civic and work experience, and
5. Related to or essential components of major cognitive strategies.

By evaluating carefully all the thinking operations and skills proposed for attention against these criteria, we can identify those that are most worthy of systematic classroom attention.6 Then we can move to integrate them into the various subject matters where appropriate instruction in them can be best provided.

Identifying the Attributes of the Thinking to Be Emphasized

As explained in Part II, every thinking operation, whether it be as complex as problem solving or conceptualizing or as discrete as judging the strength of an argument, consists of three kinds of knowledge: procedural, conditional, and declarative. Appropriate placement of these operations in a body of subject matter, a curriculum, or a course, as well as successful instruction in them, necessitates as deep as possible an understanding of these knowledge attributes or components. Where such understanding is fuzzy or lacking, we must develop it.

Becoming familiar with the components of any specific thinking operation and how it can be skillfully executed in practice requires experience in applying it in a variety of contexts as well as study and reflection. Developing this understanding and expertise occurs gradually but can be accelerated by a concerted effort with our peers to clarify exactly what constitutes the thinking operations we may be responsible for teaching.[7] By watching individuals skilled in executing these operations model them and by practicing them ourselves with peer help, if necessary, and peer feedback, we can add to our understanding of them. A number of specialists in teaching thinking have produced detailed descriptions of some of the more common important thinking operations that can be readily consulted.[8]

It is often useful for those of us who are teachers to work with a group of peers to produce written descriptions of the procedures, rules, heuristics, and conditions by and under or which these operations are applied, for every thinking operation students may need assistance in mastering.[9] Such descriptions, when completed, should be analyzed by individuals somewhat skilled in executing the operations they describe and then revised based on their comments. We should consider the resulting descriptions as tentative and evolving, and revise them periodically to reflect our developing understanding of how these operations work in practice. Assisting our students in improving their skill at executing these operations also contributes considerably toward our own understanding of and proficiency in these thinking operations. Understanding what is in a thinking operation is a task that never quite gets completed and may be engaged in throughout the planning and implementation of any effort to improve the quality of our students' thinking. But working to better understand the thinking operations we are teaching or assigned to teach is indispensable to the success of any such instructional effort.

Assigning Thinking Skills to Appropriate Subjects and Grade Levels

Because of time constraints, as well as the nature of the various subjects taught in school, all thinking operations selected for instruction cannot be taught well in all subjects. Therefore, to maximize the impact of instruction in these operations, at least in its initial stages, only a limited number of thinking skills should be introduced and taught to some degree of initial proficiency in any particular content area or subject matter. Determining which thinking operations are to receive primary instruction in each particular subject matter, then, becomes an important step in integrating thinking and subject matter.

Fitting thinking and subject matter together for instructional purposes consists essentially of matching the thinking operations selected for instruction to the subject(s) in which students will most often have need to apply or use them.[10] The most desirable thinking skill/subject-matter matches are those in which:

- Opportunities for students to employ the skill in authentic learning tasks will be numerous, frequent, and continued throughout the study of the subject.
- There is a direct functional interrelationship among the thinking skills to be emphasized in that subject.

In other words, thinking skills assigned for instruction in any specific subject matter must be those in which students will have numerous, recurring, and continued opportunities to apply in carrying out authentic learning tasks in that subject. Authentic learning tasks are those integral to achieving subject-matter learning goals as opposed to contrived exercises unrelated to achieving such goals. Thus, problem solving and hypothesis making and testing are clearly best matched with the subject areas of the physical sciences and mathematics. This is because these operations constitute the very essence of these subjects and students have many more opportunities to employ them in their study of these subjects than in the study of any other subjects. Decision making, on the other hand, as well as certain critical thinking skills—such as evaluating for bias, judging the credibility of a source, and identifying point of view—are better matched with the social studies and literature than with most other subjects. This is because they are so frequently employed in studying these subjects or are central to the subjects themselves.

Some thinking operations, however—such as argument analysis, evaluating the strength of an argument, and argument construction—can justifiably be assigned to any subject in which students actively produce knowledge, and present and justify their findings or conclusions. In each of these examples, the various thinking skills mentioned closely relate to each other functionally, thus facilitating the learning as well as improved performance of them all.

In assigning specific thinking skills or types of thinking to specific grade levels as well as to specific subject-matter areas, we must also consider the estimated difficulty of the skills for the students in the grades to which these are to be assigned. Experience indicates, of course, that most students in any grade can develop *some* degree of proficiency in virtually any cognitive operation if given enough time for appropriate instruction and practice.[11] However, the lack of time for this purpose as well as the degree of complexity and abstractness of many thinking operations makes assigning skills without regard to these factors unwise.

Thus, in the interest of student readiness and teaching efficiency and effectiveness, it seems most appropriate in matching thinking skills to subject-matter areas at specific grade levels to assign the simpler or most basic skills (e.g., classifying and seriating) to the primary grades. Reserve more abstract and complex skills (e.g., identifying certain logical fallacies or unstated assumptions) to intermediate or secondary grades. However, important thinking strategies such as decision making, problem solving, argument evaluation, and argument construction can be presented in the early grades as general procedures. In this case, only a few, key steps should be involved, gradually elaborating them into the more complex procedures as students move upward through the grades.[12]

The results of this matching of thinking skills and subject areas where they will be initially taught is usually a thinking skills/subject-matter scope and sequence. If this encompasses the entire school district or building, the scope and sequence can identify which thinking operations are to be the focus of continuing instruction in specific subjects at specific grade levels. If dealing with only a single course, it may identify which thinking skills are to be the focus of instruction in each of the units or segments of the course. Integrated thinking/subject-matter scope and sequences specify the subject areas where instruction in specific kinds of thinking is to occur; by so doing they enable us to plan our teaching appropriately. They also provide a clear overview of the overall intended instructional effort to improve the quality of student thinking in the subjects or courses specified.

Figure 10.1 presents an example of a scope and sequence for a K–12 integrated thinking/subject-matter program. This figure indicates those grade levels in various subject matters where selected thinking operations can be formally introduced and taught, the subjects in which this introductory teaching can occur, and the specific thinking skill(s) included in the sequence. In addition, it indicates how the substance of selected major thinking strategies can be elaborated upward through the grades in these subjects. In essence, this scope and sequence calls for the periodic introduction of a few new skills or strategies in pairs of selected subjects over a number of years. Continued guided practice, elaboration, and transfer of previously introduced skills can then occur in spiral fashion over subsequent years. Transfer and elaboration across subject areas at appropriate grade levels can also be an integral part of such an integrated sequence. Similar thinking skill/subject-matter scope and sequences can be prepared for specific subjects on a grade level basis, as well.[13]

Identifying Opportunities for Applying Thinking Skills in Specific Courses

Every opportunity for students to apply or employ a specific thinking operation is also a potential opportunity for providing instruction or guidance in how to execute that operation. Thus, as a first step in planning such instruction, it is necessary to determine where the learning activities and goals students will engage in or seek in a specific course will require its application. This consists of identifying as many as possible of those opportunities in a course or unit where students will have to apply that skill as a natural part of their subject-matter learning. If, for example, we are to focus on the skill of evaluating for bias, we need to search through our course or unit to find those places where students will have opportunities to evaluate information for bias as a part of their normal learning activities. If this is a social studies course, this would include any time they are using primary sources, secondary accounts, newspaper articles, editorials, and so on. If the target skill is classifying, we need to search for places in our course when students will have opportunities to apply this particular skill, such as when they will be asked to develop generalizations or conclusions.

Although it is sometimes relatively easy to infer the kinds of thinking required to achieve a specific learning goal or complete a learning activity, this is not always so. At times, a rather intensive task analysis is required for this purpose. Such a task analysis involves dissecting a proposed learning activity or goal to identify the cognitive skills that must be employed to carry it to a successful completion. To execute a learning activity involving making a generalization about something, for example, a student would have to identify examples of this "something"; evaluate data relevant to each example for credibility, accuracy, relevancy, and sufficiency; analyze the data to identify the essential attributes of each example; compare and contrast these identified attributes; infer their interrelationships; classify them into groups; infer relationships and patterns between the groups; and then

Figure 10.1 A Sample K-12 Integrated Thinking/Subject-Matter Scope and Sequence

Grade scale: K 1 2 3 4 5 6 7 8 9 10 11 12

Classify / Seriate (K) — subject area: **Reading and All Appropriate Subjects**

Observe
Compare/contrast
Classify
Seriate
Predict

Given concept examples
Identify common attributes
Classify attributes
Relate attributes to each other

Observe
Compare/contrast
Classify
Seriate
Predict

Define concept
Identify examples
Identify common attributes
Classify attributes
Relate attributes to each other
Specify critical attributes

Problem Solving — subject area: **Math and Science**

Identify a problem
Choose solution plan
Execute plan
Check answer

Selected solution plans and formulas

Recognize a problem
Represent the problem
Plan/choose a solution plan
Execute plan
Check answer/plan

Selected solution plans and formulas

Recognize a problem
Organize data
Represent the problem
Plan/choose a solution plan
Execute plan
Check answer/plan

Analysis, Synthesis, Evaluation — subject area: **Any Subject as Useful**

Analyze parts of a whole
Synthesize sentences stories
Evaluate using given criteria

Analyze parts of a whole
Synthesize paragraphs and short essays
Evaluate using self-invented criteria

Analyze relationships
Synthesize essays, papers arguments
Evaluate using multiple criteria

Decision Making — subject area: **Social Studies & Language Arts**

Define goal
Identify options
Choose best option

Define goal
Identify options
Analyze options
Rank options
Choose best option

Define goal
Identify options
Analyze options
Rank options
Evaluate top options
Choose best option

Critical Thinking — subject area: **Social Studies, Language Arts, & Science**

Fact/value claim
Relevant/irrelevant

Identify parts of an argument:
• conclusion
• reasons

Factual accuracy
Credibility of a source
Ambiguity

Identify chains of arguments

Bias
Unstated assumption
Logical fallacies

Judge strength of an argument

Logical fallacies
Logical inconsistencies

Source: Adapted from Barry K. Beyer, *Developing a Thinking Skills Program* (Boston: Allyn and Bacon, 1988), pp. 208–209.

synthesize one or more general statements that validly represent all examples of the phenomenon about which students are generalizing. Similar analysis of each of these thinking operations will clarify even more precise subordinate cognitive operations or procedures required to complete the overall activity. Such task analyses enable us to identify specific cognitive operations involved in any learning activity. Without conducting them, we cannot be sure which cognitive operations will legitimately be included in a specific learning activity or ensure that a specific thinking skill we may wish to include is a natural part of it.

At this point, we should have identified (in the order in which they will occur) most, if not all, of the activities or places in a course where students will have authentic opportunities to use the thinking skill targeted for improvement. If we are to emphasize more than one skill, then obviously we must repeat this procedure for each skill in order to identify opportunities for applying each one throughout the entire course. Initial efforts to identify these opportunities rarely identify all appropriate opportunities—more will make themselves apparent as student learning actually progresses. However, establishing as clearly as possible a sequence of perceived subject-matter embedded skill-using opportunities is important at this stage of planning.

Summary

Having completed the planning tasks described here in satisfactory fashion, we will have identified a limited number of specific thinking operations to emphasize in our curricula, matched them with appropriate subject matters at appropriate grade levels, and identified as many as possible opportunities for students to employ them in their subject-matter study in a specific course or courses. We will also have made a good start at clarifying and adding to our knowledge of how these thinking operations work when skillfully executed and to our own developing expertise in carrying them out. At this point, we can turn to integrating instruction in these thinking operations with the specific subject-matter *instruction* we propose to carry out.

INTEGRATING INSTRUCTION IN THINKING WITH INSTRUCTION IN SUBJECT MATTER

Integrating instruction in thinking with subject-matter instruction consists of providing instruction in a cognitive operation when the students are using it in the execution of a purposeful subject-matter learning activity or task. To make such instruction effective requires us to provide students with frequent, repeated, appropriately spaced opportunities to engage in that thinking. These skill-using opportunities then allow us to provide the kinds and amounts of direction, guidance, and support appropriate to improving student proficiency in that thinking. To accomplish this, we can do the following:

1. Establish a sequence of opportunities for students to apply each selected thinking operation that will provide for an appropriate schedule of skill introduction, practice, and transfer.
2. Integrate the thinking operations on which we elect to focus with other thinking operations into purposeful subject-matter learning tasks.
3. Use teaching strategies, techniques, learning materials and activities to provide the kinds of direction, guidance, practice, and support appropriate to the development of student proficiency in the skills selected for improvement.

Establishing a Skill-Using Sequence Appropriate for Instruction

As explained in the preceding chapters, helping students to improve their proficiency in any thinking skill requires those of us who are teachers to make procedures for effectively executing that skill visible and explicit. In turn, we must then provide the kinds of scaffolded, cued, and guided practice necessary for our students to be able to carry out the skill smoothly and effectively on their own in a variety of contexts. Ideally, the opportunities for student application in our subject-matter course of a thinking operation selected for such instruction will occur at intervals and in sufficient numbers to allow for such continuing instruction and practice.

Although all students benefit from numerous opportunities to practice applying a skill they are trying to improve and all benefit from the same kinds of practice, the exact amount of each kind of practice required varies. No precise amount of skill application or practice can be specified for developing proficiency in any particular thinking operation or type of thinking for any particular type of students. In fact, the amount of application or practice customarily required to master a cognitive operation varies considerably from student to student as well as from thinking skill to thinking skill.[14] It depends considerably on (1) the complexity of the cognitive operation being practiced, (2) the prior experience students have had in carrying it out on their own with whatever degree of success they could achieve, (3) the relevance of the operation to meeting their learning or personal needs, (4) their knowledge of and familiarity with the subject matter or content to which the operation is being applied, and (5) the degree to which they understand the cognitive procedures that constitute the operation. Research indicates that, for some students, as few as half a dozen practices of a particular cognitive skill are sufficient to bring about significant improvement. For others, especially cognitively at-risk students or in the case of especially complex operations, upwards of 50 or more practices may be required even to approach this goal.[15] In general, a considerable number of practice opportunities are required to develop the degree of expertise and automaticity required for the productive and efficient execution of any cognitive operation.

For example, a reasonable practice schedule for a newly introduced thinking operation might consist of four to six highly structured practice lessons in the two weeks immediately following the lesson in which the skill is to be explicitly introduced. Over this period, the interval between opportunities to practice applying the skill would be no more than one or two class days, at most. Thereafter, however, assuming this amount of concentrated, frequent practice produces an appropriate level of performance, the interval between subsequent practices can gradually be lengthened to three and later to four or five days. Eventually, perhaps, a single practice lesson each week or so may suffice for continuing to improve proficiency in this skill and for maintaining this degree of proficiency. Although no exact practice schedule can be prescribed for every thinking skill or group of students, this distribution of practice may serve as a baseline for planning. Of course, this is subject to specific adjustments resulting from how well the students actually apply the skill as they progress.

Figure 10.2 presents a sequence of opportunities for students to employ a given thinking skill over a 10-week period in a single course. In this sequence, the skill to be emphasized will or can be employed by students in those classes where a box appears (in classes 1, 3, 5, 7, etc). Such a sequence of skill-using activities provides exactly the needed frequent skill-using opportunities spaced at appropriate intervals. Such spacing provides the kind of instruction and practice necessary to assist the students in becoming somewhat proficient in executing this skill on their own, especially if we anticipate they will be encountering it in this subject-matter context for the first time.

In this sequence, the skill can thus be introduced the first time it is to be used—in class 1. The need to apply this skill in classes 3, 5, 7, and 10 then provides opportunities for scaffolding its use as students engage in the initial practice of executing it. Based on prior experience with the students for whom this sequence of lessons has been devised, as well as with teaching this skill, we may expect that after class 10, the students will be able to execute the skill without any further scaffolding. Use of the skill in classes 13, 16, 20, and 24 may then require only structured cueing, whereas in classes 28, 33, and 37, only the simplest cueing will be required. Thereafter, we can expect students to initiate and direct application of the skill (in classes 42, 45, and 50, and later) on their own. However, if students are executing the

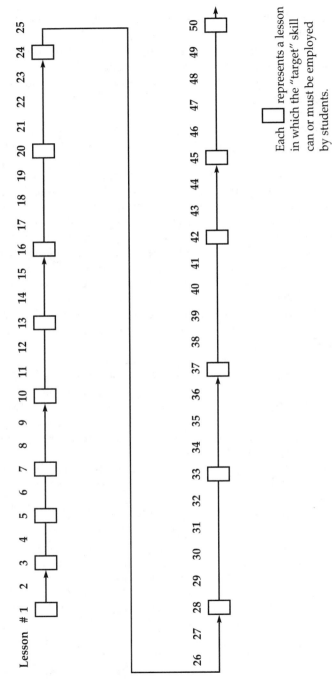

Figure 10.2 Opportunities to Apply the Same Thinking Skill in a Sequence of Subject-Matter Lessons

Each ☐ represents a lesson in which the "target" skill can or must be employed by students.

skill well, we might, at this point (lesson 42), initiate transfer of the skill and, in the lessons that follow, practice this skill in the new setting or context to which we are transferring it.[16]

Unfortunately, the opportunities we initially identify or create for applying the particular skill sometimes do not occur with enough natural frequency or in sufficient numbers to ensure that student execution of it, even with our guidance and support, will help them improve their expertise in executing it. As pointed out in Chapter 9, any thinking skill must be employed (practiced) frequently at first and then intermittently over an extended period of time in order for students to become skilled at carrying it out. When this situation arises, it is then necessary to identify and fill in any gaps in the skill-using opportunities we have identified.

What does this mean in actual practice? Suppose, for instance, the lesson sequence shown in Figure 10.2 originally contained no opportunities to apply the skill we wish to emphasize between lessons 3 and 7. Waiting until lesson 7 for a second opportunity to practice the skill might well prevent students from capitalizing on its initial introduction and practice in lessons 1 and 3, for we know that initial practice of a newly introduced skill should be quite frequent. Thus, we would fill in this gap by building into lesson 5 a subject-matter learning activity in which the application of this skill is necessary. Similarly, if there had been no opportunity to apply this skill between lessons 20 and 28, we would probably find it advisable to build in such an opportunity around lesson 24. This would allow us to assist students in maintaining the kind of proficiency in executing it we would expect them to be developing by this time.

Closing gaps in a skill-using schedule requires adding additional learning activities to provide more frequent application of the skill being emphasized. Sometimes, we can do this by scheduling additional opportunities to employ the skill between existing but too widely separated opportunities to use it. Other times, we may do this simply by extending the number of times a skill can be applied in an already existing skill-using activity. Suppose, for example, we find the skill of classifying already embedded in an activity such as this:

We are about to start our study of (country *x*). But to do so, we have to make some hypotheses about it, so we know where to concentrate our search for information. To do this:

1. List 10 products of this country.
2. *Classify* these products into at least two groups.
3. State and justify one hypothesis you can make about this country based on the groups you made.

After you have completed the above, we will find out more about this country to determine how accurate our hypotheses are.

Rather than create an entirely new activity several lessons later requiring use of classifying, we can simply elaborate this activity to provide one or two more authentic opportunities for applying this skill by inserting, between items 2 and 3, the following:

2a. Now classify these same products again, but this time into at least two groups that indicate the different amounts of labor required to produce them.

2b. Again, classify these same products into two or more groups, this time according to where they are sold once they have been produced.

By increasing the number of times these data are classified, we provide additional authentic subject-matter learning opportunities to practice applying this particular skill without creating new activities. At the same time, we help students get deeper into learning about subject matter and stimulate them to produce even more insightful hypotheses than they otherwise might.

There is one important caution to be observed as we sequence skill-using and teaching opportunities, however. We must avoid introducing instruction in new skills too close to each other. Introductory instruction and practice in new skills should be staggered, because the procedural attributes of one newly encountered thinking skill often interfere with smooth performance of another recently introduced thinking skill.[17] Thus, if we wished to introduce instruction in a second skill—especially a complex skill—in the sequence of lessons described in Figure 10.2, we should not do so until at least lessons 30 or 31, when students may be expected to have developed some degree of competence in applying the previously introduced skill. At that point, we could devote lesson 30 to this purpose, with the first practice in that skill occurring in lesson 31 and subsequent practices in lessons 32, 34, 36, and 39, when scaffolded instruction in this second new skill would not compete directly with student practice of the first skill introduced. In the early stages of learning a new thinking skill, we should do all that we can to avoid or minimize interference from instruction in other thinking skills.

The purpose of this "gap filling" is to ensure that opportunities to engage in a specific thinking skill targeted for improvement appear frequently enough and in enough number so students can remember and build on "how they did it last time" or on "what they learned last time about how to do it." Initially, practice opportunities need to be frequent, numerous, and rather concentrated over a short period. Intermittent practice opportunities can be less frequent and spaced out over a longer period. As independent practice progresses, these intervals can increase in length until they may be even as much as two to three weeks apart. Revising or elaborating a sequence of subject-matter learning activities will guarantee the appropriate continuing number and frequency of skill-using and teaching opportunities.

Integrating Multiple Thinking Operations into Subject-Matter Learning Activities

Cognitive operations—skills or strategies—identified for instruction should be combined with each other and/or other cognitive skills and strategies into purposeful subject-matter learning activities rather than be treated as isolated, discrete operations. Although a specific thinking operation requires explicit attention in the initial stage of instruction, it should be encountered even then and applied in future encounters in the context of larger thinking tasks and learning activities in which it is naturally employed.

Individuals rarely employ a single cognitive skill in isolation from other skills. We do not normally classify information and then just drop it; rather, we do something else that follows from what we learned by classifying. Few of us evaluate things for bias and stop there. We evaluate for bias as part of larger efforts to judge accuracy or credibility in an even broader effort to make hypotheses or conclusions about something. Any specific thinking operation is usually used in combination with other thinking operations to carry out more complex cognitive tasks, such as trying to comprehend or understand something or to make a decision or solve a problem or produce a product of some kind. Cognitive skills that need improving should thus be encountered in the natural course of their use in combination with other skills as students engage strategically in purposeful subject-matter learning.

The operation of detecting bias, for instance, can be embedded in a larger learning effort—perhaps one consisting of developing conclusions about some topic or event. This consists of analyzing information, which requires, in turn, evaluating that information and its sources for accuracy, relevance, credibility, point of view, and logical fallacies as well as bias, in order to ascertain its value and reliability. When students encounter thinking operations that receive special instructive emphasis in the context of their use in learning, they can identify and begin to learn the contextual cues that call into use the operation and incorporate these into the knowledge base they associate with that operation. The learning activity described earlier that embeds the skill of classifying illustrates the kind of integrated thinking operations that accomplish these goals.

Combining cognitive skills with each other in subject-matter learning activities thus provides the contextualized learning missing from the so-called content-free, skill-drill approach to improving thinking. Such an approach works against transfer and self-initiated application of a particular skill when that skill is later encountered in contexts where it should or could be used. Encountering or using a skill targeted for instruction in the context of its natural use with other skills to accomplish a substantive goal of consequence and then receiving instruction at that point in how to improve execution of that skill enhances skill learning.

Employing learning activities that require application of major cognitive strategies to generate subject-matter understandings or knowledge is one way of ensuring that a wide variety of other cognitive operations may naturally be embedded in the activity. All major cognitive strategies—such as problem solving, conceptualizing, argument construction, and so on—incorporate dozens of subordinate cognitive operations. Figure 10.3, for example, identifies some critical thinking operations that are embedded in any decision-making or in any problem-solving task of import. Of course, other operations involving analysis, synthesis, and evaluation are also embedded in each of these strategies. Engaging students in decision-making or problem-solving tasks ensures that there will be considerable—and repeated—opportunities for students to engage in, and thus for us to provide instruction or guidance in, improving any of these operations. Struc-

Figure 10.3 Some Critical Thinking Operations Incorporated in Problem Solving and Decision Making

PROBLEM SOLVING

Identifying a Problem
- Distinguishing relevant from irrelevant
- Identifying point of view
- Identifying assumptions
- Distinguishing factual claims from value judgments

Choosing/Inventing a Solution Plan
(See Decision Making)

Carrying Out the Plan
- Determining credibility of data sources
- Determining accuracy of data
- Distinguishing relevant from irrelevant
- Determining quality of reasoning

Concluding
- Determining logical consistency
- Determining strength of the argument

Checking/Evaluating
(all the above)

DECISION MAKING

Identifying a Problem or Goal
- Distinguishing relevant from irrelevant
- Identifying point of view
- Identifying assumptions

Generating Alternatives

Identifying Potential Consequences
- Determining point of view
- Identifying assumptions

Evaluating Alternatives in Terms of Their Consequences
- Distinguishing relevant from irrelevant
- Identifying assumptions
- Identifying point of view
- Distinguishing factual claims from value judgments
- Determining logical consistency
- Detecting Bias

Choosing the Best Alternative
- Detecting bias
- Identifying assumptions
- Determining the fit between alternatives and given or invented criteria

turing student learning as productive thinking tasks (such as those described in Chapters 2 and 3) provides multiple opportunities for students to engage in a number of important thinking operations.

Providing Appropriate Thinking Skill Instruction, Guidance, Practice, and Support

It is common practice in teaching to intervene when students demonstrate confusion in carrying out a task. What teacher has not had the occasion, when confronted with students stumbling through a learning task, to interrupt with a "Hold It! Wait a minute everyone! We're having trouble doing this! Let's look at what we're trying to do and see if we can figure out how to do it better!" Such interventions usually provide the quick fix needed to enable many students to carry out the assigned activity or procedure satisfactorily and move on.

This, however, is not the type of skill teaching or guidance recommended here. Although simply intervening briefly to provide remedial assistance is quite appropriate, as needed, such interventions are not effective substitutes for the continuing, systematic instruction required to bring about lasting improvement in student abilities to execute new or difficult thinking procedures.

The challenge in providing on-the-spot instruction in thinking is to provide instruction in such a way as to get appropriate focus on a particular skill-using procedure *every time* students engage in that skill until they can carry it out effectively on their own. If we intervene during our students' first encounter with a particular operation in which they need improvement, we have the opportunity to introduce it to them by making procedures for carrying it out visible and explicit. And, as suggested by Figure 10.2, subsequent opportunities for students to carry out this operation allow us to intervene each time to scaffold and later to prompt or cue its application. This instruction and assistance must continue over an extended period of time on each occasion in which students apply the skill. This continues until they can carry it out with proficiency without any outside guidance or support. Integrating instruction in thinking with subject-matter teaching and learning involves much more than a one-shot effort. Rather, it involves shifting back and forth in instructional focus, especially in the early stages of skill practice, between *what* students are learning about or with the subject matter they are studying and *how* they are executing the thinking procedures to generate that learning.[18]

The preceding pages have presented skill-teaching approaches and techniques we can use to carry out this type of integrated instruction. We can establish and maintain our classrooms as thoughtful classrooms, providing continued opportunities for productive learning and the continuing encouragement students require to sustain engagement in thinking, especially in higher-order thinking. We can help make student thinking both visible and explicit, especially in the early stages of learning a new or difficult thinking operation. We can employ skill-teaching techniques, in combination with each other and in sequences described in Chapter 9, particularly in introducing new thinking skills and scaffolding students' initial practice of them. We can also guide and support student application of newly encountered thinking operations by other appropriate scaffolding and cueing techniques as we guide them through the subsequent stages of skill practice en route to becoming autonomous thinkers. Selecting and sequencing the techniques appropriate to the level of student proficiency in executing the skill is what needs to be done at this point in our planning or teaching.

Suppose, for example, improving student execution of a particular thinking skill—perhaps the skill of evaluating for bias—is one of the continuing goals in our effort to improve the quality of their thinking. Figure 10.4 illustrates how systematic instruction in this or in any skill selected for instruction can be integrated into continuing subject-matter instruction. As shown in this figure, if we wish our students to become proficient in this skill, we must be prepared at the time they first use or are confronted with the need to use it to provide instruction in one or more explicit procedures for executing it. We can introduce the skill to them (class 1) through a directive introductory strategy involving modeling the skill and then engaging them in reflecting on how they now do it. We can then scaffold their execution of this skill as they practice carrying it out in subsequent lessons. Perhaps we do this by using a PREP practice strategy (classes 3, 5, and 7) employing a preview and rehearsal of the skill, a procedural checklist, and metacognitive reflection on what they did to carry it out. Then we can substitute a graphic organizer for the checklist—and perhaps drop rehearsal—as we employ a PEP practice strategy in the next several classes (classes 10, 13, and 16).

In subsequent activities calling for application of this skill, we then gradually withdraw the more explicit scaffolds, replacing them with, perhaps, partially completed examples and later with cued questions and, finally, perhaps a mnemonic that will provide sufficient prompts. In every one of these lessons, of course, our instruction in and discussion of the cognitive procedure on which we are focusing is always in terms of the subject matter to which the procedure is being applied, as students explain what they do to execute the skill and why. This use of subject-matter examples or details to articulate a cognitive procedure enhances the generation of subject-matter insights developed by employing the procedure. It also enables students to better comprehend the procedure itself. Organizing instruction, as described here, illustrates the infusion and immersion approaches to integrating instruction in thinking and subject matter.

Figure 10.4 Integrated Instruction in Thinking and Subject Matter

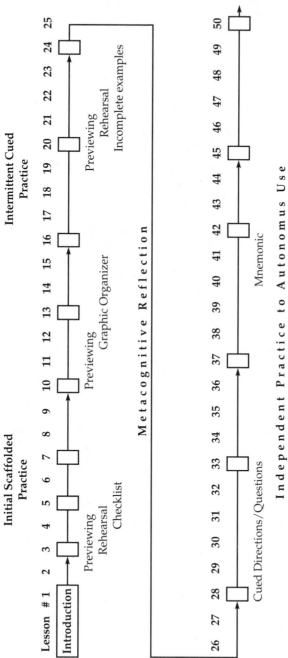

The Skill or Subject-Matter Dilemma

In combining the instructional approaches described in the preceding chapters and in integrating them with subject-matter instruction, it must be remembered that we have two goals in mind. These are (1) to improve the quality of student thinking and (2) to improve the quality (depth and sophistication) of subject-matter learning produced by such thinking. Although our ultimate goal is the latter, accomplishing it requires concerted and explicit attention simultaneously to the former. This means that the emphasis given to any single cognitive skill chosen for instruction and the subject-matter learning developed by application of that skill will vary. The emphasis will depend on where students are in the process of improving their proficiency at executing that skill. Emphasizing a skill or subject matter is not the issue; the issue is *when* and *how much* to emphasize each.

Contrary to what is often assumed, integrating instruction in thinking with subject-matter learning does *not* mean emphasizing just thinking or subject matter, or a simultaneous emphasis on both, or a simple, continuing 50–50 emphasis on each. Rather, the emphasis on and time and attention devoted to each changes as students become more proficient in executing the particular kind of thinking being emphasized. Figure 10.5 indicates the nature of this changing emphasis. It diagrams the various stages of thinking instruction in subject matter and indicates the relative emphasis and time given to each kind of learning goal—skill or subject matter—at each point. Notice that at the beginning of any effort to improve a thinking operation, most, but not all, emphasis is on the skill—what it is, how it can be done, and why. As instruction progresses through the early stages of guided practice, however, subject-matter learning receives increasing attention. For some time, both subject-matter learning and skill performance receive rather equal attention. Finally, as students demonstrate increased proficiency in applying the skill on their own and on their own initiative, full attention can be given to the subject-matter learning developed through student application of the skill.

At no point in integrated thinking/subject-matter instruction is attention devoted exclusively either to procedure or to subject matter. Both receive some attention throughout the process. However, in the initial lessons on a cognitive skill, attention should be given to the skill first and separately from attention to the subject-matter learnings developed through application of the skill. The majority of lesson time will usually be devoted to the skill. But in subsequent practice lessons, even those immediately following student introduction to the skill, we can devote the initial half or less of the lesson to the skill procedure and the remainder to

Figure 10.5 Integrating Instruction in Any Thinking Skill with Instruction in Subject Matter

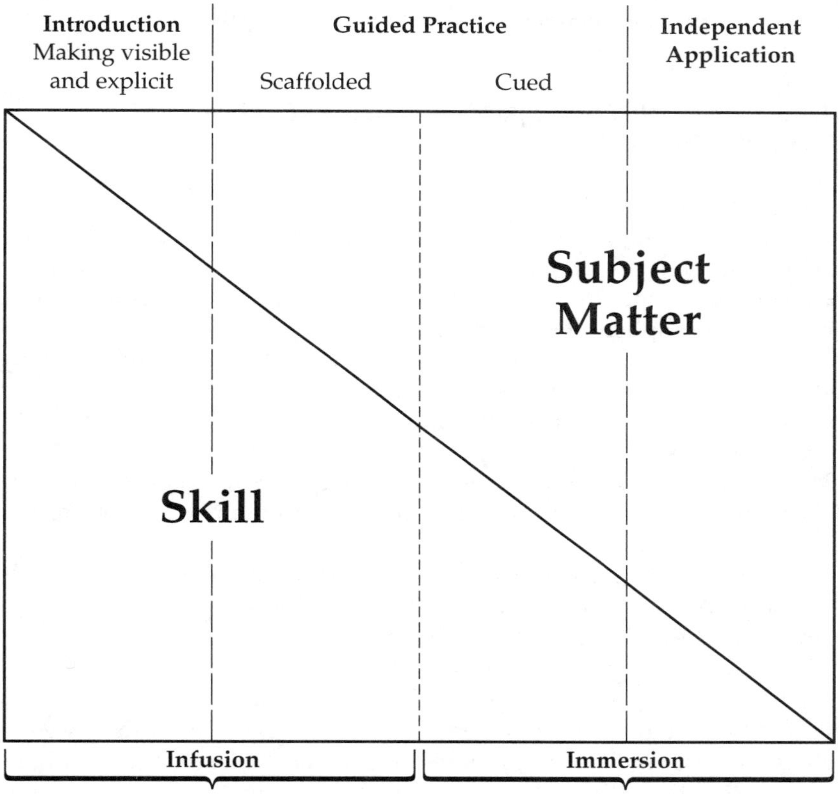

subject matter. This is especially true for skill practice lessons that occur close together in time.

In subsequent practice lessons, more time can be devoted to subject-matter discussion than to analysis of the skills employed to process that subject matter. In these lessons, we provide a subject-matter rationale for employing the skill, have students engage in an activity requiring application of the skill, and then immediately focus on one or more procedures for carrying out that skill *before* turning our attention to the subject-matter learning produced by execution of the skill. Eventually, we can focus exclusively on the subject matter being studied because students can apply the thinking operations required to do so with proficiency. Time devoted to a thinking procedure up front—even while using subject-matter content as the vehicle for carrying out the skill—pays off. We can allow much more attention and greater depth to the development of subject-matter knowledge as students improve their proficiency in executing that procedure.

INTEGRATING INSTRUCTION IN THINKING AND SUBJECT MATTER: A SUMMARY

Integrating thinking with subject-matter content consists, in part, of combining thinking with subject matter as subjects to be learned and learned about. It also consists of incorporating instruction in thinking with instruction in subject matter to direct and bring about the learning of both subjects. To accomplish this, we must ensure that the cognitive operations in which we provide instruction are those that serve authentic, meaningful subject-matter learning goals. But we must also ensure that the subject-matter learning goals and activities are those that legitimately require the application of the kinds of thinking that we believe students need to improve. In an integrated approach to improving thinking, *both* thinking and subject matter are important learning goals, and attention to both are explicit classroom activities.

Classroom lessons introducing and providing initial practice in a specific thinking skill should focus first on the thinking skill being emphasized, and then on the subject-matter conclusions, understandings, and other learning goals produced by application of that skill. However, subject matter is used and processed continuously throughout these lessons. The thinking skills being taught are always employed to achieve subject-matter learning goals. Subject matter always serves as a vehicle for practicing, applying, and elaborating these thinking operations. As students move progressively through their study of subject matter, they regularly attend, as appropriate, to specific thinking skills needing improvement. Initially, this is done in an explicit way, then through continued practice in which our mediation decreases as student proficiency in executing these skills increases. Instruction in thinking thus moves from infusion to immersion as student use of the skill moves from introduction through the various kinds of practice to autonomous application to achieve significant subject-matter learning goals.

In carrying out such integrated instruction, we must ensure that thinking is not fragmented into unrelated, discrete skills or operations. Rather, it should be presented, applied, and "taught" as components of purposeful thinking strategies and learning activities. Furthermore, we must ensure that the kind of thinking emphasized for instruction is encountered and focused on in the service of accomplishing meaningful subject-matter goals rather than as an end in itself in decontextualized exercises. Accomplishing this task requires a careful and continuous integration of instruction in both thinking and subject matter. The procedures described here provide useful ways of accomplishing this goal.

ENDNOTES

1. See, for example, Barry K. Beyer, *Developing a Thinking Skills Program* (Boston: Allyn and Bacon, 1988), pp. 106–111.

2. Robert S. Siegler, *Children's Thinking* (Englewood Cliffs, NJ: Prentice-Hall, 1986).

3. Beyer, *Developing a Thinking Skills Program*, pp. 24–26; Research and Policy Committee, *Investing in Our Children* (New York: Committee on Economic Development, 1985); Task Force on Education for Economic Growth, *Action for Excellence* (Denver: Education Commission of the States, 1983), pp. 16, 38.

4. Beyer, *Developing a Thinking Skills Program*, pp. 103–111.

5. *Ibid.*, pp. 116–117.

6. *Ibid.*, pp. 118–122.

7. *Ibid.*, pp. 125–151; Barry K. Beyer, *Teaching Thinking Skills: A Handbook for Secondary School Teachers* and *Teaching Thinking: A Handbook for Elementary School Teachers* (Boston: Allyn and Bacon, 1991), pp. 5–39.

8. Beyer, *Developing a Thinking Skills Program*, pp. 153–179, 317–352; Robin Fogarty and James Bellanca, *Teach Them Thinking* (Palatine, IL: IRI Group, 1986); Robert J. Marzano et al., *Dimensions of Thinking* (Alexandria, VA: Association for Supervision and Curriculum Development, 1988).

9. Beyer, *Developing a Thinking Skills Program*, p. 147.

10. *Ibid.*, pp. 201–205.

11. Matthew Lipman, *Thinking in Education* (New York: Cambridge University Press, 1991); David Perkins, *Smart Schools* (New York: The Free Press, 1992).

12. Beyer, *Developing a Thinking Skills Program*, pp. 194–201, 214–217.

13. *Ibid.*, pp. 194–201, 211–217; Barry K. Beyer, "Developing a Scope and Sequence for Thinking Skill Instruction," *Educational Leadership 45* 7 (April 1988): 26–30; Barry K. Beyer and Judith Dorsch Backes, "Integrating Thinking Skills into the Curriculum," *Principal* (National Association of Elementary School Principals) *69* 3 (January 1990): 18–21.

14. Barry K. Beyer, *Practical Strategies for the Teaching of Thinking* (Boston: Allyn and Bacon, 1987), pp. 139–178; Allan Collins, Jan Hawkins, and Sharon M. Carver, "A Cognitive Apprenticeship for Disadvantaged Students," in Barbara Means, Carol Chelemer and Michael S. Knapp (Eds.), *Teaching Advanced Skills to At-Risk Students* (San Francisco: Jossey-Bass, 1991), pp. 216–243.

15. Robert Pasnak, "Teaching Basic Cognitive Operations to At-Risk Students," *Human Intelligence Newsletter 10* 2 (Spring–Summer 1989): 5.

16. Beyer, *Developing a Thinking Skills Program*, pp. 235–239; Beyer, *Teaching Thinking Skills*, pp. 112–119.

17. Michael I. Posner and Steven W. Keele, "Skill Learning," in Robert M. W. Travers (Ed.), *Second Handbook of Research on Teaching* (Chicago: Rand McNally College Publishing, 1973), pp. 805–831.

18. Richard S. Prawat, "The Value of Ideas: The Immersion Approach to the Development of Thinking," *Educational Researcher*, 70 2 (March 1991): 5.

Conclusion: A Comprehensive Approach to Improving Student Thinking

There are many ways to improve the quality of student thinking and thus of student learning and achievement. But doing more of what most of us have been doing over the past years is not one of them.[1] Nor will doing these things "harder" serve to accomplish this goal.[2] However, employing the approaches presented in the preceding pages will!

Research as well as exemplary classroom practice and experience indicate that we can improve the quality of student thinking and learning by doing at least four things: (1) providing thoughtful classrooms and the thinker-friendly learning environment that supports them, (2) making thinking visible and explicit, (3) guiding and supporting student thinking through scaffolding and cueing, and (4) integrating with subject-matter learning continuing, systematic instruction in those cognitive operations with which students have difficulty or that are especially complex.

Each of the four approaches described in the preceding pages contributes significantly to improving student thinking, because each addresses a specific dimension of this task. Thoughtful classrooms provide exactly the kind of learning environment in which thinking can develop and prosper. To improve their thinking, students must have the repeated opportunities and continuing encouragement to engage in it that thoughtful classroom learning environments provide. Making thinking explicit and visible gives students a clearer understanding of how they engage in thinking and insights about what can be done to improve it. Scaffolding and cueing student application of newly encountered or difficult thinking operations provides the guidance and structured support so necessary in helping novices become more comfortable and skilled in applying these operations on their own. And employing all these approaches in a systematic way in subject-matter study provides the meaningful, purposeful context that not only motivates students to improve their thinking but that also provides them with sharper cognitive tools for improving their subject-matter learning.

Using these instructional approaches to improve student thinking is not a question of *which* to use. As useful as each by itself is to helping us achieve this goal, employing only one or even two of them is not enough. If we really wish to help our students improve their proficiency in thinking as much as they can and need to, we must combine all of these into a comprehensive, systematic instructional effort across all grade levels and in all major subjects in our schools. The result will be students who can and will think in a more rapid, precise, skillful, self-directing, and self-correcting manner and with greater confidence of success.

Although each of these approaches is a powerful method for improving student thinking, each is limited in effect when used as the sole method for attempting to accomplish this goal. For example, as important as are the opportunities and encouragement for thinking provided by a thoughtful classroom, students often cannot or do not take advantage of them because they simply do not know how to execute the thinking operations required to do so. Making thinking visible and explicit, scaffolding and cueing practice, and, in many instances, providing continuing systematic guidance and support are also necessary to empower many students to take advantage of the opportunities and encouragement provided by thoughtful classrooms. Thoughtful classrooms, by themselves, simply do not do the job that needs to be done to help students become skillful thinkers.

Clearly, making thinking visible and explicit establishes a foundation for improving thinking by alerting students to how they (as well as others) think, helping them to spot flaws and gaps in their own thinking, and alerting them to specific procedures they can adopt to close these gaps or correct these flaws. Yet, attempts to do this can hardly be successful in the absence of a thoughtful classroom, whose thinker-friendly learning environment minimizes the risks of thinking and of thinking and talking about one's thinking. Nor would either of these approaches be very productive without follow-up guidance and support for subsequent student efforts to carry out the procedures that were earlier made visible and explicit.

However, unless these approaches are embedded in continuing, systematic instruction in a variety of subject-matter contexts and settings they fail to move students toward the independent, skillful thinking essential for becoming autonomous thinkers. Unless our systematic efforts to improve thinking are carried on in the context of subject-matter learning, there is the unfortunate probability of them becoming nothing more than thought*less* skill drill. Indeed, only by integrating *all these approaches* into subject-matter learning can we bring about the kinds of improvement in learning that we and our students are capable of attaining.

In sum, the effectiveness of any one of the teaching approaches described here is enhanced by the extent to which it is employed in combination with all the others. Conversely, the effectiveness of each is limited to the extent to which it is employed in isolation from any or all of the others. Indeed, the effect on student thinking of employing all these approaches in a comprehensive effort to improve student thinking is much more than the effect of employing only one or two of them. To be most successful, any classroom or schoolwide effort to improve the quality of student thinking must not only integrate their use with subject-matter learning but also integrate their application with each other to create a comprehensive instructional effort.

IMPLEMENTING A COMPREHENSIVE APPROACH TO IMPROVING STUDENT THINKING

Implementing the approach to improving thinking described here may at first appear to be a challenging task, but it is not an impossible one. It can be done, especially when we realize that, to paraphrase an old saying, while it's hard by the yard, by the inch it's a cinch. By implementing the teaching approaches described here, one at a time, and combining them as we proceed, we can gradually and effectively incorporate all of them into our teaching to produce the comprehensive approach to improving student thinking recommended here.

For instance, if we or our colleagues are already using one or even several of these approaches, perhaps the easiest way to start is to refine what we are already doing by incorporating into this any suggestions or ideas presented here that are relevant and will help us do it better. Once a more familiar approach has been fine-tuned, we can then select one of the other approaches described here and focus on applying it while continuing to employ the approach(es) already in use. Then we can add another and so on. We can allow a semester for trying out and implementing each new approach. By proceeding in this fashion over a period of several years, we will soon be employing all of these approaches, having debugged them as necessary. By then, we will be starting to feel comfortable in employing them and doing so with some degree of expertise as a regular part of our classroom teaching.

If, on the other hand, we have never employed any of these teaching approaches consistently or seriously, combining and integrating them to improve student thinking may take somewhat longer. Introducing them all at once is obviously inappropriate. Such a policy would be overwhelming and undoubtedly lead to considerable frustration and even failure. Rather, we can implement them, one at a time, starting with efforts to establish and maintain our subject-matter classrooms as thoughtful classrooms. No matter what specific subjects we teach, we can begin to employ in a conscious, systematic way the learning activities and techniques described in Part I to create the conditions and to foster the student behaviors that make thoughtful classrooms thoughtful. Then, we can incorporate these efforts, in turn, with each of the other elements of instruction in thinking described in Parts II through IV.

By following this gradual, long-term approach over a three-year period or so, we can thus become increasingly skilled at employing all four of these teaching approaches in an integrated way and be making adaptations as appropriate. Thereafter, we should be able to employ them all, consistently, as a normal part of our everyday teaching. We will then have in place a comprehensive approach to improving student thinking that is an integral part of what we do to facilitate and ensure student learning in our classrooms.

Interestingly, implementation of these approaches is best accomplished by practicing what these pages preach. That is, to develop or refine our expertise in employing the four approaches to improving student thinking presented herein, we should use these same approaches. Our staff-development efforts should create and maintain an environment for us and our colleagues that provides encouragement and opportunities to experiment with and reflect on these various teaching approaches in a nonthreatening atmosphere. We should make visible and explicit for ourselves and our colleagues how we apply the techniques and approaches we seek to master and how they may perhaps be better applied. We should also use scaffolds and other support and guidance to assist us and our colleagues in employing these approaches as we seek to become more skilled in applying them. And, although we may initially employ some of these approaches as special exercises with our peers, we should gradually combine these with meaningful subject-matter learning activities in our classes. As we apply these approaches to the process of developing our own expertise at "teaching thinking," we can make these an integral part of our everyday subject-matter teaching.[3]

Making the instructional approaches presented here a regular feature of our own classroom teaching or of the teaching in all the classrooms in our school or school district is not likely to be an easy task. Attempting to balance the perceived demands of subject-matter teaching and learning with what it takes in time and effort to provide the kind of instruction and mediation required to improve the quality of student thinking may pose a real challenge to many of us. This challenge can be met successfully, however, by making a commitment to the importance of quality student thinking as a planned outcome of schooling as well as a tool for improving our students' academic achievements.

Developing such a commitment—on the part of school leaders as well as teachers and parents—is crucial to the success of this effort. To do so, we must overcome numerous myths and attitudes that inhibit serious efforts to improve student thinking. We have to be ever alert, for example, not to succumb to the "content coverage" syndrome that emphasizes continued mindless ingestion, storage and retrieval of so-called facts and fragments of information to the neglect of processing information to develop deeper knowledge and understanding.[4] We must reject the erroneous claim that at-risk youngsters simply can not engage in meaningful thinking or that the gifted and talented already do it better than anyone could ever hope for, and the spurious attendant myth that neither can therefore benefit from any serious effort to improve their thinking.[5] We must also reject the fallacious belief that if students have not learned how to execute complex, higher-order thinking tasks by the time they reach our classrooms, they never will, so trying to help them is a waste of time. And we must reject any temptation to succumb to the often recurring rationalization that improving student thinking is really someone else's responsibility, not ours.[6] Improving the quality of student thinking benefits all of us—students, teachers, parents, and society. And all of us can contribute to making such an improvement.

Understanding and applying consistently and continuously the approaches and techniques presented here can overcome many of the obstacles to improving thinking now confronting our students. These techniques and approaches provide powerful ways of improving student thinking—methods that many of us may have been heretofore unaware of or unfamiliar with or that have gone too long unused or underused in our classrooms. Employing these techniques as a regular part of classroom teaching may not be the only thing that needs to or can be done to improve the quality of student thinking today, but it is certainly one of the things necessary for this goal to be achieved.

WHY TRY TO IMPROVE STUDENT THINKING?

Implementing the approaches to improving student thinking presented in these pages clearly requires effort as well as commitment. Is making this effort and commitment worth it? Of course, it is. It is worth it because the quality of thinking of our students *needs* improving. It is worth it because their thinking *can* be improved. It is worth it because improving the quality of student thinking is a goal that cuts across all grade levels and subject areas and thus can unite all of us in a common school or district or statewide effort that will significantly benefit all of our students. It is worth it because systematic, comprehensive, integrated use of these approaches gives real promise of bringing about significant improvement in the quality of student subject-matter learning and achievement as well as in the quality of their thinking. And with these improvements also come improved student confidence and self-concepts.

Research clearly indicates that in subject-matter courses where we attend explicitly to the thinking operations or skills that students need to employ to carry out the learning activities in which they engage, students improve the quality of their academic achievement as well as their thinking.[7] Whereas teaching or covering only information overpowers students, helping them to improve their thinking *empowers* students. Clearly, *em*powering students as thinking, knowledgeable, productive citizens is one important goal of formal education today.

Increased student confidence and self-concept results from the use of the teaching approaches described here. This has been readily acknowledged by students themselves, as is demonstrated by the statement by a Connecticut elementary school student presented in Figure 1. Not only does this youngster make this point poignantly clear, but goes on to demonstrate this confidence by telling us exactly how to execute such a thinking task so we will not be tortured or nervous about doing it either!

In a broader sense, the value of providing systematic, comprehensive instruction in thinking as presented herein is perhaps best underscored by the following lines. They are adapted from a recent National Library Week slogan that has been prominently displayed in school libraries throughout the nation over the past several years. Comprehensive, systematic efforts to improve the quality of student thinking, using the approaches described in this book, are worthwhile because, in actuality:

The better you think, the more you learn.

The more you learn, the smarter you grow.

The smarter you grow, the stronger your voice—

When speaking your mind or making your choice.[*]

Strengthening student voices when speaking their minds and making their choices is what improving the quality of student thinking is all about. Putting into consistent classroom practice all the instructional approaches presented here can enable us to accomplish this goal. Implementing these

---

[*]Adapted and reprinted with permission from Wonderstorms, Cleveland, Ohio.

Figure 1 A Student Describes the Value of Explicit Approaches to Improving the Quality of Student Thinking

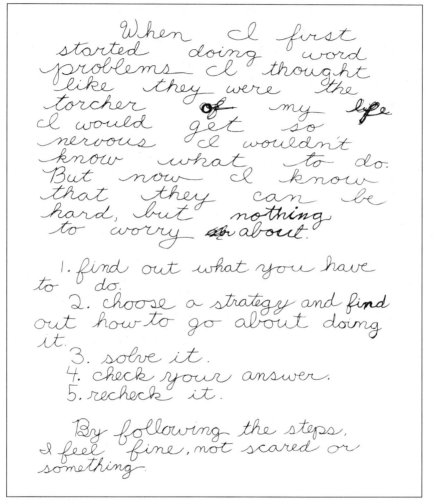

This statement is from a collection of student work assembled by educational consultant Bena Kallick. It is reprinted with her permission.

approaches may take time and effort, especially for those of us who may have to start almost from scratch. But once we have become proficient in employing these approaches as a natural part of our teaching, they will be a *permanent* fix. We, our students, and the parents of our students, as well as society as a whole, will be the ultimate beneficiaries.

ENDNOTES

1. Barry K. Beyer, "Improving Thinking Skills—Defining the Problem," *Phi Delta Kappan 65* 7 (March 1984): 486–490.

2. Rexford G. Brown, "Cultivating a Literacy of Thoughtfulness," *Thinking: The Journal of Philosophy for Children 9* 4, p. 5; Raymond Nickerson, "On Improving Thinking through Instruction," in Ernest Rothkopf (Ed.), *Review of Research in Education,* Volume 15 (Washington, DC: American Educational Research Association, 1988–89), pp. 3–9.

3. Barry K. Beyer, *Developing a Thinking Skills Program* (Boston: Allyn and Bacon, 1988), pp. 23–43.

4. Fred M. Newmann, "Can Depth Replace Coverage in the High School Curriculum?" *Phi Delta Kappan 70* 5 (January 1988): 347; David Perkins, *Smart Schools* (New York: The Free Press, 1992), p. 85; Martha Stone Wiske, "How Teaching for Understanding Changes the Rules in the Classroom," *Educational Leadership 51* 5 (February 1994): 19–21.

5. Brown, "Cultivating a Literacy," pp. 7–10.

6. *Ibid.*, pp. 5–6; Fred M. Newmann, "Higher Order Thinking in Teaching Social Studies: A Rationale for the Assessment of Classroom Thoughtfulness," *Journal of Curriculum Studies 22* 1 (January–February 1990): 41–56.

7. Carl Bereiter, "Elementary School: Necessity or Convenience?" *Elementary School Journal 73* 8 (May 1973): 435–446; Thomas H. Estes, "Reading in the Social Studies—A Review of Research in Social Studies Since 1950," in James Laffery (Ed.), *Reading in the Content Areas* (Newark, DE: International Reading Association, 1972), pp. 178–183; Norman Frederickson, "Implications of Cognitive Theory for Instruction in Problem Solving," *Review of Educational Research 54* 3 (Fall 1984): 363–407; William W. Purkey, *Self-Concept and School Achievement* (Englewood Cliffs, NJ: Prentice-Hall, 1970).

Index